Drawing the Line

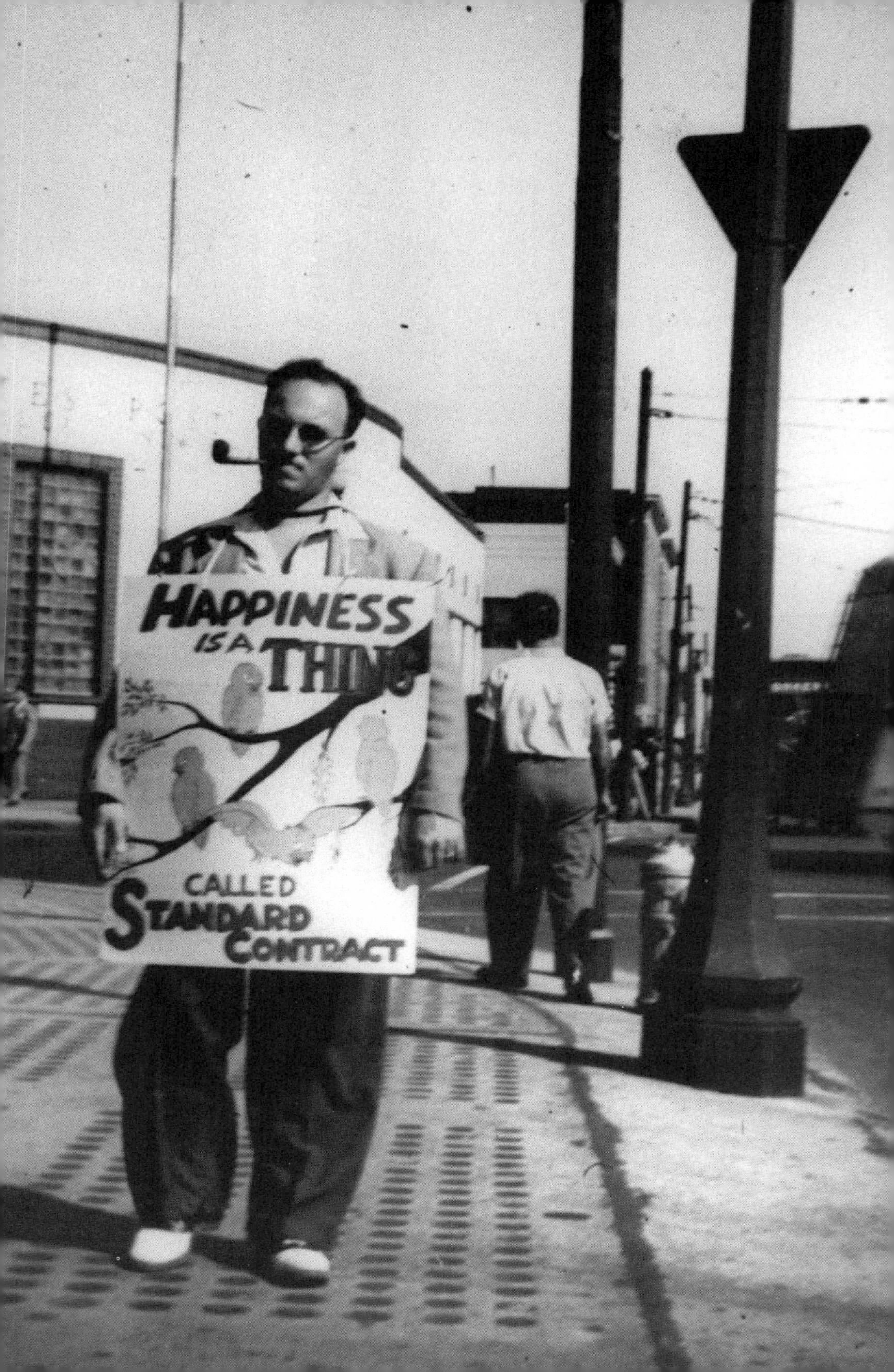
HAPPINESS
IS A THING
CALLED
STANDARD
CONTRACT

Drawing the Line

The Untold Story
of the Animation Unions
from Bosko to Bart Simpson

Tom Sito

THE UNIVERSITY PRESS OF KENTUCKY

Publication of this volume was made possible in part by a grant
from the National Endowment for the Humanities.

Scholarly publisher for the Commonwealth,
serving Bellarmine University, Berea College, Centre College of Kentucky, Eastern
Kentucky University, The Filson Historical Society, Georgetown College, Kentucky
Historical Society, Kentucky State University, Morehead State University, Murray
State University, Northern Kentucky University, Transylvania University, University
of Kentucky, University of Louisville, and Western Kentucky University.
All rights reserved.

Editorial and Sales Offices: The University Press of Kentucky
663 South Limestone Street, Lexington, Kentucky 40508–4008
www.kentuckypress.com

10 09 08 07 06   5 4 3 2 1

Frontispiece: Don Figlozzi walking picket at Terrytoons, 1947. Courtesy of MPSC
Local 839, AFL-CIO Collection, Urban Archives Center, Oviatt Library, California
State University, Northridge.

Library of Congress Cataloging-in-Publication Data
Sito, Tom, 1956-
   Drawing the line : the untold story of the animation unions from Bosko to Bart
Simpson / Tom Sito.
      p. cm.
   Includes bibliographical references and index.
   ISBN-13: 978-0-8131-2407-0 (hardcover : alk. paper)
   ISBN-10: 0-8131-2407-7 (hardcover : alk. paper) 1. Animators—Labor unions—
United States—History. I. Title.
   NC1766.U5S58 2006
   331.88'1179143340973--dc22   2006016090

 Member of the Association of
American University Presses

To my fellow animation workers—

graphite-stained fingers, strained eyes,
Cel-Vinyl paint spots in their hair
from holding the brush in their teeth,
carpal-tunnel wrist braces, shiny pants bottoms,
stooped posture, hair prematurely gray.
The least-respected, worst-paid,
yet finest artists in the world.

And especially for Pat.

Contents

List of Illustrations   ix

Acknowledgments   xiii

Introduction   1
   Why a History of Animation Unions?

1. The World of the Animation Studio   7
   The Cartoon Assembly Line

2. Suits   31
   Producers as Artists See Them

3. Hollywood Labor, 1933–1941   57
   The Birth of Cartoonists Unions

4. The Fleischer Strike   77
   A Union Busted, a Studio Destroyed

5. The Great Disney Studio Strike   101
   The Civil War of Animation

6. The War of Hollywood and the Blacklist   153
   1945–1953

7. A Bag of Oranges   197
   The Terrytoons Strike and the Great White Father

8. Lost Generations   213
   1952–1988

9. Animation and the Global Market   247
   The Runaway Wars, 1979–1982

10. Fox and Hounds   285
    The Torch Seen Passing

11. Camelot   293
    1988–2001

12. Animation . . . Isn't That All Done on Computers Now?   319
    The Digital Revolution

Conclusion   345
    Where to Now?

Appendix 1. Animation Union Leaders   353

Appendix 2. Dramatis Personae   359

Appendix 3. Glossary   373

Notes   387

Bibliography   409

Index   415

Illustrations

Don Figlozzi walking picket at Terrytoons, 1947   ii

Animator Al Eugster at his desk at Walt Disney Hyperion Studio annex, circa 1937   10

Animator Kevin Koch at his digital workstation at DreamWorks Animation, circa 2005   10

Animators clowning around on the roof of the Sullivan studio in Manhattan, 1928   14

Two of the lead animators on Disney's *Lion King* clowning around, Glendale, California, 1994   14

Inkers and painters at Walt Disney Studios, 1957   24

Disney internal memo sent to artist job applicant Frances Brewer, May 9, 1939   25

Gag cartoon of Bill Scott and Grim Natwick assassinating a production manager at Walter Lantz studio, 1947   32

Early animation producer-agent Margaret Winkler at the age of ninety-three   37

Pat Sullivan at a desk with Otto Messmer, 1928   39

Typical animation story meeting, Walt Disney studio, circa 1936   48

Floyd Norman having some fun with Pixar director John Lasseter's love of Hawaiian shirts   53

Ub Iwerks self-caricature, 1931   70

Animation camera stand at Walt Disney studio, circa 1936   71

Van Beuren inker Sadie Bodin, the first person to picket an animation studio   73

Fleischer studio crew photo, 1931   78

Fleischer studio internal newsletter, the *Fleischer Animated News*, 1935   80

CADU strike flyer, 1937   86

Illustrations

Fleischer studio strikers walking the picket line on Broadway,
1937   87

Fleischer strikers in front of Fleischer building at 1600 Broadway,
1937   88

Fleischer strikers, 1937   91

Walt Disney, circa 1941   102

Earliest known copy of the Screen Cartoonists Guild newsletter,
January 1938   105

Looney Tunes lockout, street scene outside Termite Terrace, May 1941
107

Schlesinger lockout, 1941   107

Looney Tunes lockout, 1941   109

Gag cartoon by Grim Natwick showing Walt Disney making excuses
to animators about why they weren't getting *Snow White*
bonuses   112

Union organizer Herb Sorrell, 1940, drawn by SCG president Bill
Littlejohn   116

Looking north on Buena Vista Street during the Disney strike, May
1941   122

Picketers marching against Disney   123

Storyboard artist Joe Rinaldi reading a newspaper during the Disney
strike   125

Schlesinger director Chuck Jones with his daughter Linda, 1941   127

Lunch line at Disney strikers' camp in a rural field across the street
from the studio   127

Strike leaders in their camp   128

Top animator Art Babbitt giving a speech in the strikers' camp during
the Disney strike   131

Angry Mickey with picket sign, SCG Disney strike leaflet   132

Disney strikers' newsletter with gag cartoon of Walt Disney pointing to
empty desks   134

Gangster Willie Bioff and attorney George Bresler   135

Walt Disney's appeal to his artists in an ad placed in Hollywood trade
papers   137

Animators Union response to Walt Disney's appeal   138

Gag drawing mocking Walt Disney's 1941 trip to Latin America   140

Disney strike negotiation teams   141

Illustrations

New York Daily News article, "Disney Says Reds Ruled His Artists," October 1947   146

Former IATSE official Willie Bioff's past catches up with him: he was killed by a car bomb in November 1959   157

Strikers attack a strikebreaker's car during the Battle of Burbank, 1945   161

Fire hoses are turned on strikers in front of Warner Bros. Gate 2 during the Battle of Burbank, 1945   162

CSU leaders in jail, 1945   163

CSU pamphlet during Battle of Burbank, 1945   165

Uncle Sam faces down a brutish striker in a *Los Angeles Times* editorial cartoon   167

IATSE West Coast leader Roy Brewer in 1947   170

Witness's view of the Los Angeles session of HUAC's inquiry into the motion picture industry   174

Anti-Communist pledge form that all new union officers were required to sign   180

The UPA crew in 1947   188

Gag cartoon of SCG business agent Maurice Howard reprimanding animator Grim Natwick   191

Paul Terry, old-time creator of short cartoons   198

New York union organizer Pepe Ruiz in 1944   200

Eddie Rehberg's layoff notice from Terrytoons, 1947   203

Telegram announcing the Terrytoons strike, 1947   204

Painting picket signs for the Terrytoons strike, 1947   205

Animator Theron Collier checks ideas for picket signs, 1947   205

Animator Jim Logan with picket sign, Terrytoons, 1947   206

Slap-Happy Hooligan, the union business agent, antiunion gag   207

Animator Jim Tyer and Larry Silverman at Terrytoons picket line   208

Picketers in front of Terrytoons commemorating their tenth week on strike, 1947   209

Walter Lantz crew photo, 1954   214

Background painter Anne Guenther by animator Dave Tendlar   221

TV animation genius Jay Ward and director Bill Hurtz, 1982   225

Gag drawing protesting the television hiring season   243

Lou Appet, Local 839 business agent, drawn by Dave Tendlar   245

Gag cartoon by Floyd Norman of Bill Hanna and Darth Vader

Illustrations

about Hanna-Barbera's attempts to send more production out of town   248

The Hanna-Barbera crew on the roof of the Cahuenga Boulevard studio, 1979   260

Cartoonists' picket line in front of Hanna-Barbera studio, 1979   261

Local 839 president Moe Gollub drawn by Dave Tendlar   264

Picketer Helen Barry in front of Hanna-Barbera, 1979   266

Massed pickets in front of Hanna-Barbera, 1982   267

Striking animator Harry Love making a lunch date with Joe Barbera, 1982   273

Gag drawing of Hanna-Barbera building being towed to Taiwan, 1982   275

Bill Hanna in 1990   283

Gag drawing of Jeffrey Katzenberg in Indian garb for the film *Pocahontas*   297

Disney traditional artists show their anger toward their employers in drawings   315

Pencil-pushing artist face their computer replacement in *Technological Threat*   320

Animator and effects designer John Van Vliet has some fun with people's misconceptions   337

Grim Natwick's one-hundredth birthday party, 1990   346

Picnic on the fiftieth anniversary of the Walt Disney strike, near the site of the original picketers' camp, Burbank, 1991   346

Union animators' picket line, Nickelodeon studio, 1998   347

Union animators picket Public Broadcasting System affiliate KCET to protest PBS's sending work to Canada, 2000   349

Local 839 officers in 1993   350

Acknowledgments

For someone who loves to tell stories, it was a long time before I got around to writing anything down.

Thanks to Richard Williams, Gil Miret, and Shamus Culhane for being my mentors. They gave me the greatest breaks in my career and inspired me not only to study great animation but also to learn from the life examples of the great animation artists of the past. Thanks to the UCLA Special Archives; Larry Marshal of the California State University, Northridge, Special Archives, which houses the repository of the papers of Screen Cartoonists Guild Local 852; and Steve Hulett, Jeff Massie, and the Archives of the Animation Guild Local 839. Thanks also to Linda Jones Clough and the Chuck Jones Center for Creativity, for their help. My thanks to Harvey Deneroff for his groundbreaking research into the early cartoonists guilds and the Fleischer and Terrytoon strikes; to Howard Beckerman at the School of Visual Arts, for showing me the connection between animation history and the politics of its time; and to Karl Cohen, for his work on the blacklist and censorship in his work *Forbidden Animation,* and also for rekindling in me the desire to complete this book.

Thanks to the Hollywood chapter of ASIFA (the Association internationale du film d'animation), Mike Barrier, Jerry Beck, Randy Haberkamp, Hollywood Heritage, Mark Kausler, Mike Malory, and Leonard Maltin. Joe Campana is doing some wonderful research into local Los Angeles history and the home addresses and death certificates of famous animation personnel. Thanks to Nancy Beiman for help on the title and women's issues, and to Judy Levitow for making available the union papers of her parents, Abe Levitow and Charlotte Lewis. Thanks also to Joe Adamson, Rich Arons, Bob Birchcard, Paul Buhle, John Canemaker, Andreas Deja, Mike Disa, Rick Farmiloe, Eric Goldberg, Howard Green, Glen

Acknowledgments

Keane, Bob Kurtz, Steve O. Moore, Jan Nagel, Alex Rannie, Charles Solomon, and Stephen Worth for their help and advice. And my thanks to Roberta Street and Cheryl Hoffman for editing the manuscript and stopping all those English majors from picking on my sentence structure while I'm trying to wage class warfare.

Thank you also to all the wonderful old friends I've shared a glass with who regaled me with firsthand accounts of their life and times: Pete Alvarado, Art and Barbara Babbitt, Marc and Alice Davis, George Bakes, Roy and Patty Disney, Ed Forcher, Bob Foster, Ed Friedman, Mother Mabel Gesner, Bob Givens, Joe Grant, Stan Green, Annie Guenther, Gene Hamm, Chuck Harrington, Bud Hester, Dave and Libby Hilberman, Steve and Janette Hulett, Bill Hurtz, Ollie Johnston, Dori Littel-Herrick, Bill and Fini Littlejohn, Herb Klynn, Jim Logan, Hicks Lokey, Bill Melendez, Maurice Noble, Floyd Norman, Jack Ozark, Ray Patterson, Jay Rivkin, Martha and Sol Sigall, David Switft, Iwao Takamoto, Tom Tataranowicz, Dave Tendlar, Frank Thomas, Ben Washam, Merle Welton, John Wilson, Jack Zander, and Lou Zukor, and to Rudy Zamora Jr., who shared his recollections of his father.

Without them this book would not have been possible, or at least it would have been a heckuva lot duller.

Introduction

Why a History of Animation Unions?

History [is] but myths we can all agree on.
—Napoleon Bonaparte (1769–1821)

In 20,000 B.C., Stone Age man attempted to draw movement on cave walls by drawing mammoths with multiple legs. The artists worked until their eyes went bad, they got no pay, they got no credit, and they were eventually eaten by wild animals.

Animation was born.

The animation community in the United States is not large: 5,000 people in Los Angeles, 376 in New York, and another 250 in San Francisco. To put this in context, there are 9,000 writers in the Writers Guild, 22,000 actors in the Screen Actors Guild, and 16,000 movie stagehands. Most animators are not known to the general public. For example, few know of Ub Iwerks, Grim Natwick, and Glen Keane, yet they are the animators who drew, respectively, Mickey Mouse, Betty Boop, and Ariel, the Little Mermaid. Although animators are not a big group, their influence far outweighs their number and relative anonymity. Their work generates billions of dollars. I've seen their work on everything from television cartoon shows to big-budget special-effects movies to video games. More important, they influence millions of minds and create years of memories. I daresay some of you know the personality

1

Drawing the Line

of Bugs Bunny or Bart Simpson better than that of your own brother or sister.

As I got to know animators and cartoonists better, I began to learn about the business side of drawing funny animals for a living. I discovered that making people laugh with funny pictures was as much a commodity as peddling oranges or fixing air conditioners. That there were people who drew the pictures, people who sold the funny pictures, and people who paid you to draw funny pictures. That some people made a lot of money, and some were paid very little. Gradually, I learned from older artists of the perennial struggles between the artists and businessmen and of the feuds that in particular affected the specialized world of animated cartoons.

When I became an animator in 1975, I was not a supporter of any union. I was made to join because of the movie I had just been hired to work on. Richard Williams's *Raggedy Ann & Andy* was being done under a union closed-shop contract, so I paid the fees and pledged allegiance to the Motion Picture Screen Cartoonists Local 841 New York of the International Alliance of Theatrical and Stage Employees of the United States and Canada, affiliated with the AFL-CIO. However, my heart was not in it.

I thought the animators union was some kind of club of lesser artists who closed ranks to keep young people out of the business. They extorted dues out of me with threats of fines and dismissal. I never really understood what they did for me other than endlessly annoy the employer who had been nice enough to give me a chance in the first place. In the monthly newsletters I saw photos of the overfed union bosses stuffed into ill-fitting suits, always smiling and shaking hands with one another. None of them seemed to have a neck. I read paragraph after paragraph of boring legal palaver about welfare benefits and old-age annuities. I thought, "What does all this have to do with making *cartoons*? Who needs a union? I am an *artist*, not a longshoreman. What do I need with employer-matched pension contributions?" It all seemed so bourgeois. Shortly after moving to Los Angeles in 1982, I had to walk a picket line for eight weeks in a citywide strike. After the strike, my savings dropped far enough that, for the first time, I needed a loan from my parents. I hated the whole idea of a union. I told myself, "If you're a good enough artist, you don't need a union to get work; you make your own deals."

Introduction

It wasn't until after years of being cheated, being laid off, and being assured I was part of a "family," then cheated and laid off some more, that I came to understand what my union was trying to do for me. I saw how important those defined benefits were to the older, ill artists who once were stars but now were slipping into genteel retirement. I had a gall-bladder operation that would have cost $60,000, but because of my union medical coverage, I paid only $175.

One of the few union meetings I would bother to show up for was the triennial election of officers. After the Runaway Wars of 1982 (see chapter 9), I would go to meetings to make sure they didn't nominate some jerk whose career was going nowhere and thus wanted to be a union boss so he could lord it over his betters. By the time of the meeting in 1992, I had made a bit of a reputation for myself as a Disney animator. As I walked into the packed meeting, union officer Dave Teague whispered to me, "I want to nominate you for a place on the executive board." I told him, no, I didn't want the responsibility. Then layout artist Larry Eikelberry rose and with Dave nominated me for president! I was stunned. I never asked for such a thing, but I admit the honor of it struck my vanity. Being the kid in the school yard who was never picked for ball games, it felt good to be asked. Before you could say Jiminy Cricket, I had won the election. I was head of the largest benevolent organization of animation artists, writers, and technicians in the world. Me, the union-hating cynic. Oh, well, Saint Augustine also had his doubts before conversion. . . .

As president, I determined to bring a level of pragmatism and accountability to the local, to make the union the servant of the artists, to make it *their* organization, *their* club. In the process, I raised a few eyebrows, even kicked up some dust. I was told by many old-timers that they were pleased to see a return to the aggressive leadership of the founders. That intrigued me. I wondered how we got to where we were. Why was there an animators union in Hollywood? Why did the concept of an artists union stir such passions both pro and con?

So I went to sources. I talked to people who started the cartoonists union, the old activists. What I found was not a clique of mediocre artists and thugs but a pantheon of heroes. I was told of the harsh side of some of the more famous cartoon producers. I met animators who, when they were my age and younger, had risked their careers and their fortunes for an idea: all artists will benefit when they join together for a

3

common cause, that no matter how individual an artist you think you are, the money people lump you in with the rest. They consider us a tribe of overgrown children and treat us that way; they think we are all people who want to spend our lives in dark rooms drawing ducks and bunnies. Director Bob Kurtz calls animation folks "wonderfully damaged people." So, if we were one type and one family, wouldn't we be able to do a lot of good for all of us if we spoke collectively to the big shots? As a young artist I never thought about why I had weekends off or why my company offered a fat health insurance package. I thought it was an act of nature like leaves turning colors in the fall. I came to understand that everything I ever enjoyed as an artist in a studio had to be won through demand and sometimes conflict. No boss awakes from a pleasant night's sleep and thinks, "Hmm, I think I'll grant my people an eight-hour workday."

I spoke with animators who marched in the great cartoonists' strike against Walt Disney and who went through the Hollywood blacklisting. I noticed that the animators who crossed the picket line and stuck with Walt would never look me in the eye. Their eyes strayed to the floor as they hemmed and hawed, "Well, it was a difficult time. You can't know if you weren't there." But I noticed that the animators who did go out and strike always looked back at me squarely with a look of calm inner peace. Even in old age their eyes sparkled while recounting how they brought the great studio to a halt and drove old Walt crazy.

I became fascinated with the big Disney studio strike of 1941 because it seemed to me the most neglected and underreported story in animation history. Most corporate-sanctioned accounts of the events of the summer of 1941 quickly pass over the strike to get to bigger events like World War II. Yet here was a traumatic conflict that involved hundreds of people, changed careers, spawned new studios like UPA (United Productions of America) and comic strips, and affected Walt Disney's relations with his people forever. Yet many Disney bios, if they mention it at all, dismiss it in a one-sided paragraph like, "Walt had a big happy family until a few dirty Reds came along and spoiled the fun." The more I researched and uncovered, the more story there was. It pulled in the Mafia, the FBI, the Los Angeles Police Department, and celebrities of the time like writer Dorothy Parker, matinee idol John Garfield, even Ronald Reagan. I discovered that revered names in animation like Chuck Jones; Bill Melendez, the director of *A Charlie Brown Christmas*;

Introduction

Maurice Noble; John Hubley; and Bill Scott, the voice of Bullwinkle, led second lives as passionate union supporters. My research on the Disney strike led to the story of the Max Fleischer studios strike of 1937, the Terrytoons strike of 1947, and so on. Many mainstream film historians told me they are glad someone is finally writing about it. Like Jack Nicholson in Roman Polanski's *Chinatown*, I became a detective uncovering a hidden history, a people's history of animation.

This book is a history, in part a memoir, and in part a personal reflection on my specialized field. It may not always read like an impartial account. Facts are neutral, but their presentation and order is not. Read separate biographies of Thomas Jefferson, John Adams, and Alexander Hamilton and you'll get widely divergent views of the founding of the American Republic. History is never neat and complete. I am presenting a side of animation history rarely discussed. If you want a totally impartial account, then read this book along with a corporate-approved history (which will be mostly from management's point of view), then, forgive the pun, draw your own conclusions.

This book is not a book of criticism about cartoons as art. I do not debate the qualities of Bugs Bunny and Mickey Mouse. More talented writers than I have already done that. I am not out to expose scandal or smear the reputation of some of our greatest animation legends. If some think I am irresponsibly publishing hearsay, I can only say that I was given many inflammatory stories and accusations that I left out. The historian must account for fading memories and desires to settle personal scores. Some in their old age were embarrassed by their passion and wanted to understate the record. I don't think they should be ashamed of their desire to do good. This book is not about some great man's personal prejudices; it's about how the artist handled the labor relations of his time. I may leave out some important names. If I do leave out you or your loved one, please rest assured it was not out of personal animus but from my own limited powers to do justice to so large a subject. I will probably get some things wrong. If so, I apologize, and I hope this book will be only the beginning of increased study of the subject, especially the underreported period of 1960 to 1984.

Unionism is a divisive issue. Readers will draw the conclusions they want to. The ones who hate the idea of unions will see justification in the unions' mistakes; those who support unions will see inspiration in the sacrifices made by others. Hollywood is a union town. Bugs Bunny, Mickey Mouse, Daffy Duck, Donald Duck, Goofy, Tweety, Ariel, Mr. Magoo, Fred and Wilma Flintstone, Roger Rabbit, Simba, and Shrek were all created by union men and women. Animators can't eat cartoons or pay rent with them. Animation artists risked financial loss, blacklisting, and even physical violence to create, under the swaying palm trees of Tinseltown, the highest standard of living in the animation world. And that way of life is under constant attack from the corporate media giants, more so than ever in our modern digital, global economy.

Love them or hate them, for the last century the unions are the one undeniable fact of life in Hollywood animation. For animators it is a lost piece of our history, of who we are. No one can hope to really understand the history of the American animated cartoon without knowing the unions' story. The French writer Chateaubriand said, "The Historian is entrusted with the Vengeance of the People." My hope is that because of what is written here, one day Dave Hilberman, Art Babbitt, Selby Kelly, Moe Gollub, Hicks Lokey, Bill Hurtz, and Sadie Bodin will be as renowned for their achievements as the great animation artists are renowned for theirs. I hope I can also restore a facet of the lives of some top cartoonists like Chuck Jones, Maurice Noble, Steve Bosustow, Frank Tashlin, and Ward Kimball that had been ignored by other writers, one that it is necessary to an understanding of their character, namely, their lives as labor activists.

I feel deeply honored to be able to chronicle the life and times of these great cartoonists and their struggles. My chief regret is that this book will come out too late for most of them to see. I am writing at a time when union membership is the lowest it's been since 1929. As a result, over 30 million Americans have no health coverage and millions more have no savings or retirement funds. Perhaps it is time for the public to reevaluate trade unionism as I did. Read on and judge for yourself.

1

The World of the Animation Studio

The Cartoon Assembly Line

Any nut that wants to spend hundreds of hours and
thousands of drawings to make a few feet of film is
welcome to come join the club!
—Winsor McCay

Animation is a strange art form. It is art and theater produced in industrial quantities. Many more drawings and paintings are
discarded than appear in a final film. Inspiration and creative talent are
treated like so much raw material. Who are the people who work in such
a system? An animation crew is a collection of dozens, often hundreds,
of artists, writers, technicians, and support staff closeted in some large
space, usually uncomfortable, for months, trying to create a film that looks
like it was made by one hand. When working on an animated feature-
film deadline, artists typically put in ten- to fourteen-hour days, seven
days a week. This is as true for modern digital imaging as it was for the
silent black-and-white films. Animators spend more time with their coworkers than with their own families.

In 1938, Ted Le Berthon, a newspaper columnist, wrote: "Cartoon
studios are hard-driven fable factories, jammed with sweating commercial artists who work at breakneck speed on monotonous routines at meager pay. . . . The whole strange business gets in their blood. They think
it, dream it, and live it. It is hard on their nerves. The main industrial

ailments are eyestrain, neuritis, arthritis and alcoholism."[1] I had a conversation with director Robert Zemeckis in Radio City Music Hall at the premiere of his award-winning *Who Framed Roger Rabbit?* (1988). At the wrap party, he marveled at the way an animation crew works: "I'm used to using the same crew, and we go from picture to picture. But you animation folks come together and live with each other for years! You marry each other, bear each other's children, bury each other's grandfathers, and when the film is over, *phfftt*! You scatter to the four winds."

Companies, like empires, rise, dominate, and fall. The make-or-break film becomes just another box in the stacks in a video store, or another download. Yesterday's headline-grabbing studio soon becomes just a file in a licensing attorney's office and a footnote in a film-trivia book. But the hard core of professional animators moves on from project to project. There is an old saying among animation veterans: "You always work with the same people. Only the producers change." The long hours of confinement and mutual ordeal create a camaraderie unique in filmmaking.

For example, in 1975 I first met Eric Goldberg in New York, where he was animating educational films at a small company called Teletactics. A year later we worked on the feature film *Raggedy Ann & Andy* (1977). Then Eric worked in London, and I worked in Toronto. In 1982, we worked together in Hollywood on *Ziggy's Gift*, a TV special. Back in Los Angeles, we hooked up again at Walt Disney Studios for *Aladdin* (1992) and *Pocahontas* (1995). I went on to DreamWorks SKG, then to Warner Bros., where we got together again for *Looney Tunes: Back in Action* (2003). This is typical in the film business. We sometimes call ourselves animation gypsies or migrant film workers.[2] Our social network is tight and global. If an animator takes off his toupee in Los Angeles, his animation buddies in London, Manila, Seoul, Barcelona, Orlando, Berlin, and Istanbul will know in short order.

What kind of person wants to work in this kind of field? Every studio has a kaleidoscope of colorful characters. There are all nationalities, all colors, all pressed into the same space. Traditionally animation artists have come from the quieter side of the classroom, from the ranks of the comic-book reading, reticent kids who like spending long hours in solitude.

So how did it get this way?

The World of the Animation Studio

Art by assembly line is not a new idea. Artists throughout history have used apprentices and associates for large jobs. In the seventeenth century, artists like Rubens and Van Dyck had an assembly line of underpainters, finishers, and toucher-uppers, with clients having rotating sitting appointments. Apprentices mixed colors, applied varnish, even hand-carved pencils and made paper. Michelangelo is noted in contemporary accounts as being unique because he dismissed his staff and worked on the Sistine Chapel ceiling without helpers. Earlier, there were medieval guilds of cathedral builders who crossed borders to work whenever the duke of Chartres or someone got the green light for a new job. If the contract was for length of production on a new Gothic cathedral, it must have meant 150 years worth of work. Talk about job security!

When motion pictures were invented, the young medium hired technicians from circuses and vaudeville. They came around looking for work when the big-top shows were in their winter quarters. Their special skills of hanging lights, applying makeup, and painting scenery were sorely needed in the new industry. Circus job titles—gaffer, grip, best boy—were even incorporated into film jargon.

In 1913, John Randolph Bray was making animated shorts in the manner of pioneer cartoonists Winsor McCay and Emile Cohl; that is, by making thousands of drawings alone. For example, for *The Sinking of the Lusitania* (1917), McCay and his assistant, John Fitzsimmons, took twenty-two months to make twenty-five thousand drawings. The backgrounds were drawn on the same pages as the character drawings.[3] After great exertion, Bray produced his first cartoon short, *The Artist's Dream*. He sold it to Pathé Pictures, and that led to a request for a series of animated shorts to run on a regular delivery schedule in Pathé theaters. Bray realized he needed to do things differently because the workload was far beyond his individual capacity. So he turned to the newfangled notion of the specialized production line. Frederick Taylor's landmark 1911 book, *The Principles of Scientific Management*, theorizes the concept.[4] These theories were utilized by automaker Henry Ford to develop his famous assembly line, which soon became the standard for all American heavy industry. Bray and his production manager, wife Margaret, read Taylor's book and decided to adapt the assembly-line process to making animated cartoons.

Instead of one master cartoonist drawing everything, the process

Animator Al Eugster at his desk at the Walt Disney Hyperion Studio annex, working on *Snow White and the Seven Dwarfs*, circa 1937. Eugster was a dependable staff animator who worked at many of the top studios in the golden age of animation. Besides Disney's he worked at Fleischer's, Famous, and Sullivan's and finished his career doing commercials. Every morning he lined up on his desk all the pencils he intended to use, and all the cigars he intended to smoke. Courtesy of the Al Eugster Estate and Mark Mayerson.

Animator Kevin Koch at his digital workstation on *Over the Hedge*, at DreamWorks Animation, circa 2005. Even though the equipment has changed radically, the animator faces the same creative challenges his pencil-sharpening ancestor possessed. No cigars, though. Koch became Animation Guild president in 2001. His credits include *Shrek 2* and *Madagascar.* Courtesy of DreamWorks Animation.

was broken into specific jobs. One person made up the story, another designed a character, and another animated it, that is, created the motion by drawing keyframes. (Keyframes are the animator's drawings of sequential steps of an action that, when run at film speed, look like movement.) Another artist assisted or cleaned up the drawings, others drew the remaining in-between drawings needed to complete the actions the animator designed. Still another painted the characters onto the new acetate cels developed by Earl Hurd. (Before the invention of acetate celluloids, assistants were called "blackeners" because they inked in the little black bodies of a Felix the Cat or Mickey Mouse.) Another painted background landscapes, one more photographed the drawings onto film. A similar studio was set up in the Bronx under Raoul Barré, but Bray's ideas set the stage for animation production for the rest of the twentieth century. Many of Bray's supervising artists (he called them foremen) went on to open their own studios and copy Bray's production techniques. These artists included Max Fleischer, Paul Terry, and Walter Lantz. Bray used the term "cheapmen" for artists with less-influential positions.[5]

Gregory LaCava was probably the first animation director.[6] That was in 1916 at the Hearst studio. By the early 1920s, the jobs of animation checker and storyboard artist had been created. (A checker was roughly equivalent to a proofreader, performing quality control and numbering the artwork.) A separate artist, called a layout artist, was needed to define the staging of the storyboard sketch before animating. Film editors and, later, sound editors were added. In the late 1930s, to satisfy his desire for realistic animation, Walt Disney created a separate department for special-effects animators—artists who specialized in drawing smoke, flame, water, and lightning. In the 1950s, Jay Ward, Bill Hanna, and Joe Barbera modified the theatrical-shorts production line for the special needs of large-scale television production (see chapter 7).

Bray's industrialized production line became the norm for all animated films from *Colonel Heeza Liar* in 1914 to today's $500 million digital mega hits. This system determined that the American animation studio would be an industrialized plant and not a cooperative atelier of artisans. The unions that were eventually created to support animation workers were also conceived on an industrial model created by American Federation of Labor (AF of L) founder Samuel Gompers. As a young cigar maker in 1877 Gompers witnessed the national railroad workers strikes then called the Great Upheaval. These strikes flared into ugly street battles with guns and bombs. Strikers set fire to railroad sheds, and militia fired their rifles indiscriminately into crowds of workers' families. Anarchists set off bombs in train boilers and shouted "Hurrah for anarchy" as they were hanged. The news of the American labor unrest reached Europe, where Karl Marx wondered if the worker revolution he envisioned might first start in America. Shocked by the useless carnage, Samuel Gompers conceived a new union of craftsmen governed not by a political committee but by a board of officers who could talk as equals to corporate leaders. His AF of L had an executive board elected by the membership with a president, vice president, and sergeant at arms. This became the model for all American labor unions. At first the AF of L was to be a union only of skilled craftsmen, like animators. In 1951 it joined with the Congress of Industrial Organizations (CIO), the alliance of unskilled laborers.

In the field of animation, new studio head John Randolph Bray had created a paradox. His assembly line for art created a class of workers who (still today) see themselves as individual artists yet also as part of a company that needs their output to blend into the whole. But Bray ensured that they could count on work and paychecks every week. The assembly-line system relieves artists of the burden of mastering business affairs, in addition to the skills they need in drawing, acting, natural science, action analysis, and cinema. They just go to work and let the big boss worry about making deals and signing contracts. Bray also defined the relationship of the animation studio head to his staff. He wore suits and high, starched collars and glared at his staff through his pince-nez. He set his desk on a level above his open production floor so he could bark orders down at the artists. James "Shamus" Culhane recalled Bray as cool and aloof. He said as a young boy he was afraid to even wish "Mr. Bray" a good morning.[7]

In the Depression years of the 1930s, animation was still a young industry filled with young, single people making good money while their relatives stood in breadlines. The young artists lived and worked as a team under pressure-cooker conditions for countless hours, so when the time came to loosen up and celebrate, they partied hard. In 1938 when Walt Disney threw a huge Christmas party in his studio for his staff after *Snow White*'s successful premiere, the animation crew went on a wild debauch. People got so drunk they fell out of windows. Luckily, the party was on the ground floor, so no one was hurt. But the studio was so trashed afterward that Walt decided to hold all future parties in rented space. A year later he threw a company party at a dude ranch north of Norco, California. When Walt and Roy Disney and their wives drove up to the lodge a day later, they found something more like a Roman orgy than a Christmas party. Guys and gals were running naked from room to room, and one animator drunkenly galloped a horse up a stairway and down a second-floor hallway. Maurice Noble recalls standing at the head of the stairs waving a welcome to his bosses. Walt and Roy got back in their car and left before local reporters could associate them with the wild goings-on.[8]

From 1928 to 1955, American animation exploded with the creation of a legion of characters and films as famous now as they were sixty years ago. The Max Fleischer studio had Betty Boop, Koko, and Popeye; Leon Schlesinger's studio (later Warner Bros.) had Bugs Bunny, Daffy Duck, Porky Pig, Elmer Fudd, the Road Runner, and Wile E. Coyote. Walt Disney had Mickey Mouse, Donald Duck, Goofy, and the Big Five feature-length films: *Snow White, Fantasia, Bambi, Pinocchio,* and *Dumbo*; MGM had Tom and Jerry, Droopy Dog, and the Tex Avery cartoons. Walter Lantz had Woody Woodpecker, Andy Panda, and Chilly Willy; Terrytoons had Gandy Goose, Barney Bear, Mighty Mouse, and Heckle and Jeckle. After 1945, United Productions of America (UPA) expanded the range of animation into new styles and modern interpretations with Mr. Magoo, Gerald McBoing-Boing, and the *Telltale Heart*. The skills of drawn performance and graphic storytelling reached a level of artistry envied today. It was truly a golden age.

We like to think of those times as the golden age not only of animation art but of working conditions. When modern animators think of animation workers of the 1930s and 1940s, they may rhapsodize that artists then lived on the love of cartoons and had no pressures. Today we labor under faceless and greedy corporations, ever-tightening deadlines, and distracting studio politics. Today it's all business, but in 1940 it must have been all art. Never mind Hitler, the Depression, or Jim Crow, it must have been one long party, and that's why *Pinocchio* and Tom and Jerry were so good. "Not exactly," say the artists of that age. True, they were

(Above) Animators clowning around on the roof of the Sullivan studio near West Sixty-third Street, Manhattan, 1928. Left to right, Rudy Zamora, George Cannata, Hal Walker, Al Eugster, Tom Byrne. Zamora would later gain fame for driving MGM's Fred Quimby crazy by rolling bowling balls above his head, and for annoying Walt Disney with questions like, "Hey Walt, how does this stuff move, anyhow?" Courtesy of the Al Eugster Estate and Mark Mayerson. *(Below)* Two of Disney's *Lion King* lead animators, Michael Surrey (Timon) and Tony Bancroft (Pumbaa), clowning around, Glendale, California, 1994. Courtesy of Archives of the Animation Guild, Local 839, IATSE (formerly MPSC Local 839), North Hollywood.

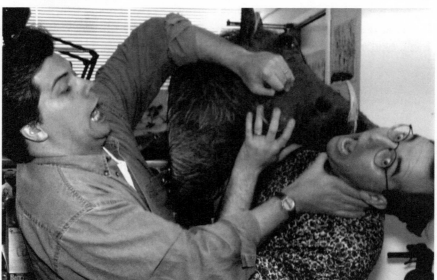

young and happy to be working at such an exciting time, but it was still a job in a factory town called Hollywood.

In the 1930s everybody worked a forty-six-hour, six-day workweek: 9:00 A.M. to 6:00 P.M., Monday through Friday, and 9:00 A.M. to 1:00 P.M. Saturday.[9] If you had a problem with that, you could go to Uncle Max or Uncle Walt and he would let you work Thursday until 11:00 P.M. instead. At Fleischer's you had to work every Friday until 9:30 P.M. Remember, this was not overtime; it was the normal weekly schedule. It was common to be told by a supervisor at 5:00 P.M., "You're working tonight," whether or not it was convenient for you. At the Iwerks studio the production manager, Emile Offerman, seemed to prefer telling the staff late on Friday afternoons that they would have to work all weekend to make up the schedule. At MGM, Tuesday nights were overtime nights. When producer Fred Quimby arranged for the commissary to set aside one table for animators, the animators took this to mean a table at the main MGM cafeteria, the art deco palace designed by Cedric Gibbons, the art director of *Gone with the Wind.* It was where Clark Gable and Judy Garland ate. The animators rushed the place and ordered steaks and chops until word got to MGM chief Louis B. Mayer. He banished the animators to the more proletarian burger grill on the lot.[10] On the plus side, though, Mayer insisted that every commissary on the MGM lot stock plenty of chicken soup, made according to his mother's recipe. Only twenty-five cents, and the soup was pretty good.

Congress passed the Fair Labor Standards Act in 1938. It stipulated an eight-hour workday and a forty-hour week; the progressive Roosevelt administration even considered a thirty-five-hour workweek. But the animation industry at first preferred to maintain its forty-six-hour week. In 1941 Walt Disney and most other studios went to a forty-hour week, more to attempt to forestall the artists from unionizing than to obey Washington. In the 1980s and 1990s many computer houses were doing the same thing for the same reason. In the 1990s, a CGI (computer animation) studio head lectured his exhausted workers on the "reality of the fifty-five-hour workweek." Hellishly long working days are equally common in live-action schedules, but the duration of the projects is shorter—usually no more than six weeks of shooting—and rest periods longer. Animation studios go on in the same pressurized mode all year round.

In the early days, any type of overtime compensation was mostly unheard of. Shamus Culhane told me Max Fleischer paid a little overtime. In 1935, the Van Beuren studio made its workers bank their extra hours as comp time, as many CGI houses do today. Nobody liked the practice back then either. Charles Mintz studios paid 60 cents a week for overtime. Claire Weeks told me that during *Snow White's* deadline rush, the studio demanded three hours extra a day, and the only compensation was a 55-cent meal ticket to Blackie's Steakhouse on Sunset Boulevard.[11] To be fair, in 1937 it was possible to buy a good meal for 55 cents.

Time clocks were standard at most studios. At MGM and Schlesinger's, a little electric bell told you when you could get up from your desk for a break; fifteen minutes later, the bell announced it was time to go back to work.[12] At Disney, workers had to get a hall pass from the supervisor to get up from their desks, even to use the restroom. Animator Ed Friedman told me he felt insulted. He was an adult, and obtaining permission to go to the restroom was like being in school. Disney kept the hall passes and a time clock for the ink-and-paint divisions until 1990. The inkers would receive the drawings with a time code: A, B, C, D, or E. The codes told them how many minutes they were expected to take to ink each drawing onto an acetate sheet, or cel: ten minutes for an A, forty minutes for an E.[13] When I worked at Hanna-Barbera in 1978, the time clock was out of use; it kept having "accidents," like people might be pouring glue and cel paint into it, so the company switched to the dreaded "late book." If you got to work late, even five minutes past the 8:30 A.M. starting time, you had to let the security guard write your name in a ledger that the high command would supposedly read at the end of the month. I never heard of anyone actually being fired for repeated entries, but we feared it enough that on any morning around 8:28 A.M., you could see people literally running up Cahuenga Boulevard to avoid that fate.

In the golden age, employee vacations were unheard of or only rarely granted. Chuck Jones recalls that at Leon Schlesinger's studio artists were allowed a weeklong vacation after they had banked at least forty-eight hours of free overtime during the year. Disney visual-development artist Bianca Marjolie took some unauthorized time to visit her mother. When she returned to the studio on June 1, 1940, she was surprised to find someone else in her office. Her personal effects were waiting out in the guard's shack. Without any warning she had been fired. Master designer

Kay Neilsen was the designer of the unique look of the Beethoven's Pastoral sequence in *Fantasia*, but when Neilsen complained about the long, "fatiguing" hours and working conditions, master designer Kay Neilsen was laid off on May 23, 1941. Designer Jules Engel concluded, "When you don't have unions, this is what happens."[14]

Health coverage didn't exist in the animation industry during the golden age because it didn't exist much of anywhere else either. If someone got really sick, the studio head, like a benevolent medieval lord, might help out. But nothing was in writing. In 1932, Iwerks's production manager, Emile Offeman, thought Godfrey Bjork, an artist with a bad heart, was taking too much time off just to goof off. Offeman hounded Bjork by phoning him at home to see if he had run off to the movies and also by sending work to his sickbed. When Bjork died of heart failure, many artists blamed Offeman.[15]

Before the unions, old-age pensions for animators didn't exist. Almost all artists and other crew members were in their twenties. In 1941, Walt Disney was just forty. Retirement seemed too far off to be a concern. The record shows that, with the exception of Disney and Warner Bros., no studio ever stayed around long enough for anyone to retire. Shamus Culhane estimates the average studio life span at about ten years, and the trend continues today. The stories of the Disney artists who became rich on Disney stock are true only for some. Regardless of their contributions to film classics, without union pensions, many golden age artists would have been destitute in their final years.

In 1941, the Walt Disney studio produced one feature and eighteen short films; Max Fleischer's produced thirty shorts.[16] To keep up with the pressures of production, artists were valued for being fast as well as good. In the silent era, Otto Messmer, Ub Iwerks, and Bill Nolan were famous as being the fastest artists in the business. Ub Iwerks, working alone, animated Walt Disney's 1929 short *The Skeleton Dance*.

At Disney in the 1990s, if you could animate five feet of film a week, you were considered a speed demon. That's roughly 40 finished drawings in 35mm film. At Warner Bros. in 1940, the weekly quota for animating Bugs Bunny was twenty-three feet a week or 276 finished drawings minimum. At MGM it was twenty-five feet, and at Iwerks studio it was thirty feet. Most of this footage was done with little or no testing. Once New York animator Vladimir "Bill" Tytla mentioned to his boss, Paul

Terry, that some guy named Walt Disney out west was letting his artists shoot pencil tests. "What's a pencil test?" Paul asked. Bill explained that it's when the animator shoots a test on film to check his animation before it gets inked and blackened. Paul dismissed the notion with a puff of his cigar. "Humph! I pay my boys to do it right the first time!" he said.[17] Fleischer animator Jack Ozark recalls that money was saved in developing fees when the studio let him pencil test his work by keeping a bucket of film developer by his desk. He would dunk his footage himself in the bucket, then look at it before the image faded to black. (There was no Hypo or fixative.)[18] The developer and nitrate films as well as the animation cels were toxic; they were also highly flammable. Most artists smoked at their desks, so it's a miracle there were not more fires or explosions. Shamus Culhane recalls an errand boy who parked his cigarette near a three-foot-tall pile of *Pinocchio* cels. Soon flames were shooting up the side of the stack, but the fire was stamped out before any artwork was damaged.

Modern animators in large studios are subject to periodic reviews by their supervisors and are discussed in personnel departments without animators' knowledge. Well, that's not a new idea. I've seen the 1940 performance review of Bill Tytla, arguably the greatest animator of the age. He gave life to Grumpy, Stromboli, the Devil on Bald Mountain, and Dumbo. But his review reads: "Bill is a terrific draughtsman but he leaves too much for the assistants and scene planners. . . . He has difficulty taking direction." Attitude problems, the favorite of supervisors. One commercial studio in the 1950s placed every animator's name on a large chart and put a check next to the name every time the artist made a mistake.[19] You can guess the fate of the artist with the most checks.

In the late 1970s, the Disney studio was known for having cels from its classic films displayed in the hallway of the Animation Building. One day someone noticed one missing. The studio was turned upside down; every artist's desk and personal belongings were vigorously searched. Eventually it was discovered that the missing character had merely slipped off its aging tape and fallen behind the cardboard mat in the frame. No apology for the overreaction was given.[20]

Part of the reason the golden-age studios were such hotbeds of creativity was competition. Chuck Jones said he wished artists would not compete with one another, but they often did. Max Fleischer and Ub

The World of the Animation Studio

Iwerks wanted to topple Walt Disney; MGM changed from one director to another, attempting to achieve a competitive edge over other studios. Because most shorts were done by a team of artists who worked together as a unit from film to film, intraunit rivalries were bound to happen. At Disney the feature animators looked down on the shorts animators. A common put-down at the studio was, "He's a good shorts animator." Even into the late 1990s the feature-film crews at Disney didn't want to be associated with the television-unit artists. At Warner Bros., the Bob Clampett, Friz Freleng, and Chuck Jones units had a hot rivalry. Some say the reason Bob left Warner's in 1945 was that after Leon Schlesinger retired, Bob lost his strongest ally against Friz and Chuck. Directors Frank Tashlin and Tex Avery left for their own reasons, and Friz and Chuck became the dominant forces in Warners' creative output, freely borrowing animators they needed from other units. At UPA, the rivalry was between the John Hubley and Bill Hurtz units. Hurtz told me he always regretted the studio's decision not to enter his masterpiece, *A Unicorn in the Garden,* for Oscar consideration for fear it would harm the chances of their other entry, Hubley's *Gerald McBoing-Boing*, which eventually won.

Still, compared to the plight of many Americans during the Great Depression and the war years, life at an animation studio was pretty good. At a time when most Americans suffered horrible poverty and waited in long breadlines and ate in soup kitchens, animation work paid reasonably well and was steady. Some animators could afford a car or even a maid. Walt Disney paid for all the art lessons for his animators from the well-known Chouinard Art Institute instructor Don Graham, and at first drove the artists to the school himself. Many are the stories of Uncle Walt, Max, or Leon helping out an artist who needed money for an operation or other emergency.

In the 1930s, before unions, artists' wages were an unregulated free-for-all from $500 a week for a top animator down to $12 for a cel painter. In 1941, animation directors were paid on average between $150 and $300 a week, animators from $50 to $250, background painters from $50 to $150 a week, story sketchers from $50 to $150 a week, inbetweeners from $30 to $75, inkers and painters from $17 to $35 a week.[21] Walt Disney, like Louis B. Mayer of MGM, boasted that his personal salary was only about $500 a week. The big money came in large, unstructured bonuses the big bosses awarded themselves. In 1939, it was estimated that 25 percent of the total revenue of the Warner Bros. studio went to several executives in the form of bonuses.[22] In 1939, Louis B. Mayer was the highest-paid executive in America, earning $1,296,000. In 1999, it was Michael Eisner of the Walt Disney Company, earning $7 million.

In the preunion 1930s, while Mayer and Jack Warner made what they made, new trainee and future Warner Bros. animator Virgil Ross was hired at $6 a week. Animator Ken Harris started at Rohmer-Grey Studios in 1930, paying the studio for the privilege of learning animation while working on films. After a few weeks, the production head told Ken he was such a good artist he would be allowed to work for nothing! Ken went home and proudly said to his mother, "Hey, Mom. Guess what! The studio's going to let me work for free."[23] Chuck Jones remembers being hired at Looney Tunes studio for $18.50 a week. Walt Disney needed to hire master animator Grim Natwick to help bolster the drive to create more humanlike animation for *Snow White*. Supposedly, while screening a Betty Boop cartoon, Walt jumped up in the theater and yelled, "We gotta get that guy!" I saw Grim Natwick's 1931 job offer. When it gets down to money, its language would sound familiar to many an animator: "Walt has seen your stuff, and while he doesn't think that much of it, he'd like to make you an offer of $150 a week." Jack Zander told me that at the MGM studio, whenever you went to producer Fred Quimby with a complaint or to ask for a raise, he would reach into a drawer of his otherwise clean desk and pull out his dreaded "footage book." He would then knit his brows and frown darkly as he perused the record of your performance thus far.[24]

In the early 1930s, before union contracts, a studio that got a lot of work would raid other studios for talent. Martha Sigall recalls Schlesinger production supervisor Ray Katz (Leon's brother-in-law) waiting at the entrance of a rival studio, asking ink-and-paint girls as they left work, "How much are you getting paid? Like to make $5 a week more?"[25] When Charles Mintz took Oswald the Lucky Rabbit away from Walt Disney, he took most of Walt's artists with him. Walt took it personally that those artists would leave him. Disney commented to Mintz, "Now watch out for them, Charlie. If they do it to me, they'll do it to you."[26]

In 1935, Max Fleischer promoted Lillian Friedman to be his first woman animator and paid her $40 a week. Her male counterparts averaged $125 a week.[27] Dave Fleischer, in his old age, claimed his studio paid artists from $1,000 to $3,000 a week, not a common salary until the 1990s, but I could find no one to corroborate Dave's statement. Cel painter Martha Sigall told me she was hired at Schlesinger's at a weekly salary of $12.75. After one year she was declared a journeyman and her salary was raised to $21 a week. After that no more raises were allowed. Inkers always made a little more: $23 a week. Inkers and painters told me that when Disney built his big, beautiful cafeteria in his big, beautiful Burbank studio in 1940, most of them couldn't afford to eat there. They still went to the lunch wagon. Art Babbitt told me of one cel painter named Helen Blume, who, on her meager salary, was supporting her children and her mother. Her husband had run off—not an uncommon occurrence during the Depression. She tried to stretch her money by skipping lunches. One day she actually passed out at her desk from hunger.[28]

At most studios whenever you wanted a raise, you had to haggle like a horse trader. Bill Melendez said Leon Schlesinger was a master at faking a heart attack over a request for more money.[29] Ben Washam said Leon loved to throw back at his workers that Ken Harris, acknowledged by his peers as the studio's master draftsman, was happy with his low rate. Washam finally went to Leon and demanded a raise for Harris. Harris got mad at Washam for doing that, but Washam said no one had a chance to get a raise until Harris got one.[30] Disney animator Virgil Partch asked his supervisor for a raise and was told, "Now's not the time. We're in the middle of production." So Partch waited and asked again. That time he was told, "Now's not the time. We're in between productions." Finally when he got his layoff notice, Partch took it into his supervisor's office and said, "Is now a good time to ask for that raise?"[31]

Animators today dream of a classic oak, handmade workstation. In the silent era, the Raoul Barré–Charles Bowers studio in the Bronx was a large room with no rugs, drapes, or heat. Animators went home when their fingers got too cold to draw.[32] In the 1930s, Fleischer, Terry, and Schlesinger equipped their studios with used office furniture and kitchen tables obtained at garage sales. Termite Terrace, as the Looney Tunes studio was derisively named, was a "barn of a building" where artists would punch a hole in the wall to toss out a Coke bottle or draw funny faces over the stains on the walls. Phil DeLara did a goofy drawing of a Japanese bomber pilot being castigated by his commander after destroying Schlesinger's, "I said ammunition dump, not animation dump!" Dave Deitich's studio was in an old pickle factory. If you dropped your pencil, it rolled to the center of the room. The floors had been built to slope toward a center drain. At Charles Mintz's studio there was a center rug that had not been cleaned for months. It was so filthy that clouds of dust would billow up when someone walked by too fast. When no amount of complaining would get the landlord to do something, one animator sprinkled grass seed into the rug and watered it. After several days, green shoots started to appear. The staff then asked the landlord, "Please come and mow the carpet."[33] No wonder animators who moved to Disney's Hyperion Studio or to MGM noted with amazement that the furniture all matched! Painter Martha Sigall told me that the first thing she noticed about going from Termite Terrace to MGM in 1943 was that at MGM they took the trash out every day.[34]

Today some studios offer free lunch and an in-house health club. Up until the film *The Great Mouse Detective* (1986), at Walt Disney you had to pitch in money to pay for coffee and bottled water, and you had to pay rent for your parking space. Some comic-book companies used to ask the artists to pay rent for their desks. At the Fleischer studio, when Dave Fleischer put his red light on outside his office, it meant he did not want to be disturbed. This meant either that he was working or, more likely, that he was having sex with his secretary or listening to racetrack calls on his big radio.[35] An executive from Paramount accused Dave of doing bookie work for his staff on the side and said that it would spoil Paramount's good reputation.[36]

In recent years Hollywood animation people complained that the producers who boss them around know nothing about animation. In the 2D boom of the 1990s (see chapter 10) many were from the Broadway stage or some corporate conglomerate. It's an opportunity for amateurs to play filmmaker without the serious risk of having a live actor storm off a picture in a rage. Cartoon people put up with a lot. Back in the golden age, Leon Schlesinger was CEO of Pacific Art & Title Company. The brothers Warner owed him a favor for helping them get the funding for their 1927 breakthrough hit, *The Jazz Singer*. When Leon Schlesinger retired in 1943, Warner Bros. replaced him with Eddie Selzer, whose only experience was arranging publicity for road shows with showgirls. With the exception of Walt Disney, animation studios were fringe operations of the Big Five, the larger Hollywood studios: Paramount, Columbia, Fox, Warner Bros., and MGM. The Big Five movie studios in turn answered to banks like the Bank of America or to Wall Street.

Some art historians fail to see artists' work in the context of the times they lived in and recognize that artists are not divorced from politics. In 1495, Leonardo Da Vinci had to flee when the French king defeated his producer, Ludovico Sforza. After Napoleon's defeat at Waterloo, artist Jacques-Louis David went into exile, and his painting was never the same. Master of the Japanese print Kitagawa Utamaro was handcuffed and beaten by a local samurai for doing some drawings of him he felt were insulting.

When the McCarthy anti-Communist hearings were extended to Hollywood in 1947, as we'll see in chapter 6, there were animators who were named and studio heads who named them. In 1936, Disney's lawyer once chewed out animator Ward Kimball for having an "Upton Sinclair for Governor" sign in his car.[37] Muckraker author Sinclair was the socialist candidate who terrified the California establishment and was the target of the first modern negative media campaign. In 1946, Chuck Jones, as a member of the liberal action committee Hollywood Independent Citizens Committee of Arts, Sciences and Professions—mercifully known as HICCASP—took some time out from drawing Bugs Bunny cartoons to paint campaign posters for a Democratic congressman, Jerry Voorhees, who was running against a GOP newcomer just out of the navy, Richard M. Nixon.[38]

I worked in 1979 at a studio hired to produce a nuclear energy commercial shortly after the Three Mile Island meltdown. The cel painters refused to work on it. The studio heads' first impulse was to fire everyone. Some women artists refused to work on the "Taarna" sequence of the film *Heavy Metal*, in which the heroine is bound, stripped, and bullwhipped by the villain, because they felt it was demeaning to women. And so it goes.

Because the American animated film emerged from the newspaper business, animators brought their white-male-dominated world with them.

Inkers and painters at Walt Disney Studios, 1957. Phyllis Craig is seated. Standing, left to right, Sylvia Cobb, unknown, Mary Tebb, and Ann Lord. Because the ink-and-paint departments of the studios were dominated by women, their offices were jokingly referred to as hen houses, YWCAs, and such. The Disney ink-and-paint unit was called Tehachapi, after the local women's prison. Courtesy of Anne Guenther and Archives of the Animation Guild Local 839, IATSE (formerly MPSC Local 839), North Hollywood.

There were a few exceptions such as Max Fleischer's head of cleanup, Edith Vernick; animators like Laverne Harding, Lillian Friedman, Retta Scott, and Ruth Kissane; and designer Mary Blair. But most women, regardless of their artistic skills, were compelled to aspire no higher than coloring, painting, and checking. In the 1930s, there was an infamous story of a woman who interviewed at Disney. She had a terrific portfolio. Her life drawing showed that she could easily be a good animator. All the male artists asked her was, "Can ya make coffee?"[39] Selby Kelly was a published illustrator of children's books when she applied to Disney in 1936. "They laughed at me and told me to go across the street to Ink & Paint," she recalled.[40] She became head of the paint-mixing lab. One well-circulated relic is a 1939 rejection letter to Frances Brewer, another artist. It stated that at Disney, "women do not do any of the creative work

WALT DISNEY PRODUCTIONS

2719 HYPERION AVENUE · HOLLYWOOD, CALIFORNIA · CABLE ADDRESS: DISNEY

May 9, 1939

Miss Frances Brewer
4412 Ventura Canyon Avenue
Van Nuys, California

Dear Miss Brewer:

Your letter of some time ago has been turned over to the Inking and Painting Department for reply.

Women do not do any of the creative work in connection with preparing the cartoons for the screen, as that work is performed entirely by young men. For this reason girls are not considered for the training school.

To qualify for the only work open to women one must be well grounded in the use of pen and ink and also of water color. The work to be done consists of tracing the characters on clear celluloid sheets with India ink and filling in the tracings on the reverse side with paint according to directions.

In order to apply for a position as "Inker" or "Painter" it is necessary that one appear at the studio on a Tuesday morning between 9:30 and 11:30, bringing samples of pen and ink and water color work. We will be glad to talk with you further should you come in.

Yours very truly,

WALT DISNEY PRODUCTIONS

By: Mary E Cleave

by HC

MEC:HC

Disney internal memo sent to artist job applicant Frances Brewer, May 9, 1939. This infamous memo has been copied and circulated by women animators for many years as a reminder of how far they've come. Courtesy of Archives of the Animation Guild Local 839, IATSE (formerly MPSC Local 839), North Hollywood.

in preparation of Cartoons for the screen; that is done by young men. . . . Your request has been forwarded to our Ink & Paint Department." In 1972, new artist Heidi Guedel was told by her roommate, Sylvia Mattinson: "This studio will never allow a woman to become an animator! I'm an Assistant Animator and that is as far as any woman has ever gotten here! The last girl who tried this [Disney] training program left in tears!"[41] Mary Blair had once been called by Walt Disney "the best artist in the studio." Within a year of Walt's death she had resigned, perhaps as a result of professional jealousy of a woman with that much importance.

The ink-and-paint departments of most studios were jokingly referred to as "hen houses" because of the overwhelming predominance of women. The Disney ink-and-paint department was nicknamed Little Tehachapi after a California women's prison.[42] Women artists were restricted by a series of dress codes and personal rules that in today's world would be seen as blatant infringement of personal privacy. The studio created a strict rule against ink-and-paint women fraternizing with male artists. It was felt that they would distract the men from their work. This is interesting because both Walt and Roy Disney married ink-and-paint artists.[43] The Penthouse Club for the animators was off-limits to women until the 1970s. When Disney expanded live-action filming to the back lot, ink-and-paint girls were strictly forbidden from talking to the live-action crews. In 1953, inker Irma Gibbs was unceremoniously fired when her supervisor found out she had been asked to go on a date with a cast member from the Disney live-action TV show *Zorro*.[44] Today, elderly ink-and-paint artists recognize in one another the "Disney shuffle." Because they were on the second floor, women were reprimanded for making too much noise when their high heels clattered as they rushed about with scenes. They were all ordered to walk softly with small steps in a shuffling gait, not picking their feet up too high.[45] People who saw them shuffling about in supermarkets wondered if their feet had been bound Chinese-style when they were children.

The Disney studio dress code was very strict: women had to wear dresses or skirts to work, and ostentatious displays of jewelry were forbidden. In 1958, Disney painter Renée Tenny showed up at work one day wearing a tasteful matching pantsuit à la Kate Hepburn in *The Philadelphia Story*. She was quickly fired.[46] It was not until 1977 that the code was relaxed enough to allow women to wear jeans to work. Background artist Annie Guenther trained a male artist named John Coleman. The studio wanted to promote John above Annie, but there was worry about the bad feelings that would ensue. The solution was to fire Annie.[47]

Nowadays everyone is sensitive to the issue of sexual harassment. In the golden age, guys who got fresh with girls were joked about as wolves and tomcats. A girl who complained about a butt pinch was called a killjoy or an old maid. One animator claimed to that he had studied optometry and promised free eye exams. Any girl who took him up on his offer found out the exam was done in the solitude of his office, where the "optometrist" insisted she had to take her shirt off for the exam. Martha Sigall tells a story of a big-breasted painter who had to endure a certain male animator who liked to reach around from behind and squeeze her breasts while she tried to paint. When she complained, she was just laughed at and called a spoilsport. Finally she came up with a solution. She lined a padded bra with sharp steel pushpins, points out, and covered it with a loosely fitted silk shirt. When the animator in question grabbed the booby traps, he let out a howl. He was cured of such behavior.

Warner Bros. character Speedy Gonzales had his origin in Frank Gonzales, an assistant animator. Gonzales managed to finish his daily drawing quota faster than anyone else so he could be the first to wander over to ink and paint to flirt with the girls. In 1953, when Chuck Jones charged designer Hawley Pratt to come up with some new characters, Hawley thought of Speedy Gonzales.[48] The real-life Speedy eventually calmed down, married, and had a long and happy career, retiring in 1987.

Since the golden age there have been some great women animators in commercial American animation. They include Retta Scott, LaVerne Harding, Ruth Kissane, Sue Kroyer, Kathy Zeilinski, Sue Nichols, Linda Miller, Nancy Beiman, Heidi Guedel, Jane Baer, Diann Landau, Vera Lanpher, Brenda Banks, Carol Millican, Anne Marie Bardwell, Caroline Cruikshank, Caroline Hu, and Theresa Wiseman. Brenda Chapman-Lima was the first woman to be a head of story, or storyboard supervisor, on Disney's *Lion King* (1995); she was later a director of *The Prince of Egypt* (2000). Vicky Jenson codirected the DreamWorks hit films *Shrek* (2001) and *Shark Tale* (2004), and Lorna Pomeroy-Cook codirected the feature *Spirit: Stallion of the Cimarron* (2002). Yvette Kaplan directed *Beavis and Butthead Do America* (1998). Many modern Hollywood producers and development executives are women. But, as of this writing, women animation artists still aren't as plentiful in U.S. studios as they are in Europe and Latin America. On occasion you still hear things like, "Hey, you're making pretty good money for a girl."

Asian and Latino artists didn't seem to have the same barriers to advancement in U.S. animation that African American and women artists have had. Rudy Zamora, Bill Melendez, Phil Roman, Iwao Takamoto, Frank Gonzales, Chris Ishii, Ray Aragon, Ruben Apodaca, and Tyrus Wong all had long and important careers alongside their Anglo counterparts. Melendez was the son of a colonel in the Mexican army who sent his son to Los Angeles for an education. Like many Mexicans from upper-class families, he had many given names: Guatamoc Guillermo José Maria Melendez. When Leon Schlesinger set a rule that animators stop using nicknames on cartoon credits, Melendez played with the rule by using two or more of his names on each film. So when you see Looney Tunes credits with G. Melendez, J. C. Melendez, or G. W. Melendez listed as animator, all refer to the same man. During World War II, Chris Ishii painted cartoon logos for air force bombers even while his family was interned at Camp Manzanar. In 1953, Terrytoons artist Bob Kuwahara created a Japanese family of mice in *Hashimoto Mouse*. Iwao Takamoto was picking strawberries in the Imperial Valley when friends advised him to get a job drawing cartoons. He rose to be a senior assistant at Disney for *Sleeping Beauty*. At Hanna-Barbera, he was the creator of Scooby-Doo, Peter Potamus, Penelope Pittstop, and the Ant Hill Mob, among many others.

African Americans had to wait until the 1950s to get into drawing jobs. In 1948, the same year Jackie Robinson took the field for a major league baseball team, Frank Braxton became the first black animation artist hired at Walt Disney.[49] He left after two months for reasons never explained. Braxton had befriended animation union president Ben Washam when they met at the office of a voice coach they were both seeing. Washam went into the office of Warner Bros. production manager Johnny Burton and said, "I hear Warners has a racist policy and won't hire blacks." Burton swung around in his chair, furious, and snapped back, "Whoever said that is a liar! That's not true!" Washam countered, "Well, then I have a young black artist out here who is terrific. I guess he came to the right place."[50] Braxton became an animator on Chuck Jones's crew and later for MGM. Friends said Braxton was aware he was one of the first black animators in America and that thought drove him to seek perfection. Many said he would have been better known had not cancer taken his life in the late 1960s.

After Braxton, Floyd Norman, hired in 1954, became the first black animator to stay at Disney and have a regular career there. Black designer Phil Mendez joked that he was hired by Disney from New York on the basis of his portfolio, and that when the Disney reps met him at the airport, they were surprised because they expected him to be Hispanic.

Animator Bob Tyler recalls that when he applied for a job at Disney in 1965, a studio exec tried to fob him off with excuses like, "You would probably be too tired from riding the bus up from Inglewood to work properly." Then, after the Watts riots and the federal Civil Rights Act of 1964 establishing hiring quotas for all corporations, the same exec called Tyler and asked sheepishly if he would consider reapplying. In 1972, Jim Simon created Wantu Animation, the first all–African American animation studio. But it was difficult to find animators, so after a while, I was working for Simon next to Bob Arkwright, whose family came over on the *Mayflower.*

Were there gay animators in the 1930s and 1940s? Undoubtedly, but they remained under deep cover. A gay could be ostracized and lose his job. Before the American Psychiatric Association reclassified it in 1973, homosexuality was considered a mental illness. A person thought to be gay could be legally committed and potentially subjected to therapies like electroshock and lobotomy. The "love that dare not speak its name" remained so in Toon Town. Disney animation producer Tom Schumacher, the first Disney employee to openly declare himself gay, did so in an article in *Out* magazine in 1994. If there were gay and lesbian animators in the golden age, their peers respected their wishes and remained discreetly silent.

Alcoholism has always been the occupational disease of animators. I recall going to a barbecue restaurant in Van Nuys near where the old DePatie-Freleng studio used to be. When asked for my drink order, I asked for a draft beer with a Jack Daniels chaser. The waitress immediately replied, "So, are you an animator too?" When I worked on *The Little Mermaid,* I had one of the older animation desks. The edges of the shelves were rimmed with metal plates to cover the burns in the oak from cigarette butts. Stan Green, assistant of now retired Milt Kahl, said to me, "Did you notice yet that the handles of your desk can open a bottle of beer perfectly and your cabinets can fit a bottle of Scotch? Don't think they are that way by a coincidence."

An artist's personal creative hunger, coupled with the game of Chutes and Ladders for which Hollywood is famous, drives many to seek solace in a bottle. Famous animators whom I won't name out of respect for their families drank themselves into an early grave or drove off cliffs or into trees. Being on top and then suddenly sitting with a portfolio next to some college student waiting to be interviewed by a producer young enough to be your daughter is more than some can bear. The pressure to succeed and, when on top, not to fall is as strong in Toon Town as in other fields. There's a well-known story about cartoonist-director Milt Gross, whose books of humorous cartoons made even Charlie Chaplin giggle. In 1938, Gross was driving his stylish convertible roadster while inebriated and crashed into the pumps of an Esso gas station. His car came to a standstill with the front end propped at a 45-degree angle against some bent gas pumps. Amazingly there was no explosion. When service attendants rushed up to him, Gross casually leaned over and mumbled, "Fill 'er up!"

There have been many suicides in animation, the most notable being that of Frank Churchill, the composer of "Who's Afraid of the Big Bad Wolf?" Some say he shot himself while seated at a piano crying, "How's this, Walt?" Others say he killed himself in a Valencia onion field that would one day be the site of the California Institute of the Arts, a regional center for both music and animation. Supposedly a Disney animator jumped off the studio water tower in 1936. In the downturn period from 1998 to 2003, there were five suicides.

There will be those among general readers who will say, "But it's just cartoons!" That attitude is another problem animation artists complain of, not being taken seriously because the work they do is typically so lighthearted. The pressures of personal performance and artistic drive are the same for the people who draw ducks and bunnies for a living as for those in seemingly more serious creative disciplines. The perennial struggle between artists and those who regard artists as merely wrists to be used and discarded is also ongoing.

2

Suits

Producers as Artists See Them

> There is something about the artist that is antipathetic
> to making a profit, except maybe in his own work.
> —Henry Miller

Much of the union story is about the relationship between the animation artist and the animation executive. In the previous chapter we have examined daily life of the animation artist; we now look at the executive.

Artists make art but they can't eat art. They have always had to earn a living like anyone else. Michelangelo was sued for breach of contract, Leonardo da Vinci's diaries record expenses and budgets as much as scientific experiments, Rembrandt and Vermeer declared bankruptcy. All the Renaissance painters and sculptors paid union dues to the Guild of Saint Luke. History records the names of great patrons of artists: Maecenas, Lorenzo de Medici, Isabella d'Este, King Louis XIV, Peggy Guggenheim, and Nelson Rockefeller, maybe because a generous patron is so rare. A more common approach is the plan Frederick the Great had for his friend the philosopher Voltaire: "We will squeeze him like a lemon and toss away the rind." Dr. Samuel Johnson defined a patron as "a wretch who supports with insolence and is paid with flattery."[1] When Michelangelo had one of his frequent arguments with his boss, Pope Julius II, a sympathetic cardinal tried to explain away the painter's temper by saying, "He is an artist. All his brains are in his fingers." Pope Julius was so incensed by the remark that he struck the cardinal with a mace,

Animators traditionally have expressed their opinions about their conditions through drawings. Gag cartoon shows Bill Scott and Grim Natwick assassinating a production manager at Walter Lantz Studio, 1947. Scott later became famous as the voice of Bullwinkle the Moose, and Natwick designed Betty Boop for Fleischer and Snow White for Disney. Courtesy of Stephen Worth.

according to the artist Georgio Vasari, who may have been embellishing a personal fantasy rather than recording an actual incident.[2]

A high-quality cartoon needs hundreds of artists, state-of-the-art technology, technical support, postproduction, distribution, and marketing. Films like *The Iron Giant* (2000) proved that even when artists could make a film of the highest quality, inadequate advertising and marketing can cause the film to fail at the box office. In 1975, the average budget for a good animated film hovered around $4 million to $10 million. Twenty-five years later, budgets have been as high as $120 million to $200 million. In the 1970s, if your animated feature did well at the box office, you sold a few toys and made some additional income from overseas screenings. Today, world distribution and marketing must be strategized from the beginning with the meticulousness of the Normandy invasion. All this requires a lot of investment capital and strong business savvy.

Enter the artist's bête noire: the businessman, the whip cracker, the suit.

To most animation artists, writers, and technicians, the ideal producer is one who signs a blank check, then leaves them alone. Such a creature is very hard to find. The sheer volume of art, money, and people needed necessitates some kind of regular support infrastructure. An environment must be created where artists are free to concentrate on work without having to be distracted by concerns about business licenses, insurance, and orders for office supplies. Yet this combination of artists and businessmen creates many misunderstandings, even conflicts. Veteran Disney painter Wilma Baker said, "In my day, we called them 'the walk-around boys.'" Shamus Culhane remembered that when he was directing Paramount Animation, he thought of executives as "a bunch of fat jerks who sat around all day chewing their cigars and annoying me with 'Why can't you give us something good like Bugs Bunny?'" Frank Tashlin recalled Leon Schlesinger's assistant at Looney Tunes, Henry Binder, as an "intelligent, bright fellow—for an executive."[3]

When we animators talk about the suits, we are talking about two types of people who work on animated films in a production capacity: the producer, who finances and arranges distribution of the film; and the production managers, who maintain the logistics of the assembly line. There are many subtypes in between, with producers acting in several roles. The current line of ascent is production assistant, the redoubtable hardworking gofer; assistant production manager, regulator for an individual department; production manager; line producer, coproducer, or, the generic term, producer, who manages the day-to-day tactical production flow; associate producer; executive producer; and vice president in charge of production—the big kahuna, Mr. or Ms. Moneybags.

When there is a single creative head like Walt Disney or Pixar's John Lasseter, the production person acts as an intermediary with the staff to keep the creative director from being pulled in too many directions at once. Producers organize and manage the production flow and deal with personnel, insurance, and legal issues. They also arrange for postproduction sound, dubbing, and prints after all the artwork is photographed. Producers are responsible for maintaining a disciplined, professional climate among dozens of volatile artistic temperaments to produce a film that seems to have been done by one hand.

Producers are also frequently the intercessors with higher-ranking executives of the studios that own the theaters and networks where the animated film will appear. These Hollywood power players have little or no interest in how the cartoons are made, only in what they cost and whether they are better than their competitors' cartoons.

After MGM closed its short-films division in 1957, Bill Hanna and Joe Barbera started their own company. They developed a limited animation system for producing large amounts of television animation cheaply. At first Joe tried to interest some of his old MGM producer friends in investing in their company. One exec, after looking at these new budgets, snapped, "You mean you coulda done your cartoons that cheap all along?"[4] No amount of explaining the difference in quality could convince him otherwise. When J. R. Bray complained to Lewis Selznick that the budget he was being given wouldn't even cover the cost of the paper necessary to do the drawings, Selznick replied, "The paper was worth more before you drew all over it."[5] When Universal Studios was in financial straits and needed to cut costs, production head Henry Henigson thundered at Walter Lantz: "Lantz! You're using too many darn pencils in your cartoon department! Do you have any idea how much pencils cost? What do you have to use so many pencils for?" When Walter explained that it takes as many as eight thousand drawings to create a cartoon, Henry shot back, "Well that's too darn many drawings. Why can't you make cartoons with two thousand drawings?"[6] Many is the animator vainly pleading today for a good-looking cartoon, only to be told by some indifferent executive, "In the end we don't care how it moves. It can look like *South Park* for all we care, just so long as it makes money."

Besides securing the finances of a picture, many times the producer must be called upon to enforce codes of professional conduct when an artist allows his self-discipline to slip. One animator refused to meet his quota because he objected to the way the rubber bands were wrapped around his scenes. Some animators get creative about the hours they work, arriving late, leaving early, and charging a full eight hours. One kept a desk at a union studio, charging eight hours worked on his time card, while simultaneously keeping another desk in another studio (this one nonunion), where he also charged for eight hours. When the non-union producer discovered this little double-dipping scam, he fired the artist. The offended chap had the nerve to call the union and complain about his treatment.

At the same time, animators abhor the condescending or exploitative producer who treats his talent like children or ignores morale. At one studio, on the day many low-paid artists were being laid off, the producer had the lack of tact to show off his new Jaguar sports car. Another producer put his exhausted staff on all-weekend overtime and then spent the same weekend water-skiing. Still another, who had an MBA from Harvard, reacted to the low morale at his studio, which had been decimated by layoffs, by hiring a feng shui specialist to add more greenery to the office. Producers like this are the reason animators joke that most of us turn Bolshevik after a few years. Anyone with a necktie should be put up against the wall. Animationnation.com, a Web site popular with animation artists, routinely refers to producers as "monkeys."

Not all people who enter the field of animation production are alike. Some truly love the medium and all its potential. Although they don't have drawing abilities themselves, they want to contribute to the creative process. Others are scalawags who see a way to exploit naïve creative types to make a quick buck in a little-understood field. For them animation could be a means to a greater end, a back door into the larger world of "serious" Hollywood film and television production.

The early part of the twentieth century saw a gold rush of entrepreneurs, carpetbaggers, immigrants, and dreamers into cartoon animation. As in the mainstream live-action world, the first animation producers were dabblers in fields like theater management, nickelodeons, or newspapers. In the 1930s, executives were usually appointed from the larger world of the mainstream Hollywood studios. In the period after the golden age, some executives who joined the shrinking field were speculators and eccentrics, but many were executives who couldn't cut it in the other realms and were banished to second-class status. In the 1990s, when it again became fashionable to be an animation executive, an alliance was forged between Broadway musical theater and animation. The industry filled with production personnel from Broadway shows and legitimate theater. Nowadays many executives from the Internet and CD-ROM games are getting involved in mainstream animation.

When animation was invented in 1900, fine artists like Picasso and Cocteau hailed it as a new form of artistic expression. In America, almost from the beginning, animation was tied to the comic art. Most of the early animators were former newspaper cartoonists. J. Stuart Blackton was a cartoonist employed by the Thomas Edison Company, Emile Cohl by Léon Gaumont, and Winsor McCay by William Randolph Hearst. The first animated shorts were attempts to advertise the sale of mass-published comic strips like "Life with Father," "The Katzenjammer Kids," and "Mutt and Jeff." Winsor McCay began in 1911 making some beautiful animated cartoons, later producing films like *Gertie the Dinosaur* (1913) and *The Sinking of the Lusitania* (1918). But by 1921 he had given up animation production. Why? because William Randolph Hearst was annoyed that McCay was focused more on his animation than on this newspaper cartooning. So McCay stopped animating to focus on his print work.

As we saw in chapter 1, cartoonist John Randolph Bray became the first true producer when he adapted the assembly-line technique to the mass production of animated cartoons. Before the artists settled in their offices on Twenty-sixth Street in New York City, they worked for a time on a farm upstate. Bray would pick his artists up in his flivver on Monday and drive them to the farm to live and work for five days, then drive them back to the city on Friday. His wife, Margaret Till Bray, became the first production manager. She ran a tight ship while running a lucrative real-estate business on the side. Bray heeded her advice above all. Shamus Culhane told me she could be a very strict disciplinarian. Disgusted because the animators seemed to spend their paychecks drinking and carousing all weekend, she began paying the artists on Monday instead of Friday to ensure they would report to work on time.[7]

Bray grasped the business potential of the new art form. He was the first animator to incorporate, and he took out patents on the most basic techniques of animation such as arcs, keys, and inbetweens. He even sued his predecessor Winsor McCay for copyright infringement.[8] (When animator Michael Sporn telephoned me in 1977 to tell me of Bray's death—at the age of 107—he joked, "Well, Tom, we can finally all animate now. It's back in the public domain.")

Suits

The first animation executives, such as Amadee Van Beuren, Charles Mintz, and Charles Winkler, were distributors who needed a steady supply of cartoon flickers to distribute to vaudeville theaters. Margaret Winkler, the "Great Live-Wire Saleslady of Warner Bros.," brokered the deals that allowed Walter Lantz, Max Fleischer, and Pat Sullivan to launch their own independent studios.[9] She enabled twenty-two-year-old Walt Disney, who had just moved from Kansas City to Hollywood, to start his studio doing the Alice in Cartoonland series. At one time she represented the two most successful cartoon series of the 1920s: Felix the Cat and Out of the Inkwell. Her brother, Charles Winkler, also was an animation executive. When Margaret married Charles Mintz, she stepped back from her career to be a full-time mother. Mintz was the distributor whose contractual machinations got the character Oswald the Lucky Rabbit away from Walt Disney, forcing him and Ub Iwerks to invent a new character—Mickey Mouse. Mintz's studio produced shorts throughout the 1930s. Had Margaret Winkler Mintz remained active, her example might have helped women gain importance early on in the

Early animation producer-agent Margaret Winkler at the age of ninety-three. Margaret Winkler was called "the Great Live-Wire Saleslady of Warner Bros." She made the initial deals that got Walt Disney's studio and Pat Sullivan their first cartoon work. Courtesy of the John Canemaker Collection.

upper levels of animated production. As it was, animation production and management remained entirely male dominated until the women's movement of the 1960s and 1970s.

Starting with *Feline Follies* in 1919, Felix the Cat was the first true animation celebrity. He was totally new, with no ties to any previously known newspaper comic strip or trademark figure. By 1925, Felix was the most popular film star after Charlie Chaplin and Rudolph Valentino. Aviator Charles Lindbergh kept a Felix doll in the *Spirit of St. Louis*, and Groucho Marx imitated the famous cat's trademark walk. Many later cartoon-character designs copied Felix's streamlined peanut shape, pipe-cleaner limbs, and the four-fingered, kid-gloved hands. There were Felix merchandise, Felix songs, and a Felix comic strip, and Felix danced the Charleston on sheet music.

Felix the Cat was the brainchild of a quiet artist, Otto Messmer, but the man who took all the credit was Pat Sullivan. He was an Australian ex-boxer who had set up his own cartoon studio in 1915. Sullivan could draw a bit, but he quickly assumed the executive role, arranging the marketing of Felix with Universal, then through Educational Films, then Paramount. Otto Messmer created the cartoons, drew the posters, and even drew the comic strip. In every case Pat Sullivan's name was the only one that appeared on the title card. Messmer even signed Pat Sullivan's name to the daily newspaper comic strip Otto drew. When Walt Disney's film *Steamboat Willie* hit big and brought sound into cartoons, Walt begged Messmer to come work for him out in California. But Messmer remained loyal to Sullivan's company. Al Eugster recalled that whenever there was a publicity photo shoot, the staff all had to shift down one seat so Sullivan could take the seat at the front desk, the only time anyone saw him at a drawing table. Yet Messmer was happy with the situation: "He was the boss, the businessman. I was the foreman, the employee."[10]

While Messmer and his staff of invisible drones worked away, Pat Sullivan and his wife, Marjorie, led the wild life of the Jazz Age. It was rumored that Marjorie Sullivan was having an affair with the couple's chauffeur. On March 21, 1932, Pat confronted her, the chauffeur stormed out, and Marjorie fell to her death from a Manhattan hotel room window.[11] It was never established with any certainty whether it was an accident or a suicide—or whether she was pushed. Whatever the reason, Pat Sullivan was destroyed by guilt and drank himself to death within a year, which,

Pat Sullivan at a desk with Otto Messmer (standing) in 1928. Sullivan had many publicity photos staged in which he was feigning interest in the animation. Frequently he made artists stand up and give him their seat at a desk so he could appear to be working. Courtesy of the John Canemaker Collection.

considering that Prohibition had made booze illegal, was not an easy thing to do. In the meantime Sullivan had failed to grasp the significance of the sound revolution, or just had not cared to notice, and soon the still-silent Felix cartoons seemed old hat. Messmer continued to draw the Felix comic strip until the studio folded. It was not until 1975 that he finally received the credit due him as the creator of Felix the Cat.

Patrick A. Powers, described by author Donald Crafton as an "erstwhile huckster," was an early partner of Carl Laemmele at Universal Pictures.[12] He distributed Sullivan's cartoons until Laemmele suspected Powers of trying to take over his company. When Laemmele confronted Powers and demanded to see the books, Powers threw them out the window. Laemmele fired him.[13] Powers went on to work for scientist and radio pioneer Lee De Forest. It wasn't long before De Forest also suspected his motives and fired him, but not before Powers lifted plans for a sound-on-film process. He then came out with a system, which he called Powers Cinephone, that was almost identical to the system De Forest was developing. Powers Cinephone was the system Walt Disney employed to make Mickey Mouse talk in his breakout 1928 film, *Steamboat Willie*.[14] Powers wanted the Disney brothers to make him a partner in their company, but they were not interested. Powers then went behind Walt's back and made a deal with Disney's top artist, Ub Iwerks, to quit and set up his own studio. After Iwerks split with Walt Disney and took most of the staff with him, Powers called a secret meeting with Walt Disney. Behind Iwerks's back, he offered to return Ub and the wayward artists if Walt would make him an equal partner in the Walt Disney studio.[15] Walt rejected the extortionate deal. Ub Iwerks's studio, with Powers behind the scenes, made shorts for several years with moderate success until closing in 1936.

Considering that Walt Disney was rooked by wheeler-dealers like Powers and Mintz, it's small wonder that he built the legal department of the Disney studio to have the reputation as one of the toughest and most efficient in the business.

In all the annals of animation, among artists Leon Schlesinger is one of the more well-liked animation executives. Stocky, affecting white suits, cigarettes, and a futile black comb-over, Schlesinger started Pacific Art & Title and helped the Warner brothers get the funding to create their hit film *The Jazz Singer* (1928). In return, the Warners granted Schlesinger exclusive rights to create cartoon shorts to go out attached to their films. Leon called them Looney Tunes and Merrie Melodies in imitation of Walt Disney's successful Silly Symphonies label. Layout artist Bob Givens told me that Leon once had most of the crew on board his sailboat for an offshore party. On the following Monday, Leon went through the studio giving people little yellow bills for their drinks.[16] Despite this and his funky workplace, Termite Terrace, his crew loved him.

What made Leon Schlesinger ideal was that as an executive he understood the separation needed between the creative and financial aspects of animation. He focused on budgets and schedules and otherwise left the artists alone. He also shielded his crew from meddling executives higher up. Studio mogul Sam Warner was reputed to have said to the Bugs Bunny creators: "I don't know what the fuck you cartoon guys do. All I know is we make Mickey Mouse."[17] The Warner artists made up a mock storyboard for a Bugs Bunny cartoon they never intended to make and pulled it out whenever Leon had to take some Warner Bros. VIPs on a tour. Schlesinger had rehearsed his spiel about the storyboard well enough that he could sound very knowledgeable on the animation process. This further helped insulate the artists from the upper echelons. And, most important, while some execs were notorious for their lack of a sense of humor, Schlesinger had a great one. When the artists created Daffy Duck, they had Mel Blanc conceive Daffy's voice as an imitation of Schlesinger's well-known lisp. When they nervously screened the first cartoon, Schlesinger stood up and said, "Jeethus Christh, that's a funny voithe! Where'd you get that voithe?"[18] Another time he interjected into a discussion on art direction: "Put more purple in. Purple ith a funny color!"[19]

After Schlesinger sold his Looney Tunes company to Warner Bros. outright and retired in 1944, Eddie Selzer was sent to manage the cartoonists. Selzer had been a low-level Warners apparatchik who arranged publicity reviews with long-legged showgirls. Gone was Schlesinger's broad smile. Writer Wilson Mizner characterized Selzer as "a mouse studying to be a rat." Selzer uttered an infamous and immortal comment when he interrupted a raucous gag session, "I don't understand what all this laughter has to do with making cartoons." Mel Blanc recalled that within a few months, most of the animators were begging Schlesinger to come back out of retirement.

Drawing the Line

Chuck Jones sparred frequently with Selzer over creative decisions. In 1947, when Jones wanted to introduce a new character named Pepe LePew, Selzer snapped, "Absolutely not! No skunks!"[20] Jones said later, "If Eddie said, no, we knew we just had to do it!" When Selzer saw the final film *For Scentimental Reasons*, he walked out of the screening room muttering, "No one is going to laugh at that shit!" The short was not only a hit and made Pepe LePew a major Warners star, but it also won an Oscar. As producer, Selzer was the one to go up on stage and collect the Oscar, which he then took home.

Over at MGM, producer Fred Quimby was an anomaly. He was a quiet Bostonian with ill-fitting dentures who dressed in out-of-date suits and starched collars that made him seem from an earlier time. Because of that big signature on the credits of every Tom and Jerry and Droopy cartoon, his name comes to us down through the decades as Mr. MGM Cartoons. But to everyone who knew him, he was at best a colorless functionary who knew little about the field he found himself in. The story is that Quimby was a former theater manager who once did a favor for MGM production chief Eddie Mannix, so Mannix set Quimby to preside over the studio shorts unit. Then Jack Chertok took over the live-action shorts like the Pete Smith Comedies and travelogues, leaving Quimby with the animation.[21] Even Jack Zander, an animator who dated Quimby's daughter for a while and so was partially immune from his anger, said of him, "Fred was a nice man, but as far as animation went, he didn't know his ass from a hot brick."[22]

Quimby saw his role as reining in expenses and answering the front office's dictum to make MGM cartoons as high quality as Walt Disney's. At first MGM cartoons were subcontracted to Hugh Harman and Rudolf Ising's HarmanIsing Studio. But when there were cost overruns and Harman demanded more creative control and more money, Fred fired them both and promoted Bill Hanna and Joe Barbera in their place. Barbera recalled that one of Quimby's first ideas was to buy the rights to the old comic strip "The Katzenjammer Kids." Barbera thought reviving these characters was a terrible idea. The Katzenjammers were funny in 1903 when German immigrant accents were quaint. But in 1937, the goose-stepping Nazis were bombing Spanish cities and putting people in concentration camps. The odds were good that no U.S. audience would see much humor in wacky Germans.

Suits

Barbera recalled: "Fred was the most dependable human being I have ever met. He would come in in the morning at ten, settle into his office, and read the trade papers. Then, at eleven he would get into his car and drive over to the studio barber for a straight-edge-razor shave followed by a liberal application of talc. Next came a leisurely lunch, after which he would return to our studio, go into our office, lie down on his couch, and take a nap. At three o'clock, he would get into his car and drive home. The routine was as inevitable as death and taxes, and everybody knew it well."[23]

When Tex Avery quit Looney Tunes and went to MGM in 1942, his first film was *Blitz Wolf,* the "Three Little Pigs" story turned into a hilarious spoof of the Nazis. At one point Quimby said to Avery. "Now go easy on the Hitler feller, Tex. After all, we don't know who's gonna win this war."[24] Barbera recalled that Quimby was embarrassed by the wildness of Avery's cartoons, which he considered vulgar. But of course whenever a MGM short won an Oscar, the only person onstage to accept it was Quimby.

Cal Howard, one of the great story artists and gagmen, lived to a great old age. He spent his final years in the Motion Picture Home in Calabasas, California. Bob Kurtz, the owner of Kurtz & Friends animation studio, was a protégé of Cal and used to take him for drives every Sunday. His route always crossed a small residential street called Quimby. Bob said it was like clockwork that whenever they crossed that street Cal would roll down his window, stick his head out and roar, "Fuck you, Quimby!!" Then he would chuckle softly to himself.[25]

By the early 1930s, studios found that the workload of production had grown too large to be handled by the creative head and executive head alone. The position of production manager or supervisor was created to oversee the workload and schedules and handle the day-to-day managing of the animators and the backend artists and techs. Production managers like Ben Sharpsteen, Don Duckwald, and Ed Hansen at Disney, Sam Buchwald at Fleischer, Emile Offeman at Iwerks, Lee Gunther at DePatie-Freleng, Jane Barbera at Hanna-Barbera, Joe Mazzucca at Filmation, and Ron Rocha at DreamWorks were admired or reviled for their handling of production pressures. The production manager is frequently stuck in the middle between the uncompromising businessman and the un-compromising creative genius and frequently gets yelled at from both sides. It's the rare person who can maintain a calm demeanor in this pressure-cooker situation. Many times production managers are used by the up-per management as hatchet men, responsible for telling people they are fired or not getting a raise or should try to come to work on time—all so the producer or creative director can smile and look chummy to the staff, even though it was he who ordered the firing or whatever. One production manager in the 1970s, before the term "sexual harassment" had gained currency, had the additional function of pimping for the pro-ducer. If the producer saw a particularly attractive ink-and-paint woman, this guy had to go to her desk and say, "Mr. —— would like to discuss production issues with you over dinner tonight. I think it would be a wise career move on your part to accept." Another production manager in the 1980s, when asked how much cubicle space to allow his staff, replied, "Seven feet by seven feet is all any artist needs and deserves!" Shamus Culhane recalled that Ben Sharpsteen was the first production manager to try to increase his importance by trying to monopolize access to Walt Disney. Culhane said, "He had it in for all the boys from New York be-cause we knew him back there. I don't wish Ben ill. I just hope he is now in Hell trying to animate with a wet noodle!"[26]

In the 1950s and 1960s, as the industry shrank and the old studio units closed, many chose not to get into animation production since it was seen as a dying field. As old studios transferred more and more production from film to television, network executives became the new powers-that-be. But the Hollywood best and brightest considered animation a career-ending one-way street. When Fred Silverman, nicknamed the "Man with the Golden Gut," fell from the head of programming at NBC, he was given an office at Hanna-Barbera where he was to run children's programming. He approved many Saturday morning kids' programs and suggested many shows like *Jabberjaws* and Steve Bochco's *Fish Police*. The creators of *Sesame Street* at the Children's Television Workshop provided the se-rious academics' perspective on children's programming, but they were a nonprofit special exception. By and large as the 1980s began, except for careerists like Friz Freleng and Lou Scheimer, the job of animation producer became a backwater for executives passing through or on the decline. It simply wasn't worth anyone's serious effort.

Suits

That changed in 1984 when Roy E. Disney and Frank Wells wrested control of the Walt Disney Company from Ron Miller. They introduced a dynamic new force into animation: the team of Jeffrey Katzenberg and Michael Eisner. These two had learned under Barry Diller the dog-eat-dog tactics of how to turn a loser studio back into a moneymaker. They were given two years to make Disney a success again and to burn, destroy, or build anything they needed to do it. (Chapter 11 tells this story in more detail.)

The hyperenergetic Katzenberg was a throwback to the aggressive creative producers of golden-age Hollywood such as Irving Thalberg and David O. Selznik. Katzenberg's motto seemed to be, "If you can't come in on Saturday, don't bother to come in on Sunday!" Katzenberg and James L. Brooks of *The Simpsons* made it chic to be an animation producer again. Their successes sparked other executives like Ted Turner, Amy Pascal, and Dawn Steel to look more seriously at their animation productions.

The Disney-Wells-Katzenberg-Eisner team saw a correlation between managing a large animation staff and managing the artists of a Broadway show. They began to handle the animation artists as a repertory company and to invite production executives from the legitimate stage in New York to handle the personnel. Some of the new execs invited were Peter Schneider, Tom Schumacher, Max Howard, Amy Pell, Kathleen Gavin, Allison Abbatte, Sarah MacArthur, Baker Bloodworth, and Jim Pentecost. I said to one of them, "I know you were a big shot in the *Les Misérables* road company, so, in Broadway terms, you've made it. If you don't mind my asking, what are you all doing here? I mean, if I loved Broadway plays and my dream was to work on Broadway, why would I then hie myself to Hollywood to torture animators?" He replied, "Well, the money is good and steady, and living out of a suitcase for two years or more can get old." The good thing was that theater people were raised in a positive working relationship between Actors Equity and the theaters. They were much more respectful of artists' everyday union issues than the usual predatory film executive or social-climbing former artist.

But as the 1990s animation gold rush continued, the more understanding producers were replaced. The new crowd was even less connected to animation but more hard-nosed. They followed their corporate headquarters' dictates to maximize profits, no matter what. In the 1970s, all the major Hollywood animation studios were run by former artists who became executives: Bill Hanna, Joe Barbera, Friz Freleng, Chuck Jones, Bill Melendez, Lou Scheimer, and the like. But by 2000, except for Pixar, all the major Hollywood animation studios were owned and operated by businessmen who could not draw a line. They operated on Richard Branson's Virgin Airlines corporate model, which preached that you did not need to know anything about your field so long as you focused on the bottom line. Suits at the studios seemed to brag of their ignorance of animation traditions and artists. Many could watch a basketball game and admire the motivation, or "hunger to win," of a team while at the same time being completely indifferent to the morale of their animation teams. One executive upbraided a colleague for being too familiar with the talent and not maintaining a managerial distance. Another once growled about having to give bonuses when a film does well. He said to me, "Give things to artists and they expect them all the time!"

The suits of the 1990s tended to ignore the loyalty that bound artists to their studios. These creative people gravitated to the studios that produced Mickey and Bugs out of love and the desire to continue the traditions. The suits viewed their artists as faceless resources to be jettisoned for cheaper labor. Cartoonists, by the nature of what they do, have to maintain a bit of their inner child to create for the child in all of us. Some of the producer teams confused the animators' horseplay with lack of seriousness on the artists' part and tended to treat their teams with a condescending attitude. One Disney animator grumbled about how, once when there was a celebration for completion of a project, part of the festivities was an inflatable kids jumpy house, provided for the adult animators. This sounds charming, but when artists had to negotiate wages or demand better conditions, the message was that they were not taken seriously. This caused great rancor among the artists.

In live action, many understand that if you leave Steven Spielberg or M. Night Shyamalan alone, he gives you a great movie. In animation these new executives insisted on arrogating to themselves the same creative control once exercised by Jeffrey Katzenberg, but without his sense of showmanship or taste. With the exception of John Lasseter's Pixar and Chris Wedge's Blue Sky, in the waning years of the twentieth century animation-studio production execs disenfranchised their creative staffs and tried to make all the major creative decisions themselves. The results were predictably poor. Tom Wolzein, a senior Wall Street media analyst writing in 2004 about the Disney Studios' problems, said, "They had a franchise, and they lost it, and I think they lost it because of a lack of decent story development."[27] Like someone wrecking a set of toy trains then blaming the equipment, the execs' only defense was to blame the artists and "their expensive union benefits." As the great Disney 2D renaissance of the 1990s started to wind down and top animators were facing layoffs, one angry animator, Dave Pruiksma, publicly referred to the management as "a skid mark in the shorts of the animation business."[28] After the film *Treasure Planet* (2002) lost the company $200 million, many Disney animators exulted in the president Tom Schumaker's transfer out of animation. This was the same Disney studio that was once famous for its employees loyalty to the company.

In March 2006 the situation at Disney seemed to improve dramatically when the studio announced that, with the outright purchase of Pixar, Ed Catmull and John Lasseter would come and head the feature animation unit. An exception to the rule in current Hollywood animation, Lasseter is a charismatic director-animator in the mold of Walt Disney of old. When Lasseter entered the Animation Building and first addressed the staff, he put the suits on notice. "If any of you here can't draw, you have no business being here," he said. When he toured Walt Disney Imagineering buildings where the theme parks are designed, he walked past the executives in charge and conferred directly with lead designers. By May at the Mouse House thirty executives had been shown the door.

One day I had lunch with veteran story artist Joe Grant. He was then in his late nineties. Joe had been at Disney since the *Three Little Pigs* in 1934 and was still drawing and contributing to movies in 2005. We spent our usual hour bitching about all the problems with the cartoon business and the Disney studio in particular. After all was said, Joe told me, "Yeah, but at the end of the day I always go back. You see, you all were working for the Disney Company, but I was working for *Walt* Disney, and that's the difference."

Animation is mass-produced magic, dreams by the yard; yet the history of animation is also a history of individual artists: Walt Disney,

Drawing the Line

Winsor McCay, Chuck Jones, Bob Clampett, Max Fleischer, Bob Abel, Osamu Tezuka, and, in our own time, Richard Williams, Don Bluth, Bruno Bozzetto, Hayao Miyazaki, John Kricfalusi, John Lasseter, Brad Bird. These artists create highly personal work, and they exercise the same type of leadership and engender the same type of fierce loyalty among their crews as a captain on a ship or a general on a battlefield. The crew considers it a terrible breach of faith to question the will of such a leader. An attack on the leader is taken as an attack on all.

In extreme cases, the individual becomes so identified with his studio that a personality cult develops. Decades after the death of Walt Disney in 1966, the impact of his personality on his studio is still palpable. A typical Disney employee has a clean-cut, youthful, can-do optimism, a down-home, soft-spoken "aw-shucks" folksiness that even people from urban centers like Brooklyn try to adopt. In his time Walt exercised con-

Typical animation story meeting, Walt Disney Studio, circa 1936, Joe Grant at right. The cartoon being discussed may be the short *Mother Goose Goes Hollywood*. Note the caricature of W. C. Fields. Newspaper cartoonist Grant was first hired for his skill at caricature. He stayed at the studio until 2005. Courtesy of Cody Cameron.

trol through creating artist-to-artist and department-to-department rivalries. He had gathered one of the finest collections of visual artists in the world, but he kept them under control by keeping them in a state of anxiety about their abilities. Among his Mouseketeers even Walt's fiercest critics still confess a warm spot for him. People who knew Walt Disney best dwell upon his warmth and forgive his actions more than they forgive their own or anyone else's.

Is this peculiar to animation? Sure, we revere the auteur live-action directors like Alfred Hitchcock, Akira Kurosawa, George Lucas, and Steven Spielberg, but studios like Universal and Twentieth Century-Fox in the main are not dependent for their survival upon one personality. No one artist is Mr. Paramount or Mr. United Artists. Even great filmmakers like Frank Capra, acknowledged as Columbia studio's single best director, was never called Mr. Columbia Pictures.

Animation seems to need not merely a coordinating chief artist but a messianic father-genius. Animators are not just loyal, they want to be members of a novitiate in a studio's worldview. Disney animator Mike Disa said that by working at Disney you for the first time became a favorite child. A simple smile from the father figure meant more than a large raise. And when the artist-leader was replaced by a mere administrator the bond was disrupted and loyalty evaporated. So what was this tangible yet mystical bond between leader and led? It was a bond of trust, tempered by experience and mutual love of their goal. The answer, I think, is centered in the psychology of the animation artist and can be traced to three roots.

First, many studio heads like Chuck Jones or Richard Williams began as the top artist among their peers. Like Alexander the Great or Henry of Navarre, the best generals lead from the front, and artists want to "follow the white plume."[29] They strive to equal or perhaps better a strong artist at the top. And a nod from the master for a good piece of animation is worth more than a big bonus. It was said Napoleon would walk among his soldiers' camp at night, pausing to share a roasted potato or a dirty joke in rough soldiers' language. He would take the medal off his own chest and pin it on a worthy private as a reward for some deed. This example made his Grande Armée follow him through the most hellish battles without a whimper. His soldiers felt he was one of them, as though the title of emperor was just another military rank.[30] Joe

Barbera would roll up his sleeves and spend late nights and weekends with his development department growing their slate of cartoon stars. Academy Award winner Richard Williams was known for his "battlefield promotions." I started on 1977's *Raggedy Ann & Andy* as a night-shift cel painter and finished the film a fully accredited animating assistant. James Baxter started 1988's *Who Framed Roger Rabbit?* as a young matte-and-inking artist fresh out of the West Surrey School of Art and finished the movie as an animator.

Ralph Bakshi set himself up in the 1960s as the bad boy of animation. Like a character full of rage out of Martin Scorsese's *Mean Streets*, he prided himself on defying the establishment and creating a new way of doing things. To his credit he accelerated advancement of women and minority animators who usually did not rise beyond assistants, and his company always paid better than any other studio at that time.

Second, the modern artist-leader long dreamed of imitating success in the tradition of strong-willed, self-made, charismatic artist-leaders like Max Fleischer, Paul Terry, Chuck Jones, and, most of all, Walt Disney. These men in turn developed their leadership style from the inspiration of cinema auteur-dictators like Erich von Stroheim and Cecil B. De Mille. But, more importantly, when these early animators were growing up, their models of success were the great comic-strip artists. At the turn of the twentieth century, America's mass media was the penny press. The large-circulation newspapers provided news and entertainment to a large population of immigrants who couldn't afford to go to the theater. Because many in the tenement slums couldn't speak English, they read the comic strips for simple, direct entertainment. Strips like "The Yellow Kid," "The Katzenjammer Kids," "Life with Father," and "Mutt and Jeff" were extremely popular.

As a result, the cartoonists who drew them became minor media celebrities. George Herriman, Elzie Seegar, George McManus, Winsor McCay, and others lived the high life wearing top hats and driving roadsters and made vaudeville appearances to cheering crowds. Raymond Outcault, the creator of Buster Brown and Tige the Dog, pioneered the first merchandising deal.

When the first animation studios were set up, newspaper syndicates like Hearst paid for flickers to boost sales. To establish security with financial backers, a studio was identified with the celebrity cartoonist who acted like he was the only artist drawing and inking the hundreds of sketches required to create one film. Also, the sense of wonder of the audience was increased if it seemed that the little birds and piggies came to life at the whim of a master wizard. This was the age of Houdini, who never revealed how he achieved his magic. So no mention was made of any of the animation workers droning away in back rooms. Winsor McCay was the original example, creating superbly drawn films, seemingly by himself. Eventually he had hired assistants and cameramen to help.

Harry Bud Fisher was the originator of the very popular comic strip "Mutt and Jeff." In 1916 Canadian Raoul Barré had an early animation studio in the Fordham section of the Bronx. But he lacked a marketable star. He jumped at the chance to sign a deal with Fisher, brokered by Charlie Bowers, to bring "Mutt and Jeff" to the screen. Soon they were making fifty-two Mutt and Jeff shorts a year, to the delight of millions of fans. But Barré soon realized he was being squeezed out of his own company and was being cheated of his share of the profits. In 1919 he quit in disgust. Shortly afterwards, Fisher got rid of Bowers as well and named the company the Bud Fisher's Mutt & Jeff Cartoon Film Corporation. One artist recalled seeing Fisher visit his animation studio only occasionally to show off to the chorus girl on his arm. As they strolled around looking at the gnomes toiling away at desks, Fisher would expound on the difficulty he had drawing an animated cartoon. Fisher by then also had a ghost artist drawing his comic strip for him. By 1921 Fisher's corporation had gone bankrupt, a victim of the cartoonist's extravagant lifestyle.[31]

Bud Fisher and, more likely, the example of Winsor McCay began the cult of the one-artist, one-studio style that must have been in the minds of young entrepreneurs like Walt Disney. Despite the vital partnership formed with his financially astute brother, Roy, by 1926 the two made the decision that their studio would no longer be called the Disney Brothers Cartoon Company, but the Walt Disney Studio. It wasn't until 1941 that the credits on Disney films were anything more than Walt's name and not until 1984 that complete roll-screen credits became the norm.

Third, the nature of running a long production and getting hundreds of artists with their different temperaments and egos to act with one mind requires a singular type of personality: a general. The battle metaphor is apt for describing a long production. Animation crews are like armies that can become demoralized short of a goal or inspired to go beyond their perceived limits and achieve things they never thought they could do. No wonder artists like Art Babbitt and Bill Tytla regretted the loss of employment at Disney. They admitted that Walt had a way of coaxing more and more out of his artists. He once critiqued one of Tytla's scenes like this, "Well, it's good. But it's not you, Bill."[32] Tytla immediately understood and redid the scene. Being the best artist among peers is not enough. To weld four hundred egos into a tool that creates art that looks like it was made by one person has little to do with the ability to draw. A strong leader is needed to bring forth good work, usually using the power of his (or her) personality alone.

Marc Davis recalled how in 1935, soon after the premiere of the successful *Who Killed Cock Robin*, a Silly Symphony short, Walt Disney took the entire company out for an Italian dinner. After the coffee and cake, he announced that the studio was going to create the first feature-length cartoon with movement so real it would be as good as live action. Davis said, "We all thought he had gone crazy, but Walt soon began to tell the story of Snow White and the Seven Dwarfs, and we were all hooked." One Disney artist said to me, "When artists saw Walt walk by in a suede sport coat, the next day everybody was wearing suede sport coats. It was spooky."[33] Walt Disney was not alone in exercising this kind of power. During the entire Max Fleischer strike (see chapter 4), no matter how heated the arguments over union issues, no one had a bad word to say about Fleischer personally. The artists blamed Paramount or production manager Sam Buchwald for management's hard fiscal line, but never the old man.

Finally, another source of the artist-leader icon may be in the relationship of medieval master artist to apprentice. The all-knowing master who has imbibed all of the ancient knowledge dispenses his wisdom to those worthy of his trust. It is ennobling to artists when they are allowed to share this sacred trust. No matter how diverse, how technologically oriented the business gets, artists know that the best way to learn the craft is under a master artist. A critique from someone who has four Oscars or who created Captain Hook carries more weight than one from some studio apparatchik whose nameplate is still wet from installation.

Floyd Norman having some fun with Pixar director John Lasseter's love of Hawaiian shirts. Norman has done many collections of his industry cartoons and was one of the first black artists at Walt Disney. Courtesy of Floyd Norman.

The main point for animators to understand is that the best interests of the messianic leader are not always their own best interests. The leader-artist by nature will put his or her interests before those of the studio or any individual; otherwise, he or she probably would not have risen to his exalted height. Some leaders, like Filmation's Lou Scheimer, genuinely fret over firing a single artist. Walt Disney said in 1941, "I hated to lay anybody off. I tried to hold on to them. They were my boys."[34] At other times such egos discard their people like so much paper and ride rough-shod over others' interests to advance their own.

This frequently happens when the issue of union membership appears. Most of the main Hollywood studios are now union signatories and have no problem with unionization. The record clearly shows that the small studios whose management thundered against signing a contract usually had something to hide. Mostly it's that they don't want representatives of the International Alliance of Theatrical and Stage Employees (IATSE) to audit their books. Any budget shenanigans may be in danger of being exposed. One nonunion studio owner once bragged, "No one sees my books till the handcuffs go on!" Also, for a studio to sign a union contract, they have to first bank the equivalent of several weeks of their artists' payroll. This is to prevent a studio from going bankrupt owing their people money. This can be a hefty amount for a studio with shallow roots. So if employers can get people to fill artists' chairs without signing a union contract, they will. If this means the health insurance and pension of the artists and their families can take a flying leap, so be it, but, hey, we're making art here, okay?

Animation people by nature have a strong streak of quiet, unquestioning loyalty. But it can be abused. So when animators hear a leader-employer warn against the dangers of unionism, they have to ask themselves whose interests the employer is speaking for. The elected union officers don't win an extra cookie when they get a studio to sign. History shows that all the animation community benefited when all the studios were playing by the union rules. But in modern times the employers at times believe their best interest is served by resisting collective bargaining. It was true in Andrew Carnegie's time, and it is true in the digital era. The push-pull of employer-union haggling over benefits is the yin and yang of Hollywood; ignoring your side encourages the other side to push harder.

Just as there's one God in Heaven and one captain on the *Pequod,* as long as there are crews, the cult of the artist-leader will continue to be a facet of animation production.

So would animation be better off if we got rid of all the producers? Not really. In the end we know that the anarchists' utopia of "no gods, no masters" is an unworkable solution. Even the most avant-garde independent film production still requires paperwork for festivals, insurance bonds, and tax statements. However, beyond the monetary needs of a film there is the hand that works to manage the team overall. Animation director and studio head Richard Williams once told me that one thing almost as satisfying as doing good work yourself was to be able to provide a climate where other artists could do their greatest work. I came to see that when I began to direct. I could steer complex scenes to talents who hungered for a challenge and I shared their pride when they were successful. I know many suits who also have this desire to see fine work created and share the artists' sense of accomplishment. After all, someone has to be around to sign the checks. For these reasons executives will always be an important part of the animation business. And so the love-hate relationship between artists and businesspeople will go on.

Hollywood Labor, 1933–1941

The Birth of Cartoonists Unions

You've gotten a great deal out of this industry. It's been good to you and what you're proposing to do is to give it away and turn it over to outside interests, and we're not going to tolerate it. We have a lot to protect here, and we are going to protect it with everything we've got.

—MGM producer Irving Thalberg
to pro-union screenwriters on May 1, 1936

By 1927, American animation had gone from experimental trick films created by a few newspaper cartoonists in their spare time to a booming business tied to the major Hollywood studios. Cartoon factories headed by men such as Walt Disney, Walter Lantz, Paul Terry, and Max Fleischer employed hundreds of artists and technicians in New York and Los Angeles.

In that year the industry threw a black-tie party in New York to celebrate its achievements by toasting the granddaddy of American animators, Winsor McCay.

There were pioneering animators before him, but Winsor McCay seemed to dwarf them all. His superb draftsmanship and imagination created films far ahead of their time. Many animators at the dinner traced their love of animation to seeing one of his films like *Gertie the*

Drawing the Line

Dinosaur (1913) or the *Sinking of the Lusitania* (1918). Although he was not, McCay seemed to be the inventor of cartoon animation, an impression he did little to discourage. Now, after decades of toil Winsor McCay was in the twilight of his prolific life.

That night, Pirroles Restaurant saw a lot of drinking bootleg liquor, laughing, and laudatory speeches. A number of animators from several studios contributed time to draw a raunchy stag cartoon called *Buried Treasure*.[1] It starred Everready Hardon, a character for whom erectile dysfunction did not seem to pose a problem. At the close of the evening's festivities, Max Fleischer invited the guest of honor to say a few appropriate remarks. Winsor McCay went to the podium and waited for silence. He then solemnly said, "I gave you an art form, and you all turned it into a business. A trade! . . . Too bad." He turned and sat down to stunned looks and some weak, scattered applause.[2]

Although theater projectionists had been unionized as early as 1908, by the Roaring Twenties unions had made few inroads into Hollywood. This was in part due to all the fast and easy money of the time as well as a national climate of antiunionism begun by Woodrow Wilson's Red Scare of 1919. The middle-class horror of anarchist terrorism and Bolshevik excesses in Russia enabled the business class, through the government, to stomp on progressive union movements like the Industrial Workers of the World (better known, perhaps, as the Wobblies). When Emma Goldman was deported to Russia during the Palmer raids of 1919 and 1920 (the crackdown on radicals, including labor union leaders, that resulted in huge mass arrests), no one recalled that she was a tireless activist for unions, women's rights, and birth control and opposed child labor. She was labeled in the press as an un-American foreign Red.[3]

President Calvin Coolidge said: "He who builds a factory builds a temple. He who works there, worships there." One of the factors that first attracted the moviemakers of the East to Los Angeles was the low-paid, nonunionized workforce. In 1914, the International Alliance of Theatrical and Stage Employees (IATSE) started the first Hollywood backstage local, Local 33.[4] In 1926, D. W. Griffith, Anita Loos, and Thomas Ince set up Photoplay Authors League. Griffith attempted an early version of the Directors Guild but gave it up after studios threatened him and others with "perpetual blacklisting."[5] Also, the issue arose as to whether the young technology of film should be unionized by the stage unions, represented by IATSE (founded by vaudeville backstage crews in 1893), or by the industrial crafts unions, the electrical workers, painters, and so on of the AF of L. In 1925, IATSE, the International Brotherhood of Electrical Workers (IBEW), the Carpenters Union, and the AF of L, while not agreeing on who was paramount, at least managed to agree on the first standard basic agreement contract to include motion picture film as well as vaudeville theatrics. However, the agreement was little adhered to. After three years of activism, by 1927 union membership was at its lowest point until the present day.

The Great Depression of 1929–1941 changed all that. The Black Tuesday stock market crash on October 29, 1929, was more than just an end of the good times of the Roaring Twenties. The system Americans and their forefathers had believed in and trusted had betrayed them. The Horatio Alger Protestant work ethic, which held that if you worked hard and saved your pennies, you would earn prosperity, seemed pointless. For the first time Americans felt that capitalism itself, as a system, might be played out. In those years, membership soared in groups that espoused radical solutions. Socialists, Communists, Fascists, and America First parties recorded their largest memberships during that time. Even Franklin D. Roosevelt's eccentric third-term vice president, Henry Wallace, said a swell model for reorganizing the American economy could be Soviet Russia.[6] Starving farmers in Kansas attacked flour mills for food. The entire city of San Francisco staged a spontaneous general strike for four days, and Gov. Frank Merriam sent army tanks to the Embarcadero. San Francisco police officers kicked over flowers and candles left on the spot where striking dockworkers were shot down and killed.[7]

The Great Depression had a psychologically leveling effect on much of society. Citizens from ditch diggers to writers like F. Scott Fitzgerald were affected by the crash. For the first time the elites of society, artists, poets, and intellectuals, made common cause with common people. All working-class stiffs, whether mural painters or animators, felt united in the fight to defeat the Depression and to bring back prosperity. The only ones who seemed unaffected by the bad times were the megarich. The clear class divisions in the United States of the early part of the twentieth century now metamorphosed into open suspicion of the business classes. Although many tycoons, like William Durant of General Motors, were ruined by the crash, the average American felt it was Morgan, Rockefeller, and those banker types who had made everyone broke. A popular song of the time was "Don't tell Mother I Work on Wall Street, She Thinks I Play Piano in a Whorehouse." When desperately poor World War I veterans marched on Washington to demand their withheld bonus pay, they were met by bayonet-wielding troops. Henry Ford stationed a machine-gun nest at his home and ordered his executives to carry sidearms for their own protection. Most labor strikes in the industrial heartland were resolved by the spilling of blood. When the progressive Franklin D. Roosevelt administration in Washington tried to get a square deal for working people, these same business titans thundered against FDR in the press as being a traitor to his own class.

In the late 1930s, the open threat abroad from Axis powers Germany, Italy, and Japan further solidified American opinion in the suspicion of the wealthy class. One of the first things Adolf Hitler did when coming to power was arrest all labor union leaders and suspend the eight-hour workday. Because of these actions and the suppression of Communists and Socialists, Hitler and Mussolini were for a time the darlings of the business class. A popular cliché of the time was "At least Mr. Mussolini can make the trains run on time." Like many a budding venture capitalist, Walt Disney called on Mussolini when visiting the Venice Film Festival in 1938.[8] That same year Walt Disney and Hal Roach were the only Hollywood producers to openly welcome Leni Riefenstahl, Hitler's favorite filmmaker, when she visited Tinseltown.[9] After Pearl Harbor brought America into World War II, the FBI raided the home of Georg Gyssling, diplomatic consul general to Los Angeles from the Third Reich. Many top entertainment industry figures were embarrassed to find their names listed in Gyssling's phone directory.[10] Movie moguls could hardly afford not to treat with these devils since their overseas box-office receipts were at stake. This seeming embrace of these evil elements abroad further united common opinion that it was us against the silk-top-hat-and-tails crowd.

The seminal moment for Hollywood came on March 8, 1933, when newly inaugurated President Roosevelt ordered a "bank holiday." Since the stock market collapse, almost one-third of the nation's banks had closed. More were teetering on the edge as account holders rushed in to withdraw their savings. FDR shut down the entire banking system for a time to arrest the momentum of the slide. Most Hollywood studios flew low to the ground financially; they depended on fast injections of cash from their investors on Wall Street. So, despite heavy film production and good returns at the box office, the major studios overnight were close to bankruptcy. Paramount and RKO for a time went into receivership. During this time, in what seemed almost a commentary, Hollywood was shaken by the Long Beach earthquake.

From MGM to Max Fleischer, the employers' solution was to pass on the problem to their employees in the form of 30 to 50 percent salary cuts despite existing agreements and personal contracts. Dan Glass, an inker at the Max Fleischer studio, wrote to his mother on March 16, 1933: "We had some more excitement at the studio. Everyone making over $15 a week got their salary cut and some of the big boys by as much as 50 percent. Word went around too that the studio might close down altogether. The Motion Picture Business is so bad. We didn't get paid last Friday (March 10th)."[11]

Teary-eyed and unshaven, studio head Louis B. Mayer explained the desperate situation of Metro-Goldwyn-Mayer to his staff.[12] Actor Lionel Barrymore shouted support: "We're with ya, L. B.!" After the applause, as Mayer went back to his office, he looked at his secretary and smiled, "So how did I do?" A week after the salary cuts, Mayer announced the hiring of his daughter's new husband, producer David O. Selznick, at a salary of $4,000 a week. The press made a joke based on the title of a best-selling Hemingway novel, "The Son-in-Law Also Rises."[13] Walt Disney got his studio attorney, Gunther Lessing, to give Walt's crew a sob story about how bad things were back east, that people went around with the seats of their pants worn out. Assistant animator Jack Kinney said, "If I had a beer, I would'a been crying in it."[14] Lessing then asked everyone to take a 15 percent pay cut. Jack Zander recalled that at Schlesinger's Looney Tunes no one was paid anything for several weeks. Finally, director Friz Freleng led a crowd to confront boss Leon Schlesinger in his office. "Leon," Freleng said, "either you pay us all now or we're walking outta here!" Zander thought, "Here I am just starting here and already I'm gonna lose my job!" After a lot of yelling and threats, Schlesinger said, "All right, you bastards. Here." He reached in his pocket and pro-

duced a wad of signed paychecks. All that was missing was the date.[15]
He expected to pay his people someday; he was just waiting to see how
long he could get away without paying. In another way of dealing with
it, Walter Lantz gravely called his staff together and solemnly told them
that Universal had asked him to make a cut. Lantz, smiling, then took off
his hat and showed everyone his head was shaved.[16]

When Warner Bros.' popular head of production, Darryl F. Zanuck,
was ordered to implement the staff salary cuts, he quit instead. He started Twentieth Century Pictures, which he later merged with Fox to create the powerhouse Twentieth Century-Fox.

Even before the salary cuts, Hollywood workers had their gripes:
strict personal contracts, stuntmen firing live ammunition at actors'
faces during filming of gangster pictures, studios laying people off before Christmas and rehiring them after the New Year to avoid paying
holiday bonuses, screen credits that were nonexistent or padded with
the boss's latest tootsies and relatives. The joke about nepotism in upper
management was that MGM stood for Mayer-Ganz-Mizpochen, which
in Yiddish means "Mayer's whole family." Ogden Nash summed up the
situation at Universal: "Carl Laemmle / Has a very large faemmle."[17]
Walt and Roy Disney let their younger brother, Ray, bicycle onto the
studio lot and sell insurance. If you wanted to look good with Walt, you
bought Ray's insurance policies. Leon Schlesinger's brother-in-law, Ray
Katz, was a production manager. Most of Max Fleischer's family seemed
to be on his payroll.

This was the climate in Hollywood as the first workers began to think
about forming unions.

As stated before, one of the unions trying to organize Hollywood film
workers was the International Alliance of Theatrical and Stage Employees. Although the union had as yet made few inroads into Hollywood,
IATSE workers were the only ones not hit by the big salary cut. Also, the
new talkies brought west a swarm of already unionized performers and
technicians from Broadway. These factors and the pro-labor Roosevelt
administration combined to unleash a flood of unionizing. The actors
and writers formed guilds in 1933, the editors and directors in 1936.
When President Roosevelt set up his famous New Deal programs to
fight the Depression, he included organizations to foster the arts, which
he thought as important as building dams and bridges. The Federal Art

Project employed theater people like Orson Welles and Clifford Odets, painters like Grant Wood and Jackson Pollock, photographers like Berenice Abbot, and poets like Langston Hughes. The first Works Progress Administration (WPA) symphony orchestra included three graybeards who were acquainted with Tchaikovsky. Many of these intellectuals maintained a strong socially leftist-progressive theme in their efforts.

Louis B. Mayer and Irving Thalberg tried to head off the rising unionization of their workers by creating the Academy of Motion Picture Arts and Sciences (AMPAS) in 1927. Few remember that before the glittering awards ceremonies, AMPAS's mission was to be an ombudsman to arbitrate employer-employee complaints; the hope was to eliminate the need for unions. However, the academy was set up and managed by studio heads. Screenwriter Dorothy Parker said: "Taking your grievances to the academy is like trying to get laid in your mother's house. Somebody's always peeking through the parlor curtains!"[18] The academy's first president, William DeMille, the brother of Cecil B., tried to hold a "squawk forum" to allow academy members to talk frankly to powerful studio executives like L. B. Mayer. The first forum turned into an ugly, heated exchange, and Mayer stormed out angrily, determined to fire all his loudmouth employees whose names he could remember. Finally, the academy's support of the industry salary cuts doomed its credibility as a labor ombudsman. The academy announced the massive salary rollbacks at the 1933 Oscar ceremony before the dinner was served.[19] It must have made for a pretty depressing party.

As the agitation for the recognition of unions grew in Hollywood, the studios didn't go quietly. When Darryl Zanuck was faced with a delegation of Fox union screenwriters, he told them, "You put a picket line in front of my studio and I'll mount a machine gun on the roof and mow you all down." Jack Warner called the screenwriters "Communists, radical bastards, and soap-box sons of bitches."[20] In 1936, Jack Warner fired writer Dalton Trumbo because of his union activity. Trumbo promptly accused Warner of blacklisting. Warner laughed, "Sure it's blacklisting, but you can't prove nothing because we got no list. We do it by phone."[21] When threats of firing and blacklisting didn't work, the ultimate union-busting response was to call in the gangsters. James Cagney was a top Hollywood actor who loudly proclaimed his desire to be part of a screen actors union. He remembered fellow actor George Raft telling him years later how studio heads had paid some hoods to stage an accident, to drop some lights on Cagney's head. I guess to the studio heads it was better to lose a movie star than to deal with a union. The studio had insurance on Cagney anyway. But then Raft stepped in. Before he became a movie star, Raft was friendly with some top mobsters, including Lucky Luciano, Ben "Bugsy" Siegel, and Owney "the Killer" Madden, owner of Harlem's famed Cotton Club. When Raft found out about the hit scheduled on Cagney, he contacted his bigger mob friends in Chicago and New York to veto the LA hoodlums and call off the hit.[22]

This was far from the first involvement of organized crime in a labor dispute. Sadly, organized crime has played a major role in American labor history. The workers needed recourse to some kind of muscle to combat the judicially approved violence of the employer establishment. Before its *On the Waterfront* reputation, labor history from the 1870s to the 1930s was filled with police and troops firing into crowds of unarmed strikers, and with the Ku Klux Klan and the Black Legion lynching union members. These murders were all winked at by the government. When budding gumshoe Dashiell Hammett joined the Pinkerton detective service in 1919, one of his first assignments was to murder Native American union organizer Frank Little. Hammett refused and the Pinkertons got a vigilante mob to lynch Little; they hanged him from a railroad trestle.[23] When union bard Joe Hill made himself a nuisance to the large Utah copper mining companies in 1915, they had him framed for a murder. Hill was executed despite pleas for mercy from President Woodrow Wilson, Helen Keller, George Bernard Shaw, and the pope. Hill's last words were, "I die as I have lived: a rebel. Don't mourn me. Organize!" Small wonder folksinger Woody Guthrie paid tribute to martyred organizers with the song "Union Graveyard."

Many unions, tired of intimidation and violence, turned first to political terrorist groups like anarchists then, via immigrant associations, to organized crime to fight fire with fire. Once unions admitted the underworld into their ranks, it proved difficult to remove. The sensational congressional hearings, led first by Sen. Robert "Fighting Bob" LaFollette Jr. in the 1940s, then by Sen. Estes Kefauver in the fifties and by Attorney General Robert Kennedy in the sixties, revealed to the world just how badly the American labor movement had been infected by organized crime, a fact often exploited by corporations.

Hollywood Labor, 1933–1941

In 1933, Hollywood studios sought revenge for IATSE's success in defying the industry-wide pay cuts.[24] They saw their chance when IATSE challenged the right of the IBEW and the Carpenters Union to organize the sound engineers. When Universal was hit by a strike, the Walter Lantz animators received no pay for the duration. The IATSE strike was defeated partly by studio-hired thugs who beat up the strikers. When IATSE president William Elliot protested to AF of L president William Green, Green said he could do nothing. The truth was that Green was a friend of the Carpenters Union president, "Big Bill" Hutcheson. The IATSE membership dropped dramatically, falling to only 174 members in Tinseltown. The IATSE rank and file began a movement to remove Elliot.

Early in the Depression, the president of IATSE Chicago Local 2 was George Browne, a man who, it was said, could drink a hundred bottles of beer in a day and who forever had black-brown streaks of chewing-tobacco juice running down the corners of his mouth.[25] Browne was trying to get soup kitchens set up for his unemployed theater people and asked Scarface Al Capone's organization for help. Capone had done this type of public relations stunt before. Although he was being sent up the river on a federal rap, his organization still managed to worm itself onto the Local 2 executive board (as happened in many union locals, as organized crime syndicates got their men elected). With Prohibition ended, Capone saw an opportunity to get his rackets into show business via IATSE. He contacted Charles "Lucky" Luciano and Mayer Lansky to enlist their New York muscle. In 1934, at its convention in Louisville, Kentucky, the weakened IATSE was compelled by the New York and Chicago crime syndicates, under Capone's lieutenant, Frank "the Enforcer" Nitti, to elect George Browne of Local 2 as the new overall international president.[26] Browne's assistant was Willard Bioff. Born as Morris Bioffsky to Russian Jewish immigrants, Bioff was a Nitti bagman and pimp who was trying to unionize Chicago's kosher butchers under Lou "Greasy Thumb" Kupchik. This was the man who was told to pack his bags for Hollywood.

Bioff demonstrated his power to Hollywood in 1935 by staging a wildcat strike of projectionists. Movie theaters from Chicago to San Francisco suddenly went black, and customers howled. When Tommy Malloy, the president of the IATSE Motion Picture Projectionists Local

110 of Chicago protested, his Packard was sprayed with machine-gun fire on Lakeshore Drive on February 4, 1935).[27] Malloy had himself become head of his union by shooting it out with hoods from the IBEW in 1916. Chicago gave Tommy Malloy one of the largest gangland funerals in the city's history. International president Browne reported at the 1936 convention, "I am happy to say the membership of Local 110 cooperated in a wholehearted way, and I am pleased to note that this organization has settled down to a proper business management." Faced with such muscle, the Hollywood studios quickly gave in.

While IATSE ranks in Hollywood swelled from 174 to 9,000 by 1937, the studio moguls learned that they could do business with Bioff and Browne. They had really never had scruples about dealing with gangsters before. Back on the East Coast before the move to Hollywood, motion picture producers employed gangsters to enforce their patent monopolies. In LA Jimmy Rosselli, Mickey Cohen, and Bugsy Siegel were frequent guests at the studio executives' dinner tables. Through the offices of top studio exec Nicholas Schenck, Bioff and Browne kept the Hollywood backstage trouble-free in exchange for a kickback of $50,000 per studio per year. Schenck, president of the National Theater chain and a player at MGM, was the go-between for the money to Bioff and Browne. In 1935, Paramount signed the first closed-shop contract with IATSE. Bioff was given $100,000 in cash as a "gift" for a job well done. When Bioff was accused of being a mobster, he denied the charges and blamed the accusations on "plutocrats in Hollywood" who were unhappy because he was "fighting for the little fellows in the picture studios."[28]

In 1937 the IATSE had defeated the Carpenters Union and the IBEW, but a new group began to claim the loyalty of Hollywood film workers. Painters' business representative Charles Lessing led six thousand studio painters, plasterers, plumbers, cooks, hairstylists, and set designers in a strike for recognition of a new independent union alliance, the Federation of Motion Picture Crafts, or FMPC. They also demanded the 10 percent pay raise IATSE had negotiated peacefully for members the year before. In the east, the striking cartoonists at the Max Fleischer studios made common cause with the FMPC, and the *New York Times* reported, "Two more famous stars joined the motion-picture walkout: Popeye and Betty Boop."[29] The newborn Screen Actors Guild (SAG) got a leg up at the expense of its brothers when it cut a deal with IATSE, agreeing to withdraw its support for the FMPC.[30] IATSE, in turn, gave up its own nascent actors' local and threatened the studios with still another nationwide projectionists' strike if SAG weren't recognized. Actors' leaders swallowed their pride for the time being and waited for an opportunity to get back at Bioff and Browne.

With IATSE and SAG on the sidelines, the studios decided to get rough with the FMPC. At the Pico Boulevard gate of Twentieth Century-Fox, the strikers fought a pitched battle with gangsters and baseball-bat-wielding thugs. The hoods all had gun permits from the Los Angeles Police Department. The studio unionists were helped in the rumble by sympathetic longshoremen from the San Pedro harbor. The longies disdained guns, preferring bare knuckles, brickbats, and tire irons. Fights broke out in front of studios all over town. A young FMPC picket captain, Herbert Sorrell, began to be noticed for his zeal in battling goons and beating up scabs. Despite their best efforts, however, the strike was broken, and FMPC collapsed. From its ashes, the more militant members of the union built a new labor alliance called the Conference of Studio Unions (CSU).

American stage actors had formed a union in 1896 first called "the White Rats" ("rats" spelled backwards is "star"). They evolved into Actors' Equity and successfully struck Broadway for recognition in 1919.[31] As noted earlier, when legitimate stage actors began moving west after moving pictures went to sound, they brought their Actors' Equity activism with them. Throughout 1933, movie actors held informal meetings about unionizing. They met at the Masquers Club on Sycamore Avenue just off Hollywood Boulevard and at Frank Morgan's house. (Morgan is the actor remembered for playing the Wizard of Oz character in the famous 1939 film.) President Roosevelt had just put the National Recovery Act (NRA) into effect to impose price controls on the collapsed economy. Much of the NRA Motion Picture Code was created under the supervision of advisers sent from the studio heads. They included clauses such as "no actor can be paid more than $100,000 a year" while studio executives had no such cap, and actors' seven-year contracts, until they were renegotiated, were to remain in effect even after they expired. Screen siren Greta Garbo called it the closest thing to white slavery ever seen. Also, according to the rules, actors' agents had to become licensed employees of the studios.

Drawing the Line

On October 8, 1933, a mass meeting of actors was held at the El Capitan Theater on Hollywood Boulevard, where one day films like *Citizen Kane*, *The Little Mermaid*, and *Finding Nemo* would premiere. A petition calling on President Roosevelt to repeal the code rules was written and signed by stars like James Cagney, Paul Muni, Gary Cooper, Jeanette MacDonald, Fredric March, and Groucho Marx. When aftershocks of the Long Beach earthquake disrupted the meeting, everyone moved to the parking lot across the street and kept the meeting going. It was decided that SAG president Frank Morgan would step down since he was seen as being too politically leftist to have a chance to persuade FDR. The new SAG president was Eddie Cantor, a vaudeville star who had made several hit movies. Cantor, a personal friend of Roosevelt, presented the petition to the president at his Warm Springs, Georgia, retreat. FDR amended the NRA code on November 27, 1937. This was the first successful collective action by Hollywood actors. For animation people, the code confirmed the forty-six-hour workweek, which most of the employers used, but called for overtime pay, which most of the employers ignored.

At Louis B. Mayer's beach house during a Sunday garden party on May 9, 1937, SAG representatives Robert Montgomery, Kenneth Thompson, Franchot Tone, and Aubrey Blair faced down Mayer, the lord of MGM, and his friend, gangster Willie Bioff. Bioff had plans to charter his own actors' local within IATSE. The actors bluffed that they had 99 percent of the actors all ready to walk out the next morning. Mayer thought it over and then gave in. That night, at the Hollywood Legion Stadium, Montgomery reported the victory to 5,000 cheering actors. The next morning, membership went up 400 percent. Goddesses of the silver screen like Greta Garbo and Jean Harlow waited in line with unemployed bit players outside SAG headquarters to get their first union cards. Only movie stars' personal service contracts would remain an issue. Individual actors fought the studios in court until the suit brought by movie star Olivia DeHavilland finally established the precedent to outlaw such contracts.

Other film workers were also beginning to see the value of speaking collectively. In 1936, when producers had asked for yet another round of staff salary cuts, a group of film directors met at King Vidor's house and pledged $100 each to establish a union. Present were Vidor, Frank Borzage, Howard Hawks, Rueben Mamoulian, Lewis Milestone, and William "Wild Bill" Wellman. They drew up bylaws for the Screen Directors Guild, which would later be the Directors Guild of America (DGA).[32] After several years of bitter negotiations and struggle, the final basic agreements recognizing the DGA were signed by guild president Frank Capra in 1940.

Screen Actors Guild, Writers Guild, Screen Directors Guild. Animation artists now wondered, why not a Screen Cartoonists Guild?

As early as 1925, Bill Nolan tried to form the first film animators' cooperative, the Associated Animators, but the cooperative never really got off the ground. (Nolan was well known as the animator who, with Otto Messmer, is credited with the creation of rubber-hose character design, the style that rejected newspaper cartoon illustration in favor of a more streamlined design for motion picture animation.) In 1932, Ub Iwerks studio animators Myron "Grim" Natwick, Shamus Culhane, Al Eugster, and ten others met at a beer saloon on Western Avenue in Hollywood. Shamus said, "A good Amontillado sherry sparked our indignation, and we decided to form a union."[33] They started to invite animators from other studios to discuss common grievances. Everyone complained about lousy working conditions, low pay, and oppressive bosses. Grim Natwick, the creator of Betty Boop and Snow White, was elected the first president. With each successive meeting, the crowd grew until they finally had to move the meeting to a Hollywood Teamsters Union hall. No animators from the Walt Disney Studio ever showed up. Yale professor Michael Denning, author of *The Cultural Front: The Laboring of American Culture in the 20th Century,* recalls one organizer telling him that "he used to have meetings with the cartoonists and could never tell what they were thinking until at the end he'd pick up scraps of paper they had drawn on—and then, from the sketches, he could figure out if he had gotten across to them."

Ub Iwerks was against any union but was not openly hostile. The creator of Mickey Mouse was an inveterate tinkerer who preferred to remain focused on developing his version of a multiplane camera out of the remains of an old Chevrolet.[34] But the other studio heads found

Ub Iwerks self-caricature, 1931. The quiet, scholarly Iwerks was the designer of Mickey Mouse and was renowned for his speed as an artist. Courtesy of ASIFA/ Hollywood Animation Archive, www.animationarchive.org.

out about the clandestine unionist gatherings and reacted by scheduling late-night overtime on the same nights. Spies and informants kept management up to date, and threats from studio managers grew. Animator Ed Friedman recalled: "You would go to work next day and your production manager would say, 'So I heard you went to that union meeting last night. You'd better lay off if you don't want to find yourself unemployed!'"[35] No one wanted to be back on a breadline, so for their own protection, the organizers were soon referring to their group not as a union but as a club. One anonymous phone call to Natwick dismissed any idea of an animators union: "Those guys don't need meetings or social clubs. You know as well as I do that all they want at night is a bottle of booze and a good whore."[36] Animators started drifting away from the meetings when no one could agree on a proper course of action. Nothing seemed to get done.

Meanwhile, it was no surprise that animation unions first found fertile ground in New York City. The major studios in the city in the 1930s

Animation camera stand at Walt Disney Studio, circa 1936. The cameras that shot animation for Walt Disney were adapted Bell and Howell cameras on custom-made upright
stands. In later years most animation cameras were developed by engineer John Oxberry
of New Rochelle, New York. In time, the generic name for an animation camera became
an Oxberry camera. Courtesy of Cody Cameron.

were Max Fleischer's and Van Beuren's, with Terrytoons way up in suburban New Rochelle. Like their West Coast brethren, Van Beuren animators Hicks Lokey, Jim Tyer, John McManus, and Bill Littlejohn started a
"club," a John Reed club of artists affiliated with the Unemployed Artists
Association (UAA). (John Reed was an American radical writer who died
in Soviet Russia. The FBI believed the John Reed clubs were monitored
by the Communist Party USA.) After Roosevelt's administration issued
its NRA regulations, the UAA changed its name to the Artists Union,
with an offshoot called the Commercial Artists and Designers Union
(CADU). In late 1934, CADU set up an animation committee called the
Animated Motion Picture Workers Union (AMPWU). In a report to the
overseer Artists Union they wrote, "We must first explore all possibilities
of shop organization, find those large numbers of workers such as fashion

sketchers, art services, textile designers and animated cartoonists who are the most exploited."[37]

Animator Izzy Klein got his brother, Phil, a job as an opaquer at Van Beuren's. Phil was a member of the Artists Union, and he soon made contact with the scattered, informal animators clubs to discuss their common problems. The artists at the Van Beuren studio seemed to have plenty to talk about. Since 1929, when they had split the studio off from Paul Terry's Terrytoons, the Van Beuren studio seemed to have fallen behind all its competitors in quality and output. None of the studio's characters, Cubby Bear, the Sunshine Makers, or the Toonerville Trolley, had captured the public's fancy the way Mickey Mouse and Betty Boop had. Future Looney Tunes director Frank Tashlin did a stint there and later was inspired to do a syndicated comic strip about the place he called "Van Boring."[38]

Van Beuren changed producers and directors frequently, looking for a team to make his studio a winner, but the mismanagement of work schedules caused his shop's cartoons to fall seriously behind and way over budget. The supervisors' solution to make up the time was to demand that everyone put in long hours of overtime nights and weekends, all for free. Animators were told that if they refused, the studio would fold and they could go on relief, the term then for public assistance like welfare. When Burt Gillett, the director of *The Three Little Pigs* (1933), left Walt Disney to run Van Beuren, everyone hoped that things would improve. Gillett tried to introduce the rigorous standards of quality he learned making Silly Symphonies at Disney, but he did this while still asking for the same low-budget deadlines made up with uncompensated extra work time. Artists saw big sections of the shorts thrown out as substandard and were forced to work unpaid overtime hours to replace them. According to several sources, the hard-drinking Gillett quickly earned a reputation for emotional outbursts and instability. The artists held regular informal sessions at the Metropole Bar a few doors from the studio to complain about their situation.

Numbers of artists, including Bill Carney, Lou Appet, and Sadie Bodin, began to meet with representatives of the AMPWU to discuss going union. Spies in the crowd soon reported everything to Gillett.[39] On February 14, 1935, Gillett called a staff meeting. He shocked everyone when he said he knew all about the union talk and that there had been a meeting. Bill Littlejohn, who was nineteen years old at the time, told me, "The big artists came out of Burt's office white as sheets."[40] The staff shrank back, intimidated, but the grumbles of discontent continued. Another snitch told Gillett that an inker named Sadie Bodin was overheard in the ladies' room encouraging her girlfriends to stand up to him and not to do the extra work. Gillett's reaction was to immediately fire her. Sadie angrily confronted Gillett. She said that since the Wagner Act had just passed in Washington, firing her for wanting a union was now against the law. Burt Gillett responded that he fired her not for organizing but merely to replace her with someone "whose attitude was better."

On April 17, 1935, Sadie Bodin and her husband became the first people ever to picket an animation studio. They stood during the lunch hour for several days on Seventh Avenue with signs reading, "Van Beuren Violates Sec. 7-A NRA by Firing Union Labor for Union Activity."[41] Her coworkers shuffled mutely past her in and out of the building, eyes down. They were all too intimidated to go out and stand with her.

Inker Sadie Bodin. This photo was taken around the time she was fired from Van Beuren studio for talking union in the ladies' room. She became the first person to picket an animation studio. Courtesy of Harvey Deneroff.

Drawing the Line

The AMPWU filed a complaint with the National Labor Relations Board (NLRB) on behalf of Bodin against Van Beuren. But when the case was heard, the union couldn't build an adequate case. Gillett argued that he was not forcing employees to work for free but had set up a system of "comp time." An employee would bank his or her hours and take the time as paid leave during down periods in the schedule. The NLRB ruled for the management of Van Beuren. Afterward another company staff meeting was held. Thin, frail Amadee Van Beuren, wheelchair-bound by a stroke, was wheeled in by his accountant to address his long-faced crew. Van Beuren tried to calm them by stating, "I am behind you one hundred percent, and I am behind Mr. Gillett one hundred and twenty percent." Instead of calming the workers, his speech made many, including Shamus Culhane, want to quit. Gillett used his victory to fire other union agitators like Phil Klein, who was blacklisted and couldn't find work at other New York studios. He went to Hollywood where another ex–New Yorker, Art Babbitt, got him a job at Walt Disney on *Snow White and the Seven Dwarfs*. Young animator Hicks Lokey expressed shame that he did not stand up for Sadie when it counted. He resolved never to be that cowardly again. The experience made him a lifelong union agitator.

Firing uppity union artists didn't make Van Beuren cartoons any better. In 1936, Van Beuren's chief distributor and financier, RKO Pictures, inked an exclusive deal with Walt Disney Studio, which had shifted its distribution needs from Columbia Pictures. So RKO dumped Van Beuren, and the studio soon went out of business. It is ironic that the studio's last shorts were finally achieving the quality needed to succeed. Amadee Van Beuren, one of the animation industry's earliest producers but now worn out before his time, died of a heart attack a year later at age fifty-eight. Burt Gillett moved back west, where he went to work for Disney and later Walter Lantz.

In Hollywood, after the failed FMPC citywide strike, the members of the broken union locals reformed in 1938 to create a new alliance called the Conference of Studio Unions.[42] As the painters union in the east had an animation division, so the West Coast branch formed its own, the Screen Cartoonists Guild Local 852, after several secret meetings of union-minded artists with organizers at El Coyote Mexican restaurant on Melrose Avenue. At this time, IATSE hadn't given much thought to organizing animation workers because, like most of live-action Holly-wood, it didn't seriously think of the animation industry as part of the film business.

Back in New York, after the failure of the Van Beuren organizing campaign, the AMPWU unraveled. The Artists Union reformed the collapsed animation movement to become the Commercial Artists and Designers Union and looked around for an AF of L parent union for amalgamation. The nearest possible fit was the Painters and Paperhang-ers Local 843, which came into existence in November 1936 as AF of L Local 20239.[43] Even after the Artists Union offices were raided by the New York Police Department and forced to close, the CADU went on with its goal of organizing all commercial artists, setting its sights on the biggest and most well-known cartoon production studio on the East Coast, the Max Fleischer studio.

4

The Fleischer Strike

A Union Busted, a Studio Destroyed

I Make Millions Laugh but the Real Joke Is My Salary
—Striking Fleischer artist's picket sign

As American industry collapsed into the Great Depression of 1929–1941 and the animation industry formed its first trade unions, it was no surprise that the first city to have a major animation strike was New York City, where many radical ideas took their form. The first striking cartoonists were the children of immigrants; ironically, their anger was directed against another immigrant who all acknowledge was a good employer.

Max Fleischer was a gentle, diminutive man who wore a three-piece suit, a gold watch chain, a Charlie Chaplin mustache, and a broad smile. His brother Dave, the taller of the two, always played the swell, wearing tailored suits and spats and driving a fancy car. It reads like a cliché now, but the Fleischer family truly lived the American dream. They came from a large Austrian-Jewish immigrant family who had achieved some success in America by inventing simple gadgets: a hook-and-eye fastener for garments, brass buttons for policemen's uniforms that snapped off for polishing. The oldest brother, Charles, created a type of coin-operated claw-digger machine like the ones still found in some arcades today.[1]

The brothers tried jobs as ushers, stage managers, and newspaper errand boys. For a while Max was an art editor for *Popular Science Monthly*. After dabbling in animation, the Fleischer brothers got jobs working for John Randolph Bray, whom they had met at the *Brooklyn Daily Eagle*. In 1917, while working on training films for the U.S. Army,

Fleischer studio crew photos, 1931. Courtesy of MPSC Local 839, AFL-CIO, Urban Archives Center, Oviatt Library, California State University, Northridge.

the brothers patented the Rotoscope.[2] It was a device used to trace live action to achieve a fluid motion much like today's digital motion capture. They created a series called Out of the Inkwell featuring Koko the Clown. Dave Fleischer pranced about in a clown suit made by his mother, and Max had his artists draw over the projected live-action frames to create realistically fluid human movement. Dave later joked that he kept the clown costume so that if their fortunes didn't improve, he could effect a quick career change.[3] Bray told Max and Dave that if they wanted to strike out on their own with their Out of the Inkwell characters, they were welcome to do so. With a deal negotiated by Margaret Winkler (see chapter 2), the Fleischer brothers left Bray and set up for themselves in Manhattan at Forty-fifth Street and Lexington Avenue.

The Out of the Inkwell series (1921–1929) was a hit and was followed by other successes like Betty Boop, Bimbo, and the bouncing-ball sing-alongs called Song Car-Tunes. Their staff was expanding, so the Fleischers moved to larger space at Broadway and Forty-ninth Street. The new location was above the Silver Slipper nightclub and next to a burlesque theater. Animators were soon slipping away from work to take in a burlesque, even resorting to laying boards so they could shimmy from fire escape to fire escape to avoid being seen by their supervisors.[4]

At first they tried their own distribution arm, Red Seal Pictures, but by 1929 the Fleischers' output was distributed exclusively through Paramount Pictures. When sound became all the rage, the Fleischers' convenient Times Square location enabled them to take advantage of the talents of many of the famous musical stars of Broadway and vaudeville. Because they worked the clubs at night, Louis Armstrong, the Mills Brothers, and Cab Calloway could spare a few hours in the afternoon to drop in and record a voice track. Most of the talent booked was also on contract to Paramount.

The top-grade musical talent combined with the New York urban settings gave Fleischer cartoons an early sophistication that set them apart from the California cartoons' more rustic barnyard settings. While Leon Schlesinger's Looney Tunes and MGM were still struggling to find an audience, Max Fleischer's output gave Walt Disney Studio its most serious challenge.[5] In 1932, the Fleischers signed a deal with King Features Syndicate to develop E. C. Segar's *Thimble Theatre* character, Popeye. King Features, in turn, could create a "Betty Boop" comic strip. Vaudeville entertainers like Mae Questel and Red Pepper Sam created the unique voices of Olive Oyl and Popeye. Ms. Oyl was an impersonation of actress Zasu Pitts. When Red Pepper Sam asked for too much money, Max fired him and promoted an assistant animator named Jack Mercer to do the voice of the spinach-eating sailor.[6] Mercer remained the voice of Popeye until his death in 1977. In 1935, Popeye surpassed Mickey Mouse as the most popular character in America. Young Americans fighting for the Spanish Republic against Franco's Fascists in the Abraham Lincoln Brigade had a regimental song that was a variation on the Popeye theme song: "In a neat little town called Jarama, we made all the fascists cry Mama! We fight for our pay, just six cents a day, and play football with a bomb-a."[7]

The bicoastal rivalry between Fleischer and Walt Disney raged for more than a decade. The studios raided each other for artists and

Fleischer studio internal newsletter *Fleischer Animated News*, 1935. Courtesy of Bronwen Barry and Archives of the Animation Guild, Local 839, IATSE (formerly the MPSC Local 839), North Hollywood.

matched innovation for innovation. When Walt Disney created Silly Symphony cartoons in Technicolor, the Fleischers responded with Color Classics, in their own two-color process. When Disney developed depth of field with his multiplane camera, the Fleischers responded with a 3D tabletop background system. When Disney created an animated feature, the Fleischers retaliated with featurettes like *Popeye Meets Sinbad the Sailor* and planned their own feature, *Gulliver's Travels*.

Much like Walt Disney in the West, Max Fleischer considered himself a papa to his staff. Sure, the pay was bad, the facilities were run-down, and screen credits were a joke. Dave Fleischer was the only director listed, when, usually, the lead animators supervised the artwork for the shorts. Dave was at most of the recording sessions and he performed the duties of line producer, but he reserved, to himself, the title director. Max would occasionally go through the studio calling out, "Who hasn't had his name on a cartoon yet?" and give credit regardless of contribution.[8] Yet, despite it all, everyone liked Max. Uncle Max could be counted on for an emergency loan if things got tough. In 1930, during the depths of the Great Depression, Fleischer was doing well enough to give his animators a Christmas bonus of $500 each. That's like getting $10,000 today. Max always threw a lavish Christmas party at the Paramount Hotel. At a time when women were discouraged from aspiring to top production jobs, Max promoted Lillian Friedman to animator, making her the first woman animator in America.[9] Shamus Culhane referred to Max as the last great Victorian gentleman.

So, if Max Fleischer's studio was one big happy family, why did so many artists, overnight, demand a union?

The answer lies in the minds of the artists present. Many of the artists were the sons and daughters of working-class immigrants who had fled the autocratic states of Europe for a land where they could stand up for themselves. The studio was ruled by one man; only Max knew what was best for all. These young people were taught by their parents that one-man rule was the reason they left the old country. Parents taught their children that if a boss couldn't respect employees' rights, they should speak out because the boss was no better than the padrone, the Junker, the szlachta, the czar. To many immigrants, it seemed that the Socialist unions and workers' organizations were the only groups that really stuck up for working people and protected their families. Before unions, ten-year-olds worked in coal mines; job safety and minority rights were unknown. There was no such thing as a weekend off. The Vanderbilts, Rockefellers, and Carnegies didn't give in out of altruism or sudden change of heart. Every right and benefit for working people was won through struggle.

We find it hard to understand the class divisions that existed then. Rich and poor acted like different species; they mistrusted each other. When anarchist Giuseppe Zangara was interviewed after trying to assassinate president-elect Franklin Delano Roosevelt, a journalist asked: "Would you shoot me?" Zangara replied innocently, "Why shoot you? You're a working man like me."[10] I knew a kid in Queens who talked about his old Uncle Gustav hiding his copy of the *Daily Worker* in a copy of the *Wall Street Journal* as he went to work. While Lucille Ball was still an infant, her grandfather, as a matter of routine, enrolled her in the American Communist Party for her future protection. He said his children needed something that could always be counted on to look after them. In the 1930s there was a thriving pro-labor culture: labor newspapers and pro-labor movies, folk songs, and radio shows. All the pro-labor, pro–New Deal, anti-Fascist groups were known collectively as the Popular Front.

During the turbulent 1930s, while Hollywood reveled in its small-town Shangri-la atmosphere, New Yorkers lived in the eye of every political and cultural storm. You couldn't go to work without running into a protest march at least once a week. Riding on the subway, taking the streetcar or getting a newspaper, you heard about the Hooverville shacks in Central Park, the Tompkins Square unemployed workers' riots, and old women and young children rummaging for food in a trash dump on Riverside Drive. People knocked on your back door begging for food. Every day Jewish New Yorkers read the *Forward*, the Yiddish Socialist newspaper. There were rent strikes, the Tammany Hall corruption, and race riots in Harlem. New York City's mayor, Fiorello LaGuardia, was a radical-reform politician. He made his name by thundering against privilege and corruption.

Of course, Max Fleischer was not a diamond-stickpin blueblood; he was a hardworking immigrant who had pulled himself up from the streets. But he was the boss. The world Max Fleischer understood was the business world of moguls like Henry Ford and Louis B. Mayer; men who ran companies like absolute monarchies, living by their own instincts. These were the men society lionized, not the tramps on the street crying, "Injustice!" when they were refused a handout. You could also make a case that Max thought like an old-fashioned Yiddish papa, the head of the family whose word was final and beyond question. Ford, Edison, and Rockefeller didn't ask employees for their opinions or listen to some outside Red troublemaker on how to treat their own people, so why should Max? On the other hand, he was paternalistic. Max wrote in 1939, "My employees could always come to me with their problems."[11]

Almost from the beginning, the artists at Max Fleischer's studio talked about forming a union.[12] Their animation cameramen were organized by IATSE Camera Local 644 in 1934, and the musicians unionized under Local 802. Dave Fleischer was a dues-paying member of 802. The Commercial Artists and Designers Union Local 20239 of the AF of L under their new president, John Hulley, tried to organize the Fleischer studio from the outside. They hired an organizer, Arthur Post, who was not an artist but a disbarred lawyer. Post kept that little detail of his résumé a secret.

There was already an informal club of animators and their personal assistants led by Dave Tendlar and Myron Waldman. Today mass-production techniques have severed the close ties animators had with their assistants in favor of a pool system or rendering software. Back then the animator and assistant were a team that lasted for years. The animators provided experience and support to those who wished to be promoted. In return, they expected and received unwavering loyalty. Dick Williams once asked Disney animator Milt Kahl how loyal he expected his assistants to be. Milt replied, "When I fart I expect them to tell me it smelled like roses!"[13]

The Fleischer Animators' Club and its subsequent involvement in events demonstrated a problem in the animation artists' ranks that continues to plague them even today. The animators and higher-paid creative artists felt themselves superior to the lower-echelon inbetweeners, opaquers, and checkers. The discussion about unionizing broke into camps based on job title. Whenever an employer wished to sabotage union members' solidarity, he only needed to separate the animators and storymen from the "backend" artists. Sixty years later the animation guild still fields complaints from animators, writers, and CGI folks who want an exclusive organization. Fragmenting the workers' interests has always played right into the hands of the bosses.

In 1935, the Fleischer animators had heard all about the union debate at nearby Van Beuren studio. Some of the pro-union artists from Van Beuren's, like Bill Carney, Hicks Lokey, Lou Appet, and Marty Taras, moved over to work for Fleischer. They made common cause with the pro-union artists already there and looked for an opportunity to unionize Fleischer's. They thought they saw it with the story of Dan Glass.[14]

Glass was a young artist who came from Arkansas to make it in the big city. After he worked his way up from opaquer to inbetweener, his health failed and he was diagnosed with pulmonary tuberculosis. Max Fleischer helped pay for his stay in a New Jersey sanatorium, but, in January 1935, Dan died. Although Dan had voluntarily added to his workload by attending drawing classes at the Art Students League three nights a week and had sent much of his meager paycheck home to his family, many employees at Fleischer's felt that the long hours, bad pay, and cramped and badly ventilated workspace contributed to Dan's demise.

The CADU launched a call for action by circulating around the studio an incendiary manifesto blaming Glass's death on the bad working conditions. The notice shouted, "Max Fleischer Killed Dan Glass!" and more in deliberately provocative language. People did start talking, but much of the talk was antiunion rather than pro-union. Animator Tom Johnson, who was Dan's friend, was particularly angry. He wrote, "I objected to your blackjack and brass-knuckled attitude. Your Communistic 'Let's-Take-It' tone that Dan himself would condemn!" Max Fleischer made sure comments like this were printed in the studio one-sheet, the *Fleischer Animated News*.

After this rebuff, the organizing efforts at Fleischer stalled for a time, then resumed in late 1936. Max started a Studio Relief Fund for needy cases like Dan Glass and figured the union issues were now laid to rest.

In 1937, two events in particular ratcheted up the labor tensions in all fields. The first was the Supreme Court upheld the Wagner Act, which stated unequivocally that workers had a right to form unions and negotiate collectively. This news opened the floodgates for workers organizing in all fields. The second was the Depression, which had been receding since 1933, returned and collapsed the economy again, despite all of FDR's New Deal policies. President Roosevelt accused the major industrialists of withholding capital to sabotage the economy so they could undermine the Wagner Act and the New Deal. The Republicans responded by calling the downturn "the Roosevelt recession." FDR was forced to lay off 50 percent of the workers on the WPA payroll. Hitler's Nazi radio in Berlin declared that the decadent American democracy could not feed its own people.

In March 1937, the CADU West Coast affiliate, the FMPC, went on strike in Hollywood for better conditions. The CADU mounted its final push to unionize the Fleischer studio. The union demanded the right to speak for Fleischer employees and set an ambitious agenda for negotiations: a reduction of the workweek from forty-four to thirty-five hours, double time for every hour worked over that limit, a closed shop, paid vacations and sick leave, and a 12 percent across-the-board raise for all departments.[15]

Fleischer refused to negotiate with the CADU and made an example by firing inbetweeners Marty Taras and Carl Wessler. Marty was accused of creating a fire hazard by giving a guy a hotfoot as a joke. Animation studios at the time were highly flammable environments because of piles of nitrate/acetate cels and paper everywhere, but smoking at desks was common. Everyone felt Marty was fired for his union activities. A delegation of inbetweeners chose Lou Appet as their spokesman and went to speak to Max and production manager Sam Buchwald, but they got nowhere.

On March 30, the footage quota on Popeye cartoons was suddenly increased with no explanation, so the artists responded with a deliberate work slowdown. Max made another example by firing another inbetweener, Tony Pinelli. The CADU asked to meet with Fleischer, but he refused. The artists complained to the National Labor Relations Board, but Fleischer's lawyer, Louis Nizer, met with the feds and said that in management's view the CADU did not represent the majority of the Fleischer employees.

On Monday, May 3, 1937, the CADU petitioned the NLRB to hold a certification election at Fleischer's to prove the union spoke for the artists. The NLRB asked Nizer if Max would agree. Nizer said Max couldn't agree because of the work slowdown already occurring at the studio. Al-

THE ARTISTS WHO DRAW US

ARE ON STRIKE!

Because though our drawings make the whole world laugh, we are forced
to work at less than even a factory wage. Some of us get as low
as $15 a week for work that requires great skill and a strain
on eyes and nerves.

Because our employer, in complete defiance of the Wagner Act, fired
18 of us for joining a union !

Because in further defiance of the Wagner Act he refuses to recognize
our Union which has attempted to negotiate with him peacefully.

Because we have been forced to work without vacations! Some of us have
worked for 6 or 7 years without time off.

Because we do not get sick leave. We can't afford to take time off at
our own expense...so we work while we're ill !

Because during the depression our wages were cut more than half. Now,
our employer admits business has improved,but he hasn't restored those pay cuts!

Because of all these reasons, we ask your support! Help us win a
decent American standard of living by writing to your local
theatre manager or the Max Fleischer Studios. Tell them that
you object to having any Fleischer pictures shown while this
firm is unfair to its employees and refuses to recognize their
labor union as specified under the Wagner Act.

Commercial Artists and Designers Union
Local 20329   American Federation of Labor
155 East 34th Street - Caledonia 5-4970

----------------------------- Tear off and Mail at once------------------------------

Manager of----------------Theatre

Address----------------------------------
----
or

Max Fleischer Studios
1600 Broadway, N.Y.C.

I object to having any Max Fleischer pictures shown (Betty Boop, Popeye,
Color Classics, etc.) at my local theatre while Mr. Fleischer is unfair
to his employees and refuses to recognize their union.

Roto-graph 817 B'way.   signed------------- ---------------

CADU strike flyer, 1937, featuring Fleischer studio cartoon stars. Courtesy
of MPSC Local 839, AFL-CIO Collection, Urban Archives Center, Oviatt
Library, California State University, Northridge.

den Getz, a pro-union artist, circulated among the rank and file copies of a leaflet he claimed Max Fleischer received. The leaflet was titled *How to Break a Strike*.[16] Pamphlets like this were common publications of the National Council of Manufacturers during the labor-turbulent 1930s. In violation of the Wagner Act, the leaflet recommended carefully chosen firings of pro-union troublemakers and the placing of armed guards at work entrances—both actions the Fleischers had taken.

On Thursday, May 6, Max fired thirteen more artists because of their union activities: Harold Abbey, Edward McCarthy, Martin Nadel, Eli Levitan, Sophie Korff, Zoltan Szenics, Sam Robinson, Beatrice Skolnick, Ellen Jensen, Monroe Halsey, Betty Palesak, Leonard Frehm, Byron Rabbitt, Irving Sirota, and E. C. Entrup.[17] Union members went to their headquarters at 135 East Thirty-fourth Street that evening and voted overwhelmingly to go on strike. The animators' club separately announced that its members would not strike, but they would honor the picket line and not show up for work. A few hotheaded conservative animators like Willard "Willie" Bowsky, Roland "Doc" Crandall, and Tom

Fleischer studio strikers walking the picket line on Broadway, 1937, Marty Taras looking at camera. Courtesy of MPSC Local 839, AFL-CIO Collection, Urban Archives Center, Oviatt Library, California State University, Northridge.

Johnson loudly declared their intention to go to work no matter what. Some people, seeing the storm clouds ahead, just left the studio altogether. Young inbetweener Jacob Kurtzberg, whom Max had given his first job as an artist, saw the crisis as a hint to pursue his dream of being a comic-book illustrator, so he quit. Inker Charles Addams went into magazine cartooning, eventually creating *The Addams Family*.

On Friday, May 7, 1937, three hundred pickets and two thousand onlookers crowded 1600 Broadway, at the north end of Times Square. It was the first major strike of an American animation studio. The CADU chose Friday at 6:30 P.M. to begin picketing because that was the time of the break before the mandatory three-hour evening work period. The lines split along job classifications. Many of the highest-paid artists went back to work; the strikers were, in the main, underpaid assistants and ink and painters, but some of the animators joined them. Dave Fleischer recalled looking down at the street from his office window and recognizing his wife's cousin marching and yelling, "Fleischer unfair!"[18] Colorful car-

Fleischer strikers, 1937, in front of Fleischer building at 1600 Broadway. Courtesy of MPSC Local 839, AFL-CIO Collection, Urban Archives Center, Oviatt Library, California State University, Northridge.

toon characters adorned picket signs reading, "I Make Millions Laugh but the Real Joke Is My Salary!" Dave noticed that the lumber for the signs was from Fleischer's own art department.

When some artists tried to cross the picket line, fistfights broke out and the New York police were called. Ten strikers were arrested for assault and disturbing the peace. Checker Ellen Jenson was arrested for biting a policeman. She said: "One officer pinned my arms back and another struck my hat off with his baton. So as I went down I sank my teeth into him."[19] Striker Helen Kligle was arrested for kicking and scratching scab employee Elizabeth Howson.[20] The few artists who did make it upstairs couldn't work much. There were not enough people to complete a single cartoon, so they sat around reading and talking. Some even spent the day shooting craps.

In his old age, Dave Fleischer told interviewers that he was unaware of any problems and was surprised by the whole thing. He claimed he knew nothing about the strike until an FBI agent informed him it was going to happen. The agent told him, "You've got a bunch of Communists here and you're going to have a strike and it's going to be a bad one." Then, he said, "All of a sudden eighty people with big signs are walking around the building. . . . It was one of the worst strikes New York City ever had."[21] Modern scholars believe this to be a bit of invention; the strike was bad, but Dave Fleischer was known for hyperbole.

The next morning, Saturday, May 8, the union petitioned Mayor Fiorello LaGuardia to protest police brutality in handling the strikers. He referred the matter to his police chief, and it ended there. The *Graf Hindenburg* zeppelin crash occurred the same day in Lakehurst, New Jersey, and the mayor and his staff may have been too distracted to worry about some crazy cartoonists' argument. The *Hindenburg* disaster and the announcement of the wedding plans of erstwhile British king Edward VIII and the American divorcée Wallis Simpson combined to push the news of the Fleischer strike back to page 6 of the *New York Times*.[22] The union had lost round one of the public relations war.

Because Max Fleischer still refused to talk to the CADU, a committee from the animators' group, including Myron Waldman, Dave Tendlar, and Hicks Lokey, tried some shuttle diplomacy, racing about between the concerned parties trying to forge a deal. After lengthy discussion they persuaded Max to accept an impartial arbitrator, something the union had wanted all along. Max added that he also was willing to rehire all the artists he fired except for his relatives. He said of firing them, "That was a pleasure." When the animators told the CADU about their meeting, Arthur Post asked that any future meetings with Fleischer studio management have a union representative present. Post was worried that the animators' unilateral action showed Max a way to split his employees' united front.

Sure enough, when the animators returned to 1600 Broadway, Max and Dave Fleischer had just completed a long strategy session with Louis Nizer. Max now told the animators he was dubious about arbitration. He added that he would accept all the union's demands about hours and wages, but to do so he would have to cut the pay of all the workers making more than $50 a week. In other words, if the top animators supported the union, Max would cut their pay. That night the supervisors phoned all of the Fleischer employees and told them to return to work on Monday, no excuses.

Arthur Post sent a telegram to the Fleischer artists explaining that this salary-cut tactic was an obvious attempt to divide them. He called for a Tuesday night meeting with the animators to discuss the problems.

From the beginning, solidarity among the senior animators was never strong. As already noted, pro-Fleischer animators like Willie Bowsky, Tom Johnson, and Doc Crandall had earlier announced they would not strike. Animators who had been promoted after the exodus of Shamus Culhane, Al Eugster, and Grim Natwick to Hollywood felt their new positions would be jeopardized by striking. Now the threat of salary cuts to support the painters and cel polishers was too much. So on Tuesday morning, sixteen animators went back to work. By week's end, almost all the senior animators had returned to work, even pro-union ones like Lokey, Friedman, and Tendlar. The only animator who stayed out on the picket line for the entire strike was Eli Brucker. Sensing victory on the horizon, Max now refused any arbitration and said he now would only rehire half of the artists he had fired, maybe. The studio sent out a call to hire scabs to replace the half of the studio still on strike. By the following week, production was close to normal.

The anger of the striking artists grew each day as they saw their friends going in to work while they stayed out. Artist Nick Tafuri (who had not joined the strike) recalled seeing Dave Fleischer and some oth-

The Fleischer Strike

Fleischer strikers, 1937. Courtesy of MPSC Local 839, AFL-CIO Collection, Urban Archives Center, Oviatt Library, California State University, Northridge.

ers go down under a pile of picket signs when they tried to break through the picket line. One supervisor, Frank Paiker, got his nose broken by unionist Lou Appet.[23] Max tried hiring taxicabs to drive his scab employees in to work. They could drive into the building's underground parking lot and thus avoid having to cross the picket line on the street. Strikers responded by gaining the sympathy of the Taxi and Chauffeurs' Union to stop the practice. Dave Fleischer's house was stink-bombed. The striker who did the bombing confessed he meant to bomb Max's house. Crowds of cartoonists went up to Max's home at the Hotel Windermere on the Upper West Side and picketed under his window. Max started carrying a gun to work and hired a bodyguard.[24]

The National Labor Relations Board, under the pro-union labor secretary Frances Perkins, had been swamped by work since the Wagner Act went into effect. The board was looking into four thousand strikes nationwide just that year alone. By June, the NLRB finally got to the Fleischer strike. Certification hearings began June 16. At first the union's attorneys laughed at how unprepared top Paramount attorney Louis Nizer was for the proceedings. They later realized it was a tactic. The longer Nizer stalled, the longer management could starve out the hapless people walking the picket lines. So Nizer dragged out the proceedings with motions about jurisdiction and interstate commerce and a petition signed by the animators asking that they be excluded from the union bargaining agreement. (The day before the hearing, Max Fleischer and Sam Buchwald had called the animators together and asked them to sign a petition they had drawn up. The petition stated that the animators did not want to be part of the CADU. Sam said that no stigma would be attached to any animator who chose not to sign, and he left the room, but when he saw some names were not on the petition, he loudly demanded to know whose names were left out. The terrified pro-union animators signed along with the pro-company ones.)

The union countered by showing the NLRB that they had signed rep cards—cards requesting union representation—from more than half the studio's employees. Nizer challenged the validity of the cards and asked that they be turned over to Sam Buchwald so he could vouch for the artists' identity. This, of course, meant Buchwald could identify union artists, who would then be purged, in violation of the Wagner Act. This request was refused, and Buchwald's animators' petition was invalidated as having been obtained through intimidation. On June 19, the NLRB adjourned the hearing and called for a certification election for all the artists employed as of April 30, 1937. The company stalled the election through appeals and points of order until August 16, when the vote was held at the Union Methodist Church on West Forty-eighth Street.[25]

On the day of the election, management posted a notice on the studio bulletin board. It declared that the NLRB election was being held "contrary to the provisions of the Wagner Act," meaning that the NLRB had invalidated the petition of the animators, and that management had "tried to negotiate but agreement was impossible because of unreasonable demands. . . . Your refusal to vote in an election under these circumstances will represent your protest against this procedure. The election at this time has no possible purpose and is binding on nobody."[26]

Although this notice scared some away, the final tally was for the union 74–0. Fourteen votes were discounted because they were by fired workers. Still, the count was 60 for the CADU and none opposed. Fleischer's filed appeals and challenges, thus delaying the final report of the NLRB until October 8.

The Fleischer Strike

Since the strike was failing to stop production of cartoons and the NLRB election was moving at a snail's pace, the CADU shifted strategy to boycotts. The union declared in the press that it was aligning itself with the FMPC strikes in Hollywood. As part of that action they appealed to the powerful American Federation of Labor to boycott Max Fleischer's chief financier, Paramount Pictures. In July, the AF of L declared a nationwide boycott of all Paramount movies. The New York Newspaper Typesetters Guild refused to run any Fleischer comic strips or ads. Even the Musicians Union Local 802, of which Dave and Lou Fleischer were members, declared a boycott and threatened them with suspension. The picket lines in front of 1600 Broadway were filled with longshoremen and striking Horn & Hardart Automat cafeteria workers. In retaliation, Max Fleischer ordered his loyal artists to get coffee at the automats. Picketers chanted, "Horn & Hardart full of slop, go and eat at a union shop!!"

Striking animation artists would sit in the lobby of the Paramount and Roxy theaters in Times Square and sing, "We're Popeye the Union Man! We're Popeye the Union Man! We'll fight to the Finish, because we can't live on Spinach."[27] On July 16, the Loews Theater chain announced it would no longer screen Fleischer cartoons. The powerful Projectionists Local 306 of the IATSE also voted to join the strike after a passionate appeal by Herman Temple. IATSE Local 644 cameramen, who ran Fleischer's animation cameras, also joined the strike and stopped filming Fleischer's animation. The IATSE had won its war with the FMPC and now saw no conflict in making common cause with union brothers against a stubborn employer. Even though IATSE was run by gangsters who promised the moguls labor peace, IATSE pressure on Paramount grew.

By autumn the boycotts seemed to have an effect. Paramount Pictures was being backed into a corner. The studio's management didn't exactly love unions, but all the boycotts and bad press were beginning to affect their mainstream motion-picture grosses. So they pressured the Fleischer brothers into cutting a deal. Mayor LaGuardia himself helped kick-start the negotiations. Interestingly enough, the chief negotiator for the management team was not Max Fleischer, but Lou Diamond, chief of Paramount's short films division. Eyewitnesses to the talks said Max looked ill, like he was suffering from nervous exhaustion or ulcers. Dave sat quietly playing with a theatrical prop sword while Lou Diamond closed the deal.

Drawing the Line

On October 19, the Fleischer studio finally recognized the CADU. Part of the delay in getting the deal signed was that, at the last minute, Max was still holding out for a separate animators' association. He encouraged some artists to resign from the union. The Paramount attorney asked why the artists needed vacation time when they had weekends off and could always go to Coney Island. In the contract Fleischer agreed to allow the CADU to represent Fleischer artists and consented to a 20 percent raise, a forty-hour week, one week of paid vacation, holidays, sick leave, and screen credits. Instead of a closed shop, the mix would be 60 percent union and 40 percent nonunion; all fired personnel would be rehired and all scabs would be fired.[28] Grievances would be addressed by a committee under the arbitration of Manhattan district attorney Thomas Dewey, the crusading, racket-busting lawyer who was to lose the 1948 presidential election to Harry Truman. This was the first artists' union contract ever signed with an animation studio. After five months of turmoil, everyone went back to work and thought that was that.

The Fleischer brothers still had one more trick up their sleeves. Both Max and Dave owned property in Florida and were being courted with tax breaks by the city of Miami to move their operations south. Max started talking seriously with the Miami Chamber of Commerce in mid-June while the strikers marched below his windows. Florida was a right-to-work state, where Governor Fred Cone boasted he'd "have all union organizers hanging from lamp posts."[29] The Fleischers convinced Paramount that in Florida the labor costs and tax breaks would lower costs and they could finish their own feature film, *Gulliver's Travels*, which would outdo Disney's *Snow White and the Seven Dwarfs*. Paramount funded Fleischer's relocation and finishing costs for *Gulliver* to the tune of $300,000. The Fleischer studio was the collateral against the loan. Dade County promised an additional $100,000 to improve roads near the studio and exempted the studio from property taxes.

So, armed with this cash infusion from Paramount, Max and Dave informed their surprised staff on January 28, 1938, that they were leaving Gotham forever. The CADU knew this was a union-busting tactic but could do nothing to stop it. Shortly before the move, Max fired Hicks Lokey for "low production." The studio began to move in the spring of

The Fleischer Strike

1938 and paid moving costs for all those who wished to relocate. Most hard-core union animators refused to move and stayed in New York; the rest were intimidated into forgoing further union activity. The pro-union workers and the union-haters were housed in separate hotels. The Fleischer loyalists were put up in the swanky Hotel Cortez, the unionists in a fleabag in Miami's red-light district. The new studio at Seventeenth and Thirtieth avenues was thirty-two thousand square feet of air-conditioned elegance. Eventually one hundred Californians and extra workers would join the hundred New Yorkers and bring the staff up to five hundred.[30]

Upon arrival in Miami, the Fleischers immediately asked for a new NLRB certification election, which they won. The efforts of another union, the United American Artists, to organize the employees were also defeated on Halloween of 1938.

The Fleischers had assured Paramount that the move to Florida and busting the union would bring down costs. Ironically, the move had the opposite effect. Everything needed for film production had to be shipped down. Every foot of negative had to be processed in New York. Shamus Culhane said the studio might just as well have been in Tibet. The studio had to pay much higher salaries than before in order to entice good artists to move with their families to distant Miami. Cartoonist Hank Ketcham recalled that while he was toiling away in the Walter Lantz inbetweener pool for $16 a week, Fleischer's Florida studio was offering $85 to $100 a week.[31] The big salaries attracted former employees like Grim Natwick (who had headed up the Snow White character animation team), Al Eugster, Dan Gordon, Cal Howard, and Shamus Culhane to leave Hollywood. Even Pinto Colvig, the voice actor for Goofy, came out to do some work. Years later, those who were there still talked with relish about the salaries Max doled out. Animator Jack Ozark told me, "It was great. I could afford a roadster and spats. I sped down the empty freeway, and if a Florida cop pulled me over I just handed him a twenty."[32]

When Fleischer alumni from the West Coast arrived in Florida, they were struck by the change in the spirit of the studio. The artists were divided into camps. The unionists stuck to themselves, getting the silent treatment from the others. The antiunionists formed a social group called the Flippers Club and had parties and picnics. Max used to be the jovial presence among his workers, but now he mostly kept to himself, associating largely with a small circle of insiders. Anyone could see he was still hurt by the whole union experience.[33]

The building boom of the 1960s made Miami the hip metropolis it is today. In the 1930s, though, it was a sleepy southern resort town. The animation artists of fast-paced, ethnically diverse Manhattan had difficulty adjusting to their new surroundings. At lunch they could go across the street from the studio and watch Seminole Indians wrestle alligators for tourist coins. Convicts did lawn work, and the big-bellied cops foiled all attempts by the artists to bring the poor men Cokes. It was also the age of segregation. At 10:00 P.M. all African Americans had to be off the street or risk being thrown in jail. When Cab Calloway went down to visit with Lou Fleischer, he received a warning in his mailbox from the local Ku Klux Klan. Some shops posted signs forbidding Jews. This was especially upsetting since many of the Fleischer employees from New York were Jewish.[34]

The expenses incurred to move the studio and train new artists soon put *Gulliver* over budget. The Fleischer shorts were falling in popularity. To accommodate the Motion Picture Production Code, Betty Boop was transformed from a sexy vamp in a black minidress to a boring hausfrau in ankle-length outfits. Lou Diamond came out again from Los Angeles in 1939, now as the official Paramount watchdog over the books. *Gulliver's Travels* didn't exactly burn up the box office, but it did well enough for Paramount to greenlight another feature. The next film, *Mr. Bug Goes to Town*, named to parody the 1936 Paramount hit *Mr. Deeds Goes to Town*, premiered shortly after the 1941 attack on Pearl Harbor. Despite music from top composer Hoagy Carmichael, *Mr. Bug* flopped badly; it seemed that with all the war news, the public had temporarily lost its taste for innocent fantasy. Paramount asked the Fleischers to do a series of Superman cartoons in high-quality, realistic style using their Rotoscope. Max warned them the series would be too expensive to be profitable, but Paramount insisted. While the average budget for a six-minute Popeye cartoon was around $16,000, the Superman shorts cost as much $50,000 each.[35] Dave Fleischer later claimed they cost $90,000. The Superman shorts gained critical acclaim but were cost prohibitive, and in spite of all his warnings, Max Fleischer wound up being blamed.

In 1942, when their contract came up for renewal, Paramount finally pulled the plug. Sensing disaster, Dave Fleischer abandoned his brothers and jumped ship to direct at Screen Gems.[36] Paramount seized the company's assets, abandoned Miami, and set up a new entity to do shorts in New York. Sam Buchwald, Izzy Sparber, and Seymour Kneitel, Max's son-in-law, ran it. It was called Famous Studios after Famous Players-Lasky, the original name of Paramount. Artists moved back to the Big Apple with suntans and a hefty pay cut.

Back on Forty-fifth Street in midtown Manhattan, Buchwald showed he had learned a lesson from the 1937 debacle and offered no resistance when union organizing efforts began again. Famous Studios quickly became a union signatory under the new Screen Cartoonists Guild, the successor of the CADU, which had largely broken up by 1941. Famous Studios later changed its name once more, to Paramount Animation Studio. The company produced Popeye shorts and Harveytoons and, later, television shows of diminishing quality. Paramount sold out to Gulf & Western, and in 1969 the studio was closed for good.

Max and Dave Fleischer sued Paramount for $15 million. Dave said that in the end Max settled "for the stupid amount of $3,000."[37] Dave sued Paramount again and named his own brother as a codefendant. In later years they would separately sue TV stations like WPIX New York and distributors like AAP (Associated Artists Productions) for cropping their names off the title cards of the Popeye and Betty Boop shorts. They usually lost. Both had smaller careers producing shorts and technical films until their retirement. Dave directed some Fox and Crow and Lil' Abner short cartoons for Screen Gems, then worked at Universal until his retirement in 1967. He continued to spar with the unions in Los Angeles and rail against the Wagner Act. Max worked for a Detroit company called Jam Handy, which had an exclusive contract to do short cartoons for General Motors automobiles. Lou Fleischer went on unemployment until he found a job grinding camera lenses for $35 a week, for a company located at 1600 Broadway, the Fleischers' old building.[38]

Max and Dave would not speak to each other for many years afterward. Dave joked in 1969 that he wanted to write a book about their relationship and call it *There's No Greater Hate than Brotherly Love*.[39] For the rest of his life, Max felt that if it weren't for the union battle, he would still have his studio. World War II and the loss of overseas profits had much to do with the bad business climate as well. Walt Disney almost went bankrupt about the same time. He only saved his studio by turning most of it over to the government for war films. Disney didn't really get back to its position of primacy until *Cinderella* in 1950.

Richard Fleischer, Max's son, became a top Hollywood director, creating films like *Fantastic Voyage* and *Tora! Tora! Tora!* He was even tapped by Max's old nemesis, Walt Disney, to direct *Twenty Thousand Leagues under the Sea.*

On January 4, 1956, Max Fleischer went out to Burbank and met Walt Disney at his studio. Perhaps one of the things they could agree on was the similar experience of dealing with striking employees. Some of Max's old employees were there and shared reminiscences and anecdotes. Richard Fleischer noticed, "My father seemed to be enjoying himself, but, in Walt's presence, he seemed diminished, and my heart broke for him. I had the feeling that Goliath had defeated David."[40] After two more attempts to restart his studio, Max retired to the San Fernando Valley.[41] He died at the Motion Picture Home in 1972. Dave Fleischer died in 1979.

Since the 1930s, Betty Boop had been merchandised exclusively by King Features, which had retained the design copyright through the old comic strip, even while the films themselves passed from distributor to distributor. King renewed the contract shortly before Max died.[42] What Max didn't see was how Betty was entering the young counterculture. A craze for 1930s nostalgia and Betty's sexy antics made millions for King Features in Betty figurines, blankets, and T-shirts. A compilation of her black-and-white pre–Production Code cartoon shorts called the *Betty Boop Cocaine Follies* packed college campuses and retro theaters in 1974–1975. In 1990, the Fleischer family heirs, with help from centenarian animator Grim Natwick, finally won a court case restoring to them the rights to Betty.

Marty Taras went on to become a great animator. Lou Appet was blacklisted and went west, where Chuck Jones got him a job at Schlesinger's. He eventually became business agent for IATSE Animation Local 839 in Hollywood. Eli Brucker was blacklisted also, but he left animation, changing to a career making dolls. Striker Harry Lampert went into comic books and at D.C. Comics was cocreator of the comic book superhero the Flash. He died in 2004. After quitting Fleischer's, inbetweener Jacob Kurtzberg changed his name to Jack Kirby. In 1941 he teamed with Stan Lee and Joe Simon and created the Marvel superhero comic publishing empire, giving birth to characters like Captain America, Thor, and the Fantastic Four. To comic-book lovers he was Jack "the King" Kirby. In his final years he returned to animation periodically to design TV series for the studio Ruby & Spears.

Lillian Friedman married and moved to Troy, New York, leaving the business.[43] Hicks Lokey went on to Walt Disney, animated on *Pinocchio* and *Fantasia* and marched in the 1941 Disney strike (see chapter 5). In the spirit of "if you can't beat 'em, join 'em," pro-management artists Tom Johnson and Edith Vernick became officers of the union. Edith even ran for business agent in 1948 and 1950. Dave Tendlar served as a loyal executive board member for many years and later, at Hanna-Barbera, walked picket lines in the Runaway Wars of 1979 and 1982. The CADU was not happy with the high-handed way Arthur Post had handled the strike, so he was fired. Willie Bowsky chafed at the reputation he had as a hard-nose, even being called pro-Nazi by some. He enlisted in the army to fight in World War II, even though at thirty-nine he was almost over the age limit. In 1944, on the day after D-Day, a German tank firing from the hedgerows of Normandy killed him.

Animation would not return to Florida until Walt Disney Studios opened a studio as part of an attraction at Disney World theme park from 1989 to 2003. The studio created hit films like *Mulan, Lilo & Stitch,* and *Brother Bear*. In 1993, I helped the artists there organize their own union, the Motion Picture Screen Cartoonists Local 843, IATSE. In this formerly segregated state, its first president, James Parris, was an African American.

Despite a few bright spots, like the TV commercial boom in the 1950s, *Sesame Street* work in the 1970s, and Blue Sky and J. J. Sedelmier today, New York City was never the animation powerhouse it was when the Fleischers reigned supreme.

The Fleischer strike was the first major labor strike in animation history. It demonstrated all the tactics and problems that would dominate labor-management conflicts in animation for the next sixty years: employee anger over working conditions but apathy about joining organizations to do anything about the conditions; suspicion of outside labor organizations; artists' denial of basic business realities; employers trying to stay friends with their staff while acting tough behind the workers' backs; official rhetoric about "free choice" masking strong-arm tactics;

intimidation of workers; flouting of government laws and oversight; gestures calculated to pit artists against artists; and stonewalling negotiations while waiting for the artists and their families to starve. All these things occur with depressing regularity in studios up to the present day, whether cartoons are done with pencils or pixels. Like all conflicts, the Max Fleischer strike could have been avoided. Many said afterward that if Max had simply recognized the union and offered a token raise or agreed to arbitration, the strike would not have happened. But that would be asking for some pretty forward thinking from a businessman of those times, even one as well loved as Max Fleischer. Myron Waldman summed it up: "It was sad, the whole damn thing."[44]

5 The Great Disney Studio Strike

The Civil War of Animation

ANIMATOR: "Who do you think you are, God?"
ROY DISNEY: "Nah, I'm just his brother."
—Bob Thomas, *Building a Company*

Probably no single event in the history of Hollywood cartoons has been more subject to spin and hurt feelings than the Great Disney cartoonists' strike of 1941. It was an event that splintered the unity of the animation community and affected hundreds of careers. The strike spawned new studios, new creative styles and characters, and new comic strips and changed the world of animation forever. For the people who were there, it was a defining moment in their careers. Friendships were broken, and many carried their anger for the rest of their lives. Trying to piece together the complete picture of what happened is a task worthy of the judge in the film *Rashomon*.

In 1919, a Kansas City kid just out of the army went to his local library and checked out Edwin Lutz's *Animated Cartoons: How They Are Made*. The youth kept the book for so long, the librarian upbraided him for monopolizing it.[1] He could draw a little, and soon he and his brother started up their own cartoon flicker business. In 1923, he moved to Hollywood to direct live-action movies, but, getting nowhere fast, he resumed his animation production. It was the first animation studio on the

Walt Disney, circa 1941. This famous drawing was admired for capturing Walt in one of his darker moods. But the artist who did it has never come forward. Courtesy ASIFA/ Hollywood Animation Archive, www.animationarchive.org.

West Coast. He brought with him future animation greats: Ub Iwerks, Friz Freleng, Hugh Harman, Rudolf Ising, and Carl Stalling.

The rest of the Walt Disney story is well documented: Mickey Mouse, Donald Duck, and Goofy; Technicolor films; feature-length cartoons; Oscars. Mickey Mouse was so popular that a popular advertising slogan of the 1930s was the plaintive whine of a movie theater patron when he discovered that some other cartoon was playing: "What? No Mickey Mouse?" Even MGM's legendary mogul Louis B. Mayer said, "There are only two true geniuses in Hollywood today: Garbo and that damn Mouse!"[2]

By 1941, Walt Disney had left all his competitors far behind and was a Hollywood celebrity. He dressed well, drove a fashionable Packard, and sported a small Clark Gable mustache that was très chic. He played polo with movie stars at the Riviera Polo Club, was photographed by Richard Avedon, and escorted glitterati like Charlie Chaplin and H. G. Wells around his cartoon factory. Thomas Mann inspected the storyboards for the *Sorcerer's Apprentice*. Orson Welles once pitched to Walt the idea of making a movie of *The Little Prince* by Antoine Saint-Exupéry. Disney sent him off in a half-joking way, "I don't think there's room for two geniuses in this company!"[3] "Who's Afraid of the Big Bad Wolf?"—the song heard first in the 1933 Silly Symphony called *The Three Little Pigs*—became the rallying anthem in America's battle to recover from the Great Depression. Although Walt Disney's cartoon studio was not considered one of the Big Five major Hollywood studios, the moguls did invite him to their regular conferences to shape policy for the motion picture industry. Disney was the only animation studio head at the secret meeting called by Louis B. Mayer to discuss what to do about the feud between publishing titan William Randolph Hearst and rogue wunderkind Orson Welles over the film *Citizen Kane*.

Walt Disney and his more financially minded brother, Roy, survived the rough and tumble of independent filmmaking. They were repeatedly cheated by distributors and raided of their top talent. They fought off attempts by bigger studios to turn their business into a fiefdom the way Paramount pulled the strings of Max Fleischer's studio or Universal owned Walter Lantz. On more than one occasion, Walt Disney was close to bankruptcy. He admitted that in 1931 he had a nervous breakdown over the strain.[4] Like many successful self-made businessmen, the Disney brothers felt a pride of achievement tempered by a hard edge of experience. They wouldn't stomach any outsiders telling them how to handle their employees.

Yet the 1930s film workers' drive to form unions and have a voice in their futures would soon reach even the Disney magic kingdom.

After the Ub Iwerks studio artists began having secret meetings in 1932, Los Angeles animation artists attempted several times to organize themselves into a union (see chapter 3). Looney Tunes painter Martha Sigall recalled that when she was hired in 1936, her supervisor, Art Goble, immediately invited her to attend one of their clandestine union meetings.[5] In 1936, Looney Tunes gagman Ted Pierce was union president and director Frank Tashlin was vice president. Sometimes they held secret meetings in El Coyote Restaurant on Melrose Boulevard, sometimes in the Hollywood Mormon Temple across from Grauman's Chinese Theatre. Tashlin recalled: "We used to meet in cellars—it was like Communist cell meetings. The salaries were terrible then. So we started this union, and it was tough going; everyone was afraid to join." Supervisors would find out about the meetings from snitches and threaten their artists with dismissal. If outside organizers came on too forcefully or seemed too openly Communist, the more reticent shied away.[6] Finally, inspired in part by the other backstage unions like those for writers and directors and the example of the Fleischer cartoonists striking in the east, in 1938 the Los Angeles cartoonists openly declared themselves the Screen Cartoonists Guild, Brotherhood of Painters, Decorators and Paperhangers of America Local 852, as a chapter of the Conference of Studio Unions. In 1939, an NLRB ruling awarded the SCG jurisdiction over all levels of production of animation from writing to painting. Animation cameramen were to be in the Cameramen's Union Local 695, and editors were in the Screen Editors Guild.[7]

After several years of slowly building infrastructure and goodwill, new SCG president and MGM animator Bill Littlejohn and the other leaders planned an organizing blitz on cartoon studios. By early 1941, they quickly signed contracts with Walter Lantz and independent producer George Pal. An artist himself, but no stranger to the financial pressures of production, Walter Lantz was refreshingly cooperative in signing a union contract with his artists. Littlejohn and a young inbetweener named Pepe Ruiz then went to work trying to convince MGM artists to sign with the guild. Some of the organizers the AF of L sent to help were experienced in the roughhouse school of 1930s industrial actions and were not used to talking to cartoonists. Gus Arriola, who in later years created the comic strip "Gordo," was then an animation assistant at MGM. His future wife, Frances Servier, was an animation painter. He recalls: "We didn't want to join the union. Our objection was not to the union so much as to the threatening methods they used with everyone. . . . Frances and I were among the last ones to join. We were taken for a walk out in the MGM back lot by one of the tough union guys, and he said if we didn't join the union, we weren't going to walk through that front door to work. So we did. Under protest, we joined. And the funny part of it was that by joining, I doubled my salary. This all happened just when I was transferred out of the animation department to the storyboard department, and because of the new job classification, story sketchman, I was qualified for a different salary. My salary jumped

THE ANIMATOR 5¢

January 3, 1938   Official Publication Screen Cartoon Guild   Vol.I-No.8

OPEN MEETING FOR ALL CARTOONISTS SET FOR ROOSEVELT HOTEL'S ACADEMY LOUNGE

McWILLIAMS AND BODLE TO REPORT ON COMPANY ORGANIZATIONS AND GUILD NEGOTIATIONS
AT SCHLESINGER STUDIOS

The SCREEN CARTOON GUILD invites all artists employed in animated cartoon studios to attend an open meeting Wednesday night, Jan. 5, at 8 o'clock at the Academy Lounge of Hollywood Roosevelt Hotel.

Speakers representing the Screen Set Designers and the Screen Publicists Guild will report on negotiations pending with producers. Other speakers will include George Bodle, of the Pacific Coast Labor Bureau and Carey McWilliams, attorney for the Screen Cartoon Guild.

Mr. Bodle is at present representing the SCREEN CARTOON GUILD in its negotiations with the Leon Schlesinger Studio. The S.C.G. has on file with the regional National Labor Relations Board a complaint against this studio for refusal to bargain collectively with the Guild in spite of the fact that the Guild represents 98 % of its employees. Mr. Bodle will give a resume of these first negotiations with any cartoon producer on the Pacific Coast. (Artists in the Max Fleischer Studios in New York were victorious in the recent strike at the "Popeye Factory")

Carey McWilliams is the attorney who led the attack on the I.A.T.S.E. officialdom in the recent investigation into labor racketeering in the Motion Picture Industry. He will discuss company unions and the N.L.R.B.

This meeting is open to all cartoonists in the animated cartoon industry whether members of the Guild or not. Members and officials of individual studio organizations are urged to attend.

UNITED WE STAND---DIVIDED WE FALL--
INTO THE LAP OF THE I.A.T.S.E.!!!!!!

To clear up the confusion arising from the attempted separate company organizations in some cartoon studios, the ANIMATOR offers these facts:

1. There is no protection for cartoonists in organizations which are fostered, controlled or influenced directly or indirectly, in whole or in part by their employers or by others acting in or for their behalf.

2. Such organizations DO NOT guarantee bargaining rights nor are they recognized by the NLRB as bargaining agents.

3. By splitting the movement for a unified organization to effectively fight the I.A.T.S.E., these company organizations are actually delivering the artists employed in making animated cartoons into the hands of the I.A. dictatorship.

In those studios where separate organizations have been started, the members should suggest that the SCREEN CARTOON GUILD be contacted for a conference. The SCREEN CARTOON GUILD stands ready to meet with a committee representing any studio, for the purpose of explaining the Guild set-up, its aims and policies.

The SCREEN CARTOON GUILD has sent a letter to the executive committee of the Disney employees' organization inviting them to set a date for a joint conference to discuss mutual problems of vital importance to both organizations.

The SCREEN CARTOON GUILD is the only bonafide organization representing all of the studios in the Animated Cartoon Industry.

PRODUCERS GO BEGGING FOR ANIMATORS

With the opening of two new Animated Cartoon Studios, there is an increasing demand for trained cartoonists. The Ub Iwerks Studio has just landed a sweet contract for fifty shorts for British release. Ub is on a search for good men and women artists, competing with the newly organized 'toon fac' at MGM Studios. Phenomenal coming out party of Disney's Snow White and the Seven Dwarfs creates a new field for the business. Disney has two new features scheduled.

COME TO THE OPEN MEETING AT ROOSEVELT'S ACADEMY LOUNGE, WEDNESDAY NIGHT AT 8:00
WRITE FOR GUILD INFORMATION --- 1930 No. Normandie Ave. or Phone NO. 16938.

Earliest known copy of Screen Cartoonists Guild newsletter, January 1938. Notice that one of its first blasts is at the rival union, the IATSE. From the estate of Grim Natwick, collection of the author.

from $32.50 a week to $65—overnight. Because of the union. So I can't complain about the union."[8]

One way or another Littlejohn convinced 90 percent of his fellow MGM animation employees to vote to go union. According to the federal government's new rules for organizing, if that many employees ask for representation, an election is not necessary. MGM was immediately compelled to sign a contract. This caused production head Fred Quimby to angrily raise everyone's weekly footage quota from twenty feet to twenty-fve feet. Animator Rudy Zamora responded by taking his bowling ball upstairs to Milt Gross's old room over Quimby's office to practice bowling. After a few frames, Quimby fired Rudy.[9]

That May, Leon Schlesinger responded to the union agitation with a lockout of his Looney Tunes and Merry Melodies artists. When the first negotiations began, a Warner executive sneered at director Chuck Jones, "We're not a charity here!" Chuck was stung by the disrespectful remark from a member of management for whom he had worked with such dedication. Jones became one of the few animation directors to be wholeheartedly pro-union. The distinction between employee and management for animation directors is ambiguous. Animation directors may draw, like their staff, but they may also hire and fire, like management. So they may fancy themselves as being above the union fracas, but they can have their pay docked or be fired like any other employee. Even today some animation supervisors adopt this elitist attitude—until they are laid off. By contrast, Jones took a leadership role in the unionizing efforts at Warner Bros. This lockout lasted only six days; then Schlesinger surrendered. "Our own little Six-Day War," noted Jones.[10] When Schlesinger signed the SCG contract, he smiled, looked up at the union leaders and chuckled, "Now, how about Disney's?"[11]

How about Disney's, indeed. The entire cartoon industry understood that the real decision of whether animation artists could ever function as a union labor force would be made at Disney's. All the SCG successes up to that point brought its membership to just 115. There were more than 800 Disney artists. Those artists felt themselves the aristocracy of their profession, with Uncle Walt the benevolent master over all. Artists were grateful to Walt for plowing profits back into upgrading the studio's working conditions and paying for drawing teachers like Don Graham to show them how to polish their skills. To a profession that was made

(*Above*) Looney Tunes lockout, street scene outside Termite Terrace, May 1941. Courtesy of MPSC Local 839, AFL-CIO Collection, Urban Archives Center, Oviatt Library, California State University, Northridge (*Below*) Schlesinger lockout, 1941. Sitting outside the locked front door, left to right, animator Ben Washam, cameraman Roy Laupenberger, animator Rudy Larriva, painter Sue Gee, background artist Paul Marin, and standing, inker Martha Sigall. Courtesy of MPSC Local 839, AFL-CIO Collection, Urban Archives Center, Oviatt Library, California State University, Northridge.

to feel inferior to fine artists Disney brought a new respect. What other cartoon studio would bring in Frank Lloyd Wright to discuss aesthetics with its employees? Walt frequently had his artists and their families up to his Los Feliz house for pool parties. He threw western-style barbecues and picnics. Everyone knew Walt could be counted on to help anyone in trouble. While work in other studios was seasonal or from project to project, Disney employees were rarely laid off. While other studios were housed in dingy industrial spaces with cheap garage-sale furniture, Disney's studio had custom-designed matching furniture, volleyball courts, and a softball field. It wasn't a job; it was like one big family. Disney inbetweener Jim McDermott, writing under the pseudonym J. M. Ryan, illustrated, if not exaggerated, the psychological atmosphere in his controversial 1971 novel, *The Rat Factory*:

> "You're here to draw the Rat!" cried the cop.
> The trainees cheered.
> "You shall be paid eleven U.S. dollars every week, issued free
> pencils and paper and allowed fifteen consecutive minutes for
> lunch!"
> They cheered again.
> "A six-day workweek, and we won't let the Reds change it to five,
> will we?"
> "No!" They roared.[12]

As in many other studios before unionization, Disney studio pay scales were arbitrary, regardless of personal contracts. Management assumed the right to raise or cut salaries or bestow bonuses with no notice or consultation. A top animator could be paid $200 a week while a cel painter earned $12 a week. One union leaflet repeated the charge that the average Disney artist, at $18 a week, was paid less than a house painter, who earned $20 a week.[13] Background painter Jay Rivkin recalled that Disney offered her $16 a week; her unemployment insurance paid $18 a week. Selby Kelly gave up a $20-a-week job as a drugstore clerk to work for Disney at $16 a week. Dave Hilberman was being paid $90 a week to do layout on *Fantasia*, and the production manager told him, "Cheer up. Walt really thinks you deserve $120 a week but things are tight right now."[14] Looney Tunes director Frank Tashlin took a pay cut to work at

The Great Disney Studio Strike

Looney Tunes lockout, 1941. Locked-out artists standing on Van Ness Avenue include top directors Friz Freleng (in hat) and Tex Avery (to his right), who ponder their next move. Betty Burke is the woman in sunglasses and white outfit. Photograph by Chuck Jones. Courtesy of the Chuck Jones Center for Creativity.

Disney. "When you went to Walt's, no matter where you came from, you had to learn what they called humility. Which meant that your chevrons had to be ripped off you, and the drums rolled. When I left Leon [Schlesinger]'s, I was making $150 a week and when I got to Disney's I was making just $50." Walt's former friend Ub Iwerks, the man who designed Mickey Mouse, returned to work at the studio in 1940. Despite his immense stature in the industry and early importance to the company, he was started at just $75 a week.[15] Small wonder that when Max Fleischer began dangling big paychecks to get artists to move to Florida, a number of Disney animators quit, "part of the magic" or not. Directing animator Art Babbitt was outraged when the studio refused a $2.50 a week raise for his assistant Bill Hurtz. When Babbitt asked Walt about it, Walt snapped back, "Why don't you mind your own goddamn business. If he was worth it he'd be getting it."[16] Art finally augmented Hurtz's salary out of his own pocket. This was all flat-rate salary whether you worked the forty-six-hour regular week or around-the-clock overtime. Top animator Ward Kimball recalled the life of a lower-paid inbetweener at Disney: "We had straw bosses in the inbetween department who made us work overtime when it was 95 degrees outside. We used to strip to our waists to keep cool and work for nothing so some supervisor could win a package of cigarettes, because he'd promised to get a picture out on time."[17]

The Disney studio instituted a system of profit sharing in 1933 and then canceled it abruptly in 1936 when work started on *Snow White and the Seven Dwarfs*. Walt also dispensed and withheld bonuses as rewards with no defined pattern but totally on his personal whim. He saw it as being a good guy without recognizing that this arbitrariness might cause anger. Without anything in writing, an artist's financial security and that of his family was totally at the mercy of one man's caprice. Even though the artist had signed a contract, there was no organization to police the agreement, just a studio management that freely ignored its provisions as it suited the conditions of the moment. Imagine trying to buy a house or planning to start a family under such circumstances. In union-contract studios, two warnings and two weeks' notice were required before a worker was fired. Walt Disney reserved the right to fire anyone, anytime it suited him. For example, in the 1930s he encouraged his artists to go to the premiere of their short cartoons at the Alex Theater in Glendale, then come back for a critique. These sessions were a free-for-all of creative opinions and exchanges that sometimes left egos bruised. Only once did Walt direct a short himself instead of relying on his usual directors, Wilfred Jackson, Clyde Geromini, Dave Hand, and Ben Sharpsteen. When the hard critique started to come after the screening at the Alex, Walt got so angry he fired Rudy Zamora and another artist who spoke their minds too freely.[18] He fired animator Rudolf Ising in 1927 for falling asleep on the animation camera stand and accidentally starting the shutter clicking. Ising later said, "I felt like leaving anyway." Disney employees were so worried about losing their steady jobs during the Depression that, some confessed, when they played a friendly company softball game they were careful not to throw Walt out at first base when he'd hit an easily fielded ground ball.[19]

Nor could artists entertain the thought of fame making up for their lack of security; they worked in virtual anonymity. For the most part,

The Great Disney Studio Strike

Walt Disney's name was the only one allowed on the credits. The public, if they thought about it at all, might well have assumed that Walt drew all the cartoons himself. But he had stopped drawing professionally in the early 1920s. Even his famous signature was designed by an art director. When young character designer Ken Anderson started at the studio, Walt told him, "There's just one thing we're selling here, and that's the name Walt Disney. If you can buy that and work for it, then you're my man. But if you got any ideas of selling the name Ken Anderson, it's best for you to leave right now!"[20]

In 1937, the Walt Disney animation crew pushed themselves to the limit to finish the big feature-film project *Snow White and the Seven Dwarfs,* nicknamed "Disney's Folly." Everyone knew that Walt was gambling the studio and all their jobs on one big project. One day, when they projected the unfinished work-in-progress reels for the artists' feedback, one anonymous wag wrote, "Why don't we stick to shorts?" This bugged Walt, who had hocked everything he had, including his house and car, to finish the project. Years later when animator Milt Kahl criticized an idea of his, Walt would erupt, "So *you're* the son of a bitch who said we should stick to shorts?" *Snow White* animators, painters, techs, everyone, put in twelve-hour days and seven-day weeks without overtime pay.[21] When the budget ran out, many worked without any salary at all. After the actual creation of the artwork was done, the artists themselves fanned out across Los Angeles to thumbtack up the little square posters announcing the opening day. Walt promised his exhausted staff that their sacrifices to finish *Snow White and the Seven Dwarfs* would be repaid with big bonuses from the profits. Whether Walt or someone else made the actual promise and to how many it was made is uncertain, but the fact that it was promised is a given.[22] Not only did *Snow White and the Seven Dwarfs* become a success, it was a phenomenal success, earning four times the box office of any other film in 1938, even though the majority of tickets sold were low-priced kiddie matinee tickets. Many theaters initially refused to run *Snow White* because they balked at paying the same rental fees for a cartoon as for a live-action feature. The film was the story of the year. It was awarded a special Academy Award—one Oscar and seven little ones. Famed Russian filmmaker

Sergei Eisenstein declared Snow White "the greatest motion picture ever made!"[23]

For most of the hardworking employees, the eagerly anticipated share of the profits from *Snow White* never materialized. On the advice of his financial planners, Walt Disney withheld the profits in order to pursue his aggressive expansion plans, like the big $4.5 million air-conditioned studio being built in Burbank. The new studio featured the Penthouse Club, where the top artists could get milkshakes and a back-rub.[24] There was even a personal trainer, Carl Johnson, who was on the 1912 Swedish Olympic team. But this was all for the artists who could afford it. Most of the staff had trouble affording the cafeteria and used a sandwich wagon instead. Despite good intentions, all the Penthouse Club did was to create more envy among the lower-paid echelons. The word that some of the artists, but not all, had been awarded some bonus

Gag cartoon by Grim Natwick showing Walt Disney making excuses to animators Fred Moore, Natwick, and Art Babbitt about why they weren't getting *Snow White* bonuses. The reference to numbers is to studio project production numbers. Courtesy of Stephen Worth.

money further inflamed workers. Ted Le Berthon wrote in his bylined column in the *Los Angeles Evening News* on August 1, 1938: "According to one Disney Studio employee, a recent story in a movie trade paper stating that part of the profits of 'Snow White' were to go to the employees, turned out to be an erroneous and unauthorized story. But she said, she had never seen it corrected anywhere, except on a bulletin board at Disney's. Many outsiders, she says, still think the profit sharing story is true, and are glowing sweetly and tenderly over it, while the employees gnash their teeth."[25]

Disney artists saw that artists at studios all around them, like Walter Lantz and MGM, had signed with the new Screen Cartoonists Guild, and that all their people were enjoying the benefits regardless of status. The Disney hallways soon rang with arguments not over story content or design but over whether to go union.

Meanwhile, in Europe the clouds of war were growing ever more ominous. In September 1939, while Disney artists were packing boxes for the move to Burbank, Hitler's panzer divisions were rolling through Europe and the imperial Japanese armies were overrunning Asia. The war created a financial crisis for Hollywood and for the Walt Disney Studio in particular. At that time, overseas markets accounted for as much as 45 percent of the Disney studio's income, but it's hard to take in a movie while you are dodging Stuka dive-bombers. On September 3, 1939, when the infant BBC television station shut down for the war's duration, the last program run was the short *Mickey's Gala Premiere.*[26] By summer 1940 the Third Reich had imposed a ban on all Hollywood movies. Since the Germans had conquered most of Europe, it meant that theaters from Norway to Greece were closed to Disney products. The overseas revenue dried up to almost nothing. In addition, the U.S. public, concerned about current events, was losing its taste for the kind of escapist fantasy so popular during the Depression.

Walt Disney's next feature film, *Pinocchio* (1940), despite its exquisite quality, did poorly at the box office. A second film released in 1940 also fared poorly. *Fantasia* was conceived as a daring experiment in locational stereophonic sound, FantaSound, but this idea was only realized in the 1990s digital Dolby sound era. In 1940, FantaSound was so far ahead of its time that few theaters would pay to retool their sound systems for it. *Fantasia* not only flopped at the box office but was also ridiculed by the hoity-toity New York film critics, who laughed it off as a kitschy attempt at high culture. Also, the once unique Disney short cartoons were losing ground to the newer, more aggressive styles of Warner Bros.' Looney Tunes and MGM's Tom & Jerry. Walt Disney kept borrowing to recoup losses and in 1940 went public with a stock offering. Disney stock opened at $25 a share and quickly plummeted to $3.[27] By 1941, the Disney studio was $5 million in debt, its worst financial year proportionately since 1927, that is, before Mickey Mouse was created. By March, the studio's chief financier, the Bank of America, was sounding alarm bells.

The business situation naturally affected the atmosphere in the studio. As time wore on, Walt the jocular fellow artist became Mr. Disney the worry-wracked capitalist. The small Kansas City company of friends had become a big industrial plant of hundreds of workers. Walt may still have thought of himself as just one of the guys, but to everyone else he was the boss. He grew increasingly isolated from his artists. Those who managed to spot him were those who worked nights or weekends. Then he could be seen walking around the empty tables looking to see what work was being done.[28]

Throughout this period, the unionization debate continued. Union leaflets mysteriously appeared on peoples' desks. They had provocative messages like: "When you arrive at Disney's you may find your roommate is no longer at his desk. The Blitzkrieg struck him last night without warning! . . . These men had no inkling of their dismissal. They were unceremoniously thrown out. . . . The Screen Cartoonists Guild Contract is your only insurance against these blitzkrieg tactics!"[29]

Walt Disney's attorney, Gunther Lessing (ten years Walt's senior), who once represented Mexican revolutionary Pancho Villa in El Paso, had a Texas frontiersman's innate distrust of unions. They smacked of big East Coast gangsterism to him. Director Jack Kinney thought Gunny "terribly egotistical and a very poor attorney. He only got the job in the first place because he loaned Walt money when he was starting out."[30] Nevertheless, Lessing exercised considerable influence over Disney. He had represented the Disney brothers ever since Charles Mintz took Oswald the Lucky Rabbit away from them in 1927.[31] Harry Tytle said that after that debacle it was Lessing who encouraged the Disney brothers

The Great Disney Studio Strike

to build the name Walt Disney into a nationally recognized name brand. That way it could never be stolen the way Oswald had been. Animator Ward Kimball said, "Walt believed everything Gunny told him, and some of it was wrong. Gunnie would read a Hearst editorial [equivalent to supermarket tabloid exaggeration] and report it as a fact to Walt—and Walt believed him."[32] Lessing urged a hard fiscal conservatism with the employees. He introduced Walt to unsavory characters like Willie Bioff, a gangster in the Frank Nitti mob, who was the preferred "union expert" of many Hollywood studio executives, among them MGM's Louis B. Mayer or Nicholas Schenck.

By 1940 Walt Disney Studio already had closed-shop union contracts in several fields (musicians, cameramen, and makeup, for example), but these were pinpricks compared to the hundreds of his animators going union. In January 1941, when the SCG announced its stepped-up organizing campaign, Gunther Lessing encouraged Walt Disney[33] to head it off by reducing the official workweek from forty-six to forty hours a week. Lessing had already overseen the creation of a sham company union, the Federation of Screen Cartoonists. Animator Al Eugster noted in his diary, "Jan 27th 1938—I went to the American Legion Hall. Meeting by Disney employees to establish an organization to protect us from any outside union. Meeting lasted from 8 to 11. Art Babbitt was chairman." (In 1957, Al wrote in the margin next to that entry: "How ridiculous that seems now.")[34] After receiving 602 employee rep cards, the NLRB certified the federation in July 1938.[35]

Enter the Brutus of our drama. Arthur Babbitt was one of the most highly respected and highly paid animators of the studio. Art took the character originally named Dippy Dog out of the ranks of minor characters, renamed him Goofy, and made him the equal of Mickey Mouse and Donald Duck. His work on the short *Country Cousin* was considered a breakthrough in personality characterization. He animated Gepetto, the Wicked Queen, and the Chinese Mushrooms in *Fantasia*. Professor R. K. Field of Harvard University, in his 1942 study of Disney animation, *The Art of Walt Disney*, called Art Babbitt "the greatest animator of them all." Babbitt did a lot to get the studio art training programs under way. While many people stood in breadlines, Art had a house with

Herb Sorrell, union organizer, leader of the CSU, and director of the Disney Cartoonists Strike, as drawn by Bill Littlejohn. Sorrell could give a punch as well as take one, but his charm left a lasting impression on all who knew him. Courtesy of MPSC Local 839, AFL-CIO Collection, Urban Archives Center, Oviatt Library, California State University, Northridge.

servants and two autos. A blunt little bantam of a man, Babbitt looked at the world through his hawklike squint with a Davy Crockett–like sense of what was right. He wore a stopwatch on his wrist. He was much like Walt in that he could be a good friend or a bad enemy. His friends called him "Bones." I once looked at Babbitt's desk and noticed he kept a 1937 photo of the entire Disney animation crew with names written on all the faces. Over his own face was written "The Troublemaker."

At first Babbitt enthusiastically accepted the offer to be the federation's president. He sincerely desired to be a spokesman for his fellow artists, but he soon came to realize that the Disney Federation of Screen Cartoonists was nothing more than a corporate smoke screen. The studio refused to seriously negotiate wages, contracts, or conditions with him. Gunther Lessing called the shots for the federation.[36] None of the artists from the other animation studios would even consider joining the sham operation. Yet, in official correspondence with the NLRB and the press, the company maintained that the federation was indeed a bona fide labor union.

Finally, during a slump after the box-office failure of *Fantasia,* what the animators got instead of the promised bonuses was layoffs. Animator Preston Blair's layoff notice was on studio stationery adorned with the dancing alligators and hippos of *Fantasia* that Preston himself had animated.

Labor organizer Herbert Sorrell, head of the Conference of Studio Unions, heard of the frustration of the Disney artists. He was invited by SCG president Bill Littlejohn to help. From Local 644 of the painters' union, Sorrell brought over attorney George Bodle to help handle the SCG's legal affairs. Herb Sorrell was a big, tough, ex-prizefighter who described himself as "just a poor dumb painter," but he had the charisma of a natural leader that inspired thousands of film workers to follow him. Father George Dunne wrote, "To watch Sorrell thinking something through is a fascinating spectacle. It is like watching the powerful gears of a bulldozer slowly meshing, laboriously gaining strength, painfully struggling with the obstacle, and thrusting relentlessly forward to the goal."[37]

Like teamster Jimmy Hoffa, his contemporary, Sorrell learned his stuff in the violent world of 1930s industrial union organizing. He had the boxer's classic broken nose, thick neck, and cauliflower ears, and a roguish smile. When Littlejohn mentioned that one of the animators resisting joining the union at MGM was Jack Zander, Sorrell quipped, "Well, he can't very well animate with a broken arm, can he?" Zander got the message and joined, becoming a union president himself in 1938.[38] In Sorrell the union now had an additional dynamic, if uncompromising, force to match Lessing and the company.

Together with Littlejohn, Sorrell worked to get Walt Disney artists to abandon the company union and sign cards requesting membership in the independent Screen Cartoonists Guild. After meeting Sorrell, Art Babbitt was convinced, and, by virtue of his status in the industry, soon became the movement's leader. With Babbitt and Sorrell on one side and Lessing on the other, it was certain that the situation would quickly pass beyond the casual family atmosphere.

In summer 1940, Sorrell and Littlejohn sent Leon Schlesinger ink-and-paint artist and guild secretary Charlotte Darling to sound out Bill Tytla's former assistant and layout man Dave Hilberman. She asked him if the Disney employees would go union. Hilberman held a secret meeting at his Beachwood Canyon house.[39] He explained to the artists assembled that if a majority of the studio employees were to sign representation cards, the federal government would acknowledge their union, and Walt would have to agree. He said this was how it was done, and artists would not be fired but would be protected by the federal Wagner Act of 1935, if this was what they really wanted. To Hilberman's surprise, the artists started to sign cards by the dozen.[40] One of the first artists to sign was layout assistant Moe Gollub, who would lead the union in the Runaway Wars of 1979 and 1982 (see chapter 9).[41]

When Hilberman, Littlejohn, Babbitt, Bodle, and Sorrell had about 400 cards out of a staff of 560, they went to Disney's offices to ask for recognition. To their surprise, Gunther Lessing told them Walt Disney refused to meet with them and the management refused to accept the results of the cards. They wanted to ask the NLRB for time to verify the authenticity of the count. The studio also denied that Sorrell or the American Federation of Labor had any official right to speak for Disney employees.[42] Lessing demanded time to organize a secret ballot for the workers, figuring the time could be used to pressure individual voters to change their minds.

Hilberman, Babbitt, and Sorrell announced a mass meeting for all

Walt Disney artists at the Hollywood Roosevelt Hotel to discuss the situation. Walt Disney soon heard about it and demanded that the meeting be delayed so he could hold his own staff meeting first. The Hollywood Roosevelt meeting was set for February 21, 1941.[43] On February 11 at Studio Theater A, Walt Disney stood before his assembled employees and personally appealed to them not to unionize. He labored to make the speech meet all the parameters set by the NLRB regulations. At first he spoke to their sense of pride and loyalty. "Everything you are going to hear is entirely from me. There was no gag meeting or anything to write this thing. It's all me."[44] Then he tried to be chummy: "It's my nature to be democratic. I want to be just another guy working in this plant—which I am." But he soon turned angry and condescending, insisting that only he knew what was best for them. "It's the law of the universe that the strong shall survive and the weak must fall by the way, and I don't care what idealistic plan is cooked up, nothing can change that!" Many said he sounded more like a businessman than an artist. At one point, when Walt ran out of entreaties, he declared, "If you boys sign with the union . . . I'll . . . I'll never let you swim in my pool again!" Background artist Al Dempster shot back, "Walt, swimming in your pool doesn't feed my kids or pay my rent!"[45] Hilberman called it the "law of the jungle speech." Assistant animator Bill Melendez recalled, "If only Walt had leveled with us about how bad things were, we might have gone along. But instead he patronized us and called all union talk Communist."[46] Even Walt's staunchest apologists admitted the speech was a disaster. It only made matters worse.

The union rally at the Hollywood Roosevelt went off as scheduled. The day before, Lessing warned of potential reprisals against anyone who dared attend. The ballroom was packed anyway. Guest speakers included famed Hollywood screenwriters Donald Ogden Stewart and Dorothy Parker. Parker said things like: "Remember Union is not a four letter word! And the greatest word in the English language is *organize!*" Finally: "Mr. Disney is going to have to decide if he is a man or a mouse!"[47] The evening was a great success. More than ever an overwhelming majority of Disney employees wanted to be recognized as part of the Screen Cartoonists Guild.

Art Babbitt now officially resigned from the presidency of the Federation of Screen Cartoonists to join the SCG's effort. Other top artists followed his example: master animator Bill Tytla; effects animator Jack Buckley; designer Selby Kelly; story artists Bill Peet, Thorton "T" Hee, and Joe Rinaldi; layout man Zack Schwartz; art director John Hubley; and background stylist Maurice Noble. Walt Disney was shocked at what he considered a personal betrayal. Lower-echelon painters and inbetweeners were one thing, but these were his stalwarts, his stars! On May 15, 1941, the Federation of Screen Cartoonists was declared dissolved.[48] One more sham organization, the American Independent Cartoonists Union, was formed, but no one took it seriously.

As Babbitt argued more vigorously for the studio to recognize the right of the SCG to represent Disney artists, he began to be harassed. He got threatening calls to lay off the union stuff or else. Walt once said to him during an exchange, "You and your Commie friends live in a world so small you don't really understand what is going on around you!" On the day Babbitt was scheduled to appear before the NLRB to testify about the studio's attitude to unionization, two detectives from the Burbank Police Department showed up at his home office and arrested him. (The head of Disney Studio security was the brother-in-law of Elmer Adams, Burbank chief of police.) The detectives claimed the arrest was on a concealed-weapons charge. Babbitt never owned a weapon and was released soon after. But the warning was clear: Back off now![49]

The Screen Editors Guild had filed a complaint with the NLRB on March 28, 1941, that Walt Disney Studio was refusing to negotiate in good faith. The Publicists Guild soon launched a similar complaint.[50] On May 26, the SCG's general membership voted to authorize a strike for the Walt Disney unit. On May 27, several of the Disney studio's corporate backers, including Richard Story, an attorney for the Boston law firm Kidder-Peabody, and Joseph Rosenberg of the Bank of America, had a meeting with Walt Disney to urge him to make a deal and recognize the animators' union.[51] Walt flat out refused.

There was a final meeting on May 28, 1941, between Walt Disney studio and the Screen Cartoonists Guild negotiation team in Walt's executive offices on the Burbank lot. The bright California sun and chirping birds contrasted with the dark emotions seething in the room. Walt Disney continued to prevaricate and question Sorrell's legal right to speak for his artists. He asked once again for a few weeks for the Labor Department to verify Sorrell's credentials and set up a secret election. Guild attorney George Bodle recalled that every time he tried to offer something, all he'd get back from the other side was the low growl, "You boys won't get away with this."

To a veteran negotiator like Herb Sorrell it was now time to play hardball. He went right in Walt's face and angrily threatened a walkout. Sorrell yelled at Disney, "I can make a dust bowl of your studio!"[52] This was a scary allusion to a born midwesterner. The meeting broke up in an angry impasse. As an experienced negotiator, I know that yelling, threats, and strong language are standard operating procedure. Management and I have often screamed at each other and then gone out for a beer together later. But it seems Walt took this all personally. Maybe he was still more of an artist than a businessman after all. After the meeting broke up, Walt stormed back to his office and immediately fired Babbitt and sixteen other pro-union artists. In an amazing bit of arrogance, Lessing sent Babbitt a memo in which he openly stated that the reason for the termination of employment was for union activity. This was a blatant violation of the Wagner Act. Lessing had studio police escort the fired artists off the premises, as still occasionally happens. Babbitt, with a box of his personal belongings in hand, scowled at the studio cops giving him the bum's rush, "Can you at least wait until I get my pencils?"[53] Crowds of sullen, silent artists gathered in the hallways to watch the sorry procession as Art and the others, flanked by security guards, carried their stuff out to their cars. A Toon Town *via dolorosa*: the creator of Goofy was being fired, for them.

That night, the Walt Disney Studio employees held an emergency meeting at the Hollywood Legion Hall. The hall was jammed, standing room only, and reeked of cigarette smoke and fiery speeches. After a rousing speech by Herb Sorrell, Art Babbitt's assistant on *Fantasia*, Bill Hurtz, rose and made the final motion to strike. The motion was seconded and carried to thunderous applause. The following morning, May 29, 1941, was hot and dry. When Walt Disney turned his car on to Buena Vista Boulevard, he found the entrance to his studio choked with a crowd of three hundred picketers. Every couple of feet artists stood on soapboxes and made angry speeches to knots of cheering picketers and scribbling reporters.[54] Colorful hand-painted signs bobbed up and down in the clear blue skies of Burbank: "Disney Unfair," "One Genius vs 600 Guinea Pigs," "We Had No Scabs at Schlesinger's," "Leonardo, Michelangelo and Titian Were Union Men," and a picture of Pluto with the title "I'd Rather Be a Dog Than a Scab!"

Later accounts of this event stated that Walt Disney was surprised, or shocked when he saw the picket line.[55] This hardly seems credible since he must have been aware of the guild strike vote on May 26, and he was in strategy meetings with Bank of America attorneys on May 27 about a potential labor action. An internal memo from Lessing mentioned that as early as April 7 the studio anticipated a strike. If Walt was shocked, it must have been the surprise of a man in deep denial about his situation. Standard tactics in union negotiations are threats, bluff, and counterbluff. Maybe he was confident that despite all the bluster from Sorrell and Babbitt, in the end his people, his boys and girls, would never actually do something like this to him.

Although more than two-thirds of the artistic staff signed representa-

Looking north on Buena Vista Street during the Disney strike, May 1941. Courtesy of Los Angeles Times Photographic Archive, Department of Special Collections, Charles E. Young Research Library, UCLA.

tion cards, only half actually walked out on strike. The numbers are debatable, but out of 1,293 employees, 600 artists and the rest clerical and support staff, perhaps 373 went out on strike. Walt Disney later claimed 293 walked and 427 went back to work. Lessing made Disney believe it was even fewer, which may have influenced Walt's decision to tough it out. The attorney cockily assured Walt the strike wouldn't last twenty-four hours. Walt broke out a few bottles of Harvey's Bristol Cream, and all toasted a quick resolution.[56]

While management celebrated inside, the employees approaching the Buena Vista gates had to make a choice they would remember the rest of their lives. Regardless of personal politics, this had all become the real thing. Should you go out and picket, risking unemployment and blacklisting during the Depression? Or cross the picket line, go in to work, and earn the lasting hatred of your friends? The more artists who refused to work, the better the union's chances of shutting down production to force a compromise. The more people who went in to work,

Picketers marching against Disney. Left to right, Looney Tunes animator Emery Hawkins (looking up), Disney artist Volus Jones (reading newspaper), MGM animator Dan McGinnis (hands in pockets). Courtesy of Los Angeles Times Photographic Archive, Department of Special Collections, Charles E. Young Research Library, UCLA.

the greater the chances that the studio would hold out until you and your family starved. Then, with your bank account empty, you would slink back in and beg for your job back. This was the choice that now confronted every Disney worker. Imagine walking through a shoving, seething mob that was yelling, "Scab! Commie! Don't go in! Join the line, brother! Traitor! Fink!"

All the artists who became known as the Nine Old Men—Frank Thomas, Ollie Johnston, John Lounsbery, Marc Davis, Ward Kimball, Wolfgang Reitherman, Les Clark, Milt Kahl, and Eric Larson—crossed the picket line and went back to work. Top animator Ward Kimball was very liberal and came from a family of union sympathizers. That morning when the picket went up, he and Fred Moore argued for ninety minutes over what to do. In the end they both crossed the line.[57] Art Babbitt said that it must have been an agonizing decision for Kimball to make. As he walked through the gate, an assistant yelled at him, "Ward! Don't do it! The strike will fail if you go in!" Kimball growled back, "If I don't go in *Dumbo* won't get made and the studio will fail!" Ward's best friend, animator Walt Kelly, did go out to picket. The two were never close again thereafter. Animator Bernie Wolf recalled his old friend, Bill Tytla, stopping him before he crossed and "call[ing] me every name in the book."[58] Interestingly, recent histories refer to Tytla as politically apathetic toward the guild, but he didn't want to let his friends down.

Character design department supervisor Joe Grant had once been the best man at Tytla's wedding. Now he was inside like the other supervisors anxiously watching their crews marching down the street. Grant recalled that whenever he needed to consult his story team about some point regarding *Dumbo*, he would walk out beyond the wall to the picket line where they were marching. As his people would walk around past him he would pull them out of the line to get their input. A local newspaper article of the time noted that all four of the Nisei artists went out on strike: Chris Ishii, Tom Okamoto, Masao Kawaguchi, and James Tanaka.[59] Political tensions between the United States and Japan were on the rise, so whether this piece was meant to show loyalty to American institutions or subversive behavior is open to conjecture. Hugo D'Arcy, an Italian count and the studio's head of sanitation, went out on strike. Assistant animator Hank Ketcham was a striker, while his roommate, Dick Kinney, was for Walt because Kinney's brother, Jack, was a super-

Disney strikers. Storyboard artist Joe Rinaldi is seen reading a newspaper. Rinaldi was one of the rare artists who was completely forgiven by Walt and allowed back to work without any trouble. Courtesy of MPSC Local 839, AFL-CIO Collection, Urban Archives Center, Oviatt Library, California State University, Northridge.

vising director. Dick Kinney, in his old Mercury convertible, would drop Ketcham off a block from the studio and proceed through the jeering strikers' line while Ketcham checked in with the organizers and shouldered his sign.[60]

Former Warner Bros. director Frank Tashlin had spent the last two years as a Disney story artist. When the strike began, he had just given his notice to take a job managing a new animation unit forming at Screen Gems Pictures. "I'm management—but management, on the way to the studio, would stop by Disney and walk in the picket line and call Walt dirty names when he drove through in his Packard. Then I'd go to Screen Gems, down on Seward [Avenue]. I hired the picketers and built a new studio out of them."[61]

Along with the top-echelon artist-supervisors crossing the picket line in defiance of their friends were some bottom-echelon cel painters and polishers who in the end felt they couldn't afford to lose their jobs. Bill

Melendez recalled, "We went out on strike to help those poor girls, and now here they were crossing the line!"[62]

At first the atmosphere on the picket line was jovial and irreverent, as cartoonists are by nature. All the animation artists from the other studios came to join their friends on the Disney picket line. Starting on June 5, every Wednesday the Warner Bros. animators, led by Chuck Jones, joined their brethren while dressed up as characters from the French Revolution and carrying on their shoulders a guillotine with an effigy of lawyer Lessing in the business position. Their picket signs read, "Liberté, Fraternité, Closed-Shoppité."[63] They all sang a song to the melody of the French anthem "La Marseillaise":

> Come on you faithful sons of liberty,
> We're here to give you moral aid.
> We will put the ax to Gunther Lessing,
> And the mess of boners he's made.
>
> Come on, you're doing swell!
> The scabs can go to Hell!
> March on, march on
> There's sure to be,
> A final victory![64]

Another time, everyone dressed in black mourning and feigned crying. They were celebrating the death of the company union, the federation. Chuck Jones and Friz Freleng came up with the idea of Warner Bros. picketers driving their cars slowly up and down both sides of Buena Vista Boulevard, creating a traffic jam to prevent scab artists from getting into the lot.[65]

The strikers pitched a camp in the weed-grown field across the street, a field that a few years later would be the site of St. Joseph's Hospital. The chefs of the nearby Toluca Lake restaurants, when off duty, would cook meals at a makeshift soup kitchen for free. Animator Ed Friedman brought in cantaloupes from the farms of San Fernando, north of the city.[66] The striking animators played poker, sandlot baseball, and ping-pong to pass the time. Late at night, by a clump of trees called the Knoll, a sing-along started in front of a bonfire. Hollywood celebrity activists

Schlesinger director Chuck Jones with his daughter Linda, 1941. Courtesy of the Chuck Jones Center for Creativity.

Lunch line at Disney strikers' camp in rural field across the street from the studio. Several years later St. Joseph's Hospital was built on this site. Courtesy of MPSC Local 839, AFL-CIO Collection, Urban Archives Center, Oviatt Library, California State University, Northridge.

made speeches. Bill Littlejohn flew his small plane overhead and did victory rolls to the cheers of the picketers.

Dorothy Parker invited the wives of strikers to her cramped Hollywood flat for drinks to bolster their sagging morale. Bill Tytla's wife, Adrienne, wondered why a famous nonconformist writer like Parker would host a "hen-party" of house-bound, child-bearing, middle-class women. She herself may have wondered, since Adrienne recalled Parker spent the evening drinking heavily and making quips like, "Having no children, I grow fingernails."[67]

But as the weeks dragged on and nobody seemed willing to give in, the mood got ugly. As in the Fleischer strike four years before, friendships were broken. Everyone had to pick a side. You were either for Walt or for the union, a scab or a Red; no one could be neutral. One antiunion

Strike leaders in their camp. Left to right, SCG attorney George Bodle (second from left), animator Bill Tytla (third from left), layout artist Dave Hilberman (fourth from left), Art Babbitt (fifth from left, back to camera), Selby Kelly, others unknown. Courtesy of MPSC Local 839, AFL-CIO Collection, Urban Archives Center, Oviatt Library, California State University, Northridge.

painter marched up to the curb and flung a fistful of pennies at the strikers, yelling, "You want money? Here!"[68] Striking animator Cliff Nordberg found a way into the studio back lot via the storm drains in an attempt to cause mischief.[69] In the tents, striker families were down to eating bologna sandwiches. An anonymous collection of antiunion workers calling themselves the Committee of 21 stealthily circulated leaflets that accused strike leaders of heinous crimes and Communism. They referred to the striking top animators in the most derogatory of terms; for example, they called Bill Littlejohn "Bill Littleguy."

Inside, while the steady Roy Disney quietly worked to restart negotiations, Walt was at first bewildered. But his confusion and hurt feelings soon turned to anger. Artists close to Walt, like Ward Kimball and Dave Hand, urged him to make a deal with the strikers but were brushed off. Director Jack Kinney noticed Walt had sent a publicity photographer to climb up on top of a wall and snap photos of the picketers. He had his photo lab enlarge the prints. Then in the solitude of his office he could more easily identify individuals from the large prints and rant against their ingratitude. Sucking long drags on his Marlboro cigarette Disney would rage, "Damn. I didn't think he'd go against me! That sonofabitch. I trusted him and he went out on me. What's his gripe? Well, we can get along without him!"[70] This was in violation of federal law regarding random disciplining individual employees during arbitration. The pro-Walt animators working on *Dumbo* added a new sequence to the film: drunken clowns laughing and spouting labor slogans in an insulting parody of their brother union artists: "Oh, we're gonna hit the big boss for a raise!"

When striking assistant animator David Swift had had enough of his leaders' increasingly militant tone and went back to work, unionists, including John Hubley, scratched David's car with keys.[71] Striker Hank Ketcham was put off by Sorrell's speeches about the violence necessary to win at General Motors and other industrial debacles. He felt they had nothing to do with him as an artist. He went back to work and was called by his friends "the King of Finks."[72] Once someone even poured gasoline around some strikers and threatened to light a match. Striking assistant Bill Hurtz romanced his fiancée, Mary, who was on the secretarial staff, through a hole in the studio fence. The strikers' publicity team (Sam Cobean, Willis Pyle, and Reg Massie) wanted to make their wedding a big publicity event, but Bill and Mary opted for a private service. Inside, Walt Disney tried to belittle the unionists and their effect on him. On June 11, he told reporters, "The men in here are all my top artists, which I can't say the same for those out there."[73]

One hot day while famous actors John Garfield and Frank Morgan (*The Wizard of Oz*) were addressing the strikers' camp, Babbitt noticed Walt driving his elegant Packard through the picket lines. Art jumped up on a flatbed truck, grabbed a bullhorn, and shouted, "There he is, the Great Man! He wants brotherhood for all except himself! Shame on you, Walt Disney!" Disney leapt out of his car and stripped off his jacket. A fistfight would have ensued had not cooler heads separated them.[74]

Dave Hilberman recalled Walt Disney once gunning the Packard's engine and braking just short of him, showing how much Walt would like to hit him. One night when a rumor circulated that paid goons were going to beat up the strikers, Sorrell sent a gang of Lockheed aircraft mechanics, monkey wrenches in hand, to guard the strikers' tents.[75] The rumor of violence luckily turned out to be just that, a rumor. Despite the rancor, the Disney studio strike never descended to the level of violence all too common in some others of the era.

One morning, animator Bill Tytla ran into Walt Disney at a local breakfast counter.[76] In this unguarded moment, the two had a cordial conversation. They mused, "If we can sit down and talk now, why can't we do this to end this strike?" Tytla realized that, because he was a friend of both Babbitt and Disney, he was in a unique position to break the deadlock. He went home to change his clothes for a real meeting with Disney at the studio. But, just before he left, he got a call from Disney's office. Someone there had talked Walt out of it and broke off the meeting. Years later the cancellation was blamed on union leaders.

In later years Disney claimed no other unions went on strike. But the striking cartoonists got support from labor groups outside the animation world.[77] On June 3, the Screen Editors Guild called a strike at Disney. On July 11, Pat Sommerset of the Screen Actors Guild announced that SAG had voted to donate $1,000 a week to the cartoonists' support fund and that no actor would cross the Disney picket lines. On June 13, the American Federation of Labor called for a boycott of all Disney films and merchandise. On June 19, the animation units at Screen Gems and Columbia Pictures under Frank Tashlin's leadership signed SCG union

Top animator Art Babbitt standing in the Disney strikers' camp giving a speech. The camp was set up across the street in a field. Public meetings were held on a small rise called the Knoll. Courtesy of MPSC Local 839, AFL-CIO Collection, Urban Archives Center, Oviatt Library, California State University, Northridge.

Angry Mickey with picket sign, SCG Disney strike leaflet. The guild maintained a printing press and kept their members and the public informed through flyers. Courtesy of MPSC Local 839, AFL-CIO Collection, Urban Archives Center, Oviatt Library, California State University, Northridge.

contracts. The Printing Council refused to print the "Mickey Mouse" comic strip, and the Technicolor Corporation, whose founder, Herbert Kalmus, had a longtime relationship with Disney, announced that they would refuse to develop any more Disney footage. This held up the completion of the final reels of *Bambi*.

Babbitt was doing everything he could think of to keep strikers from being starved back to work. He had heard there was going to be a big meeting in Burbank of all the Congress of Industrial Organization's (CIO's) local leaders in the west, so he went to plead for help. Art was so politically naïve he did not know that his guild was an AF of L affiliate and that the AF of L and the CIO at that time were bitter rivals. Babbitt found out his mistake as he was invited up to speak, but, rather than back away, he went right at it. "I suppose you're CIO and I'm AF of L. I don't know what those damned initials mean. All I know is I'm pro-union and my people are on strike and need your help."[78] He left the meeting convinced he had wasted his time, when a big tough guy called from the hallway, "Hey, come on back. You got everything you wanted!" A few days later a Monsignor O'Dwyer of the Roman Catholic Archdiocese of Los Angeles, who was also in that meeting, sent food aid from Catholic Charities.

In August, the Teamsters Union joined the boycott. All the bad press increased the pressure on Walt Disney so much that it brought him close to another nervous breakdown. One time a secretary saw Walt sitting in his office crying uncontrollably.[79]

Ironically, the Disney theatrical release slated for this time was *The Reluctant Dragon*, which featured a mockumentary about the fun life at the wonderful Disney studio. At the Hollywood premiere at the Pantages Theatre on June 20, 1941, strikers ringed the theater chanting, "The Reluctant Disney!" and carrying a huge segmented sign shaped like the Reluctant Dragon character but with Walt's head and the word "unfair." Disney artist and future head of UPA Steve Bosustow and his wife, Audrey, got out of a chauffeured limo in formal evening wear: top hat and tails for him, silk evening gown for her. Their chauffeur, Maurice Noble, then ceremoniously handed them their picket signs and they proceeded to picket, to the delight of the crowd.[80] The Hollywood Police Department closed off a stretch of Hollywood Boulevard around the theater for fear of rampaging cartoonists.[81]

R.K.O. NOTIFIED OF M.P.P. STAND ON RELEASE OF DISNEY FILMS

Yesterday Herb Sorrell, Acting Business Agent for the Screen Cartoon Guild, in a personal interview, as well as in a letter, officially notified Mr. Sid Rogell, high R.K.O. official that unless that studio ceased to distribute Disney films until the strike is over, serious action would have to be taken against R.K.O. Productions.

SYMPATHETIC GUILDS ON LINE TONIGHT

As you all know, representatives of every union in the film industry are walking on the picket line with us here tonight and every member of the Screen Cartoon Guild is, of course, here as well.

SOUP KITCHEN RUNNING FULL BLAST

The soup kitchen which literally sprang into existence overnight in the grove is now in full operation and is equipped to feed everybody. There is no need for anybody to go hungry!

DID YOU KNOW :

That 12 more insiders walked out to join our ranks yesterday!

That Bill Littlejohn is contributing $25 a week for the duration of the strike!

That the Culinary Workers have donated the services of a union chef at our soup kitchen as long as the strike lasts!

That the soup kitchen served 511 hamburgers, 634 cups of coffee, and 29 lbs. of coleslaw this noon!

"----and production has increased
three hundred and fifty percent!"

That the studio has been smuggling food through the picket lines in private cars!

That Herb Sorrell is contributing twenty-five dollars a week for the duration of the strike.

That the faked-up photo of the parking lot which the studio realeased got plenty of laughs from the newspaper men!

That the Fed-boys have even tried to get a charter from the Actor's Guild!

---o---

Disney strikers' newsletter with gag cartoon of Walt Disney pointing to empty desks and telling a reporter, "And production has increased . . .". Courtesy of MPSC Local 839, AFL-CIO Collection, Urban Archives Center, Oviatt Library, California State University, Northridge.

The Great Disney Studio Strike

When *The Reluctant Dragon* opened at the Palace Theater in New York, the theater was ringed with picketers from United American Artists, the Screen Publicists Guild, the Screen Readers Guild, and the Film Company Office Workers Union. Marching with a picket sign was Donald Ogden Stewart, the Academy Award–winning screenwriter of *Kitty Foyle*. The star of *The Reluctant Dragon,* writer Robert Benchley, had recently been the best man at Stewart's wedding. The resulting bad publicity helped *The Reluctant Dragon* flop at the box office, costing the studio a further $100,000 loss.

Back in Hollywood, other events were brewing. Since the 1937 FMPC strikes, SAG president George Montgomery had hired detectives to accumulate as much information as they could on IATSE leader Willie Bioff's underworld activities. SAG joined forces with with *Variety* editor George Ungar, who also investigated Bioff. When the gumshoes

Gangster Willie Bioff (left), with his attorney, George Bresler, being booked downtown. Bioff was sent by the mob-controlled IATSE leadership to Hollywood to take over the labor unions. Courtesy of Los Angeles Times Photographic Archive, Department of Special Collections, Charles E. Young Research Library, UCLA.

had gathered enough information, Montgomery and Ungar turned all their evidence over to the Justice Department. On May 23, 1941, Bioff was indicted by a federal grand jury for racketeering. He knew he was in big trouble. Out later on $50,000 bail, he realized he needed to do something big to show the studio heads and the feds he was still a force to be reckoned with. He thought his opportunity would be to intercede in the Disney studio strike then making headlines in all the papers.

On June 30, Disney representatives sent a note to the union leaders asking them to meet once more to hammer out an agreement. The SCG leaders received the invitation at their meeting hall at Sunset Boulevard and Highland. Bill Littlejohn, Art Babbitt, George Bodle, and Herb Sorrell got in one car. Dave Hilberman got into another that was being driven by one of Willie Bioff's hoods. The four men thought they were headed for the strike headquarters at the Hollywood Roosevelt Hotel, but Bodle suddenly noticed on the invitation that they were really supposed to go to Bioff's secluded ranch in San Fernando Valley. This would have certainly meant a gangster-style shakedown and perhaps even a working-over. The union leaders had everyone get out of the cars; Hilberman told his driver to let him out or he would jump out of the moving car.[82]

Bioff's federal indictment was made public the next day. Did Disney management and the other studio heads know about this attempt at strong-arm tactics or was this Bioff's own scheme? At about this time Walt Disney was visited by the FBI regarding "the possible criminal violation on the part of [name deleted] or others in which an effort might have been made to extort monies from the Disney Studio in settlement of a strike[.]" Walt Disney later denied that anyone ever demanded or received a payoff. According to the FBI report filed on July 21, 1941, Walt told the G-men that due to the slowdown of the overseas box office, he was forced to lay off nineteen workers. These workers began a whispering campaign that management intended to lay off two hundred more people, Disney said, and that was the cause of the general strike. Walt Disney told a different version later to the House Committee on Un-American Activities (HUAC) when he testified in 1947.[83]

On July 2, Walt Disney Studio management announced that it was entering negotiations to end to the strike, exclusively with union rep Willie Bioff. Babbitt, Sorrell, and the guild leadership were thunderstruck. Bioff had no right to speak for them and no mandate from their

To My Employees on Strike:

I believe you are entitled to know why you are not working today. I offered your leaders the following terms:

(1) All employees to be reinstated to former positions.

(2) No discrimination.

(3) Recognition of your Union.

(4) Closed shop.

(5) 50% retroactive pay for the time on strike—something without precedent in the American labor movement.

(6) Increase in wages to make yours the highest salary scale in the cartoon industry.

(7) Two weeks' vacation with pay.

I believe that you have been misled and misinformed about the real issues underlying the strike at the studio. I am positively convinced that Communistic agitation, leadership, and activities have brought about this strike, and has persuaded you to reject this fair and equitable settlement.

I address you in this manner because I have no other means of reaching you.

WALT DISNEY
Hollywood, California
July 2nd, 1941

Walt Disney appeals to his artists in an ad placed in Hollywood trade papers. Courtesy of MPSC Local 839, AFL-CIO Collection, Urban Archives Center, Oviatt Library, California State University, Northridge.

Dear Walt:

If you meant what you said in your trade paper announcement yesterday, we believe this strike can be settled.

You made an offer of settlement. As a basis for negotiations the offer sounds reasonable.

Your letter in the trade papers was our first written notice of your offer. Prior to that we were told by Willie Bioff that you would agree to certain terms.

We cannot accept the intervention of a character like Bioff, who now is under indictment for extortion and who has been a disgrace to Organized Labor.

We meet openly at 10 A.M. every morning across the street from the Studio. You are invited to come over to speak to us at any time. The door is open for negotiations except at Willie Bioff's ranch.

We address you in this manner because we have no other means of reaching you.

Sincerely,

YOUR STRIKING EMPLOYEES.

Animators Union response to Walt Disney's appeal. Courtesy of MPSC Local 839, AFL-CIO Collection, Urban Archives Center, Oviatt Library, California State University, Northridge.

members. The *Daily Variety* announced, "Bioff Blocks Strike Washup, SCG Walks Out as Hoodlums Walk In."[84] Bioff contacted Art Babbitt and tried to buy him off with a hefty bonus and an additional $50 a week raise. Art responded, "Mr. Bioff, I already make so much damn money I don't know what to do with it!"[85] On July 10, splashy headlines in *Variety* and the *Hollywood Reporter* announced that a deal had been signed.[86]

The Great Disney Studio Strike

The SCG loudly protested the unfair settlement and asked the U.S. Department of Labor to intervene. The studio complained in the press that the union was the real cause of the stall in negotiations. The studio issued a leaflet to the marchers in Walt Disney's name, claiming that the Disney studio was giving in to all demands but their union leaders still refused to stop the strike. Walt now leveled a new charge: "I believe you have been misled and misinformed about the real issues underlying the strike at the studio. I am positively convinced that Communist agitation, leadership and activities have brought about this strike, and have persuaded you to reject this fair and equitable settlement."[87]Against the advice of more level heads, Walt had this statement printed in the trade press, with dire consequences for all Hollywood (see chapter 6).

The union leaders voted to resume picketing July 14. Word about the war in Cartoonland finally reached Washington, D.C., which up until then was more concerned with wars in Europe and the Pacific. On July 15, President Roosevelt sent a federal mediator, Judge Stanley White, to arbitrate a settlement. Walt Disney angrily rejected the federal arbitration. He also refused to negotiate when Art Babbitt was in the room. Clearly, nothing could be done while the Old Man was boiling mad.

A face-saving tactic was concocted to get Walt out of town so a deal could be struck. He had been invited by Nelson Rockefeller to tour Latin America on a goodwill mission funded by the State Department. Washington was worried that the military governments of Brazil, Chile, and Argentina would side with the Axis powers in the war. Rockefeller was sent to mollify the South American governments with anything they wanted to keep out of the war. Among other things, they asked for Donald Duck. Urged on by his brother, Walt finally agreed to go. Gunther Lessing, who had assured Walt that the strike would not last twenty-four hours, now told him, "Don't worry Walt. I can take care of this. I know the boys [the federal mediators] over there. I play golf with them, and we'll make a deal under the table."[88] On August 17, Walt Disney left town for the tour, taking with him fifteen of his most loyal artists, including Frank Thomas, Ollie Johnston, Ward Kimball, Fred Moore, Marc Davis, Norm Ferguson, and Lee and Mary Blair. The AF of L contacted the heads of the labor unions in the South American countries to be visited. At several stops the Disney plane was met by picketing longshoremen. Of course that little detail was omitted in the studio documentary of the trip. The

Disney strike: gag drawing mocking Walt Disney's 1941 trip to Latin America. Picket signs read "Malo," "Malo Deesney," etc. AF of L artist next to Walt says: "Boy-o-boy. Get publicity on this to New York at once. What a reception. Gee I wish I could read Spanish!!!" Artist unknown. Courtesy of MPSC Local 839, AFL-CIO Collection, Urban Archives Center, Oviatt Library, California State University, Northridge.

South American trip was touted as a great success and the films *Saludos Amigos* and *The Three Caballeros* were the eventual result.

Back in Burbank the negotiations between management and the union remained deadlocked. A frustrated Judge White told Sorrell, "Herb, the only way you're going to move that stubborn cuss [Walt] is to go over his head. Do you know anybody like that?" Sorrell replied, "I know the Gianinni brothers of the Bank of America, and I know Disney is deeply in debt to them." "Well, there's your answer," White said.[89]

Sorrell did talk secretly to the Bank of America. Whereas the bank managers had formerly urged a hard line, now they saw no purpose in continuing the bruising battle with the unions. The Department of Labor sent ace mediator Judge James F. Casey, who had previously settled the violent General Motors Strike of 1937. The Disney studio was fi-

Disney strike negotiation teams. Front, left to right, Herb Sorrell, federal judge Stanley White, Disney counsel Gunther Lessing. Rear: SCG counsel George Bodle, White assistant Marsha Lambertin. Courtesy of Los Angeles Times Photographic Archive, Department of Special Collections, Charles E. Young Research Library, UCLA.

nally forced to settle and recognize the SCG. At long last a deal was announced on July 28.

Everyone wanted to go back to work, but one final glitch held up the deal. The studio announced a new round of layoffs. The ratio was 207 union workers getting the boot to only 29 scabs. After the union balked at the layoffs, Roy Disney ordered all studio production shut down.[90]

Judge Casey now ordered all sides to Washington to arbitrate the details. Once in the nation's capital, Casey ruled for the union in every instance. The jurisdiction of the Screen Cartoonists Guild, the Screen Editors Guild, and the Screen Publicists Guild was acknowledged, wages and hours were standardized, and complete screen credits were to be listed on films. The great bulk of Disney employees' pay rates doubled, or more, retroactive to May 29, the first day of the walkout. An animator making $35 a week would now be making $85 a week. The studio reopened, and everyone finally went back to work on September 21, 1941.

When Walt Disney returned from Latin America in October, his first reaction was to hop an express train to Washington to try and get the federal rulings overturned.[91] He failed at that. After the ninety-day arbitration period ended, Walt immediately fired a number of the union leaders, including Art Babbitt. This was once again a violation of the Wagner Act. The studio claimed Babbitt was let go for artistic inadequacy.[92] Babbitt showed the court some of his animation drawings from *Snow White* and *Fantasia*. The court made the studio rehire all of the artists fired. Appeals of the ruling went as high as the U.S. Court of Appeals for the Ninth Circuit; the U.S. Supreme Court refused to review the case to reverse the Ninth Circuit's ruling in favor of Babbitt.[93]

Roy Disney finally convinced Walt that, although the settlement was lousy, they were trying to buck a national trend and that unions were definitely in the saddle. The Disney brothers gave up fighting, and the Walt Disney Studio stayed a union shop thereafter. To avoid further grief, Walt even made sure that the groundskeepers and caterers were unionized. He had a meeting with his remaining staff and told them things were going to be different from then on. One wise-guy artist in the crowd piped up, "Does that mean we don't have to buy insurance from your brother Ray anymore?"[94]

The Walt Disney Studio strike was seen in Hollywood as a great victory for Herb Sorrell and the Conference of Studio Unions. Sorrell now moved on to challenge IATSE for the right to represent all backstage artists and technicians in Hollywood, but among the Disney animators no one seemed to want to forgive or forget. The pro-management artists felt the family atmosphere of the studio had been destroyed by a lot of outsiders, troublemakers, and Reds. The Penthouse Club was closed for a time, and a row of time clocks was installed. No more employee parties around Walt's pool. No more polo with the crew. No one wanted to work together until the Pearl Harbor attack several weeks later compelled opposing artists to work side by side in the army's First Motion Picture

Unit (FMPU), making training films. Frank Thomas, who was pro-Walt, worked next to John Hubley, who was pro-union, and so on. But bad feelings persisted.

Because the studio was making training films, the army draft board awarded the remaining Disney employees a 2A deferment for doing war work. Disney sent a list of artists who could be exempted from that list and drafted. Just by coincidence, of course, they were all union men.[95]

Slowly, the pro-union Disney artists were made to feel unwanted and drifted away from the studio. Whenever there was a staff cutback, the union supporters were always the first to go. The pro-unionists who tried to stay got the silent treatment. In a close working space where tempers are high and tensions exist, it's difficult to concentrate, and the stress level can be unbearable. Art director Maurice Noble told me no one wanted to speak to him, even in the men's room. Noble's desk was moved from a spacious third-floor office to a dank closet where he had to get up on a stool to see out a small window. Noble quit and went on to Warner Bros., where he attained immortality designing the unique look of Chuck Jones's classic Road Runner & Coyote series and *The Grinch Who Stole Christmas*.[96]

Walt Disney and Art Babbitt continued to feud. It was said that Walt put Babbitt on projects knowing he never intended to make them. It was just calculated to frustrate Babbitt and waste his energies. Babbitt finally got the message and left to join the Marines. He returned to Disney's in December 1945 as stipulated in the War Reemployment Act, which guaranteed returning servicemen their jobs. He animated on some Goofy shorts but left again, registering a complaint of bias with the War Reemployment Board.[97] He organized several union artists to mount a class-action lawsuit against Disney for unpaid overtime. Artists complained of being compelled to work mandatory Saturdays and evenings for free. Some claimed that when they wrote sixty or eighty hours on their time cards, someone in management erased the number and wrote in forty hours. They produced their personal service contracts for inspection. Upon studying them, one judge commented, "These are the worst Yellow-Dog contracts I have ever seen!"[98] A yellow-dog contract is one that heavily favors the employer. Despite these sympathies, after two years in court the plaintiffs got only about $100 dollars each.[99]

So one by one they left. Among them: Bill Tytla, Bill Scott, Jules

Engel, Frank Tashlin, Ade Woolery, Selby Kelly, John Hubley, Harry Reeves, Zack Schwartz, Bill Scott, Bill Hurtz, Phil Klein, Phil Eastman, Dave Hilberman, Steve Bosustow, Aurelius Battaglia, Hicks Lokey, Ed Forcher.

Director Dave Hand had negotiated for management alongside Lessing and Roy Disney, but, because he seemingly sympathized with the strikers, Walt ended their association. Hand moved to England to found the cartoon studio GBS for J. Arthur Rank. Joe Grant said that Walt was left so personally hurt that he even looked with suspicion at his loyal artists.[100] Walt later said, "In the end, the strike was a good thing because it cleaned house over there better than I could have ever done."[101]

Some who left created comic strips: Hank Ketcham did "Dennis the Menace"; Walt Kelly, "Pogo"; George Baker, "Sad Sack"; and Don Tobin, "The Little Woman." Sam Cobean and Claude Smith moved east to become top cartoonists at the *New Yorker*. Cobean published several books of his *New Yorker* cartoons, including *The Naked Eye;* he died in a car crash in 1957. Many other artists regrouped under Frank Tashlin at Screen Gems, then at the new studio, United Productions of America (UPA), to create *Mr. Magoo* and *Gerald McBoing-Boing*. Chris Ishii left and, after a successful career at UPA, designed the *Snow White* parody for Woody Allen's 1977 hit film *Annie Hall*. David Swift went on to a career in live-action direction, starting with the *Mr. Peepers* television show starring Wally Cox. Perhaps because Swift crossed the picket line, Walt remembered him fondly when he came back to the Disney studio in the 1950s. He directed the successful Hayley Mills films like *Pollyanna* and *The Parent Trap*. Later, at United Artists he directed the popular comedies *How to Succeed in Business without Really Trying* and *Good Neighbor Sam*. Frank Tashlin went on to direct such memorable live-action comedies as *Cinderfella, Will Success Spoil Rock Hunter?* and *The Disorderly Orderly*. Tashlin joked years later, "I got into a fight with Walt. I always pick the wrong people to fight with."[102]

Bill Tytla went to Terrytoons, then Famous Studios, and later owned his own commercial place, but he never fully regained his mastery of the medium. He disliked the artistic trends of the UPA-inspired graphic-stylized animation in the 1950s. His assistant, George Bakes, said Tytla once had to create a commercial for Doxee Clam Chowder. All the client wanted was a simple rendition of a school of fish swimming past the product. That meant a held cel panning across the screen with a two-drawing cycle of wiggling tailfins. Tytla instead produced beautifully three-dimensional animated fish like the Persian Dance in *Fantasia*. The client hated it, because it looked "old-fashioned."[103] In 1965, Tytla supervised the Warners animation crew to produce *The Incredible Mr. Limpett*, but artists there, such as Ben Washam, told me Bill's heart just wasn't in it.[104] His passion was for the full-out character animation that could only be done at Walt Disney Studio. He repeatedly applied to get back into Disney's, but the studio never agreed. As late as June 1968, two years after Walt's death, Tytla went so far as to offer to animate a test for free to get his old job back. On August 27, 1968, Disney exec W. H. Andersen sent a rejection in writing, "We have only enough animation for our present staff." Tytla died in Connecticut later that December.[105]

Bill Littlejohn served several terms as SCG president and had a long and fruitful career animating important scenes in former Disney animation assistant Bill Melendez's television special *A Charlie Brown Christmas* and award-winning John and Faith Hubley shorts like *The Hole*, *Cockaboody*, *The Tender Game*, and *A Doonesbury Special*.

As he walked out of the Buena Vista gates for the last time, Melendez agonized, "I'm leaving Disney; my career is over!"[106] He went on to be a top animator for Bob Clampett's Looney Tunes shorts and later became famous for directing the Charlie Brown television specials.

So what was lost to the studio? Many film critics agree the strike ended the experimental period of Disney animation. Before this time you could not say that Disney had an in-house style. The wonderful thing about the Big Five Disney features was that no two looked alike: *Pinocchio* has a different style and tone from *Bambi*; *Fantasia* looks nothing like *Dumbo*, and so on. The mass exodus of these individualists may have affected the overall look of the films. To be sure, new talent—Mary Blair, Ken Anderson, Milt Kahl—filled the void. However, an obvious conformity in style emerged in the mid-1940s, and the Disney style has remained ever since.

Walt Disney joined politically conservative groups like the Society for the Preservation of American Ideals and in later years became a Republican. When HUAC began to investigate Communist subversion in Hollywood, he was one of the first friendly witnesses to testify, on October 24, 1947.[107] Once under oath, Walt Disney did not go into the financial

Communists Tried to Capture Mickey Mouse, Says Disney

By RUTH MONTGOMERY
of THE NEWS Bureau

Washington, D. C., Oct. 24.—Producer Walt Disney today told the House Committee on Un-American Activities that Communists once took over his studio. He also called the League of Women Voters a Communist front organization. The mustached cartoonist said the Commie invasion occurred last year during a strike called at his plant by Herbert K. Sorrell.

Sorrell, president of the Conference of Studio Unions which has plagued Hollywood with a jurisdictional strike for more than a year, was identified by Disney as a "Communist."

"He admitted to me that Communist money financed his strike in 1937," Disney said. "I believe that Sorrell is a Communist because of all the things I have heard, and because when he pulled the strike on my studio the first people to smear me were the Communist front organizations — the League of Women Voters, the Peoples World, PM and the Daily Worker."

Asked later if he intended to include the League of Women Voters, the creator and director of "Mickey Mouse," "Donald Duck" and other animated cartoons and he would stand by his testimony.

Renegade Commie 'Disappeared'.

Two other witnesses testified as to alleged subversive influences in Hollywood. Oliver Carlson, political science instructor at the University of California, electrified the committee with testimony that a lifelong friend who sought to resign from the Communist Party

(Continued on page 18, col. 1)

Cartoonist Walt Disney draws some of his characters for two young fans before testifying at Washington yesterday. Children are Bud Stripling (left), daughter of House committee's chief counsel, and Jerry Wheeler, son of a committee investigator.

Reds Tried to Capture Mickey, Disney Testifies

(Continued from page 3)

"disappeared" in Hollywood and has not been heard from since.

He identified the missing Red as Ely Jacobson, former director of the Workers School in New York and Hollywood, who was ordered to direct Red infiltration in the movie industry. Carlson charged that Commies have also heavily infiltrated the teaching staff of public schools in Los Angeles.

Mrs. Lela Rogers, mother of actress Ginger Rogers, revealed that she and her daughter turned down the script of Theodore Dreiser's "Sister Carrie" because it "lent itself to Communism."

As assistant to the late RKO president Charles Koerner, she said she also tried to block the purchase of Richard Llewellyn's "None but the Lonely Heart" for the same reason. Despite her objections, she said, RKO bought it for Cary Grant. Clifford Odets, "whom I consider a Communist," was hired to write and direct it.

The three witnesses joined the long parade of anti-Communist actors, directors, writers and pro-

The Defense Airs Its Case

Hollywood, Oct. 24 (U.P).—Twenty-eight motion-picture celebrities will be cut in from Washington, New York and Hollywood on a radio program Sunday to answer charges that the movie colony has a strong Red element.

The show, "Hollywood Fights Back," sponsored by the Committee for the First Amendment and written and directed by Norman Corwin, will be broadcast at 8 P. M. New York time. Stars will include Katharine Hepburn, Frank Sinatra, Rita Hayworth and Humphrey Bogart.

Communist leader in New York), and Kyle Crichton, an editor of 'Collier's' magazine, who writes for the communistic 'New Masses' under the name of Robert Forsythe."

He said Jacobson later phoned him, was "terribly agitated," and said he wanted to leave the party but was afraid he would be killed. Carlson said he never heard of him again.

In 1940, Carlson continued, Communists set up an educational institution in Hollywood called The Peoples' Educational Center. He said the teaching staff is composed primarily of Communists, who teach would-be directors and script writers how to feed the Commie line into films.

"The director is a New York Communist named Sidney Davison," he revealed, "and among the teachers and directors are such well known Reds as John Howard Lawson, Helmer Bergman, Frank Tuttle, Sandra Gurney and Herbert Biberman.

Know Their Box Office.

"When you hear Katharine Hepburn speak at Communist rallies," he said gravely, "you can be sure there'll be thousands there instead of the hundreds that the party workers could pull. It makes Com-

Mrs. Lela Rogers, mother of Ginger, as she testified before House committee yesterday.

New York Daily News article, October 1947. Courtesy of Daily News Archives.

reasons behind the strike or repeat his FBI testimony about the whispering campaign of the nineteen laid-off workers. Rather, he declared that Communists instigated the strike at his studio. He went further and charged that the SCG and the League of Women Voters were subverting the spirit of Mickey Mouse with Communism.

He said the problem at his studio "was not a labor problem at all. They called my plant a sweatshop, which it is not. Sorrell warned me that he would make a dust bowl out of my place. . . . The thing that I resent most is that they [Communists] are able to get into these unions, take them over, and represent to the world that a group of people who are in my plant, who are good 100% Americans, are trapped by this group, and they are represented to the world as supporting all of these ideologies and it is not so, and I feel they really oughta be smoked out."[108]

He named Herb Sorrell and SCG business agents William Pomerance and Maurice Howard as Communists who smeared the good name of his studio. Disney said, "If Sorrell is not a Communist then he oughta be." SCG attorney and former Writers Guild of America secretary William Pomerance had indeed been a member of the Communist Party, but he was not employed by the union at the time of the strike. In his testimony, Walt Disney bungled the name of the League of Women Voters, calling them instead the "League of Women Shoppers." The following day he had second thoughts and tried to retract his charge against this group, sending out a press release to that effect. The apology was rejected by the league's chairperson, Anna Lori Strauss, who said Walt Disney "ha[d] made it difficult for the very forces of democracy which he is interested in preserving."[109]

Walt also named layout artist Dave Hilberman as "the brains of the strike," although everyone knew Art Babbitt and Bill Hurtz were equally important in the strike leadership. Walt Disney called Hilberman a Communist. When asked for proof, Walt admitted that all he knew was that "he was a man without religion, and I know he visited Moscow once." As an art student in 1931, Hilberman did travel to Soviet Russia. He was accepted to the experimental Leningrad Conservatory of Art and met writer Maxim Gorky. Not speaking Russian, he soon grew homesick and left.[110]

In the twenties and thirties, many Western intellectuals, particularly Jews, were curious about the Soviet workers' utopia that had overthrown the anti-Semitic terror of the czars. After all, hadn't Leon Trotsky once lived in the Bronx? Ramsay MacDonald, George Bernard Shaw, Bud Schulberg, Alexander Woolcott, Maurice Rapf, Al Hirschfeld, and even Harpo Marx had all visited Russia. They hoped they were witnessing the birth of the future. Once there, though, most were disillusioned by the reality of the centralized Soviet police state. When Joseph Stalin signed the nonaggression pact with Hitler in 1939, he ordered Communist party cells worldwide to stop criticizing the Nazis. This caused disillusioned liberals in Europe and America to leave the party in droves. The charge of being Communist dogged Hilberman and his artist wife, Libby, for the rest of their long lives.

Walt Disney completed his testimony to the committee. Then he made sure the newspapers photographed him sketching cartoon characters for two children of HUAC attorneys.[111]

As time wore on, the situation at the studio was slowly getting back to normal. A number of artists who picketed were welcomed back: story artists Joe Rinaldi and Bill Peet, character designer T. Hee, effects anima-tor Jack Buckley, animation supervisor Ken Peterson, and background artist Al Dempster. Walt even hired screenwriter Maurice Rapf to do rewrites on *Song of the South, So Dear to My Heart*, and *Cinderella*. Rapf was well known in Hollywood as a Jewish radical Communist who had been an important figure in the Screen Writers Guild. Walt knew all this when he hired Rapf but felt his progressive credentials would help circumvent criticism about the potentially racist themes of *Song of the South*. After leaving the studio, Rapf was investigated by HUAC, then blacklisted.[112]

The one person Walt Disney would never forgive was Art Babbitt. Ever since Babbitt made Walt lose his cool on the street in front of hundreds of his people it had become a personal score between the two men. Production manager Harry Tytle recalled that Walt once told him that of all their characters, the one he never liked was Goofy, the charac-ter most often associated with Babbitt.[113]

Meanwhile, the artists who sided with Walt showed they cared about their fellow artists by participating in union politics. Animators Frank Thomas, Ollie Johnston, and John Hench served on the guild's executive board as early as 1942, and Eric Larson was president in 1943.[114] Ward Kimball organized a concert of his famous Dixieland band, the Firehouse Five, as a benefit for the SCG in 1945. Gunther Lessing, the attorney who gave Disney so much bad advice on handling the strikers, was kept on as head of the legal department until his retirement in 1950.[115] Ward Kimball said that Lessing was never really influential again. Disney at-torneys learned to get things done by ignoring him. Instead of believing everything he said, Walt would now dismiss Lessing's ideas with, "Gunny doesn't know his ass . . ."

For the rest of his life, Walt Disney stuck to his version of the trau-matic events of the summer of 1941. Studio-approved histories of the period downplay the strike's importance and instead emphasize the trip to Latin America and the studio's wartime contributions.

Art Babbitt had a long, if diminished, career at other studios. He became one of the foremost teachers of character animation. He suf-fered a nervous breakdown in 1964 but recovered and returned to work. His lectures to the Richard Williams studio in 1973 helped spark the renaissance of London animation. But Walt Disney had one final way to get back at his old enemy: oblivion. Hollywood loves to custom-tailor its heritage, and no studio outdid Walt Disney in customizing its own mythology. The full resources of the studio's publicity machine were employed in an Orwellian effort to erase any contributions Babbitt ever made to the Walt Disney story. In books, documentaries, and TV shows, the name of the creator of Goofy was expunged. In most officially sanctioned histories of the company, it's hard to find signs that Babbitt was ever there at all.

Indeed, Disney tried to see that Babbitt was ostracized in the larger community. Babbitt once showed me a letter from the Disney Company in regard to a 1974 offer from Jack Hannah, chairman of the animation department at California Institute of the Arts, to have the animator guest lecture at the school. CalArts is the college the Walt Disney Company created out of Chouinard Art Institute. Babbitt was acknowledged as one of the best animation teachers in the world, and he lectured frequently at the University of Southern California, UCLA, and the Cartoonists Union. But this letter declared that if Babbitt set one foot on the campus of CalArts, the Disney Company would withdraw its millions in annual financial support. This was eight years after Walt's death, six years after Roy's death, and thirty-three years after the strike.

I recall a 1978 meeting with a young man in his twenties who was in Disney's animation training program. Making conversation about various veteran animators we worked with, I mentioned that I had had the chance to work with Art Babbitt. The young man didn't say, "You mean the animator of Goofy and Geppetto?" He said, "Oh, him. Wasn't he that troublemaker?" This was a man born long after the strike and with no real knowledge of it.

The feud finally ended when Roy's son, Roy Edward Disney, reached out to Babbitt and reconciled with him in 1989, writing him a note that said, "I want to give you some long overdue thanks for making *Fantasia* the classic that it is." Babbitt was touched by this gesture and kept Roy's note in his wallet for the remaining years of his life.

Many kept to Walt Disney's view of the strike long after his death in 1966. Historians have dutifully recorded as fact the made-for-press claim that the Federation of Screen Cartoonists was a legitimate union and not the company puppet the U.S. government declared it to be. Historians have recorded as fact the rhetoric Walt gave the press in the heat of the moment that no artists of any importance other than Babbitt and Tytla went out on strike. This claim runs counter to the reputations of all the great art directors, animators, and award winners named here.

But memories are long, even if the rancor fades over time. In 1988, during the celebrations marking the sixtieth birthday of Mickey Mouse at Disneyland, ninety-eight-year-old animator Grim Natwick paused to ask seventy-eight-year-old Frank Thomas, "Hey Frank, did you ever get your *Snow White* bonus?"[116]

So, was Walt Disney a bad man? Not really. He was a businessman of his time. As a typical Midwestern, middle-class boy, he was raised with the examples of successful self-made moguls like Henry Ford and J. P. Morgan. Walt Disney was generous and warm to his friends but cold to those he felt were trying to impose their will on him, even if it was a collective will. If we can fault him for anything, it is being patronizing when he should have been understanding and making everything a personal feud when he should have been businesslike. He was a man who, more successfully than any other, balanced being a hot-blooded emotional artist and a cold-blooded pragmatic businessman. But, in this one episode, his instincts faltered: when artists expected to see the fellow artist, he showed them his business side, and, when businessmen expected to work with the businessman, he gave them the emotional artist.

In the end, what was gained from the 1941 strike? What was gained was the foundation of a self-governing community of animation professionals. Once the great Walt Disney Studio recognized the union, all remaining animation studios in Hollywood quickly fell into line. By New Year's Day of 1942, U.S. animation was 90 percent unionized. The strikers' victory laid the foundation for the highest standard of living in the animation world: a reliable wage scale, standardized workplace rules of conduct, a place where the rank-and-file artist could take his grievance to his superiors without fear of retribution, the best benefits, and the best social safety nets—guaranteed in writing, not based on the whim of a potentate. When animators around the world bargain with their employers for better conditions and pay, they look to the Hollywood animators as the standard. What was gained was respect. American workers were not born to work on their knees, grateful for their chains, no matter how benevolent the despot. Looking back, Ward Kimball, one of the Nine Old

Men, said, "I was quite liberal, yet I didn't go out on strike. But I knew something had to be done. And I agree to this day that it was a good thing that it happened."[117]

Art Babbitt died in 1991. He had asked that Frank Thomas give his eulogy. I was the one who had to call Thomas and give him Babbitt's last request. I said, "Frank, I'm just the messenger, but Barbara [Babbitt] told me one of Art's last wishes was that you would speak at his funeral." He was very moved by the gesture, "Hmmm . . . that's . . . interesting." Although they had lived in opposite camps, Frank came to the service and gave a moving speech. Art was buried in Forest Lawn Cemetery in the Hollywood Hills. Because he was a World War II veteran, the Marines sent an honor guard to the interment. The white hilltop mausoleum, where Hollywood greats like Bette Davis, Stan Laurel, and Liberace sleep, overlooks the Burbank area. The Disney studio is plainly visible in the valley below. As the Marines fired their twenty-one-gun salute, Bill Hurtz leaned over to me and whispered, "If Art had his way, those guys would lower their rifles slightly."

6

The War of Hollywood and the Blacklist

1945–1953

With the world at war, labor in Hollywood should be at peace. That is not possible so long as Communists continue to exercise some control within the Screen Cartoonists Guild!
— Conservative screenwriter Martin Berkeley, 1951

Animators don't work in a separate universe. Their livelihoods were affected just as much by outside conditions as those of any toolmaker or bus driver. To understand how the U.S. cartoon business changed in the 1940s, in this chapter we examine the broader political and social turmoil that engulfed mainstream Hollywood. The rival backstage live-action unions battling for dominance brought their struggle to a violent climax that dragged the animation community into the maelstrom. At the same time, the political currents flowing in Washington also had an impact on the fate of U.S. animation and its unions. These external conditions had just as much to do with the final shape of the animation community as the talent of a Chuck Jones or the innovation of a UPA.

In 1938, the corporate leaders who made up the National Association of Manufacturers (NAM) were at a loss as to how to stop the increasingly successful unionization of the American labor force. They had tried tear gas, blacklisting, the militia, the Ku Klux Klan (and its northern equivalent, the Black Legion), immigrant strikebreakers, and vigilante murder; yet more Americans than ever were joining unions. NAM leaders went to the research group the Rand Corporation for a solution.[1] For this union problem, the Rand eggheads came up with a set of instructions called the Mohawk Valley rules. It advised that companies shouldn't try to defeat unions in the streets; instead, they said, the way to defeat unions is in the press. To turn public sympathy from strikers, the mass media should be used to hammer home the idea that labor strikes are something un-American, even though Abraham Lincoln wrote, "Thank God we have a system where workers could go on strike." The Mohawk guidelines suggested that there is something inherently socialist in all that workers' brotherhood stuff. It just doesn't mix with the good old U.S. spirit of individual enterprise. Overjoyed with the study, NAM and the U.S. Chamber of Commerce immediately had ten thousand copies of the Mohawk Valley rules printed and distributed to company boardrooms nationwide.

The rules, however, were sidelined temporarily while World War II raged. Conflicts between nations at times take precedence over conflicts of class. Because of the national emergency, management and unions on December 14, 1941, declared a labor truce. For the duration, wages and prices were frozen and extra working hours were mandatory. American animators heeded the call just like workers in other fields. They served in all branches of the military. Many went into the Signal Corps, headquartered in Culver City, California, and Herald Square, New York. There they created training films on everything from learning new radar to avoiding venereal disease. They participated in camp shows for soldiers and made films and publicity art to spur war bond sales. Martha Sigall and the Schlesinger ink-and-paint girls volunteered time washing coffee cups at the Hollywood Canteen on Sunset Boulevard, and Ivar Street. Artists constructed enemy cities in miniature so bombardiers could practice. Animators Chris Ishii and Iwao Takamoto painted regimental mascots and nose-cone art, even from their Japanese internment camp in desert-like Manzanar.

It was understood that private life was put on hold for the duration. As Rick told Ilse in *Casablanca*, "The problems of three little people don't mean a hill of beans in this crazy world." But by the summer of 1945, the war against Hitler was won and the defeat of Japan was only a matter of time. The War Labor Board, which had supervised the management-labor truce, disbanded, and American unions began to think again about conditions at home. Employers doing defense work had seen their profits grow 400 percent, while wages had not risen since Pearl Harbor. Not surprisingly, employers could not see any reason to change. Soon the United States was rocked by nationwide rail, steel, and coal strikes. President Harry S. Truman, who had been saluting management-labor harmony, was by 1946 threatening to nationalize some heavy industry and draft striking workers into the navy.

The Hollywood movie industry had boomed during the war, but it had its own labor problems. Besides the independent "glamour guilds"—DGA (directors), WGA (writers), and SAG (actors)—two rival labor organizations claimed jurisdiction over all other behind-the-scenes movie workers. They were the International Alliance of Theatrical and Stage Employees (IATSE) and the Conference of Studio Unions (CSU). The CSU was the blanket organization that guided the fate of the Screen Cartoonists Guild.

To review a bit from previous chapters, the IATSE started in New York in 1893 to protect the rights of vaudeville stage folks. Being the first to organize stagehands and movie theater projectionists on an industry-wide scale made IATSE into a national organization. The union was badly beaten up in 1933 when trying to organize sound workers, dropping to just 175 members in Hollywood. At that time, mobsters like Al Capone took advantage of IATSE's weakness to get a puppet president, George Browne, elected in 1934. Browne tainted IATSE with mob corruption. He sent his lieutenant, Willie Bioff, to Hollywood to help extend the Mafia's power in the entertainment business via the unions.

By 1940, Browne and Bioff were implicated in a scheme involving Nicholas Schenck, head of Loews Movie Theaters, which owned MGM, to shake down Hollywood's big studios for hundreds of thousands of dollars, threatening them with "union problems" if they didn't cooperate. In 1941, Senator "Fighting Bob" LaFollette's committee helped send Browne and Bioff to prison for racketeering. Bioff said, "We had about 20% of Hollywood when we got in trouble. If we hadn't gotten loused up, we'd have had 50%. I had Hollywood dancing to my tune."[2] Bioff tried to hijack the Walt Disney cartoonists' strike negotiations to demonstrate his influence and so affect his plea bargain. But it didn't work, so

Browne and Bioff went to Alcatraz. After serving two years on the Rock, Bioff turned government witness. He said he wasn't doing it for himself, that he wanted to do his part in the war against Hitler. He took the witness stand and sang so well that he accomplished something even Elliot Ness and the Untouchables couldn't do. Frank "the Enforcer" Nitti, heir to Big Al Capone and the gangster king of Chicago, was finally indicted. The day before he was to turn himself in, Nitti was seen taking a walk down a railroad track near the Riverside tuberculosis sanitarium in Cook County, Illinois. After downing a little flask of bourbon, he called to some nearby railroad employees. He waved his 32mm pistol at them and called them to witness that he was doing himself in and was not whacked by any up-and-comer. Then he put the pistol to his head and pulled the trigger. Interestingly, while Browne and Bioff were in jail, Nicholas Schenck, who was also convicted in the Hollywood extortion case, was pardoned by President Truman and resumed his powerful position in the industry.[3]

After his early release from prison, George Browne retired to suburban Chicago and lived quietly the rest of his life. For helping bring down Nitti, Bioff went into the federal witness protection program. He changed his name to Bill Nelson and moved to Tucson, where he became a pillar of the community. For a while he was the entertainment director for the Riviera Casino and a personal friend of conservative Republican senator Barry Goldwater.[4] But the Mob never forgets. On November 4, 1959, Willie left his suburban home, waved goodbye to his wife, and got into his Ford pickup. When he turned the key in the ignition, there was a deafening explosion. The force of the blast demolished the truck.[5] Willie was killed instantly, his body blown about twenty-five feet away. When the Tucson police arrived, they found Mrs. Bioff up in a lemon tree. Police wondered if she was mad with grief, but she explained that Willie was wearing a large diamond ring on his finger when he blew up, and she thought she saw his hand fly into the tree.[6]

The IATSE declared itself free of organized crime with the imprisonment of Browne and Bioff in 1941, but the taint remained because the new president, a pudgy Brooklynite named Bill Walsh, was once on Browne's executive board.[7] The IATSE rebuilt, and by 1945 it was sixteen

The War of Hollywood and the Blacklist

Former IATSE official Willard Bioff was killed outside his Arizona home by a bomb in his truck, November 1959. After informing on the mob Bioff went into the federal witness protection program and changed his name to Nelson. But the mob tracked him down. Courtesy of Herald Examiner Photography Collection, Special Collections, Doheny Library, University of Southern California.

thousand strong in Hollywood alone. It had triumphed over rivals such as the Teamsters, the International Brotherhood of Electrical Workers (IBEW), the Communications Workers of America, and the Federation of Motion Picture Crafts (FMPC) alliance of unions.

The CSU formed in 1937 after the defeat of the FMPC and other anti-IATSE coalitions. It was considered much more militant than its predecessors. Many CSU members had belonged to John Reed clubs and other progressive, socialist organizations. Their charismatic leader ("just a poor dumb painter," as he described himself) was Herbert Sorrell. From his position as business agent of Scene Painters Local 644, Sorrell by 1945 had built up the CSU to nine locals totaling nine thousand workers. He had several victories under his belt, including the Walt Disney cartoonists' strike. The Screen Cartoonists Guild Local 852 was a proud pillar of the CSU. Everyone knew that sooner or later a showdown would occur between IATSE and the CSU.

The flash point came on March 12, 1945. Since 1943 IATSE and the CSU had both claimed jurisdiction over some seventeen set dressers, the movie equivalent of interior decorators.[8] The set dressers had voted to go with CSU Local 1421, and the NLRB sanctioned the election, but the producers refused to abide by the results. Herb Sorrell tried to strike over the issue in 1944 but was stopped by the War Labor Board, which was enforcing the wartime truce. But now the war was almost over, and the War Labor Board was closing its offices. Sorrell called for a city-wide strike. His nine thousand CSU members put down their tools and walked off the job at all the major studios. The following day, IATSE president Richard Walsh ordered his sixteen thousand members to cross the CSU picket lines and go back to work. On April 5, the studios distributed blue leaflets created on hand-cranked mimeograph machines. The leaflets said that all the employees then out on strike were fired. The IATSE leadership stated it to the press even more bluntly: "The IATSE and the Conference cannot exist together in Hollywood. It is War to the Finish!"[9]

All of Hollywood chose sides. The studio heads lined up with IATSE. They remembered that the IATSE controlled the thousands of motion picture projectionists, and Richard Walsh already had his projectionist locals across the country ready to strike if the producers caved in to the CSU demands. The Big Five knew Walsh could, at a word, make every movie screen in America and Canada go black. Besides, the moguls found they could do business with the IATSE leaders, while Sorrell and the wild-eyed young romantics around him seemed like loose cannons. The Screen Cartoonists Guild and the CIO voted to honor the CSU pickets; the AF of L and Teamsters voted to support IATSE. Sorrell told the SCG that its members could sit out this strike because their own fight for recognition had financially exhausted them.[10] But many animators came on their own to support the strikers. Actor Salka Viertel recalled that on the first day of picketing at the Warner Bros. studio lot in Burbank many screenwriters and their secretaries met across the street in the Copper Penny Coffee Shop to discuss what to do. Because of her unique world-view, author Ayn Rand was able to convince many writers' secretaries to cross, and they convinced their WGA screenwriter-bosses.[11] Long-time union supporters Frank Sinatra, the Three Stooges, Judy Garland, and Lucille Ball crossed the CSU picket lines, while Bette Davis, Eddie "Rochester" Anderson, Roy Rogers, Dale Evans, and heavyweight boxer Joe Louis supported the strikers.[12] Peter Lorre suspended his production of the Warner Bros. film *The Verdict* because of the threat of violence—and because he didn't want to be called a scab.[13]

The strike went on for eight months. Many film workers saw their savings drain away while strikebreakers shoved their way past picketers into heavily guarded studios to continue production. Thirty films were being made across Hollywood at the time. The major studios augmented security by hiring goons. Thanks to connections downtown, these tough guys were immediately granted Los Angeles Police Department licenses to carry guns. Many were moonlighting LAPD and Burbank police offi-cers on the studios' payrolls, earning double overtime to bust heads. Like something out of a James Elroy novel, the LAPD had a unit of rogue detectives called the Red Squad, whose off-duty job was to harass sus-pected Communists, civil rights workers, union organizers, immigrant advocates, and any others that city hall deemed undesirable.[14]

One thing nobody in the CSU could see at the time was that liberal pro-labor federal authorities would not come to the rescue as they had in years past. FDR was dead, President Truman's new administration was unsure, and the country's mood was swinging conservative. "New Dealer" was fast becoming an undesirable label. Cries of "Justice for the working man" were drowned by calls to root out subversion and un-Americanism. The newly implemented Mohawk Valley rules began to have an impact. Even labor unions like the United Auto Workers purged progressives from their governing boards and demanded war on Communist subver-sion. FDR's pro-labor secretary of labor, Frances Perkins, was gone. The NLRB, which had acted swiftly and decisively under Perkins, procrasti-nated, sitting on the sidelines for months.

In 1944, IATSE president Richard Walsh appointed a representative with no mob ties to fight for the alliance's interests in Hollywood. His name was Roy Brewer. He was a projectionist from Nebraska who had risen in IATSE leadership ranks. A passionate anti-Communist, Brewer had worked in the government and joined the Society for the Preservation of American Ideals, the conservative Hollywood group organized by Walt Disney, Louis B. Mayer, Gary Cooper, and John Wayne. Brewer quickly went before the cameras and microphones and hammered on Herb Sorrell and the CSU's Communist background. Brewer raged: "Is this a Labor Strike? No! It is a political strike! It was the result of a long range program instituted many years ago by a 'certain political party' to take over and control organized labor in the Motion Picture Industry![15] Ironically, in June the American Communist daily newspaper, *People's World*, came out against the CSU strike. The paper followed the party line that the wartime labor truce was still in effect.

By October, a thousand replacement workers were getting the films made, and strike stories had dropped out of the newspapers. The federal government denied the strikers unemployment insurance benefits. The CSU realized it had to do something big to regain the public's sympathy. The first week of the month, the Indian summer baked Los Angeles with dry 100-degree heat. At an October 4 CSU meeting at the American Legion Hall on Highland Boulevard, tempers flared. The idea was floated that instead of picketing generally all around Hollywood, perhaps the union should single out one studio for a mass demonstration, an overwhelming display of power. A Local 644 studio carpenter named Tony Schiavene jumped up onto the platform and shouted, "Give me a thousand pickets tomorrow morning and we'll close Warner's tight!"[16] Wild cheers carried the motion.

Of all the studios Warner Bros. seems an odd choice for this showdown. Warner Bros.' reputation was as the socially liberal studio, the film arm of Franklin Roosevelt's New Deal. While Louis B. Mayer and the other Big Five bosses were well-known right-wingers, Jack Warner was considered one of the few progressive Democrats in an executive producer's chair. But what happened on October 5, 1945, would change his politics forever.

The Battle of Burbank began at 5:00 A.M. when forty pickets appeared at the Warner Bros. studio gate on Barham Boulevard in Burbank.[17] By noon their numbers had grown to over two thousand, blocking Barham as well as West Olive Boulevard, the main road from Burbank to Hollywood. The CSU had invited several church groups, including Quakers

The War of Hollywood and the Blacklist

Battle of Burbank, 1945. Strikers attacking a strikebreaker's car attempting to enter the Warner Bros. gate. Courtesy of Los Angeles Times Photographic Archive, Department of Special Collections, Charles E. Young Research Library, UCLA.

and Unitarians, to witness the violence that appeared to be imminent. At 1:00 P.M., when IATSE workers tried to enter Gate 2 after lunch, scuffling broke out. The violence escalated as the pickets overturned autos and started fistfights. For the big men who built movie sets and carried heavy klieg lights, flipping over a Chevrolet sedan was no problem.

Although the bulk of the film workers there worked in live action, many animation guild members were in the crowd as volunteers. Animation checkers Reg and Nancy Massie recalled going into the Copper Penny Coffee shop for lunch after a morning of picketing and watching the protest outside turn into a full-scale riot.[18] Animator Ed Friedman was on the other side of the studio lot at Water Tower Gate 4, but he could hear shouts and commotion coming from the other side of the L-shaped studio lot.

At 1:30, dozens of police and strikebreakers emerged from the sound-stages by Gate 2 and formed a dense phalanx to confront the picketers. The Burbank Police Department called on the Hollywood and Glendale police departments, as well as off-duty LAPD officers. Additional tough guys were recruited from the Main Street Gym, a hangout for boxers. Burbank police chief Elmer Adams stepped forward with a bullhorn and called on the crowd to disperse "in the name of the People of the State of California!"[19] A moment later, the Warner Bros. studio fire hoses were turned on the crowd. With a roar, the two armies rushed together in a battle scene worthy of a Cecil B. DeMille spectacle. But this was not a movie. Through clouds of tear gas and water spray, three thousand pickets and police battled in the streets of beautiful downtown Burbank. They brandished clubs, blackjacks, monkey wrenches, and chains. Sev-

Fire hoses turned on strikers in front of Warner Bros. Gate 2, during the Battle of Burbank, 1945. Courtesy of Los Angeles Times Photographic Archive, Department of Special Collections, Charles E. Young Research Library, UCLA.

enty people were injured. One striking set painter was stabbed in the nose with a penknife; production secretary Helen McCall was hit in the eye with a tear-gas bomb.[20] At Gate 4, a U.S. Marine officer trying to conduct some government business at the studio got out of his jeep and threatened all sides with an M-1 rifle if he were not allowed to pass. The crowds parted for him.[21]

Jack Warner and the studio's senior management stood on the rooftop of a soundstage and supervised the action like generals. *Los Angeles Times* news photos of the riot still bear the editors' grease-pencil marks to show where to crop the studio execs out of the published photo because showing them would be bad publicity. Blainey Matthews, chief of Warner Bros. security, posted sharpshooters behind the large movie bill-

CSU leaders in jail, 1945. Herb Sorrell second from left, John Morley far left, MGM background painter Johnny Johnson partially hidden, third from right. Courtesy of University of Southern California, on behalf of the USC Specialized Libraries and Archival Collections

boards up and down the boulevard in case the rioters broke onto studio grounds and started to cause serious damage. The strikers knew this and made a joke of the current studio slogan "Better Films through Better Citizenship," changing it to "Better Films through Better Marksmanship."[22] Herb Sorrell got a black eye and, with a group of CSU leaders, was arrested for incitement to riot. He was later acquitted of the charge but given sixteen days in jail for the misdemeanor "failure to disperse." Among the rioters thrown into paddy wagons were two SCG members: Tex Avery's MGM background artist John Johnson and animator John Morley.[23] The Looney Tunes animators of Warner Bros. were not affected by the violence because their studio was located off the Burbank lot. A court order was immediately issued to halt the demonstrations in front of Warner Bros.

That Sunday, October 6, six hundred picketers, "thick as sardines" and wearing gas masks, were back at the gate in defiance of the court order. They sprinkled copies of it on the ground so they could symbolically step on the order. Student filmmakers from the University of Southern California and UCLA came to march in support of the striking film workers.[24] Hundreds of members of the Lockheed Lodge of the International Association of Machinists (IAM) arrived on the scene led by members carrying a huge American flag.[25] Meanwhile, the war of words in the press continued. Roy Brewer declared in the *Los Angeles Times* that Sorrell and the Communists were "boring out the CSU from within" to take it over.[26] Orange County councilman Republican Jack Tenney tried to link Sorrell and the CSU to anti-Semitism, the Communist Party, the German-American Bund, and even the Ku Klux Klan. If that were true, it would be a curious bit of ideological contortionism.

The following Monday became known as Black Monday. At 6:00 A.M., at Warner Bros. Soundstage 3, the raising of the American flag was the signal for 350 heavily armed IATSE men and studio thugs to form a line six abreast and charge the pickets at the Olive Avenue entrance.[27] Arthur Silver of the trailer department saw a huge truck filled with "50 goons stripped to the waist with leather bands. It was unreal; these guys were monsters and determined to break the strike."[28] Eighty people went to the hospital because of the storm of fists, clubs, and lighted flares. Blainey Matthews, whose usual duties as studio security chief included fixing parking tickets and drying out a drunken Humphrey Bogart, now stood

CSU pamphlet during Battle of Burbank, 1945, Collection of the author.

his ground fearlessly in the center of the brawl, directing his truncheon-swinging forces. A Universal Studios production secretary was arrested for wielding a blackjack. Warner dance director LeRoy Prinz was knocked senseless and woke up in the studio infirmary. Warner casting executive Steve Trilling wrote that the siege at the studio "resembled the one at Stalingrad."[29] The Burbank police fired shots into the air to break up the riot.

On the fifth day, October 10, Burbank police arrested 307 more pickets and piled them into buses for the trip to the station. When the bus drivers, who were all Teamsters, learned that the cargo they were hired to transport was arrested strikers, they pulled over and walked away from their buses, to the cheers of their passengers. A large number of women who were arrested sang folk songs as they were fingerprinted. All this rough stuff involving women and students softened the image of the CSU in the eyes of the public at large. Most newspapers, with the exception of the conservative *Los Angeles Times,* now openly favored the CSU.

The public outcry over the violence finally moved Washington to intercede. By the end of October, after 238 days, the NLRB settled the strike in favor of the CSU. "The Dove of Peace alighted, at last, upon the fortress of Burbank," said Steve Trilling.[30] But the victory was costly: the CSU's coffers were empty, and neither side seemed ready to forgive or forget. Hollywood publicity departments turned out official spin on the strikes as the Red Menace and a greater threat to the American way of life than Hitler or Tojo. MGM executive Eddie Mannix testified to a House subcommittee, "We never had a dispute with labor in Hollywood until these unions came to town." The record shows there had been labor activity in Hollywood since 1914, and the first strike was in 1926. A political cartoon in the *Los Angeles Times* showed an angry Uncle Sam facing down a thuggish brute called "Big Labor." Gesturing toward the prostrate forty-eight states, Sam declares, "This is my union!" Warner's now asked Blainey Matthews to use his contacts within the FBI to begin background checks on employees who had gone out on strike.[31] W. R. Wilkerson, publisher of the *Hollywood Reporter,* wrote, "If it were not for the good right arm of the IATSE, represented by Dick Walsh and Roy Brewer, studio labor would have been in the Commie Column!"

Seven months later, a new argument between the IATSE and the

Which Union?

Los Angeles Times editorial cartoon. Uncle Sam faces down a brutish striker. Courtesy of Los Angeles Times Photographic Archive, Department of Special Collections, Charles E. Young Research Library, UCLA.

Drawing the Line

CSU broke out over studio machinists. Herb Sorrell called another city-wide strike on July 1, 1946. The following day, SAG vice president Ronald Reagan (who had taken to carrying a 32mm Smith and Wesson under his jacket) brokered a temporary compromise nicknamed the "Peace Treaty of Beverly Hills."[32] As part of this settlement, CSU members had won an amazing 25 percent pay raise. The SCG earned a two-week warning for dismissals, among other increased benefits.

Herb Sorrell and Roy Brewer were still not satisfied. At the Beverly Hills talks, sympathetic movie star Gene Kelly had warned Sorrell, "You are being shortsighted. You risk suicide." Since the 1945 strike, the powerful Hollywood Carpenters Union had folded itself into the CSU, swelling its ranks to more than nine thousand and giving Sorrell new hope he could win. A dispute now broke out over IATSE carpenters. CSU carpenters refused to work on hot sets built by IATSE artisans. (In cinema jargon a hot set was a live-action movie set that was being used for several days. When it was a hot set, for the sake of visual continuity during breaks no one would be allowed to touch anything—a cigarette, a glass, paper—unless an actor had moved it on film.)

Herb Sorrell called upon his exhausted and bankrupt CSU to hit the bricks once again in October 1946, the third major citywide strike in two years. More violence occurred on the streets in front of MGM and Fox but with diminishing impact. Under a court injunction to limit the number of pickets to no more than 8 at any studio gate, Sorrell sent 1,000 pickets to lay siege to Columbia. The police arrested 610 and 80 were injured.[33] Secretaries, production assistants, and executive assistants found themselves stranded in the studio offices all day. Many used the time to party on the company dime. Warner employees recalled spending the day playing craps and cards. An RKO executive returning from out of town found his office littered with empty liquor bottles and used condoms. Obviously, some employees were making the most of a bad situation and had a party.[34]

On October 7, 1946, the Battle of the Mirrors took place in front of Republic Pictures in the Studio City area. Picketing lighting technicians disrupted an outdoor shoot by holding up large reflectors that filled camera lenses with blinding sunlight. The IATSE crew retaliated by using the reflectors to shoot sunlight back across the street. This bizarre solar duel went on all day.[35] On October 30, shots were fired at Herb Sorrell's car as he backed out of his driveway. Not only was the shooting not investigated, but the chief of the Glendale Police Department accused Sorrell of making up the story to gain sympathy.

All sides appealed to the American Federation of Labor for mediation.[36] AF of L president William Green sent three judges to investigate: Bill Dougherty of the American Postal Workers Union, Felix Knight of the Barbers Union Local 939, and William Birthright of the Trainmen's Union. This unlikely committee had no real understanding of the film industry. They came to Hollywood, toured only one studio, Paramount, then took the first train home. They quickly wrote a vague decision that satisfied no one. When a delegation from the Screen Actors Guild confronted the AF of L president about the inadequacy of his actions, Green surprised them by bursting into tears, "What can I do?" he shouted. "We are a federation of independent unions. I have no power to do anything!" SAG vice president Ronald Reagan ran into Herb Sorrell in the lobby of Green's building. Reagan said Sorrell told him, "It doesn't matter what he [Green] does! When it ends up, there will be only one man running labor in Hollywood and that man will be me."[37]

As if to pour gasoline on the fire, in 1946 the Central Committee of the American Communist Party, in clumsy Stalinist fashion, urged greater central control and a hard line now that the war was over. This alienated traditional leftists like SAG officers George Murphy, Robert Montgomery, and Ronald Reagan. Actor Sterling Hayden (Brig. Gen. Jack D. Ripper in *Dr. Strangelove or: How I Learned to Stop Worrying and Love the Bomb*) admitted joining the Communist Party in June 1946 to help move SAG toward the CSU.[38] In a mass meeting at Hollywood Legion Stadium on December 19, 1946, the actors gathered to debate the situation. Film stars Edward G. Robinson, Katherine Hepburn, and Paul Henreid all argued to support the CSU strike. Then Ronald Reagan got up and gave one of the best speeches of his career. Hedda Hopper called it a "flabbergasting performance." He even convinced Sterling Hayden. SAG officially voted to condemn the CSU actions as Communist inspired and led all the remaining neutral film unions into the IATSE camp.[39] When Robert Montgomery and Franchot Tone became independent producers, Ronald Reagan moved up to the presidency of SAG. He had been visited at home several times by FBI agents and had clandestinely agreed to cooperate with them. He was named informant T-10.

IATSE West Coast leader Roy Brewer in 1947. Courtesy of University of Southern California, on behalf of the USC Specialized Libraries and Archival Collections.

This final CSU strike dragged on for the rest of 1946 and long into 1947. It was the fight to the finish that Roy Brewer and Herb Sorrell wanted, but the livelihoods of hundreds of loyal union film workers were the cost. The SCG continued to stay on the sidelines, giving monetary support and volunteer pickets. However, exhaustion had set in, and many rank-and-file animators were growing impatient with their leadership's dedication to what was being generally perceived as an increasingly extremist cause.

On March 2, 1947, Herb Sorrell and his wife were going to a union meeting in a church on Brand Boulevard in Glendale when Sorrell was picked up by what he thought were policemen. "I didn't resist," he said later, "because I thought we were going to a police station. [One of the men] put handcuffs on me. When I got into the car somebody hit me on the side of the head." He was driven up into the dark hills on Mullholland Drive, given a good working over, and then left on the side of the road.[40] No one was ever arrested or prosecuted for this incident. Someone shot holes in the gas tank of a private plane he used, hoping it would crash with him in it. It seemed the government, police, studio management, and the IATSE were all stacked up against the CSU. The Catholic Archdiocese of Los Angeles at one point tried to arbitrate the IATSE-CSU battle.[41] Archbishop John Joseph Cantwell called for a sit-down meeting with all the aggrieved parties on Labor Day 1947, but the producers ignored the summons.

After three years of labor strife, the CSU was broke, exhausted, and stripped of support and public sympathy. In October 1947, one by one, the CSU member locals voted to abandon their picket lines and go back to work. Sorrell was impeached by the executive board of his own local, Local 644, Scene Painters. He resigned and then tried to sue them for $20,000 in back pay. He lost. Walt Disney exulted, "Wow, they licked him good!"[42] By 1949, the CSU had disintegrated, leaving the IATSE as the sole Hollywood backstage-crafts union.

Texas Republican congressman Martin Dies first tried to tie show business to liberal subversion when he led the attack on FDR's Federal Theater Project in 1937. Hollywood liberals joined the theater folk of New York to denounce the attempt. In June 1939, the Federal Theater was shut down when Congress cut off funding. Martin Dies then got himself appointed to chair the House Committee on Un-American Activities (HUAC), which had been created on March 25, originally to investigate the threat of Nazi infiltration on the American waterfront through immigrant associations.[43] During World War I it was common for Germans to sabotage ships carrying munitions destined for the western front. In the Black Tom Pier explosion in 1916, German spies detonated 2 million pounds of explosives on a New Jersey wharf. That blast rattled the office windows of Wall Street and knocked loose the arm of the Statue of Liberty. So with America about to be involved in a new world war, the U.S. government was worried about Italian immigrants and American pro–Nazi Bund members on the waterfront. They might give information about convoy sailing times to U-boats lying in wait just outside American harbors. By 1944, with the threat of German spy rings diminishing, Dies shifted the emphasis of HUAC from Nazis to Communist infiltration.

This directional shift was encouraged by FBI director J. Edgar Hoover. The colorful little bureaucrat hated Communists since, as a clerk in the Treasury Department, he had organized the Palmer raids of Woodrow Wilson's Red Scare in 1919. The FBI now began to circulate research studies charging that Communists were making inroads in the American arts and entertainment fields, that Moscow had targeted Hollywood for conquest through subversion as early as 1936.

Conservative congressmen had chafed for years at the cozy relationship between the Jewish-immigrant Hollywood studio heads and the progressive Roosevelt administration. On the Sunday night before election day in 1940 and again in 1944, Warner Bros. had produced on nationwide radio a huge variety show in support of reelecting Franklin Roosevelt. Dozens of top Hollywood stars, including Humphrey Bogart, Lena Horne, Judy Garland, and Katherine Hepburn, urged Americans to vote Democratic. Warner Bros. also made films for the Roosevelt administration in which the ghosts of Abraham Lincoln, George Washington, and Woodrow Wilson praised the policies of the New Deal. Lincoln would say, "At last we have some *real* leadership in Washington again!" More than once Republican congressman tried to retaliate by investigating the motion-picture business but got nowhere. In Hollywood a group of like-minded conservatives such as Gary Cooper, John Wayne, Hedda Hopper, Ward Bond, Louis B. Mayer, and Walt Disney formed the Society for the Preservation of American Ideals. By 1940, the society joined the FBI and the American Legion in urging HUAC to shift the focus of their investigations from American Fascists to American Communists.

While the Disney Studio strike raged in 1941, Walt Disney paid for a large ad in *Daily Variety* (July 13, 1941). He stated in the ad, "I am positively convinced that Communist agitation, leadership and activities have brought about this strike."[44] This charge was taken up by Jack Tenney, a politician from Orange County, California. The rotund Tenney, who composed the song "Mexicali Rose," was chairman of the Joint Fact-Finding Committee on Un-American Activities of the California legislature.[45] Tenney's first subpoena went to Herb Sorrell. Tenney got nowhere because he had no proof, and his witnesses were nothing more than a few disgruntled conservative American Legionnaires and some personal friends. Tenney's committee was stymied, but for the short time he had the spotlight, he thundered in the press, calling again and again for Washington to investigate Hollywood subversion.

In 1944, WGA activist-screenwriter Dudley Nichols hosted a mass political rally of entertainment luminaries for Vice President Henry Wallace at Hollywood Legion Stadium. This caused the Society for the Preservation of American Ideals to again call publicly for Washington to come and chase the Commies out of Movieland.[46] It had seemed a futile exercise, but in the 1946 midterm congressional elections the mood of the nation swung sharply to the right. Franklin D. Roosevelt was dead, many of his New Deal lieutenants were leaving, and his enemies, the Republican conservatives, were dominant in what President Truman called the "Do-Nothing" Eightieth Congress. The shoe was now, finally, on the other foot. These men knew that investigating Russian spies in the U.S. Department of Game and Fisheries didn't get the headlines the way chasing spies in Hollywood did. At last it was payback time.

Immediately after the elections, the McCormick Press's *Chicago Tribune* and its affiliate, the *New York Daily News*, published an incendiary two-week-long exposé on Communist subversion in Hollywood. The accusation was that powerful "foreigners," meaning Jews who ruled Hollywood, had colluded with the New Deal Democrats to make the late President Roosevelt the Joseph Stalin of America.[47] The powerful Hearst national newspaper chain took up the crusade. "The enquiry into the Hollywood community would uncover the greatest hotbed of subversive activities ever seen in the United States!" Initially, the *Los Angeles Times* defended the film industry: "The assertions that leftists control Hollywood, or its output, is sheer nonsense. . . . The content of motion pictures [is] controlled by producers and studio executives. In the main this group is as left wing as the chairman of General Motors."[48] But the

Witness's view of the Los Angeles session of the HUAC inquiry into the motion picture industry. Chairman J. Parnell Thomas is second from the right. Missing from the photo is the one representative from California, Rep. Richard Nixon. Courtesy of University of Southern California, on behalf of the USC Specialized Libraries and Archival Collections

paper soon changed its view and also loudly demanded the rooting out of subversives. HUAC promised a new series of hearings for 1947.

In May 1947, the committee set up preliminary hearings at the downtown Biltmore Hotel under the gavel of New Jersey Republican judge J. Parnell Thomas. In his testimony Jack Warner, a friendly witness, said the Epstein brothers, the writers of *Casablanca*, might be Commies; he then asked if he could please keep his testimony a secret. "Jesus, I couldn't even get a laugh outta them," he said to his son Jack Jr.[49] Judge Thomas went to the press and loudly proclaimed a crisis. He said hundreds of prominent Hollywood celebrities were known Red agents. HUAC published a list of forty-one people subpoenaed to appear at the larger hearings in Washington that fall. Nineteen announced they would refuse to cooperate. Between May and October, when the hearings were supposed to begin, these award-winning writers, directors, and actors were roasted in the press as stooges of Moscow, and members of the Hollywood community were questioned by the FBI. UPA background painter Jay Rivkin lived with her husband and child down the block from writer Gordon Kahn, one of the group that would come to be called the Hollywood Ten. One night, when her husband was away, two FBI men knocked on Jay's door. "They were 'the proverbial men in the dark hats,' right out of Central Casting." They wanted to question her about "her neighbor up the block," but she refused. "I was cool, but after they left, I was so nervous, I couldn't stop shaking."[50] When the G-men interviewed Dorothy Parker, she laughed, "Take control of Hollywood for Moscow? I can't even get my poodle to listen to me."

On Saturday, October 18, Thomas reconvened the HUAC hearings in the huge House Caucus Room with three hundred members of the media, movie cameras, and theater lights packing the high-ceilinged room. This was the same room that saw the 1912 inquiry into the *Titanic* disaster and the investigation into the Teapot Dome scandal in 1923 and would one day see the Watergate (1973), Iran-contra (1986), and Monica Lewinsky (1998) hearings. Chairman Thomas sat in the middle, perched on a Washington, D.C., municipal telephone book topped with a red silk pillow so he could be seen above the rostrum. Many witnesses came in wearing sunglasses, not because they were being cool Hollywood-types, but because the large movie camera lights were blinding. *Daily Variety* called it "a Congress-eye view of Hollywood that P. T. Barnum would have staged." The first few days saw a parade of friendly witnesses, including Jack Warner (again), Louis B. Mayer, Roy Brewer, Adolph Menjou, Gary Cooper, and Walt Disney (see chapter 5).

On October 27, the committee started calling the unfriendly witnesses: left-wing screenwriters like Berthold Brecht, Alvah Bessie, Abe Polonsky, Waldo Salt, Ring Lardner, Howard Biberman, and Dalton Trumbo. Whereas the friendly witnesses were allowed to make a public statement, these people were not allowed to speak, and their lawyers were not allowed to speak on their behalf or to cross-examine their accusers. John Howard Lawson, former president of the Screen Writers Guild, got into a screaming match with Judge Thomas and was ordered removed by the guards. If Lawson thought he was going to move everyone with his eloquence, like Jimmy Stewart in *Mr. Smith Goes to Washington*, he was mistaken. He was dragged off shouting, "This is the beginning of an American concentration camp!"[51] All the other unfriendly witnesses had similar ugly exchanges. They would try to appeal for their constitutional rights and be silenced by the loud, banging gavel and the dull refrain, "Answer the question! Are you now or have you ever been a member of the communist party?" The hearings were adjourned after ten of nineteen witnesses invoked their Fifth Amendment rights against self-incrimination. Their refusal to cooperate made headlines in newspapers around the world. These ten were called the Hollywood Ten. Their common thread was that they were all one-time union activists for the Writers Guild.

On October 26, a number of leading Hollywood celebrities, including Humphrey Bogart, Lauren Bacall, Gene Kelly, Danny Kaye, and John Huston, flew to Washington to do a nationwide radio show called *Hollywood Fights Back*. The day of the performance Judge Thomas announced that the FBI had captured a Russian spy who was ready to tell what he knew. This Russian spy was never produced in the flesh. Much later it was revealed that he was a KGB agent named Lipnin who was arrested in Los Angeles for trying to infiltrate the Los Alamos nuclear project, but he had nothing to do with Hollywood. Still, the story helped to knock the movie stars' political message off the front page for a day. Five days later, the headlines screamed that a real atomic spy had confessed. Los Alamos scientist Klaus Fuchs admitted he passed the plans for the Nagasaki plutonium bomb to Russia. Again, Fuchs had no connections to show business, but in the public's mind, the fear of impending mushroom clouds over America outweighed the concerns of a few pampered movie people. In Washington no one took the Hollywood stars seriously. One Washington reporter silenced Danny Kaye's statement on the hearings by yelling sarcastically, "Hey, Danny, why don't ya' tell us a joke?" The Hollywood celebrities tried to give a petition to the only HUAC member who was from California, freshman congressman Richard M. Nixon, but his office informed them the representative was out of town. The celebrities, outmaneuvered, went home empty handed and angry. "As politicians we stink!" Humphrey Bogart confessed.[52]

As noted in chapter 3, the social climate of the 1930s was one of flirtation with leftist ideas. The concept of class strata was much more palpable. If you were for civil rights, for national unemployment insurance, for banning child labor; if you felt Hitler and Mussolini had to be stopped; or if you just liked to see someone poke a finger into the face of the powerful, then at one time or another it is likely that you would have attended a meeting sponsored by the American Communist Party (CP/USA). Many of the progressive charities of the Popular Front formed in the 1930s, like the Hollywood Democratic League, Spanish and Chinese War Relief, the Anti-Nazi League, the Hollywood Independent Citizens Committee of the Arts, Sciences and Professions (HICCASP), and the Committee for the First Amendment probably had one or two CP/USA members. Writer Robert Benchley wrote about Hollywood to friends back at the Algonquin Roundtable, "Everyone here seems to be on a committee to free the Scottsboro Boys or aid Jews in Germany or help the Screen Writers Guild."[53] Any association like this would have been enough to implicate you during the later period when Senator Joseph McCarthy saw a Red under every bed. Even Walt Disney donated money to a memorial rally for Art Young, a cartoonist whose work was a feature of the radical publication *The New Masses*.[54] FBI agents pointed this out to Uncle Walt when they came knocking on his door in 1944. Sol Sigall said that when he returned from the army in 1945, his wife, Martha, an MGM animation painter, said to him, "Why don't you go to this veterans' rally at Hollywood Legion Stadium? They are supposed to discuss benefits and Ronald Reagan is supposed to talk." He went, but when he returned, he said, "Don't ever send me to any meeting like that ever again! Those were the biggest collection of Reds I ever saw!"[55]

The Hollywood social scene sparkled with dinner parties where political activism was served with every course. The phrase was "Dearie, are you political?" Special dinner guests included European exiles. Among famous leftists at the parties were Bertold Brecht, Thomas Mann, Igor Stavinsky, and Sergei Eisenstein. The wartime alliance of Russia and America to defeat Hitler granted an air of legitimacy to the liberal elite's flirtation with Soviet Communism. Screenwriter Paul Jarrico attended his first Communist Party meeting at the Hillcrest Country Club.[56] One screenwriter said the prettiest girls attended CP dances. Animation writer Maurice Rapf said, "I never knew anyone in the party, in all the years

I was associated with it . . . that was ever seeking anything but humanistic goals."[57]

The animation community was not immune to this heady intellectual climate. The key to understanding these animators is that, although they drew funny ducks and bunnies for a living, many considered themselves artists first. They had studied drawing and painting at Chouinard, the Art Institute of Chicago, or the Art Students League of New York alongside "serious artists." Hollywood artists' house parties sizzled with discussions of new techniques and trends. In the mid–twentieth century, any discussion of modern art would inevitably go from Picasso, Dali, and the Bauhaus to the Mexican Communist muralists Diego Rivera and Siqueiros to Soviet futurists and the Revolutionary Theatre of Gorky and Mayakovsky. They would ask friends just back from Mexico City how Frida Kahlo and Leon Trotsky were. Disney animator Bill Tytla when young had been a painter living the bohemian life in New York's Greenwich Village. There in 1912 he knew John Reed, radical writer and a founder of the American Communist Party.[58] Selby Kelly said, "Everything in life is politics, you can't just stay out of it."[59]

On November 24, 1947, the House of Representatives voted 400 to 17 to charge the Hollywood Ten (also called the Unfriendly Ten) with contempt of Congress. That same day in New York City, representatives of all the Hollywood studios met at the Waldorf Astoria to try to decide how to respond to the HUAC situation. Present at the conference were Louis B. Mayer of MGM, Sam Goldwyn and Harry Cohn of Columbia, Jack Warner of Warner Bros., and Darryl Zanuck of Twentieth Century-Fox. Also in attendance were Barney Balaban of MGM and Sam Katz of Paramount, both of whom had been implicated years before in the old union kickback rackets with Browne and Bioff. Bioff's other old partner, Nicholas Schenck, was there as well.

The studio heads liked to think of themselves as absolute rulers, but the truth was that they were answerable to their shareholders, who were now loudly demanding something be done about Red infiltration in the movie industry. Initially, spokesman Eric Johnston, president of the Association of Motion Picture and Theatrical Producers, told the press, "As long as I live, I will never be a party to anything as un-American as a blacklist."[60] On Nov 26, 1947, the studio heads formulated the Waldorf statement or, as we call it, the Hollywood blacklist. Nothing was ever written down. It was an understanding among the studio heads that any film employee who refused to cooperate with HUAC was to be fired and never hired again. Producers' spokesman Eric Johnston released a new statement: "We will forthwith discharge and, never again, willingly employ a Communist. . . . Loyalty oaths in the industry will now become mandatory." The day after the Waldorf statement, MGM fired several top writers, including Donald Ogden Stewart, who had helped the Disney cartoonists with their strike. By the end of the month, seven hundred people were fired at MGM alone.

Soon the studios were blacklisting people such as Edward G. Robinson, Gale Sondergard, Charlie Chaplin, Zero Mostel, Howard Da Silva, Paul Henried, John Garfield, lots of union leaders, and anybody who ever owned a Paul Robeson record. Old studio mogul Sam Goldwyn was indignant at what was going on. Just as he once refused to accommodate Nazi filmmaker Leni Riefenstahl, now he called the committee "a bunch of one-track-mind dirt-sniffers."[61] But Goldwyn was the exception. All the other major studio heads eagerly lined up to testify and prove their patriotism by turning in their employees. Young Sidney Poitier was blacklisted just for being friends with black activist–actor Canada Lee. Yip Harburg, who wrote lyrics for hit songs like "Somewhere Over the Rainbow" for *The Wizard of Oz*, was blacklisted. Some say it was because the committee thought his song "Happiness Is a Thing Called Joe" referred to Joe Stalin. Congress quickly passed the Smith Act, which said you could be fired from your job if you were even suspected of once being a Communist. Truman tried to veto it, but his veto was overridden.

Because of the McCarran-Walters Act (1952), filmmaker John Grierson, founder of the National Film Board of Canada, was denied a visa to cross into the United States. In September 1945 a Soviet cipher clerk named Igor Gouzenko had defected to Canada. He shocked the country when he produced documents mentioning Grierson. Grierson testified twice in Canada and was further investigated by the FBI and was cleared of any Soviet connection, but the taint remained. The National Film Board of Canada purged dozens of leftist artists, and its entire infrastructure had to be rebuilt. Star animator and former Communist Party member Norman McClaren was shielded from dismissal or prosecution by Grierson on the advice of Canadian prime minister MacKenzie King himself.[62]

After weeks of being roasted in the press, movie stars Humphrey

UNITED STATES OF AMERICA
NATIONAL LABOR RELATIONS BOARD

AFFIDAVIT OF NONCOMMUNIST UNION OFFICER
(See instructions on reverse)

The undersigned, being duly sworn, deposes and says:

1. I am a responsible officer of the union named below.

2. I am not a member of the Communist Party or affiliated with such party.

3. I do not believe in, and I am not a member of nor do I support any organization that believes in or teaches, the overthrow of the United States Government by force or by any illegal or unconstitutional methods.

Motion Picture Screen Cartoonists, Local 839, IATSE
(Full name of union, including local name and number)

International Alliance of Theatrical Stage Employes and Moving Picture Machine Operators of the United States and Canada
(Full name of national or international union of which local is a constituent unit)

Signature ....

Residence .. 11161 Aqua Vista St.,
(Number and street)

North Hollywood, Calif.
(City and State)

(The notary public or other person authorized by law to administer oaths must fill in completely all blank spaces below.)

Subscribed and sworn to before me this .... day of ...... March 19 54

A notary public or other person authorized by law to administer oaths and take acknowledgments in and

for the county of ...... Los Angeles ...., State of ...... California

My commission expires ....

....
(Signature)

[SEAL]

Anti-Communist pledge form all new union officers were required to sign. After passage of the Smith Act all public officers were compelled to sign some kind of document stating their loyalty. Courtesy of Archives of the Animation Guild, Local 839, IATSE, North Hollywood.

The War of Hollywood and the Blacklist

Bogart and Lauren Bacall made a public statement denouncing Communism and saying their participation in *Hollywood Fights Back* was a big mistake. Bogart later apologized to his friend director John Huston: "You just don't know what the pressure is like." Huston wrote, "The whole town is running for cover."[63] According to historians, despite all the fuss, out of a Hollywood workforce of 30,000 only 324 people were ever proven to be Communist Party members.[64] In a 1971 *Playboy* magazine interview, conservative-leaning actor John Wayne pooh-poohed it all: "There was no blacklist. That was a lot of horseshit. The only thing our side did, that was anywhere near a blacklist, was just running a lot of people out of the business."[65]

In January 1948, Roy Brewer went before HUAC and produced proof that Herb Sorrell had signed a Communist Party card in 1930.[66] It said Herbert Stewart on the card, but, he alleged, Stewart was Sorrell's mother's maiden name. J. Edgar Hoover declared the party card genuine.[67] The card was copied after the Los Angeles Police Department's Red Squad seized it in a 1937 raid on the FMPC offices. Herb Sorrell had once showed Art Babbitt how easy it was to doctor a CP/USA card. He created one with J. Edgar Hoover's name on it. Despite such parlor tricks, HUAC was convinced, and the accusation stuck. Sorrell had already been sacked from the leadership of Local 644. As a result of the new Taft-Hartley Act, which banned any proven Communist from holding union office, Herb Sorrell was permanently driven from Hollywood.

The archbishop's office in Los Angeles commissioned a young Jesuit scholar, Father George Dunne, to write an analysis of the Hollywood labor dispute. He interviewed all the participants, reviewed all the records, and in 1949 produced a pamphlet called *A Study in Immorality*. It was so scathingly critical of the Hollywood studios, IATSE, the City of Los Angeles government, and the Los Angeles Police Department that it was quickly suppressed. The archdiocese had Father Dunne shipped off to a mission in the desert of New Mexico. Robert DeNiro dramatized this event in the 1981 film *True Confessions*, written by Joan Didion and Father Dunne's nephew, John Gregory Dunne.

Until the late 1940s, the large San Fernando Valley north of Hollywood was mostly citrus orchards and hobby farms for the movie colony. Humphrey Bogart and Lauren Bacall had a getaway cottage in North Holly-wood; Ronald Reagan owned a horse ranch in Northridge. As World War II was reaching an end, the burgeoning population of Los Angeles saw the sleepy fields of the valley as prime land for development. On May 9, 1945, the day after the war in Europe ended, industrialists Henry Kaiser and Fritz Burns announced a grand venture to build tens of thousands of mass-produced tract homes on the West Coast.[68] A veteran could put $500 down and get a two-bedroom, two-car-garage home for as little as $10,000. Before the war less than a third of Americans owned their own home. People who lived crammed in stuffy apartments and flophouses dreamed of a big backyard with their own fruit trees and barbecues.

As soon as the announcement came that the valley was going to be opened up for residential development, the SCG issued a statement.[69] It was the union's intention to create a planned community of suburban tract homes in the dairy farms and alfalfa fields of the northern area of the valley township of Van Nuys. The land, bordered by Sherman Way, Vanowen, White Oak, and Louise boulevards, was to be purchased by a coalition of animation union members and their families. There was a plan for an SCG community center, ball fields, and an elementary school for the little animators who were sure to come. The plan was called the Screen Cartoonists Guild Community Homes Project. The SCG solicited investments from the membership to pay architect Gregory Ain, planners, and initial security deposits. Because of the wartime labor peace, most animators' salaries had been frozen. Despite the tight money, many dug deep into their savings to invest in the plan. Originally there were 39 families committing to the plan; soon that number grew to 104, and eventually to 150. One family even mortgaged its little starter house in hope of getting something better. With this money the permits were granted, and ground was soon broken.

But nothing was ever built. By 1949, the plan collapsed, and no animation people would ever inhabit the dream community. There would be no cartoon commune. What happened?

Even though as early as 1911 AF of L president Samuel Gompers cooperated with corporate leaders to extend racist Jim Crow regulations to unions, the radical union and socialist movements were integrated. SCG Local 852 was conceived and run as a completely integrated local.

The War of Hollywood and the Blacklist

But the small communities in San Fernando Valley had created zoning laws that seemed more appropriate to Old Dixie than Hollywood. Since 1911, restrictive covenants had been put in place to ensure that the neighborhoods remained all white. The covenants stated: "This Property can never at any time be sold, conveyed, leased or rented to any persons other than those whose blood is entirely of the Caucasian Race. . . . No Japanese, Chinese, Mexican, Hindu, or any person of the Ethiopian, Indian, Mongolian race shall be deemed to be Caucasian."[70] Exceptions could be made for servants and employees.

Mexican immigrants who worked in the fields and fruit-packing houses were confined to a valley neighborhood of Pacoima referred to as Cholo Town, the home of early rock-and-roll star Ritchie Valens. The 1950 census shows that of 402,538 people living in the San Fernando Valley, only 2,654 were black and another 2,189 were Asian and Hispanic. Real-estate brokers and developers colluded with the racist covenants. They refused to show homes to minorities outside of Pacoima, and landlords refused to rent apartments to nonwhites. When American-born Disney artist Wah Ming Chang tried to marry his sweetheart, Glenella Taylor, he was prevented by a local municipal code that forbade interracial marriage. They traveled to that bastion of liberalism, the state of Texas, to get hitched.[71]

Among the SCG families wanting to move to the planned community were four black families, several Asian families, and many proud Hispanic artists like Bill Melendez, Rudy Zamora, and Frank Gonzales. When they heard of the problem posed by the restrictive covenants, some of them volunteered to withdraw so the others could go on. But almost all of their union brothers and sisters agreed that they must all go together or none at all. The situation especially incensed Bill Scott, animation writer and SCG executive board member. To Bill it was a matter of principle. No one could boss guild members around or tell them who they could or could not live next to.[72]

The legal battle was joined. The SCG case would be fought in the courts while the competing Hollywood unions fought in the streets. Ironically, the final blow to the Cartoonists Community Project was dealt by the U.S. government. In the conservative political climate, the Federal Housing Authority (FHA) refused to grant the SCG final housing loans. The FHA's materials argued that stable neighborhoods required "like people living with like." The housing authority's ruling was final and could not be appealed.

Even the U.S. Supreme Court's 1948 decision in *Shelley v. Kraemer*, a case originating in the Missouri Supreme Court, had little effect in Los Angeles. The U.S. Supreme Court essentially ruled that courts cannot enforce restrictive covenants that prohibit people of a certain race from buying or occupying property because such judicial action violates the Fourteenth Amendment. But the *Shelley* ruling didn't address private enforcement of such discriminatory covenants. Communities continued to enforce racial covenants themselves, in part by putting pressure on builders who sold to minorities.

By 1949, after four years of lawsuits, legal fees, and hearings, the Community Homes plan finally collapsed. Most of the union families lost their deposits. MGM inker Martha Sigall and her husband, Sol, lost $500, the equivalent of losing thousands today. Many lost even more. Other developers took over the property and built houses on the Community Homes Project sites. Despite the proximity to swinging radical Hollywood, the San Fernando Valley would remain a conservative, all-white bastion until the 1960s. In 1961, the Rice family became the first black family to move into Northridge, northwest of Van Nuys. In 1962, the first African American was admitted to the San Fernando Valley Association of Realtors. In 1968 Congress passed the Fair Housing Act, abolishing all preexisting covenants. As late as 1977, there were still stories about Ku Klux Klan activity in the area of Sylmar in the northwest valley.

The dream of an all-cartoonists community remained just that, a dream.

The Screen Cartoonists Guild Local 852 finally cut loose from the wreckage of the CSU and tried to go it alone like SAG, the WGA (successor to the Screen Writers Guild), and the DGA. Former SCG business attorney Bill Pomerance, layout artist Dave Hilberman, John Hubley, and Phil Eastman were all accused by HUAC. The guild's next business agent, Maurice Howard, also found himself subpoenaed. These men left the guild leadership, but the taint of Communism remained. Eventually, a group of conservative artists grew tired of what they perceived as the SCG's militant leadership. Urged on by Disney assistant animators Dave

Hilary and Larry Kilty, they opened a dialogue with the IATSE. When they felt large enough and strong enough, they began openly collecting IATSE rep cards. The AF of L had a policy of not allowing its locals to pirate members from one another, but when the SCG went independent, the AF of L looked the other way. By late 1951, the dissident group had enough cards to petition the NLRB for a special certification election, and the now conservative NLRB agreed to it. It was now the SCG versus the IATSE in a winner-take-all vote.

Guild stalwarts like writer Bill Scott and animator Bill Littlejohn argued passionately against voting for the IATSE. At a spirited open debate on November 12, 1951, IATSE West Coast leader Roy Brewer told the cartoonists, "In the IA you will have a union which will be your own, but with the assistance of all other AF of L unions in the industry behind you in your efforts to improve conditions for the cartoonists."[73] Littlejohn tried to get Herb Sorrell invited, but he was banned because of his Communist blacklisting. Littlejohn kept hitting the IATSE on its old links to mob corruption and the producers. He produced Father Dunne's book as evidence. At one point the meeting grew heated. Roy Brewer, red faced, yelled at animator Bill Melendez, "You are pathologically unfit to work in this industry!"

Two months later, on January 7, 1952, the IATSE held a big pre-election rally for the cartoonists at Troupers Hall. The IATSE called the SCG "the last Communist-dominated union in the studio field." Among the luminaries who addressed them was SAG president Ronald Reagan. He said it was "high time that labor worked together in a common effort to advance the Motion Picture industry." Reagan also praised Roy Brewer for his "sound labor leadership."[74] The next night the Screen Cartoonists Guild held a similar rally. SCG president Bill Scott argued in the words of nineteenth-century Irish patriot John Curran, "It is the common fate of the Indolent to see their rights become a prey to the Active. The condition upon which God hath given Liberty to Man is Vigilance."[75]

Ballots were sent out on January 9. The votes were counted under federal supervision, and the result was announced on January 21, 1952. Five hundred cartoonists voted for the IATSE, two hundred for the SCG, and twelve for "no union."[76] Smaller studios like UPA were solidly behind the SCG, but the great bulk of animation workers, Disney employees and most Warner Bros. and MGM artists, swung the vote for the

IATSE. Guild people complained that Walt Disney himself had urged his people to vote for the IATSE as his final revenge for their victorious strike in 1941.

The first meeting of the Motion Picture Screen Cartoonists (MPSC) Local 839, IATSE was held on March 7, 1952, at Larchmont Hall in Hollywood. Roy Brewer formally inducted four hundred cartoonists into the IATSE. They elected Bill Shippeck as their first president and Don Hillary as business agent.[77] After some paperwork, Local 839, IATSE was formally chartered on January 17, 1953. Among the charter members signing were top Disney artists like Milt Kahl, Les Clark, and John Hench. MPSC Local 841 was set up in New York after SCG leader Pepe Ruiz saw how the wind was blowing and merged his SCG local into the IATSE. There was soon an MPSC local in Chicago as well. To sweeten the pot, the IATSE allowed the pension and benefit hours accrued by the cartoonists in the SCG to fold into their new IATSE health and pension plans. This idea was championed by Don Hilary. One member told me later, "I was always pro-Guild, but I must admit the benefits in the IATSE local were immediate and much better." HUAC subpoenaed the SCG's new attorney, Milton Tyre, on February 8, 1952.[78]

SCG Local 852 announced, despite its truncated numbers, that it was still viable and possessed contracts with five television production houses. Animation in Hollywood would now have to get along with two unions.

United Productions of America was a studio formed in 1944 by renegade Disney and Warner Bros. union activists who wanted to explore new artistic styles. Through Columbia Studios, UPA distributed some brilliant cartoons. Every animator sick of cutesy cat-chases-the-rat cartoons flocked to UPA. Animators there talked about Sören Kierkegaard, the Bauhaus, and new trends in art like the work of Piet Mondrian and Jackson Pollock. Former Looney Tunes gagman Ted Pierce would thunder at story meetings, "Are we discussing anything funny? I do funny!"[79] Art Babbitt took a background painter's cardboard palette with random multicolor drips and drabs and framed it on a wall. He invited the "arteests" to expound on the aesthetic virtues of the new work. Despite such clowning around, the revolutionary styles and subject matter of

UPA broke new ground and affected animation done around the world. Arguably, no studio since Walt Disney exerted such a great influence on world animation. Director Gene Deitch wrote, "UPA was born at a time before cynicism set into our culture. We all really *believed*."[80] Small wonder Warner Bros. director Friz Freleng joked, "When I die, I don't want to go to Heaven, I want to go to UPA."

Yet the blacklist reached out to the UPA happy home as well. While the studio attracted the newest styles, it encouraged the same politically progressive thinking seen in much of the rest of the community. Background painter Jay Rivkin wondered during her first week if there were any other politically minded artists among her office mates. So she walked through the hallway singing "Spanish songs," meaning Spanish civil war songs from the Abraham Lincoln Brigade: "Fly Higher, and higher and hi-yer! Our emblem is the Soviet Star!" In no time at all, many voices joined in with her from the other offices. Because the little Los Angeles River drifted by both UPA and Disney, Walt liked to refer to UPA as "the Commies down river."

On July 29, 1946, Steve Bosustow, a former assistant who had walked the Disney picket line, bought out his UPA partners, Dave Hilberman and Zack Schwartz.[81] Columbia chief Harry Cohn, who owned 20 percent of UPA's stock and their vital distribution deal, ordered Bosustow to enforce the blacklist. The alternative would be to lose all their contracts. Union activists and other suspected Reds like Hilberman, Schwartz, Bill Scott, Armen Schaeffer, and Phil Eastman were hounded out of the studio. The HUAC probes reached New York and chased away the advertising clients of UPA's East Coast branch. On May 2, 1952, remaining artists wrote Bosustow a letter affirming loyalty and admitting any remaining ties to leftist organizations they may have once had. Columbia forced UPA to rehire a publicist named Charles Daggett after he had testified as a friendly witness. The staff saw Academy Award–winning director John Hubley's firing on May 31, 1952, as a particularly ominous sign. Bosustow reported all his actions to HUAC and then joined the conservative Hollywood Producers Association to allay any fears about his own political views. The Producers Association had an exclusive contract deal with the IATSE, so by signing with them Bosustow disenfranchised the SCG from UPA.[82] Bosustow's former leftist party affiliations were successfully covered up. UPA would survive, cartoons would continue to be made,

The UPA crew in 1947. Producer Steve Bosustow is to the far left, behind the woman wearing a cross pendant. Art director Jules Engel is in the front row. Behind Engel and to his right is production manager Herb Klynn. Behind Engel and to his left is director John Hubley. Behind Hubley and to his right is director Bill Hurtz, wearing a bow tie. Behind Hubley and to his left is animator Rudy Larriva, wearing a checked shirt. Behind Larriva is animator Bobe Cannon. Bill Scott is in the back row, third from left and partially hidden behind the man wearing glasses; he is wearing glasses and his trademark Teddy Roosevelt smile. To Scott's right is writer Phil Eastman. To Eastman's right is animator Pete Burness, wearing a black shirt. Art Babbitt is in the back row, third from the right, wearing round glasses. Courtesy of Archives of the Animation Guild, Local 839, IATSE, North Hollywood.

but the dynamic spirit was gone. Artists, such as Jules Engel, who supported Bosustow's moves to save the studio remained apart from the others. It was just another toon factory now. "After that episode I think I lost heart," Bosustow later confessed, "It was never the same after that."

Dave Hilberman and Zack Schwartz had an offer from the Soviet Union to form an animation studio in Moscow, but they went to Madison Avenue instead.[83] With Phil Eastman they moved to New York and started a commercial studio called Tempo. Many progressive artists moved east, where the studio blacklist wasn't as strong, and the new media of television and commercial advertising needed old Hollywood experience more than doctrinal purity. In 1953, however, there was a new round of HUAC hearings on show business, and this time New York was not spared. In 1954, an article by legendary Red-baiting newspaper columnist Walter Winchell about Reds in advertising named Tempo Animation Studio specifically as run by Commies. He got his information from an anti-Communist pamphlet written by two former FBI men. The text was published in the January 1953 issue of *Counterattack* magazine. Jack O'Brien of the *New York Journal*, a Hearst paper, also took up the cry that the Commie cartoonists should be exposed. The FBI announced there would be an investigation, and Tempo's clients soon broke off all contact. The FBI never followed through, but Tempo closed its doors, laying off 150 artists. Speedy Alka-Seltzer and the Jolly Green Giant were safe from Communist subversion.

In Detroit there was an animation studio of five hundred named the Jam Handy Organization (JHO). It was owned by a well-meaning old Christian Scientist named Jamison Handy. Jam Handy had on its payroll the elderly cartoon master Max Fleischer, who found a refuge there after losing his own studio. JHO held a contract to do technical and promotional shorts for General Motors. It also produced some government shorts, which was why HUAC came knocking in early 1951. Young designer Gene Deitch had moved there from UPA to direct his first films. A bohemian hep-cat, Deitch had enjoyed the artistic freedom of UPA and was even trying to grow his first beatnik beard. One day Deitch was called into the personnel office to face a lieutenant commander of the U.S. Navy in his full dress blues with a chest full of multicolored service ribbons. The officer informed Deitch that the Pentagon had denied him access to work on their films because "he was a member of the Communist Party, an organization dedicated to the overthrow of the government of the United States of America by force and violence." When Deitch protested his innocence the officer drily explained, "Your case has been thoroughly investigated." Deitch had to take a train down to the Pentagon and explain himself. It turned out the only evidence against him was reports that in Los Angeles Gene and his wife liked to have come-one-come-all jazz-record parties at their house. Some of the guests may have been CP/USA members or other radical types. "There was probably some political talk, mostly about Negro rights." After trying to get him to identify names on a list, his interrogators let him go and one month later restored his security clearances. "My only guess is they must have figured I was too young, naïve and nutty to be of any real danger to my country."[84]

Disney writer Phil Eastman had not worked for over a year since he was fired from UPA when he was subpoenaed to appear before HUAC on March 24, 1953. At the hearing, he took the Fifth. Then he added how his many-times great-grandmother was convicted of being a witch. "I believe she would not have been convicted of witchcraft had she had the privilege of the Fifth Amendment available to her. . . . I not only *do* stand on my privilege but I am *proud* to stand on it!" After that, Eastman could count on not finding work in Hollywood, so he moved to New York, where he sought out his old friend and former union activist Shamus Culhane. Shamus gave Phil a job writing commercials—ironically, for the U.S. Air Force. He hid Eastman in the back office while he worked: "Nobody in our office ever informed. We coulda been out of business in 48 hours" if he was found out.[85] Eastman joined the publishing company of his friend Ted Geisel (Dr. Seuss), where he created popular children's books like *Go, Dog, Go!* By 1953, John Hubley had his own studio in New York and was one of the hottest directors of TV ads. The producers of the musical *Finian's Rainbow* wanted an independently financed animated feature of the play. Hubley had started storyboards and lined up Frank Sinatra and Ella Fitzgerald for voices, Bill Tytla was to head the animation team and started to round up top talent. But the project was suddenly stripped of its funding and canceled. The blacklist was given as the reason.

Former Disney striker Walt Kelly landed himself a job as a political cartoonist on the fledgling newspaper the *New York Star*. From 1948 onward, he used his pen-and-ink skill to pillory the tyranny of the blacklist and won the admiration of future progressive cartoonists like Jules Feiffer.

Gag cartoon of SCG business agent Maurice Howard reprimanding animator Grim Natwick for wanting to relocate to help start UPA East, 1948. Courtesy of Stephen Worth.

In his *New York Star* cartoons you could see the beginnings of his greatest creation, "Pogo." He published a small book of lampoons about McCarthy, calling the book *The Jack Acid Society Black Book*. When an editor from Providence, Rhode Island, banned his cartoons, saying, "Politics has no place on the comics page!" Kelly struck back by creating a character called Miss Sis Boombah—"a Political Chicken from Providence R.I." Kelly's phone was tapped. A 1953 FBI memo reported that an agent was interviewing a reporter who was convinced that Kelly's "Pogo" characters eccentric way of speaking, especially that of baby groundhog, Grundoon, was actually a secret Russian code.[86]

The Hollywood blacklist and HUAC hearings were not one cataclysmic event; their effects went on for years. If you were heroic and defied the committee in 1947, by 1953 you had been unable to find a job in your line of work at your normal salary for more than five years. The big difference between the 1953 and the 1947 HUAC hearings was that in 1947 the friendly witnesses were in the main crackpot conservatives and nervous studio executives; now those naming names were blacklisted artists who had suffered the ruin of their careers and were desperate. The 1951 execution of the "atomic spies" Julius and Ethel Rosenberg further frightened the show business community. The government was not playing games anymore. The fact that the Rosenbergs were East Coast Jews unleashed a new national flood of anti-Semitic writings. President Truman never invited first Israeli prime minister David Ben-Gurion to the White House because he and the Zionist kibbutz movement were considered socialists too friendly with Moscow.

By 1953, SCG activist and UPA founder Zack Schwartz had finally had enough. He called Roy Brewer and made a mea culpa, and Brewer got him in to see the committee. On May 7, 1953, Schwartz went before HUAC and named names. He didn't name anyone who hadn't already been named; his humiliation was staged more for show. His employment situation improved, but he was ostracized by his close friends like Dave and Libby Hilberman. For the rest of their long lives, UPA veterans Herb Klynn and Paul Julian always referred to him with distaste. After they heard of his testimonial, Schwartz's own parents sat shiva for him. (Shiva, the Jewish ceremony of mourning is for one who has died, can also be used for informants—for example, for someone who turns in fellow Jews to the Gentiles.)[87] Zack Schwartz went on to teach at Sheridan Animation School in Canada and the Film Institute in Tel Aviv, where he was inspirational to generations of young artists. He retired to a kibbutz and died in 2003.

Charlotte Darling, another top SCG leader, also testified (on March 26 and June 2, 1953).[88] She gave a long list of names, including Dave Hilberman, John Hubley, Bill Pomerance, Zack Schwartz, Phil Klein, and SCG business agent Maurice Howard. Many of her fellow painters were amazed because she had seemed the most leftist of all. She was forever hanging out in the ladies' room smoking and raising money for the Nationalists in Spain.[89]

There is an anecdote that at this time one of the Hollywood Ten, Lester Cole, was doing time in prison. He and his cell mate, a real criminal, sat listening to the HUAC hearings on the radio. After hearing a number of people turn in their friends, the hoodlum looked up at Cole and said, "Hey, if you is one a dem Reds, lemme give ya a woid of advice. Any organization wit dat many finks in it can't be any good!" Director Billy Wilder joked: "Blacklist-schmacklist! As long as everyone works. Of the Unfriendly Ten only two ever had any talent. . . . The rest were just unfriendly."

Martha Sigall and Bill Scott said a sad thing about this period was that everyone knew the FBI had infiltrated Communist cells for years and probably had all the names they needed; they just wanted to put on a public spectacle to whip up funding to extend their investigations. By 1953, HUAC was not really out to find any more Communists but to get even with the liberals who defied them in 1947. Roy Brewer became the big man in town. All former activists and CSU members who wanted to get their names off the blacklist and work again started by making an appointment with IATSE chief Roy Brewer. Several artists, including Bill Hurtz and Bill Scott, declared that HUAC was corrupt. It was a well-known secret in Hollywood that $5,000 got your case dossier moved from the bottom to the top of the stack. It was estimated that producer Harry Cohn of Columbia doled out $30,000 a year in bribes to keep his personnel working unmolested. Bill Melendez was told $1,000 would keep him out of trouble.

Democratic president Harry Truman's antiunion policies and his tacit acceptance of the McCarthy Red chasers annoyed many Hollywood liberals. In the 1948 presidential elections, the last of the old New Dealers and Popular Front rallied behind the third-party candidacy of FDR's old third-term vice president, Henry Wallace, and his running mate, Chet Taylor, the Singing Cowboy. Bill Melendez recalled that Warner Bros. producer Eddie Selzer warned all cartoonists on the Warner lot to stop wearing "Wallace for President" buttons to work.[90] Because his relationship with Selzer was already strained, Chuck Jones complied and focused his energy on cartoons, to the annoyance of Melendez. Henry Wallace and the Republican Thomas Dewey were defeated, and Harry Truman was reelected.

The blacklist dominated Hollywood through the 1950s. Much of the town's intellectual talent fled to New York to work on plays and television, or to Europe, where the postwar living was cheap and neorealist cinema was hot. Writers produced hit movies like *Bridge on the River Kwai*, under assumed names. When the leading anti-Communist crusader, Wisconsin Republican senator Joseph McCarthy was humiliated on national television during the Army-McCarthy hearings in the spring of 1954 and then censured by Congress, HUAC's power at last was broken.

The committee still had enough juice in 1956 to drag John Hubley in to testify on July 5, 1956. He was uncooperative and was blacklisted. Hubley continued to work in New York. Behind an eccentric front man named Earl Klein, Hubley's studio created commercials and later branched into independent film. Faith, John Hubley's wife and partner, later said: "I know this sounds totally irreverent but I think Johnny's life was made by the Blacklist. . . . It was very harmful to him of course, but in a practical way it got him out of being a successful director in the studio system and into being an independent, and I don't think he would have done it otherwise."[91]

At the peak of the cold war, Hubley, with other union activist friends Bill Hurtz and Bill Littlejohn, helped create the American branch of an international animators' society beginning in Europe. Conceived in 1956, the Association Internationale du Film d'Animation (ASIFA) was granted a charter by the United Nations in 1961. Other founders included Fydor Khytruk of Russia, Marcel Jankovic of Hungary, Paul Grimault of Belgium, and John Halas of the UK. They elected Canadian animator Norman McClaren as their first chairman. ASIFA branches soon spread around the world to every city where animation was being done. It was a way that information and exciting new works could be shared across ideological borders. John and Faith Hubley were big supporters of the ASIFA movement. They won many awards, including Oscars for their avant-garde short films *MoonBird, The Hole,* and *Cockaboody*. John Hubley died in 1977.

HUAC finally suspended its operations in 1958. Judge J. Parnell Thomas was convicted of embezzlement and put in the same Danbury, Connecticut, prison that housed Hollywood Ten writer John Howard Lawson. When asked if he minded, Lawson laughed, "Nah, it's good to see him here among his own kind."[92] Finally, in 1960, for the movie *Spartacus*, producer and star Kirk Douglas brought blacklisted Hollywood Ten screenwriter Dalton Trumbo out in the open for rewrites. It is considered, for all intents and purposes, the official end of the blacklist.

The War of Hollywood and the Blacklist

Hollywood was left with a hangover from politics. Everyone just wanted to forget the whole McCarthy era ever happened. Except for an occasional celebrity stumping for a candidate or driving an electric car, Hollywood never again organized en masse for a political cause. The dinner parties that had simmered with political talk now fizzed with local gossip. Film magazines like *Confidential* went back to reporting what movie star was sleeping around: "For One Glorious Afternoon, I was Rock (Hudson's) Mate!" Hollywood unions never got involved in national politics again, with the exception of SAG's support of striking air traffic controllers fired by former SAG president Ronald Reagan in 1983.

Very few films were made about the blacklist, and even those were watered down for fear of arousing old passions. Martin Ritt's comedy *The Front*, starring Woody Allen, was a notable exception. Hollywood Ten writer Abraham Polonsky wrote the film *Under Suspicion* (1991) about his blacklist experiences but withdrew his name when producer Irwin Winkler insisted on changing his lead character from a card-carrying Communist to a "misguided liberal." A 2004 film called *One of the Hollywood Ten* with Jeff Goldblum portraying blacklisted director Herbert Beiberman failed to find an audience.

In 2000 director Elia Kazan received an honorary Oscar for his life's work. Although Kazan directed some of Hollywood's greatest films, he did so after naming names to HUAC, ruining many of his friends. Unlike other informers, he never expressed any remorse for his actions. When visibly uncomfortable Martin Scorsese and Robert DeNiro, longtime friends of Hollywood Ten writer Waldo Salt, stood on stage to present the award to Kazan, only about half the theater applauded.[93] The television monitors at the Academy Awards accentuated the sound of the applause and focused on the few standing celebrities. When former president Ronald Reagan died in 2004, most eulogies, including an NBC/Showtime channel TV dramatization of his life, carefully omitted any mention of his HUAC or FBI activities, such as doing commercials for the Crusade for Freedom, a Commie-chasing charity. They ignored his SAG union leadership as well. After defeating Roy Brewer for the presidency in 1954, Richard Walsh led the IATSE through many happy years. (In the 1954 campaign, Brewer accused Walsh of being too cozy with employers, but he lost anyway.) The elderly Walsh received a standing ovation at the IATSE Centennial Convention in 1993. Brewer lived into the new millennium. In a 2002 article in the *Los Angeles Daily News*, Brewer praised the patriotism of the just-deceased Elia Kazan. Herbert Sorrell died in obscurity in Florida. His 1961 memoir, "You Don't Choose Your Friends," was never published and is locked in a university archive.

Hollywood had many strikes and lockouts in the next fifty years but nothing on a scale as huge as the War of Hollywood. The animation community licked its wounds and prepared to go forward, now with two rival unions. Soon it was common practice for animators to carry two union cards, an SCG card and an MPSC card.

The amazing thing about these years—1945 to 1953—was that in the midst of all the uncertainty, mistrust, and financial hardship, Hollywood animators still produced some of the most well-loved cartoons of all time: Tex Avery's *Northwest Hounded Police*, Chuck Jones's *Rabbit Fire* and *The Roadrunner and Wile E. Coyote*, Disney's *Cinderella* and *Peter Pan*, UPA's *Mr. Magoo* and *Rooty-Toot-Toot*. It says something for the human spirit that no matter what the turbulence of the times, artists will strive to pursue their craft, sometimes to the level of genius.

7

A Bag of Oranges

The Terrytoons Strike and the Great White Father

He kept all the money; he got all the glory. . . . He's
going to take it with him when he dies.
                    —Terrytoon artist Mannie Davis

In 1914, long before Winsor McCay had made his sour conclusions about the animation business, he was the guest at yet another
New York cartoonists' dinner party. In the audience was Paul Terry, a
young newcomer from San Mateo, California, who was searching for his
place in cartoons. As he watched McCay lecture and show his masterpiece, *Gertie the Dinosaur,* Terry was inspired. "And all at once it consolidated, right there." He knew what he wanted to do.[1]

He immediately began drawing and bought an old, secondhand
camera. He produced a small short, *Little Herman* (1915), and sold it
to Tannhauser Pictures. Almost at once he began to learn the harder
lessons of the business. He pitched cartoon ideas to William Randolph
Hearst, who at the time wasn't interested, then to "Mutt and Jeff" creator
Bud Fisher. He even animated a pilot film on spec that Fisher happily
used onstage, but Fisher gave the contract for the series to Charlie Bowers.[2] When Terry set up his shop, one of his first visitors was Margaret
Bray, who immediately threatened him with a lawsuit if he didn't pay the
fee for her husband's animation patents.[3] Terry wound up working for
J. R. Bray for a while, then did a stint in the army during World War I,
making films for the army medical corps.

Drawing the Line

Paul Terry, old-time creator of short cartoons. His artists called him the Great White Father. Courtesy of National Cartoonists Society.

After getting out of the service, Terry set up a studio in New York with Earl Hurd, Frank Moser, Hugh Shields, and his brother, John Terry. Later they were joined by animator Mannie Davis and young neophytes Art Babbitt and Bill Tytla. Terry started a series called Aesop's Fables, later working in his character Farmer Al Falfa. He concentrated on creating shorts in volume at a furious pace. While other studios did a six-minute short over six weeks to three months, for the next eight years Terrytoons' staff of twenty turned out one short every two weeks. Jack Zander recalled, "Every other Tuesday without fail, we would all get up and march to the projection room and see a new picture. I don't know how the hell he did it." Terry kept a file of stock jokes, and his direction consisted of comments like, "Put two mice in. If one mouse is funny, two mice will be twice as funny."[4]

As he grew older and successful, Terry grew jaded with respect to the way his product was treated by his distributors. "You'd sign up a theater for 26 pictures. When you got to December you saw they only used 18 or 15 or 20 of them because they didn't have enough room. . . . The quality of the pictures didn't make any difference. They're sold like ribbons."[5]

As the years wore on, while studios like Disney, Warners, and MGM rose to the heights and others, like Sullivan, Van Beuren, and Fleischer collapsed, Terrytoons continued on its steady pace. By the 1940s Ter-

A Bag of Oranges

rytoons studio had become a venerable institution in the northern New York suburban community of New Rochelle.[6] Terry, known to his employees as the Great White Father, had a reputation for cheapness that would have made the legendarily tightfisted John D. Rockefeller proud. Terry made no bones about the fact that he did not consider himself in competition with Walt Disney. He just wanted to make cartoons in the same frugal little way he had been making them since 1921. "Let Disney's be the Tiffany's of this business; I want to be the Woolworths" was one of Paul Terry's sayings.[7] Another was, "If Disney is making chicken pâté, then we are making chickenshit!" The Terrytoons shorts like *Mighty Mouse, Heckle and Jeckle, Gandy Goose,* and *Ickle Meets Pickle* were cheap yet charming in their way.

The main animation industry considered Paul Terry's studio a backwater. Famous artists like Bill Tytla, Art Babbitt, Cal Howard, and Joe Barbera had left Terrytoons years before for more exciting places. They usually returned only when they needed a place to temporarily hang their hats. Paul Terry didn't care. He had a hard core of veterans who stayed with him for decades. Terry joked, "If they worked there shorter than 25 years, they were considered newcomers."[8]

The studio space at 271 North Avenue was described as a big, drafty loft, much cheaper than office space in midtown Manhattan where all the other animation houses were located. For office furniture, Terry scouted local neighborhood garage sales for tables and chairs. While the rest of animation was changing to the newest acrylics paints, Terry kept his background artists using watercolor and the cel painters using doctored house paint. The cartoons all sounded the same because music director Phil Scheib's scores were much the same as they had been twenty years earlier. Sameness was especially true of the salaries. Assistant animator Jim Logan said that as late as 1946 Terrytoons was still paying Depression era wages.[9] The average rate for an animator at Terrytoons in the 1940s was $95 a week.[10] It was $150–$500 elsewhere. Instead of overtime pay, Terry gave employees a bag of oranges, from his own farm in Florida.[11] To the day he retired, Terry allowed no screen credits other than his own name. Terrytoons did not suffer the violent ups and downs of the other studios because not much was attempted. The studio lived in a vacuum; it was a throwback to an earlier era, the era of J. R. Bray and Pat Sullivan, of spittoons and sleeve garters.

New York union organizer Pepe Ruiz in 1944. Pepe eventually moved to New York to be business agent of the East Coast guild and finally Local 841. Drawing by MGM animator Irv Spence. Courtesy of www.filboidsudge.com/blogspot.

In 1943, the victorious Screen Cartoonists Guild of Hollywood under president and Disney animator Eric Larson sent union organizers to New York City to start a new East Coast local.[12] Union activity in New York had been in a holding pattern since the Commercial Artists and Designers Union collapsed after the Fleischer studio left for Florida. The new CSU local was called the Screen Cartoonists Guild Local 1461 New York. The new business agent was Pepe Ruiz, the hero of the MGM organizing effort.

The New York SCG immediately went after the Fleischer personnel returning from their Florida sojourn to reorganize as Famous Studios.

A Bag of Oranges

Famous production head Sam Buchwald recalled all too well the tragic consequences of Max Fleischer's fight with the strikers in 1937. He wanted no more trouble. He quickly signed a contract for his Famous employees. Ruiz then collected a majority of rep cards for Terrytoons. He frequently mentioned Sam's cooperation. Union cards were even sent to animators serving overseas in the military. Animation assistant Jim Logan recalled being handed his SCG card in mail delivered to him while he was squatting in a slit trench in Kumming, China, being dive-bombed by enemy Zeroes.[13]

But if the other New York studios went along with the new guild, Terry didn't prove so cooperative. He first fired two of his employees, SCG president Gordon Whittier and then vice president Johnny Gentilella, for their union activities. This was a violation of the Wagner Act, so the NLRB forced Terry to rehire both men. The pro-labor Roosevelt administration told Terry to keep his nose clean if he wanted to keep those big lucrative government contracts for wartime training films. In 1944, with a majority of his employees ready to vote union, Terry reluctantly signed a contract. The contract would not cost that much more anyway, because the AF of L and the CIO had declared a national labor peace in 1941 and supported the U.S. government's freezing wages for the duration of World War II. Terry decided to make up the additional cost of the union contract by firing his two highest-paid animation directors, Izzy Klein and Bill Tytla. To him they were both union loving troublemakers anyway. Terry handed them their termination notices personally. Tytla crumpled his and rushed out of the building. For a man who was once the top animator at Walt Disney Studio, the mortification of being axed by a nickel-and-dime operation like Terry's was just too much to bear.[14]

When the contract expired on June 30, 1945, Paul Terry refused to sign another. World War II was ending, and so were Terrytoon's government contracts. And government attitudes were shifting; the "corporate liberal" NLRB staffers in Washington, under the new Truman administration, were pro-business and feared the unchecked growth of big labor. Terry reckoned that doing business with this pushy union in the recession-weakened postwar economy was too expensive for one of his stingy nature.

After the old contract ran out, Terry conducted a campaign of delay. Whenever the SCG wanted to sit down and negotiate, Terry's management stalled, prevaricated, or was not in town. These delaying tactics went on for months, driving his workers crazy. The year 1945 went into 1946, then 1947. Terry's workers watched the rest of the animation business all around them get raises and benefits. Terry meanwhile stockpiled extra cartoon shorts. Clearly both sides were preparing for war.

By April 1947, the Terrytoons artists had had enough. They wanted serious action. Paul Terry's way of showing them who was boss was to lock everyone out of the studio on Thursday, April 21, 1947. After two weeks, the studio opened as usual, but the unionists had recognized the warning shot across their bow. The SCG petitioned the NLRB, saying that Terrytoons had conducted an illegal lockout and had refused to bargain in good faith. The feds sent a conciliator named Frank Walsh (no relation to the IATSE president of the time, Dick Walsh) to arbitrate. Walsh brought both sides to the table, negotiated what he thought was a fair deal, and left by May 1. Once Walsh was gone, Terry refused to sign the final papers. The SCG held a meeting at the local YMCA to decide what to do. As before at Van Beuren, Fleischer, and Disney, tempers flared. Story supervisor Tony Morrison resigned from the guild on the spot. He declared, "This strike will be deadly for everybody that works here. The studio ha[s] piled up a backlog of cartoons that could keep them going for a year or more. It will be disastrous, Terry could just let everyone go and still release these films."[15]

On Friday, May 16, Paul Terry fired artists Eddie Rehberg, Don Figlozzi, Clifford "Red" Augustson, Carlo Vinci, and Theron Collier. Picket lines went up outside 271 North Avenue on Monday, May 19. Jim Tyer, Jim Logan, Milt Stein, Jim Rasinski, Lou Silverman, and the Eletto brothers picked up picket signs and joined the march. The studio had never had more than two hundred employees. There were only nine senior animators (Terry called them his regulars). Some artists sided with Terry and crossed the line to work, but most walked picket. On May 21, Terry's vice president in charge of production, Bill Weiss, declared all the striking artists fired and put ads in the local newspapers. Weiss even contacted local high schools and Sara Lawrence College to look for replacement artists.

People in New Rochelle liked Terry and liked having his "movie studio" in their little suburban town. It gave this sleepy little outer province of Gotham some glamour. The local newspaper called it Hollywood East.

 **TERRYTOONS**
· **Inc** ·
271·NORTH AVENUE
NEW ROCHELLE·NEW YORK

May 15th 1947

Mr. Edwin W. Rehberg
42 May Street
New Rochelle, N.Y.

Dear Sir:-

We are sorry to notify you that prevailing
business conditions require us to terminate
your employment. Lay-offs are being made
in accordance with departmental seniority.

When business conditions warrent it, we will
notify you to return. Failure to return on
forty-eight (48) hours notice to your last
known address will be regarded as demonstrating
your desire to leave Terrytoons Inc permanently.

We deliver herewith your wages to and including
May 16th 1947. Your services will not be required
on that day.

Please be assured that we will make every effort
to re-avail ourselves of your services at the
earliest possible date.

Very truly yours
Terrytoons Inc
By
President.

Eddie Rehberg's layoff notice, 1947. Rehberg was one of Terry's top artists but was also one of the union leaders, so his dismissal could not have been about his work. Courtesy of MPSC Local 839, AFL-CIO Collection, Urban Archives Center, Oviatt Library, California State University, Northridge.

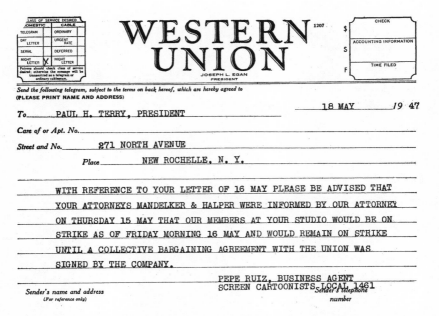

Telegram announcing the Terrytoons strike, 1947. Courtesy of MPSC Local 839, AFL-CIO Collection, Urban Archives Center, Oviatt Library, California State University, Northridge.

Terry added to those good feelings with many charitable acts for the community (a contrast with his pinchpenny ways with his employees). So the town's mayor and Chamber of Commerce were completely on his side. In the new era of cold-war conservatism, any labor disturbance was seen as Communist inspired. The good people of New Rochelle passing by the picket line spat at the strikers and yelled at them, "You dirty Reds! Go home to Russia!"[16] To men and women on the picket line who had recently returned from the service in the war, this was particularly upsetting. Jim Logan recalled, "We were ordered not to answer any comments made to us by passers by. If we didn't follow the rules, we would be arrested and put in jail."[17]

When the union tried the Fleischer strike tactic of picketing the local Roxy Theater that was showing a Mighty Mouse cartoon, they were hit with the new Taft-Hartley Act, which forbade ancillary pickets. When the strikers hired a truck with a loudspeaker for a rally in front of the studio,

(Above) Painting picket signs, 1947. Left to right, Cliff "Red" Augustson, Jim Tyer, Eddie Rehberg. Courtesy of MPSC Local 839, AFL-CIO Collection, Urban Archives Center, Oviatt Library, California State University, Northridge. *(Below)* Animator Theron Collier checks ideas for picket signs, 1947. Courtesy of MPSC Local 839, AFL-CIO Collection, Urban Archives Center, Oviatt Library, California State University, Northridge.

Animator Jim Logan with picket sign, Terrytoons, 1947. "I had just come out of the army after being bombed by the Japanese, and here I am with a picket sign with people yelling at me: 'You Goddamn Red! Go home to Russia!'" Courtesy of MPSC Local 839, AFL-CIO Collection, Urban Archives Center, Oviatt Library, California State University, Northridge.

A Bag of Oranges

Slap-Happy Hooligan, the union business agent, antiunion gag. Courtesy of MPSC Local 839, AFL-CIO Collection, Urban Archives Center, Oviatt Library, California State University, Northridge.

the New Rochelle City Council refused to grant a permit on the grounds that the noise would disturb the peace. Picketers were restricted to a set area of the sidewalk. One of the few outlets remaining to the cartoonists was to draw derogatory caricatures of management for use as publicity in newspapers. They drew Terry as an insincere lion in a top hat and suit and Bill Weiss as his pet monkey.

Minutes of meetings from the SCG archives read with a disturbing matter-of-factness:

"June 16th: William Weiss knocked down camera saying to newsman 'I don't want my picture taken!' Thumbed his nose at the photographer and went inside. Scab artists threw cigarette butts, water and buns out the 5th story windows onto strikers. Ed Rehberg hit with bun."[18] In the tenth week of the strike, picketers held a ten-week anniversary party on the curb that brought the police down on them. They were ordered to stop conga-line dancing while waving a large birthday cake on a pole. The strike had now lasted longer than any previous cartoonists' strike and showed no signs of ending.

Pepe Ruiz called his West Coast allies. Herb Sorrell, the hero of the Hollywood strikes, could not be of much help. He had immolated his CSU unions in three big citywide strikes by fighting the IATSE. By 1947, Sorrell's power base was gone. He had been expelled from his own local union and was fighting indictments for conspiracy. The CSU leaders were being arrested and subpoenaed by the House Committee on Un-American Activities. The Hollywood blacklist was forming. The West Coast SCG Local 852 was trying to go it alone as an independent union

Animator Jim Tyer (with hat) and Larry Silverman at Terrytoons picket line. The quirky animation style of Jim Tyer was a great influence on animators like John Kricfalusi and David Silverman. Courtesy of MPSC Local 839, AFL-CIO Collection, Urban Archives Center, Oviatt Library, California State University, Northridge.

A Bag of Oranges

like SAG or WGA. No help could come from the west beyond expressions of sympathy.

By November the leaves had turned colors, the cold New Rochelle winter had arrived, and the picket line was dwindling down to one or two strikers. Terry and Weiss sensed victory. They petitioned the NLRB for a new election to decertify the SCG. Terry had secret meetings with a number of key animators. He told them he was old and was planning to retire. He promised them that if they broke ranks and went back to work, he would sell them his studio. On November 15, Terry's remaining striking regulars—Jim Tyer, Joe Rasinski, Carlo Vinci, and Theron Collier—crossed the picket line and went to work. The rest of the strikers thundered and called for expulsion and fines, but they were helpless. The only power a union has in a strike is to stop an employer's production until he gives in. With all the animators returned to work, Terrytoons was functioning at full capacity without the remaining strikers.

Picketing was suspended on December 10, and on December 19

Picketers in front of Terrytoons commemorating their tenth week on strike, 1947. Courtesy of MPSC Local 839, AFL-CIO Collection, Urban Archives Center, Oviatt Library, California State University, Northridge.

the strike was declared officially over.[19] The broken and hungry artists, their savings exhausted, slunk back to work. The decertification election was put aside and never held. Why bother? The management had won without it. Terry then went back on his word to the scab animators and changed his mind about retiring. In a final supreme irony, two years later Terry and Weiss decided things would be easier with a union contract, so they signed one after all.

In 1952, Terry sold his library of old theatrical cartoon shorts to television. The CBS television network bought them all, even the silents. I recall that when I was a child watching TV in the 1950s, I saw Terrytoon's Farmer Al Falfa cartoons, black-and-white silent cartoons with a recording of Brahms's Hungarian Rhapsody playing endlessly in the background. Even at that tender age, I noticed the sound-picture sync was off. Terry told an interviewer, "They've [the old cartoons] done better in television than we ever did in theaters."[20] In 1955, he stunned his crew when he sold the entire company, lock, stock, and barrel, to CBS for $3.5 million. The old man bought Disney stock with the money, retired to Rye, New York, and died rich in 1971. CBS retained the services of Bill Weiss as producer-administrator.

The weakened eastern branch of the SCG was told in 1951 that Roy Brewer, the anti-Commie-crusading IATSE executive, was now turning his attention to them. Brewer had just created a new Los Angeles local, the Motion Picture Screen Cartoonists Local 839, and got a majority of artists and techs to leave SCG Local 852, for MPSC 839. Brewer colluded with the producers in using the anti-Communist HUAC hearings to blacklist activists in the enemy guilds. Now not only was Brewer coming east, HUAC was going to set up in Washington for a fresh round of Red-baiting. Particular attention would be paid to the New York television and advertising community. The New York SCG membership wasn't nearly as strong as the Hollywood contingent. Pepe Ruiz and his board saw the way the wind was blowing and opened talks with the IATSE. The SCG Local 1461, ceased to be, and on April 16, 1952, the Screen Cartoonists Local 841, New York, IATSE, came into being.[21] Ruiz continued as business agent, John Gentilella as president, and Fleischer strike veteran Izzy Klein as vice president. Without argument, Terrytoons quickly signed a contract with the new IATSE union. The contract was identical to the 1947 SCG one.

It is ironic that almost as soon as Terry cashed in his chips and re-

A Bag of Oranges

tired, Terrytoons had its most creative period. In the year of the CBS sale, Bill Weiss hired Gene Deitch as creative director. The thirty-one-year-old UPA star was not polite in his opinion of the studio's output up to that point: "For thirty years they had been making the crassest of unadulterated crap."[22]

In his two years there, Gene Deitch filled the studio with new ideas and people like famed writer-cartoonist Jules Feiffer. The studio that seemed stuck in a time warp suddenly scored big hits with unconventional characters: Flebus, Sidney the Elephant, Deputy Dawg, Mushmouse, Hector Heathcote, and Tom Terrific. Japanese-American artist Bob Kuwahara created Hashimoto Mouse, the first Asian character in American animation that wasn't a racial stereotype.

Some traditions never really die. Successful or not, when Deitch argued with Bob Weiss once too often, Weiss fired him. After a CBS exec dismissed Feiffer's script for the feature *Easy Winners* as "a little more Dostoyevsky than Peter Pan," Feiffer quit.[23] Terrytoons went on a few more years until Viacom, then a young CBS affiliate, closed the studio in 1968. And the artists Terry promised to sell his business to if they went against their friends and helped him break the strike? In the end they got nothing.

Pepe Ruiz continued for some years as business agent of the IATSE Local 841. In 1968, he was voted out of office in a dispute between union animation artists and optical cameramen, who were becoming a growing force in the local (see chapter 8). In 1993, Ruiz was run over and killed by rhythm-and-blues singer Wilson Pickett, who was driving while intoxicated.[24]

At twenty-eight weeks, the Terrytoons strike was the longest in animation history. It would not be the last time that artists were convinced to go against their friends, thinking their loyalty to management would be rewarded, only to come up short in the end. The Great White Father had the last laugh. Pro-management artist Mannie Davis said in the year before the old man died: "He got everything. He got all the money: he got all the glory. He had everybody's talent—he inherited that all for himself. He kept it; he's going to take it with him when he dies. I might sound a little bitter, but I am."[25]

8

Lost Generations

1952–1988

Everyone cried and cried. We thought the end of the
world had come.
                    —Anne Guenther, Disney background artist

When I entered the animation business in 1975, I noticed
something curious: All the animators and directors were in their fifties
and sixties, but all their assistants were in their teens and twenties. Only a
few were in early middle age. There seemed to be a twenty-year gap between the golden age generation (1930s) and the baby boomers (1970s).
Why was that?

The odds are that if you graduated from school any time between
1958 and 1975 and you wanted to become an animator, you were told
you were crazy. The business of animated cartoons was said to be dying.
The big Hollywood studio empires were collapsing, and peripheral operations like their animation units were among the first things to be jettisoned. At the same time the smaller independent animation producers
were all struggling to undercut each other. Few seriously thought the art
of animation had much of a future. Small wonder animators who lived
through that period often refer to themselves as the "lost generation."[1]

Part of the reason behind the success of 1930s Hollywood was block
booking. Movies were shown in theaters as part of a package deal. If a
theater manager, say in Wyoming, wanted to show *Dark Victory* (1939),

Walter Lantz crew photo in 1954. Archives of the Animation Guild, Local 839, IATSE (formerly MPSC Local 839), North Hollywood.

starring Bette Davis, he had to show an entire package: the B movie, the newsreel, the short subject, and the short cartoon. He had no choice, and most of the theaters in North America were all franchise chains of the big studios anyway. The small independent theaters were frequently shut out of getting high-profile movies and had to run inferior or obscure pictures. The Hollywood movie factories controlled every aspect of production, from concept to screening to an audience.

In 1938, independent movie theater owners brought suit against the Big Five major movie studios, saying this practice was a monopoly. The Society of Independent Motion Picture Producers (SIMPP), a group organized in 1942 and that had Roy Disney and Gunther Lessing on its executive board, supported the case. The case was titled *United States v. Paramount,* with Paramount representing all the other major studios.[2] Like all big Department of Justice cases the lawsuit took years to make its way through the courts, finally emerging in 1948, coincidentally the same year that television sets began to appear in homes in significant numbers.[3] The Supreme Court ruled that the motion picture industry had indeed become a monopoly and was thus in violation of the Sherman Antitrust Act. The Court ordered the Big Five studios to sell their theater chains and to end the block-booking system. Harry Warner urged his colleagues to fight the ruling. But when Howard Hughes caved in and signed the consent decree, selling off RKO's theaters nationwide, the floodgates were open and all the others followed suit.

Lessing declared, "This is a Declaration of Independence as far as independent motion picture producers are concerned." But it was also a mortal blow to the Hollywood studio system. Theater owners, once they were free to choose, opted to drop the short films, newsreels, and other items so they could get in more showings of the main feature and thus draw more paying customers. Audiences by then were getting their news and short comedies from television. In 1949, even with hits like *Treasure of the Sierra Madre,* Warner Bros. reported a 50 percent drop in revenue from the previous year.[4]

The rising cost of creating more novel cartoon shorts hurt profitability. As early as 1941 Walter Lantz worried aloud whether the days of the theatrical short cartoon were numbered. By the 1950s Walt Disney said, "There was no money in the short subject. You sold them in bunches, like bananas."[5] In the period 1947–1961, the cost for a good-quality Hollywood short cartoon was around $50,000 to $90,000, and the studios were demanding budgets be slashed to just $6,500 by 1961. These kinds of cuts throttled quality and forced animators to think of more simplified styles. Ten years before Hanna and Barbera created the "limited" system of TV animation Chuck Jones tried to use graphic artistic styles as a way to economize. Animator Ben Washam said that, when you think of it, even the Road Runner and Wile E. Coyote cartoons could be considered limited animation, because they utilized lots of head shots, repeated use of running cycles, and long holds.

Besides the financial problems, a kind of artistic exhaustion had set in. Many animators complained of the endless cat-chases-the-rat slapstick formula and desired personal growth. This is why UPA blossomed in the late 1940s. Bill Hurtz declared at the world animation retrospective at Montreal's Expo '67: "Seventy-five percent of the people in animation are tired out, anyway. They don't give a damn about advancing the medium."[6] Art Babbitt said at one of the first of his lectures at the 839 union hall, "Animation is 50 years behind where it should be."[7]

At the beginning of the 1950s, to fill the early morning hours, local television stations like KTLA in Los Angeles and WNEW in New York began running large blocks of pre-1948 short cartoons. Sagging movie studios dumped their large libraries of short cartoons on independent distributors for peanuts to feed the new television stations. Commonwealth TV, Walter O. Gutlohn, Official Films, and Library Films bought up silent Felix the Cat cartoons, Van Beurens, and Terrytoons, which they sold with a rudimentary soundtrack interspersed in a live show hosted by the Merry Mailman, Sonny Fox, Chuck McCann, or Captain Kangaroo. The cereal and toy companies soon saw that there was a huge audience of children spending every morning and every afternoon transfixed before the tube watching cartoons. This was especially true on Saturday mornings while mom and dad got a few extra hours of shut-eye. Saturday morning network shows were mostly live affairs until the 1953 *Winky-Dink and You*. These elements combined to create the programming time block known as Saturday morning kid-vid.

The Big Five studios at first tried to boycott television. Fledgling networks like ABC that were lacking experienced personnel, improvised, promoting photographers to be camera operators. Walt Disney, ever the innovator, had been interested in television since the mid-1940s. In 1951, after hiring the research firm C. J. Roche to study the potential of the medium, Disney Studio created an animated special called *One Hour in Wonderland*. In 1954, Disney was the first major studio to break ranks with the other Hollywood studios, and began the *Disneyland* show. It showcased Disney films and the new Disneyland amusement park. The studio also spun off a new animation crew to do animation for the show as well as TV commercials. An entire postwar generation of children was raised on animation that would yield benefits twenty years later in the form of a new generation of classic animators.

While politicians in Washington were breaking up the Hollywood monopolies, they also dealt a heavy blow to organized labor. Senator Robert Taft Jr. had his eye on the Republican nomination for president in 1948 and got himself appointed to the Senate Special Committee on Labor and Public Welfare. It held hearings on the recent waves of postwar national strikes and was in charge of redrawing the rules for organized labor. Conservative businessmen hoped for a repeal of the Wagner Act. After lengthy hearings, Senator Taft created the Taft-Hartley Act and steered it into law on June 23, 1947, over President Truman's veto.[8]

The Taft-Hartley Act outlawed several key tactics used successfully by unions. It forbade jurisdictional strikes of the sort seen in the CSU-IATSE battle in 1945, wildcat strikes, and sympathy strikes of related industries. The strikes at Disney in 1941 and at Fleischer in 1937 were won with the help of related unions like the AF of L, printers, taxi drivers, and projectionists. Under the new rules, those two victories would have been impossible. Taft-Hartley also denied NLRB protection for supervisors and foremen who wanted to organize their own unions. This is why today most production people work long hours for no overtime pay. The politicians also considered labor peace more important than labor democracy, so the new rules consolidated more arbitrary power in the hands of labor union national presidents than ever before. The act also demanded loyalty oaths and forbade Communists from serving in labor management, which decapitated most of the more militant leadership from their rank and file. Labor would find it more difficult to strike and win a strike nationally. The momentum of labor organizing of unskilled and immigrant workers was slowed. President Truman, with his policy of corporate liberalism, was all for curbing the growing national power of labor, but even he called the Taft-Hartley Act the "Slave-Labor Act."

As the effects of the *Paramount* decision and the rise of television continued to be felt, the major Hollywood studios found it harder and harder to stay profitable. By the 1960s, studios began to divest their large resources. "They're selling the family china," Barney Balaban said.[9] Dorothy's ruby slippers, Sam Spade's trench coat, and Charles Foster Kane's childhood sled went on the auction block. The back lots were bulldozed to become parking lots and shopping malls. This divestment included the animation units. In 1957 MGM fired Bill Hanna and Joe Barbera and closed its animation unit after one hundred cartoon shots and fifty Oscars. No longer would late-shift animators jostle actors in the Culver Lot commissary for

217

a 25-cent bowl of Mama Mayer's chicken soup and some saltine crackers. No longer would inkers and painters work while listening out of their windows to talents such as Gene Kelly in the black tarp soundstage next door filming *Singing in the Rain*. The studio packed up all the thousands of beautiful animation drawings and background paintings and had them buried in a landfill. Priceless to collectors today, back then they were treated like garbage taking up too much space.

Independents underwent change as well. Hungarian-born George Pal did stop-motion shorts like *Jasper* and *Tubby the Tuba* for Paramount. In 1950 he produced a low-budget sci-fi live-action film, *Destination Moon*, that was a hit with audiences. Pal moved into live-action effects films and never looked back.

Warner Bros.' Looney Tunes and Merrie Melodies units endured into the 1950s, producing superb short cartoons like *Duck Amuck* and *Wabbit Fire*. Then, on June 15, 1953, Warner Bros. shut down its animation unit. The studio planned to work off a backlog of cartoon shorts and wanted to dabble in 3D technology as the answer to defeating television, "as though they expected future generations to be born with one green retina and one blue," Chuck Jones joked as he received his pink slip.[10] The animation staff shrank to ten, including Friz Freleng and Warren Foster. That December, Warner Bros. sold Termite Terrace, among their other Hollywood buildings, to Paramount to build a new television facility, KTLA (today the building is a warehouse). Warners then had the tens of thousands of Looney Tunes and Merrie Melodies animation drawings and paintings in storage incinerated.

The truncated Warner Bros. animation crew produced one Bugs Bunny short in 3D, *Lumberjack Rabbit*. But public interest in the 3D fad was disappointing. Meanwhile, Chuck Jones went to look for work at the Walt Disney studio. "Walt liked me, despite my being a leader of the 1941 strike," Jones later said.[11] Walt showed the animator all around the facility, but at the end of the tour, Jones confessed, "I see all the different jobs but honestly, Walt, the only job I would really want is yours!"[12]

One year later, Warner Bros. realized its mistake and restored the animation unit. Since Termite Terrace was gone, returning artists were set up in a new building on the Burbank studio lot so far in the back that if you went any farther you'd be in the Los Angeles River. The artists considered the facility sterile. Mike Maltese walked through the halls yelling, "Calling Dr. Kildare!"[13] The returned Looney Tunes crew soon found they were doing fewer shorts and more television bridges, stitching their old short cartoons into half-hour TV episodes for *The Bugs Bunny Show*. In 1956, Jack Warner thought he scored a business coup by selling the entire library of black-and-white Looney Tunes short cartoons to Associated Artists and the rest to United Artists for a total of $4 million. In the decades after, the beloved old shorts made hundreds of millions of dollars before Ted Turner returned the library to Warner Bros. when he merged with the studio in 1990.

By now Chuck Jones was so bored that he and his wife, Dorothy, on the side wrote and produced an animated feature for UPA called *Gay Puree* (released through Columbia Pictures in 1962). Judy Garland, Paul Frees, and Robert Goulet provided the voices. Warners upper management found out and was not amused. On July 23, 1962, in a climactic confrontation in Warner's office, Jack Warner thundered at Chuck, "Your name and Warner Bros. will never be associated ever again!" Chuck came to love the irony of that remark: in his golden years he became the living personification of Warner Bros. animation, and his frog from *One Froggy Evening* is now the Time Warner Corporation's mascot—and in *Variety's* jargon, Warner TV is called the Frog. Meanwhile the name Jack Warner is remembered today mainly by film historians. Friz Freleng soon left as well. He teamed up with Warner executive David DePatie and founded DePatie-Freleng Productions.

In 1963, the remaining Warner Bros. animators were assigned the task to create the live-action–animation combinations for the Don Knotts film *The Incredible Mr. Limpett* (1964). Their director was Disney legend Bill Tytla, who had founded his own commercial house in New York after leaving Terrytoons, as their director. As they were completing this task, the call was going out for most of them to join the newly formed DePatie-Freleng partnership, which was already leasing space on the Warner Bros. lot.[14] DePatie-Freleng began by doing theatrical shorts like *The Pink Panther*, but their mainstay was soon Saturday morning TV. They moved to a larger facility in Van Nuys, adjacent to the Van Nuys airport. In 1967, Jack, the last of the original Warner brothers, retired after selling his remaining film library to Seven Arts, a Canadian distribution company. Mel Blanc recalled doing his last *Looney Tunes* voice in 1969. As the decline in animation continued, Terrytoons shut down in 1968 and Paramount Studios, the successor of Fleischer's, ceased operation in 1969. Walter Lantz, independent since leaving Universal, created the last original theatrical short cartoons in 1972. Much of Lantz's stored artwork wound up in a landfill as well.

That left the Walt Disney Studio as the remaining big player in theatrical animation. The studio had built a loyal fan base that looked forward to every Disney release. Disney staked a lot on the success of *Sleeping Beauty* (1959). It took eight years to make and had the largest crew ever hired and the largest budget yet for a cartoon—about $4 million, double the average budget of the studio's previous three films. All the stops were pulled out, and all the tricks then known were used to make the visuals stunning, with tour de force performances by master artists like Eyvind Earl and Marc Davis. But the final result, while adored by animation fans, was controversial. Assistant animator Bud Hester recalled coming out of the premiere of *Sleeping Beauty* with Milt Kahl. They were standing in the lobby when Walt walked by and growled: "Well, Milt, so *that's* what I spent $4 million for?"[15] *Sleeping Beauty* opened to disappointing box-office revenues while at the same time Disney's low-budget live-action films like *The Shaggy Dog* and *The Absent-Minded Professor* were chalking up significant profits. The experience finally soured Walt Disney on big-budget animation. He confessed to animator Eric Larsen, "I don't think we can continue; it's just too expensive."

Disney artists spoke of the layoff after the completion of *Sleeping Beauty* as among the darkest days of their careers. Other studios rose and fell while artists bounced from job to job, but at Walt Disney no one ever seemed to leave. Disney tended to shift people around from shorts to television to theme-park design rather than lay them off. Animator John Lounsbery said, "All our lives we work at Disney. When we get sick they move us across the street to Saint Joseph's. When we die they send us next door to Forest Lawn." It wasn't just a job anymore; it was a philosophy, a way of life. After the *Sleeping Beauty* layoffs, the studio personnel roster dropped from five hundred to just seventy-five artists. People who had worked at Disney for thirty years found pink slips on their desks. The psychological effect was devastating. Anne Guenther recalled, "Everyone cried and cried. We thought the end of the world had come."[16] Dick Anthony, an inker, went into the woods and shot himself.

Background painter
Anne Guenther by
animator Dave Tendlar.
Tendlar was a top Max
Fleischer animator
but by the time of this
drawing was working
in television at Hanna-
Barbera. Guenther was
a background artist at
Walt Disney and Hanna-
Barbera. Courtesy of the
Tendlar family.

He had never worked anywhere else and didn't know where to go to find another job.

Some young Disney artists took the layoffs as a sign of the times and left of their own accord. Women assistants like Marlene Robinson figured they would never get promoted to animator in the reduced circumstances. Don Bluth took the time to do Mormon missionary work and some Saturday morning TV work. The remaining positions became stratified under a strict seniority. Someone had to retire or die before anyone could move up. All hiring ceased. Even into the 1970s the crew on *Aristocats* was by and large still made up of the veterans from the days of *Bambi* and *Pinocchio*. The Walt Disney animation unit would hire only twenty-one new artists between the years 1960 and 1976.

Even though the studio went ahead with films like *101 Dalmatians, The Sword in the Stone,* and *The Jungle Book,* Walt Disney's heart just didn't seem to be in it anymore. His new passion had become his theme parks. In 1966 the years of stress and chain smoking caught up with him. Walter Elias Disney died of lung cancer and acute circulatory collapse at the age of sixty-five in Saint Joseph's Hospital, built on the site where twenty-five years earlier Art Babbitt and the strikers had pitched their tents. Artist Elmer Plummer recalls the last time he saw the Old Master. Walt had escaped his sickbed and donned a crisp new suit; he was found wandering the hallways of his beloved studio, not even realizing in his pain and weakness that he was barefoot. He asked Elmer, "How are you?" Plummer replied that he was okay. Walt said, "If you ever get sick, don't ever go to a hospital, just go off somewhere and die." Plummer said, "Don't worry. I couldn't afford it working for you." Disney smiled.[17] He was taken to his hospital room where he died alone.

It seems poetic that as Walt Disney lay dying, the old Hyperion Studio facility was razed to build a shopping center. The mute, threadbare rooms where Snow White, Donald Duck, and Goofy were born, where artists conversed with Charlie Chaplin and Frank Lloyd Wright, were bulldozed to rubble. No trace remained but memory and the antics of Mickey on the screen.

Because the last film Walt Disney supervised, *The Jungle Book* (1967), was a hit, it spared the animation division for a time from cost-cutting studio execs. After Walt's death, Roy Disney took over and saw through the creation of Disney World in Orlando, Florida. After Roy's death in 1970, Walt's son-in-law, Ron Miller, assumed leadership of the Magic Kingdom. UPA, which had entered the 1950s breaking new ground stylistically, by the 1960s was also in bad shape. Steve Bosustow had bought out the original partners in 1946 and guided the studio through the blacklist and the collapse of the large studios. In 1959, UPA lost its exclusive distribution contract with Columbia. Bosustow sold UPA to a businessman named Henry Saperstein, who turned the emphasis from theatrical shorts to making the television shows like *Mr. Magoo* and *The Dick Tracy Show*. Animator Carl Bell recalled: "One Friday we saw Steve and Mr. Saperstein having drinks on the veranda outside the studio overlooking the LA River. Afterwards they called a staff meeting and told us not to worry; our jobs were in no danger. The following Monday the pink slips were handed out."[18] The last UPA films were made in 1967. Henry Saperstein relinquished direct control of UPA in 1972 but he kept doing various business deals until he sold all the rights to Classic Media in 2000 and retired.

While theatrical cartoons declined, the 1950s and 1960s became the golden age of television. Animation people fleeing the studio breakups moved into the new territory of commercial advertising. Many moved to New York and Chicago to be near the big advertising agencies and further away from the Hollywood blacklist. Across the country old studio veterans like Shamus Culhane, Gene Deitch, Bobe Cannon, Art Babbitt, Abe Levitow, Mike Lah, Armen Schaeffer, Ruth Kissane, Tex Avery, Bill Tytla, Jack Zander, Ade Woolery, Fred Crippen, and Bill Littlejohn formed new companies: Pelican, Format, Gantray-Lawrence, Cambria, Playhouse, Ovation, Quartet. The creative energy to explore new filmmaking horizons that seemed to leave UPA now flowered at these small, ten- to twenty-people houses. Instead of admiring scenes from *Dumbo* or *Fantasia*, animation enthusiasts were talking about Culhane's Muriel Cigar girl, Hubley's Marky Maypo, or Littlejohn's Tigerpaws for Firestone Tires. (When Prime Minister Winston Churchill was asked what he thought about American television, he is reputed to have replied, "Not much, but I do like those dancing cigars.") Hanna-Barbera had Fred Flintstone and Barney Rubble selling everything from cereal to cigarettes. Warner Bros. had Looney Tunes artists doing commercials for Blatz beer. Even the venerable Walt Disney Studio got into the act, forming a commercial unit to do Mickey and Pluto plugging candy bars and Nash-Rambler automobiles. By the 1960s, wage scales were reversed: work in commercials paid the highest, television Saturday-morning 1animation paid second highest, and, unless you were one of Walt's old guard, theatrical feature work paid the lowest.

Producing the large quantity of animation required for television was a challenge. In the old system it took six to eight weeks to create six minutes' worth of film. Now in as little as eight months, artists had to create animation for sixteen half-hour programs. Now instead of producing five to twenty feet each week, animators had to churn out eighty to a hundred feet. Starting in 1949 with *Crusader Rabbit,* Bay Area producer Jay Ward explored ways to meet it. His formula of strong writing and good performances with former radio actors on the soundtrack combined with simple UPA-style visuals made for some memorable television. While Jiminy Cricket needed up to twenty colors of paint, characters in *Crusader Rabbit* needed only one color besides black and white. On November 19, 1959, Ward broke out with *Rocky and His Friends.* It was a huge hit, and Ward proudly built a gift shop on the Sunset Strip named the Dudley Do-Right Emporium. It was graced with a large statue of Bullwinkle holding Rocky. Hanna-Barbera, DePatie-Freleng, Snowball (Bob Clampett's company), and Filmation turned out dozens of great TV shows: *The Flintstones, The Jetsons, Beany & Cecil, Scooby-Doo, The Pink Panther, Johnny Quest.* Hanna-Barbera's system of limited animation offered other shortcuts: stylized minimal motion, reused stock runs and walks, and emphasis on clever gag writing and voice talent. Starting with the show *Ruff & Ready* in 1957, Hanna-Barbera's streamlining of J. R. Bray's production line became the model to be copied by the entire TV animation industry.

At first the quality-oriented character animators derided the quantitative approach of TV houses like Hanna-Barbera. One background artist told me that working for Hanna-Barbera was "the last resort." Bill Hurtz said, "They move animation around like real estate. Hanna-Barbera are the real-estate agents. It's all very competent. Very professional."[19] The minimum pay for a journeyman animator was $250 a week—not great, but it was steady. Overtime rules were circumvented by establishing a bonus footage system. Animators earned $10 for every foot over the eighty-foot-a-week quota. Artists weren't asked to work nights, but many did, hoping to get bonus money. Higher rates were paid for the series title sequence. Hanna-Barbera knew that a big, high-energy opening title hooked the kids to watch the rest.

In the 1960s at Hanna-Barbera and the other TV animation houses it was not unusual for one animator to turn out over one hundred feet a week of limited animation. Bob Kurtz said that at Fred Crippen's studio, animator Bill Hutten could animate an entire *Roger Ramjet* short himself in one day. Although the quality was not on a par with Disney's, the work was steady and paid well. Soon Hanna-Barbera filled its rosters with the notables of animation: Art Babbitt, Irv Spence, Mike Maltese,

Lost Generations

TV animation genius Jay Ward, left, and director Bill Hurtz, 1982. Courtesy of ASIFA/
Hollywood Animation Archive, www.animationarchive.org

Dave Tendlar, Dick Bickenbach, Ken Muse, Ray Patterson, Ed Barge,
Hal Ambro, Nick Nichols, Lefty Callahan, Bill Keil, Bill Schipek, Walt
Peregoy. Because these people were masters of the intricacies of timing
and pose, they knew exactly where to take a shortcut yet still keep the
overall show looking good.

While New York continued to be the center of TV commercials,
Los Angeles became the generator of Saturday-morning kid-vid: *Peter
Potamus*, *Magilla Gorilla*, *The Wacky Racers*, *Penelope Pittstop & the
Ant Hill Mob*, *The Superfriends*, *The Groovie Ghoulies*, *The Herculoids*,

Drawing the Line

DynoMutt, The Amazing Chan and the Chan Clan, The Ant and the Aardvark, Scooby-Doo, The Bugs Bunny/Road Runner Hour, and more. British comic Eddie Izzard joked that *Scooby Doo* (1969) had become the common denominator of mankind, that no matter where in the world you were, if you could impersonate Don Messick's Scooby Doo voice "Roobie Doooo!!" you would be understood.[20] Other cities and countries attempted the format but couldn't compete with the efficiency of the Hollywood infrastructure in turning out hours of low-budget toons at a dependable rate. In 1971, the PBS series *Sesame Street* and its clones (*Multiplication Rock* and *Zoom*) needed a lot of fresh new animation from small East Coast studios, but, despite funding from the National Endowment for the Arts, Children's Television Workshop used only the lowest budgets and encouraged studios to underbid one another.

The stretch of Cahuenga Boulevard in the pass between Hollywood and the San Fernando Valley was known as "Animation Alley." Director Jack Kinney of Kinney Aldquist Studio recalled, "Hanna-Barbera's big studio [was] at 3400 Cahuenga with Ray Patin's four doors down, Les Novros next door. Nearby, Gus Jekel's Filmfair, Chuck Couch, Filmation, Foto-Kem Lab, Chuck Hawes Camera Service, Marian O'Callahan's Ink & Paint Service and the Screen Cartoonists Guild."[21] Los Angeles animation was now seasonal work. The three networks OK'd new TV series in March; animators and support staff were hired in April; they created the sixteen or so episodes and got laid off in November. How you got by until the following spring was your problem. You tried to fill in the winter with freelance commercials, an industrial or educational film or, if you were lucky, you got on the crew of one of Chuck Jones,'s, Bill Melendez's, or Leo Salkin's TV specials.

When MGM management realized the mistake they made in getting rid of Hanna and Barbera, they approached Tex Avery once more. They asked him if he would head a new unit to bring the classic MGM characters to television for them: Tom and Jerry, Wolfy and the Girl, Chilly Willy, and Droopy. Of course this would all have to be done in the new stylized, low-budget animation system. Tex Avery refused. "I loved those characters too much to do that to them," he explained.[22] Chuck Jones agreed to do a new series of Tom and Jerry cartoons through his studio.

In addition to the regular series, the 1960s was also the age of great television half-hour specials. Usually they came at the holiday season, and viewing them became an annual tradition for many families. This meant they could deliver a guaranteed audience share for advertisers. In 1956 UPA veteran John Wilson directed an animated version of Igor Stravinsky's *Petrushka* with Stravinsky himself conducting. In 1962, Abe Levitow at UPA pioneered the format of a one-hour TV special with *Mr. Magoo's Christmas Carol.* Former SCG president and Clampett animator Bill Melendez brought to life the famous *Peanuts* characters of Charles Schulz in a series of TV specials starting with *A Charlie Brown Christmas* (1965). *A Charlie Brown Christmas* has run every year without fail for some forty years. Chuck Jones, now with his own company, followed with *The Grinch Who Stole Christmas* (1966). He went on to create a series of successful TV specials for CBS, including *Rikki Tikki Tavi, A Cricket in Times Square, Carnival of the Animals,* and *The White Seal.* One Chuck Jones assistant described what he felt he knew was a secret of Jones's new success in the TV-special market: When he was a young director in the 1940s Jones would befriend and play golf with many young Warner Bros. minor executives. As he moved on, the men all became senior programming managers at the television networks. Jones would only have to call up an old friend to get a meeting to pitch a half-hour of prime time. Stop-motion animators Rankin and Bass created classics with *Rudolph the Red-Nosed Reindeer* (1964) and *Frosty the Snowman* (1969). Like *Grinch* and *Charlie Brown,* both run every year, and woe to the program scheduled at the same time!

The refreshing iconoclasm of Jay Ward's TV shows *Rocky & Bullwinkle* and *George of the Jungle* had faded by the 1970s. Ward felt hemmed in by network restrictions forcing his sophisticated satire into kiddie fare. He fought network standards and practices, he fought ad agencies. The federal government once came to the studio and confiscated the 1964 Dudley Do-Right parody of the Interior Department's character Smokey the Bear, called Stokey the Bear, a pyromaniac. Storyman Al Kilgore explained: "This was before Watergate when you didn't know you could seriously fight the federal government. These guys in dark suits just showed up and confiscated the film can!" Later, when doing the Quisp and Quake cereal campaigns, Ward had to answer charges from Madison Ave ad agencies that the character Quake could be perceived as gay. The reason given was that he was a handsome, clean-shaven coal miner with blonde hair and metal wristbands. Ergo . . . Kilgore recalled telling the clients: "You call Ward and tell him that! I'm not going to bother him with something so stupid!" They finally found an executive underling willing to make the call. Al said he never found out what Jay said to the exec in response, but it was so nasty, the man threw the phone away as though it had suddenly grown red hot. Jay ended the "Rocky & Bullwinkle" comic strip with Boris and Natasha being shot in a Potsylvanian concentration camp while trying to escape dressed as Mary Poppins and a child flying off the water tank. The stress took a toll on Ward's health, and in the 1970s he scaled back his activities to restoring silent films. In 1985 after the deaths of Ward and Bill Scott, Jay Ward Productions ceased making animated films. The big statue of Rocky and Bullwinkle on the Sunset Strip was allowed to deteriorate until neighborhood preservationists restored it.

Theatrical feature films continued to struggle. After the master's death Disney played to its dependable family audience, and the animation unit seemed to move ahead on autopilot, pumping out—*Aristocats* (1970), *Robin Hood* (1973), *The Rescuers* (1977), and *Pete's Dragon* (1977), among others. For other studios a profitable release for a feature film was a long throw of the dice, to say the least. The Briton George Dunning's film *The Yellow Submarine* (1968), featuring the music of the Beatles, made 1960s pop art and psychedelic design a critical success and influenced commercial spots for years, but it made few inroads at the box office. *The Yellow Submarine* actually sparked a riot in Singapore: teens attacked the stage when they saw the film was not the real Beatles but a cartoon. Other efforts at the time like *The Man Called Flintstone* (1966); *Shinbone Alley* (1971), cowritten by Mel Brooks; *Charlotte's Web* (1973); and *Heidi's Song* (1982) didn't generate enough audience to impress the moneymen. The surprise film of the 1970s was from Italy. Bruno Bozzetto's *Allegro non troppo* was a wildly imaginative spoof of Disney's *Fantasia*.[23] Despite its popularity in colleges and revival houses, it also failed make the box office needed to attract the U.S. money guys, although the film did do well enough in Europe that Bozzetto's studio was deluged with commercial work. All the extra work in the studio prevented Bozzetto from getting back to do another feature or sequel to his hit.

In the 1970s the two big exceptions, with a hint of things to come, were the studios of Ralph Bakshi and Richard Williams. While most animators had settled into a workaday norm that eschewed art for speed, these two brash young artists kept much of the quality of technique alive. Twenty-nine-year-old Bakshi was made a director at CBS in 1969 and embraced the counterculture-rebel persona then en vogue. Producer Steve Krantz, the husband of romance novelist Judith Krantz, had gotten the rights to Robert Crumb's *Fritz the Cat*, then the most famous underground comic book in America. Bakshi and Krantz announced that *Fritz* would be the first animated cartoon to get an X rating from motion pictures' National Board of Review, the strongest warning for sex and violence. They saw the rating as increasing the public's interest, this being the age of the sexual revolution. Film intelligentsia, wanting to be hip, were flocking to porn films like *Deep Throat* and *Behind the Green Door.*[24] So while Disney was releasing the hopelessly outdated kiddie comedy *The Aristocats,* the X-rated *Fritz* was just right for the times. When escorting potential distributors around his studio, Ralph instructed his artists to leave out on the tables the most sexually explicit artwork.

Production on *Fritz the Cat* was started in New York then moved to Hollywood for completion. Ralph remained so homesick for the streets of Gotham that he had a giant photostat of Manhattan pasted inside his Sunset Boulevard office windows so he didn't have to look at the Hollywood skyline. The Bakshi studio in Los Angeles was at Sunset Boulevard and Ivar Avenue near a Hollywood talent agency. The glass walls of the studio looked onto the rooftop of the agency. For some reason people never realize that when looking at a glass office building from the outside there are hundreds of people looking back out at you, hidden by the mirrored glass. Often whenever the talent agent was boinking some would-be starlet in his rooftop hot tub, dozens of Bakshi animators would be pressed to the glass watching and cheering.

Fritz the Cat and *Heavy Traffic,* Bakshi's follow-up autobiographical film, did very well at the box office. Critics hailed him as the bad boy of animation. In 1971, *Fritz* was the first animated feature film screened at the Cannes Film Festival, and Ralph appeared on the cover of *Newsweek.* Cartoonist-creator Robert Crumb was bitter about the final result; he felt that Fritz had become too Hollywood. In his next comic book he killed Fritz by having a bird-girlfriend stab him in the head with an ice pick. Next to the body the caption read "Violence in the Media."

Drawing the Line

Steve Krantz tried to follow up with a sequel called *Nine Lives of Fritz the Cat*. But by then he and Ralph had gone their separate ways. Krantz instead used another veteran Hollywood animation director, Bob Taylor. *Nine Lives* suffered greatly for the lack of the Bakshi touch. It failed at the box office.

Ralph Bakshi wanted the best animators to work for him, like MGM great Irv Spence and Famous Studios' Marty Taras. But he ran into difficulty because of the diminishing pool of retiring golden-age artists. Also, his abrasive personality and bullish business practices offended many. Some old-timers labeled him a "vulgarian." So Ralph was forced to look far afield of the normal pool of artists. He broke glass ceilings by aggressively hiring young artists including women and minorities. Among the were Louis Scarborough, Lenord Robinson, and Brenda Banks, the fi African American woman animator. Ralph hired animation prodigy A Vitello, who was so young that when he tried to enter a local theater to see *Fritz* he was turned away for being underage. He mingled these newcomers with older vets like Irv Spence, Marty Taras, Jim Logan, and Walt Peregoy. It was said that working for Bakshi could be an emotional roller coaster. The volatile director could fire you on Friday, and then call you at home on Monday to castigate you further for not coming in to work. Yet he always paid well. When most studios were paying animators $500 to $800 a week, Bakshi paid some of his animators up to $2,000 a week.[25] He almost always worked under a union contract and paid benefits.

African American designer Phil Mendez recalled Bakshi dragging him up to the most crime-ridden parts of Harlem in the dead of night to soak up local atmosphere. Mendez joked about how he had worked his way downtown through great effort; now he didn't want to return to his old neighborhood. In one dank, seedy bar on West 125th Street, Bakshi went up to a tough-looking black man and said, "Put 'er dere, my soul brudda!" The man looked at Bakshi, looked at his drink, spat in his drink, made Bakshi drink it, and then threw him into the street. Of course, instead of being upset, Bakshi was ecstatic, savoring the experience.[26]

After the successes of *Fritz* and *Traffic*, Bakshi stumbled in 1974 with *Coonskin*, his attempt to illustrate the experience of black urban violence. The film featured wild stereotypes like an Aunt Jemima who flipped pancakes at people. The film critic for the *Wall Street Journal* called it Bakshi's "most serious and mature work to date," but others, including the Council on Racial Equality (CORE), branded the film as racist. On November 12, 1974, when Ralph prescreened the film at the Museum of Modern Art (MOMA) in New York, CORE activists picketed and tried to disrupt the screening. It was the custom at MOMA for the filmmaker to stand on stage after a screening and intellectually defend his film. When Bakshi got up, the postscreening discussion quickly degenerated into a screaming match. Protesters wrestled Bakshi for the microphone, and for the first time in MOMA's history police were called to quell a disturbance. It's one of the regrets of my life that I skipped the screening to finish some freelance work. Barry Diller, the head of Paramount, was in that audience and was shocked by what happened. Distributor Paramount quickly distanced itself from the film.

Coonskin flopped dismally. Production was suspended on Bakshi's next urban film, *Hey Good Lookin'*, and his studio almost went under. His next films, *Wizards* and *The Lord of the Rings* (1977), focused on sword-and-sorcery fantasy, a genre that was less likely to be politically offensive. In the mid-1980s Bakshi returned to TV to revive the old Terrytoons character *Mighty Mouse*. On this show he gave opportunity and impetus to a new group of young artists—Lynne Naylor, Bob Camp, Chris Riccardi, and Jim Smith—led by an eccentric Canadian, John Kricfalusi. Dressed like a retro-escapee from the *Steve Allen Show* and perfecting Bakshi's penchant for the outrageous, Kricfalusi would inherit the mantle of bad boy and create his own hit series, *Ren & Stimpy*.

At the same time, an unusual commercial studio in London headed by Richard Williams was turning heads in the animation world. Canadian-born Williams had visited Disney in the 1950s and befriended master animators like Milt Kahl and Grim Natwick. He developed a consuming passion for high-quality personality animation when it was in steep decline. Moving back to London, he began producing breathtakingly beautiful commercials, even if they lost him money. He urged his artists at 13 Soho Square on to greater personal achievement whether the client appreciated it or not. Like the monks in Umberto Eco's novel *The Name of the Rose* who toiled thanklessly to preserve the wisdom of ancient civilizations for generations yet unborn, Dick Williams embarked on a program to preserve the skills of Hollywood animation's golden age. He began with a close collaboration with Chuck Jones in 1971 to produce the Oscar-winning short *A Christmas Carol*. In 1973, Williams all but closed down his studio and paid for experienced golden-age animators like Art Babbitt, Grim Natwick, and Warner's Ken Harris to train his young staff.

Many of these artists, including Richard Perdum, Jill Thomas, Oscar Grillo, Tony White, Ted Rockley, Russell Hall, and Eric Goldberg, would move on to form new studios and invigorate old ones. Like the children of the dragon's teeth, wherever you threw them, studios popped up. Williams's influence started a spirited competition between studios for high quality and craftsmanship, giving London dominance in the European commercial market. But Williams saw himself as an outpost of the mainstream film industry. The Williams influence reached back to Hollywood and helped bring about the Hollywood animation renaissance through films like the 1988 hit *Who Framed Roger Rabbit?*

Back in the golden age, training was mostly done on the job. In the 1930s, the Walt Disney Studio set up a drawing program under a demanding demagogue named George Drake to create inbetweeners for the clean-up department. The program was discontinued after the 1941 strike. In 1937, as the Fleischer strike raged, animator Eli Brucker conducted animation classes for the inbetweeners to improve their skills.[27] In the 1930s and 1940s, each new artistic breakthrough was disseminated informally. For instance, when Schlesinger's Looney Tunes crew came back from the black-tie premiere of Disney's *Snow White and the Seven Dwarfs*, Chuck Jones was inspired to strive toward more natural fluid movement with a gentle character called Sniffles.

In the early days of animation, artists shared little information outside their studio. Like the Kansas City trumpeters who were so worried about young Miles Davis that they gave him bad advice to keep him down, some animators didn't want to let out too many professional secrets. Early union president Grim Natwick studied life drawing at the Ecole des beaux-arts in Paris in the 1920s. When he returned to animate in the United States, the results of that experience were apparent. He was the first animator to turn characters in a 3D manner. Whereas other animators would change direction of a running character by letting it run off screen, then flop the drawings and run him back in the other way,

Natwick could turn the character around in the frame. He also was the first to master the subtleties of the female form.

In the mid-1930s, animator Art Babbitt began to hold informal life-drawing classes in his home. Artists passed the hat to pay to hire models. Walt Disney heard about it and decided to move the sessions into the studio and make them official. Walt was worried that newspapers might get word that his artists had naked women posing in their houses. In those days in many cities an artist was ordered by law to post a sign on his front door that read A.I.R.—Artist in Residence. That sign warned decent neighbors that there was a fellow inside with naked women models and bongo playing and all such goings on. So in 1935, Disney brought art instructor Don Graham into the studio to teach his artists the finer points of draftsmanship. The program quickly expanded, and the overall quality of the studio's work grew by leaps and bounds. It was the secret to Disney's studio outdoing every other studio in the world in terms of quality. The program was interrupted, however, by the strike, World War II, and the tough postwar period.

The Disney instruction courses continued at the Chouinard Art Institute near Westlake Park, renamed MacArthur Park for the World War II general. Chouinard was founded in 1921 by Nelbert Chouinard and boasted luminary artists such as Edward Ruscha and David Siquieros. It provided the animation business with many of its great animation instructors; it offered classes by Disney legends like Don Graham and Marc Davis, along with radical, iconoclastic young artists like Bob Kurtz, who said, "If there is a Heaven I want there to be a Chouinard there."[28]

The first true film school was set up in 1929 at the University of Southern California. Silent-movie stars Mary Pickford and Douglas Fairbanks funded it. Eugene Coe was one of the mainstays in the development of the animation course, and Art Babbitt was a frequent lecturer. In the mid-1940s, Bill Tytla's assistant at Disney and a Disney striker, William Schull, started an animation course at UCLA that became the UCLA Animation Workshop. Schull, like many animation artists of that time, was steeped in what came to be called the UPA revolution. Many wanted to explore new ways of storytelling and new styles beyond realism—neo-expressionism and abstracts.

In 1969, the Disney Company paid for creation of a new institution by blending the Chouinard Institute with the Los Angeles Conservatory of Music and calling it the California Institute of the Arts, or simply Cal-Arts. Chouinard students were lodged in the Villa Cabrini School while awaiting the completion of the Valencia campus. One legend says that CalArts was on the site of the onion field where famous Disney song composer Frank Churchill shot himself in 1942 after being let go. Called by many the foyer of Disney, CalArts quickly earned a national reputation in the world of advanced musical composition. Beyond the Character Animation Department, old UPA designer and union activist Jules Engel branched off into a separate program first called Film Graphics, then Experimental Animation. This program enabled students to explore the aesthetic, nontraditional aspects of animation. Jules's program produced many great abstract artists like Sara Petty, Christine Panushka, and Vibeke Sorenson. The Experimental Animation program did a lot to change the perception of CalArts as being no more than a vocational training school for Disney cartoonists.

By the 1970s, the veterans of the Walt Disney Studio noticed something new: they were getting old. Some wanted to retire. Others, like John Hench and Marc Davis, wanted to explore challenges in fields other than animation, such as theme-park design. Who would carry on all the innovations developed at Disney? Would they all disappear in one generation? Shamus Culhane, in New York, rhetorically asked, "Twenty years from now, whom will you hire?"[29] The days of Walt driving artists to drawing class in his jalopy and the old inbetweening school of George Drake were long gone. So in 1972, the studio put top animator and ex–SCG president Eric Larson at the head of an internal training program. The twenty-one trainees hired by 1975 read like a who's who of contemporary animation greats: John Musker, Andy Gaskill, Dan Haskett, Mike McKinney, Ron Clements, Brad Bird, Ron Husband, Glen Keane, Mark Henn, Randy Cartwright, Michael Cedeno, Heidi Guedel, Phil Young, Randy Cook, Hendel Butoy, Phil Nibbelink, Chuck Harvey, John Lasseter, Dave Spafford, Linda Miller, Lorna Pomeroy-Cook, Diann Landau, and others.

At Warner Bros., art director Maurice Noble took many young artists under his wing. They were nicknamed the Noble Boys and included future director Rob Minkoff, Don Hall, Harry Sabin, and Kelly Asbury. Hanna-Barbera created a training program under veteran artist Harry Love. When I worked at Hanna-Barbera, an open secret was "Benny's class." Every Tuesday night after work, veteran animator and old union president Ben Washam taught a class in his garage to any budding animators who bothered to show up. I ASKED him why he didn't charge for such sophisticated training. He replied in his modest way that animation had been very good to him, and this was his way of paying animation back. So he sat with a toothpick in his mouth and taught classic Warner Bros. animation to us wide-eyed novices. Washam had been planning a book on his animation technique when he died in 1985.

Because the skills of an animator can be intuitive, many gifted artists have difficulty putting into words what they are doing. Milt Kahl was one of these. Disney occasionally asked top artists to present to the department a chalk talk about some new technique. Kahl, asked to make such a presentation one day, stood in front of the class and stammered and grunted a while; finally he said: "Aw, just fucking *draw!*"[30]

Outside Hollywood, animation schools were few before 1990. In New York the Cartoonists and Illustrators School started by newspaper editorial cartoonist Bill Gallo became the School of Visual Arts in 1960. Shamus Culhane started its animation program and was followed by industry professionals like Gil Miret, Howard Beckerman, Marty Abrahams, and Don Duga. Industrial Arts, from which Ralph Bakshi graduated, became the New York High School of Art and Design in 1949. Although it did not have an official animation program, New York's Pratt College produced notable animation figures like Eric Goldberg and David Silverman. Sheridan College in Ontario, Canada, was started in 1969 by Jack Porter and William Firth. Bill Martsegis, Bill Matthews, Kaij Pindal, and old unionist Zack Schwartz developed the animation program. Sheridan produced excellent animators like Chuck Gamage, Dave Brewster, Wendy Perdue, Robin Budd, Charlie Bonifacio, and John Kricfalusi. These were the main incubators for the animation business until the 2D renaissance of the 1990s sparked a boom in animation courses in universities across the United States and Canada. One of the difficulties of making the young comprehend their place in the animation business is the failure of animation instructors to adequately explain to their charges the realities of the market. The lingering disillusionment over the idealism destroyed by the HUAC blacklist and the collusion of some mainstream unions may have affected many pros when it came to telling their students about the cold, cruel business world outside. It was easier to focus on technique and the quest for self-expression and never mind the realities of the market. As the old, leftist pros retired, their place was taken by teachers who had begun their careers as independent filmmakers, moving sand, scratching on film, or other nontraditional, award-winning, abstract personal styles. Because these teachers' experience was with the film-festival and foundation-grant world rather than the big studios, their experience of trade unionism was limited. So when students asked about the commercial business, many instructors preached about uncompromising quality and the freedom to create. The idea was that if you were very good, CEOs would drop to their knees and shower you with money. Even when the violent political upheaval of the 1960s convulsed most U.S. campuses, for artists the emphasis remained on self-improvement rather than collective social action. Icons of political art like Diego Rivera were replaced by inward-looking artists like Andy Warhol and Mark Rothko. All unions except for Cesar Chavez's United Farm Workers were lumped together as big establishment fat cats. In the 1960s, several attempts to unionize the booming world of New York comic-book artists were defeated. This was achieved mostly through the appeal to the counterculture, the "I am an arteest and need no one" argument. So Spiderman, Superman, and Vampirella were safe from Dr. Doom and safe from guaranteed wage minimums and health benefits.

In 1971, Walt Disney Productions brought a plagiarism lawsuit against a group of wild-eyed hippie cartoonists called the Air Pirates for copyright infringement. They included *Dirty Duck* creator Bobby London and *Ods Bodkins* artists Dan O'Neill, Shary Flanniken, Gary Halgren, and Ted Richards. The Disney Company accused the Air Pirates of selling two underground comic books using their characters Mickey, Donald, and Goofy in various racy scenes: shooting up drugs, having sex, and so on. The Air Pirates argued that the Disney characters had become public icons and as such could be subject to parody. The Disney lawyers contended that it was just simple plagiarism. If they had called the figures Mickey Moose or Mickey Moth, perhaps the Air Pirates would have had a case, but it was in print as Mickey Mouse. The Air Pirates tried to fund their legal defense by passing the hat at comic-book festivals: "Our Toes Are Being Stepped on by a 100-Ton Mouse!" But they didn't raise much beyond a few doobies and a roller-skate key. Dan O'Neill also had fun marketing belt buckles and T-shirts with the logo MLF: the Mouse Liberation Front. The Walt Disney corporation won its case on September 5, 1978, although the remaining Pirates claim it was an out-of-court settlement between the judge and lawyers.[31] What is unique is that for the first time no thought was given to any collective or united response. There were no appeals to any union to arbitrate. Such a course of action was not even considered.

Students were not taught that the reason Hollywood salaries were high and conditions were good was that artists and craftspeople had presented a united front of mutual interest to the mighty. While many skilled film workers like directors and actors understand the need to stick together, today's animators for some reason think they are all unique and on their own. It is a surprise to many to hear that famous Hollywood talents like Joan Crawford, Groucho Marx, Bela Lugosi, and James Cagney were staunch union supporters. A bio film done by filmmaker Alan Rudolph about writer Dorothy Parker (*Mrs. Parker and Her Dangerous Circle,* 1994) focused on her alcohol abuse and troubled love life rather than her union activism and progressive politics. There's no mention of her support for the Walt Disney strikers. Even today in most union-hating animation studios, it is not uncommon for the lead directors to have DGA cards and the writers WGA cards, and all the sound crew and editors are union.

In the 1950s, 1960s, and 1970s, American labor unions also underwent a transition. In the mid-1950s, American labor union membership peaked at 54 percent. The small locals of miners and teamsters riding on the running boards of trucks waving ax handles became huge national organizations with offices in Washington, D.C. In becoming huge, though, much was lost. Big establishment power brokers replaced the grassroots organizing of impoverished minorities and immigrants. Once Walter Reuther of the autoworkers union sponsored Martin Luther King Jr.'s Poor People's March on Washington and King was in Memphis to help striking garbagemen when he was shot. But by 1968 unions seemed out of touch with the public, who saw George Meany and Jimmy Hoffa, big national power brokers with shadowy mob ties, talking tough to Vice President Richard Nixon and President John F. Kennedy. In their well-pressed suits and pinky rings, they were indistinguishable from the corporate leaders they claimed to oppose. Unlike their grandfathers, the unionists of the 1960s didn't want to make common cause with the youth peace movement, progressives, beats, or hippies. Immigrants, the original foot soldiers of the radical unions of the 1890s, were frozen out by seniority bylaws and resumed their old role as unorganized strikebreakers. For the leaders of Big Labor, clout was wielded in boardrooms, not in the streets with folk guitars. After the blacklist and the Taft-Hartley Act, national unions went overboard in loudly pronouncing their devotion to conservative American ideals, patriotism, God, and apple pie. Union strategies were no longer about progressive issues but local issues: adding a few more pennies to the health-and-welfare fund, getting an extra coffee break.

The huge postwar baby-boom generation entering the job market seemed to be left cold by the whole union image. Union members were the dumpy hardhat guys who beat up antiwar protesters. Union leaders enforced seniority rules to keep out young people—except their own children. Many unions were slow to desegregate. To the new generation it seemed too pro establishment to support a labor union.

In Hollywood animation, the two rival unions, MPSC Local 839 (with 1,100 active members in 1970) and the SCG Local 852 (300 active members in 1970), continued to make steady gains in wages and benefits. Through negotiations, they won coffee breaks for the artists: a fifteen-minute period at 10:00 A.M. and another at 3:00 P.M. MPSC Local 841, New York went to a thirty-five-hour workweek, and fifteen additional minutes' free time was allowed on Fridays to do banking. A seniority roster saw to it that the pool of new jobs was funneled first to union members.

The ancillary world of live-action storyboard artists was represented by IATSE Local 790. To answer the needs of the growing advertising field in the Midwest, in 1960 IATSE chartered its third MPSC, Local 732, Chicago. This local focused on the small local commercial market and rarely compared notes with its sisters on the coasts, so much so that it's difficult today to find a unionist who recalls the local. MPSC Local 841, New York began representing many cameramen and technicians who operated the machines needed for the burgeoning art of visual effects. Products need sparkles, spaceships need lights and rocket fire, lasers need beams; all these then were optical effects. In Los Angeles, Oxberry or large animation rostrum camera operators and optical cameramen were represented by Local 659, Camera—today Local 600.

By the late 1960s, New York optical cameramen became a significant voice in the direction of the local, causing some animators to feel slighted. In 1968, after losing an election, longtime Local 841 business agent Pepe Ruiz resigned, to be replaced by Al Shapiro. By the 1970s, the optical camera people elected optical cameraman Dick Rauh as president of Local 841, and in 1975 optical camera assistant Gerald Salvio became business agent. The boom in special effects opticals after the film *Star Wars* saw the influence of animators in New York local affairs dwindle further. Local 16, San Francisco, a mixed-craft local (meaning one that represented numerous job classifications), led by Ed Powell, strove to represent animation in the Bay Area, including George Lucas's growing effects house, Industrial Light & Magic.

One of the more unusual characters in the story of animation unions was Larry Kilty.[32] A compact, black-haired former Disney assistant, Kilty had a long and checkered history. He liked to dress in snappy suits and lunch at the ritzy Smoke House. All who knew him remarked on his easygoing charisma. He was one of the first to lobby animators to forsake the CSU guild in favor of the IATSE. But on August 23, 1953, in the first year of MPSC's existence, he was expelled from the union for unspecified reasons. He drifted back into the SCG and by 1958 was its business agent. He was forced out when it was revealed that he was using his position as business agent to try to maneuver the SCG back into the IATSE and unification with the MPSC. Guild leaders learned that Kilty secretly attended an MPSC executive board meeting on May 2, 1958. It was said that at the meeting the SCG business agent derided the guild leadership and announced he would shortly be bringing the SCG into the IATSE. That was preparatory to his declaring himself a candidate for the job of retiring Local 839 business agent Dave Hilary. This was not just for the sake of unity. At the time anyone could see the major film studios were in trouble, and the SCG had contracts with many of the small but aggressive television units like that headed by Jay Ward. SCG business agent Kilty was brought up on charges by former president Bill Littlejohn on June 16, but Kilty's term had expired. He left before the charges could be brought to trial.

Drawing the Line

Without pausing a beat, Kilty reentered the MPSC Local 839 in time to win the business agent job. Many artists maintained double cards in the locals, but Kilty was the only person other than Pepe Ruiz to be a business agent in both rival unions. By the mid-1960s, many in 839's union management felt Kilty was abusing his position, but nothing could be proven. He was very good at manipulating the technical details of union management and Robert's Rules of Order. At one particularly contentious executive board meeting in the summer of 1965, Kilty ended discussion of some impropriety by announcing the lack of a quorum and walking out. Disney animator and local president Charlie Downs threw up his hands and resigned in disgust. Willie Ito, vice president, ran the local until the hotheaded Downs could be convinced to return to his office.[33]

For over a decade, Kilty pursued an idea he called the Animation Basic: that MPSC Local 839 would regroup and combine with the SCG as a new unit under the IATSE. The combined organization would also have jurisdiction over animation camera and editing that was then represented by other locals. The Motion Picture and Television Fund would create a separate section just for animation workers. And this superlocal would be under his guidance. Was Kilty motivated by a desire to heal the destructive rift between the animation unions? Or did he seek to be a big man in town like Bioff, Sorrell, and Brewer once were? We'll never know. The SCG remained hostile, and the camera and editing unions did not see the value of losing dues-paying members from their own ranks. So the idea remained just that, an idea.

Most film workers got straight salary whether a film flopped or became a phenomenon. Studios could exploit a film for years in rereleases and TV sales, and nobody made money but the execs. In the 1940s, some major Hollywood actors like James Cagney and Bette Davis formed their own production companies to negotiate a more equitable share of a film's profits. In 1953, James Stewart won the first backend percentage deal—a deal that would give him a share of the final profits—to star in the movie *Winchester 73*. Lew Wasserman, agent head of MCA productions and a mentor of a kid named Steven Spielberg, brokered the deal. In 1960, after several high-profile strikes, the Screen Actor's Guild under president Ronald Reagan won profit residuals for its members. The writers and directors guilds soon won their own slices of the pie. By 1969, young activists in the MPSC also wanted to make their claim for film profits. If writers, actors, directors, and even extras could get residuals for their toil, why couldn't animators? Didn't the cartoons they drew ten or twenty years ago still make money for studios like they were brand-new? They also wanted a tough anti-runaway clause to ensure that their work would not be sent out of town. They also demanded a solution to the seasonal nature of television work that left half the membership unemployed for four months a year.

Everyone seemed up for a strike in 1969.[34] Local 839 president Lou Appet and executive board member Corny Cole had several meetings with SCG leaders Bill Hurtz and Bill Littlejohn to see if they could form a united front to win residuals. The guild leaders were polite but unresponsive. Corny said that only later did he understand the deep mistrust these men still felt toward the IATSE.[35] Richard Walsh and Roy Brewer, who led the IATSE during the blacklist era, were still in power. The SCG members considered MPSC business agent Larry Kilty an opportunistic turncoat. No matter how enlightened the new activists of Local 839 seemed to be, old memories of the SCG were still fresh.

Animation producers defeated the 1969 residuals drive through skillful manipulation of the old animosity between animators, painters, and cameramen. Some at the time felt that Larry Kilty had been bribed to defeat the demand for residuals. Because of the large numbers of ink-and-paint artists needed on a film, they constituted more than half of the total number of the voting membership. Because old chauvinistic glass ceilings barred women from being animators or directors, most of the ink-and-paint crews were women; some were single mothers. Larry Kilty saw the residuals debacle as an intolerable distraction from his master plan for the Animation Basic local. He and his confederates spent many evenings having informal dinners with painters. They argued convincingly that there was no need to risk their steady employment to strike so that male animators could make even more money. The MPSC leaders, who were mostly animators, had heard about the meetings but were powerless to stop them. Animator Mark Kausler recalled, "Bill Hanna knew of this and aided the Kilty's efforts by selectively laying off some ink-and-paint girls for two weeks, then calling them back for a week, then laying them off for a week again. These women losing work became demoralized and anxious for their incomes."

The suspicion between the job categories quickly broke into full flower. At the next general membership meeting, many of the inkers and painters announced that they would not support any move to strike for residuals. The animators and cleanup artists would remember this feud. When the Runaway Wars broke out in 1979 (see chapter 9), some of them saw the issue as solely the problem of inkers and painters because at that time most of the work going out of town was ink and paint. So they withheld their support for the union's struggle. The defeated strike caused heavy loss of ink-and-paint jobs to overseas, but they also caused animation and cleanup jobs to leave town.

As 1969 moved into 1970, the negotiations between Local 839 and the producers seemed to have reached a stalemate. Then old IATSE international president Richard Walsh visited the contract negotiations.[36] The studios and Walsh must have realized that if a relatively small IATSE local like the animators could win residuals, then the larger mainstream union locals like editors, cameramen, and even grips and projectionists, might demand residuals as well. Many IATSE contracts with smaller businesses had me-too clauses in their basic contracts that would drag their profits into the residual pool along with those of the major studios. It seemed to the owners a stampede to ruin would occur. When Walsh sat down at the table on the union side, the Local 839 militants hoped a big gun like him would help turn the tide in their favor. Larry Kilty still had hopes for his Animation Basic scheme.

To their chagrin, the old gentleman only mouthed some vague platitudes about how Lucky Lindy Lindbergh was also told things were impossible yet he persevered. Then Walsh, with Kilty, broke the deadlock and quickly closed a deal with the producers. The final results were far below everyone's expectations: no residuals, no basic or animation superlocal, or no runaway clause, just a few increases in minimum pay. When MPSC members were told about the results, they cried collusion and rejected the contract offer on August 7. One rash member was quoted in the press accusing Walsh of "whip-cracking."[37] Local 839 president Lou Appet recommended a strike vote, but it was defeated. Walsh agreed to go back and negotiate further. But he threatened disciplinary actions

WHOSE S.O.B.?*

Gag drawing protesting the television hiring season, printed in the MPSC 839 newsletter, 1970, business agent Larry Kilty on the right. Television animation studios hired and fired based on the seasonal needs of the major TV networks. An animator could look forward to spending October to March on unemployment. Courtesy of Archives of the Animation Guild, Local 839, IATSE (formerly MPSC Local 839), North Hollywood, and Mark Kausler.

against the MPSC—for example, seizing the general fund and pension funds—if the union continued to be uppity. Another mild contract was quickly negotiated with some more token bump-ups in salary rates. But the issue of residuals never was brought up again.

By now "Guilty Kilty" was so unpopular that the defeat of the residuals drive was the last straw. After being business agent for more than a decade, he sized up the mood and wisely decided not to run for another term. When a new Local 839 administration, led by president Harry "Bud" Hester and business agent Lou Appet, looked into the local's books, they were shocked by what they saw.[38] Kilty had padded his expenses, paid an unauthorized retirement bonus to his outgoing assistant, Lona Ipsen, and awarded himself additional severance pay on leaving office. Executive board member Anne Guenther recalled that many blamed Kilty for the disappearance of money collected for a charity art sale. The MPSC Executive Board held a special trial on May 10, 1972, and formally expelled Kilty for misappropriation of union funds. Kilty denounced the board as a kangaroo court and charged bigotry, comparing his own plight with the Norman Lear sitcom *All in the Family:* "Prejudice is in vogue with sitcoms now. . . . Maybe we should call this All in the Union!"[39] This is a strange charge since everyone involved was of Caucasian European ancestry. Kilty then filed his own charges with the IATSE and the NLRB against board members Charlie Downs, Hester, Guenther, Lou Kearns, and Appet. Both cases were thrown out, and the IATSE endorsed the executive board's judgment against Kilty. The NLRB explained that a business agent is an elected official who understood his time in office was limited, so the concept of severance pay was not applicable.[40] Rejected and defeated on all sides, Kilty finally left town. He moved north to Monterey, California, and worked for a commercial studio called Aptos with fellow ex-Disneyite Bob Carlson. Friends there said he remained bitter about what happened. The board members remained equally angry at him. Kilty died in 2002.

The best chance in a generation to win residuals was gone. For the next twenty years whenever a contract needed to be negotiated, the MPSC would list the residuals demand in its bullet points but with no results. In 1979, when the entire animation community went out on strike, former union president Ben Washam told me it was already too late. "We had our chance in 1969, we had the entire business in town," he

Lost Generations

Lou Appet, Local 839 business agent, drawing by Dave Tendlar. Appet was an early union activist at Fleischer and after coming west was Local 839's business agent in the 1970s. Courtesy of the Tendlar family

said. "The studios could do nothing because we had all the cards. But we didn't stick together. We blew it."[41]

In 1970, the Screen Cartoonists Guild Local 852, surprised the rest of the animation community by announcing that it was affiliating under the national Teamsters Union as Local 986. The downtown mixed-crafts local under the Teamsters was nicknamed Anderson's Raiders, after their business agent, Andy Anderson. After years of going it alone the SCG members feared their members' clamor for reconciliation with the IATSE, in part because of the IATSE's superior health insurance. So affiliating with the Teamsters was their solution. SCG members voted five to one to amalgamate. MPSC artists nicknamed them the truck-driving cartoonists. The Teamsters were happy to add another local under their umbrella, but they really couldn't offer much beyond low-cost car insurance. As the few remaining SCG contract employers—UPA, Jay Ward—slipped under the waves, the SCG quietly died also. Bill Melendez Productions was the last SCG contract house. In 1979, guild secretary Jim Carmichael donated most of the guild's important papers to the library at California State University, Northridge. In the next decade, when new animation studios tried to work outside the MPSC Local 839 contract, among their key personnel could be found some old SCG members. They still could not stomach coming into the IATSE.

The Hollywood animation community survived strikes, the blacklist, the breakup of the major studio system, and the transition from theatrical shorts to television production. A new generation was rising to fill the ranks of the retiring golden-age artists. While the old masters had taught their young charges all they knew about fluid movement, acting on paper, comedy, and cinema, they left out or ignored questions about unions and their value. Maybe they were burned out on it all, disillusioned, or angry. With the guild just about gone, many former SCG animators still could not find it within themselves to make peace with the IATSE local, and vice versa. Whatever the reasons, the result was that the younger artists grew up not knowing the role unions had played in creating the best lifestyle for animation cartoonists in the world. They thought their benefits and wage scales were a natural occurrence that would always be around, like leaves turning colors in autumn. No matter how little they cared to participate in union affairs, no one was concerned. The party would go on forever.

This delusion would bear bitter fruit in 1979 and 1982.

9

Animation and the Global Market

The Runaway Wars, 1979–1982

I get my shows painted in China for $16 a week.
When you get it that cheap, call me.
　　　　　　　　—Bill Hanna in response to a salesman
　　　　　　　　hawking a digital paint system

There was no decree that Hollywood, a small town of orange growers situated on the western edge of the Great American Desert, would come to dominate the world's media. The social, political, and creative reasons for that evolution are too large a subject to be explored here. Suffice it to say that the cataclysm of World War I, the subsequent global depression, and America's emergence as the world's economic superpower caused a physical as well as aesthetic weakening of many competing film communities. Backed by America's corporate muscle, Hollywood's film output soon overwhelmed all competitors. Hollywood's message of pleasure and escapism became the world's preferred distraction. Hollywood's image of what it was to be American—carefully crafted by immigrants—became America's accepted image at home and abroad. One English writer warned in 1921, "The world is in danger of becoming Americanized, through the import of their photoplays."[1]

Cartoonists around the world began experimenting with animated cartoons at about the same time as J. Stuart Blackton and Winsor McCay: Emile Cohl in France, Walter Booth in England, Victor Bergdahl

Gag cartoon by Floyd Norman of Bill Hanna and Darth Vader, teasing Hanna-Barbera's attempts to send more production out of town. Courtesy of the artist.

in Sweden, Ladislas Starevitch in Russia. Disney fans may be surprised to learn that *Snow White and the Seven Dwarfs* was not the first animated feature. German Lotte Reiniger created *The Adventures of Prince Achmed* almost a decade before (1926), and there was an Argentine feature called *El apostol* by Quirino Cristiani as early as 1917. While most studios in St. Petersburg or Paris remained the exclusive ateliers of a few artists, American animation embraced J. R. Bray's industrial mass-production model. With ties first to major press and publishing empires like William Randolph Hearst, then to huge movie studios, American animation gained predominance in the world alongside live action. The ongoing serial nature of the American comic strip combined with the burgeoning Hollywood star system to enable Felix the Cat, Koko the Clown, and later Mickey Mouse to become international stars. Through the universal language of mime they became as important a Hollywood

Animation and the Global Market

export as the flesh-and-blood stars like Charlie Chaplin and Mary Pickford. In the 1930s, Walt Disney's shift in creative emphasis from graphic experimentation to the development of more lifelike performances pushed America's theatrical cartoons to set a high standard, outdistancing all international efforts.

Abroad, small regional studios, some relying on state funding, some on advertising revenue, simply couldn't compete with the juggernaut of the American economy. During World War II, the Nazi regime tried to prove it could produce films as good as American ones. After all, wasn't "Snow White" a folk tale of German origin? Why let the decadent, *untermenschen* democracies interpret their story to good Aryan children? Reich Minister of Propaganda Joseph Goebbels tried to form a consortium of animation studios in occupied Europe to collaborate to create a cartoon to rival Herr Disney's efforts. Led by Dutch director Egbert Van Putten, artists from Prague, Amsterdam, and Paris produced *Reynard the Fox* (1943).[2] Hitler had disbanded all trade unions and suspended the eight-hour workday, so there was not much trouble about unions in his cartoon studios. The animators were given the choice of working on the film or being sent to a slave labor camp.

Cartoons animated in Vichy France portrayed an evil Donald Duck dropping American bombs on the homes of the innocent. Future Hubley animator Tissa David recalled animating in a small studio in Budapest while bombs rained down. "There were so many air raids interrupting my work, after a while I gave up going down to the shelter and took my chances remaining at my desk," she said.[3] In Japan, one of the first feature films, Momotaro's *God Blessed Sea Warriors* (1943), by Mituyo Seo, sowed seeds of the future style called anime. The film's climax showed the Japanese heroes, all anthropomorphized teddy bears and bunnies with samurai swords, accepting the surrender of a scraggly Popeye and Bluto. When he needed the sound of enemy voices, Seo recorded interviews with British prisoners of war, sprinkling their casual comments incongruously throughout the action sequences. Despite these efforts, the Axis cartoons just couldn't replace the output of the Hollywood cartoon. Italian dictator Benito Mussolini's children still cried for their Topolino—Mickey Mouse. Luftwaffe air ace Adolf Galland had Mickey Mouse painted on the side of his Messerschmidt ME109G fighter plane.[4]

For years Hollywood animation studios had pulled in talented artists from around the world, but no one saw the need to use animation produced in other countries. The animation of other nations was too culturally specific to appeal beyond their own borders or too experimental for the kind of mass audience Hollywood was after. Besides, the technology did not then exist to permit easy delivery and opportunity for revisions. The foreign shorts were good for international festivals and advertising local products, but they would not do for American audiences. But studios and their corporate sponsors wondered how they could utilize the low-paid artists and technicians beyond Hollywood. The appeal of low-budget, deregulated mainstream film production was given the blanket name "runaway production."

The controversy over runaway production was never about an individual nation's cinematic culture. No one in Hollywood complained when Sylvain Chomet's film *The Triplets of Belleville* (2003) or Hiyao Miyazaki's *Spirited Away* (2002) did well in U.S. theaters. It was never a case of xenophobia. Many of America's finest animation artists—Stuart Blackton, Max Fleischer, Jules Engel, and more—were immigrants. It was about American studios exporting American work for American markets to a lower-paid workforce abroad. In the 1950s, the difference in salaries couldn't offset huge shipping costs, logistical problems, customs duties, and communication issues. After the world wars, ravaged nations like Britain imposed heavy trade tariffs on film and the amount of money that could be taken out of the country. As America reached out to bolster the economies of the world, the American economy evolved into a world economy, and the world poured back in to do business.

In 1948, the Supreme Court's *Paramount* decision fatally wounded the short cartoon. This was when U.S. animation studios began to seriously study, among other options, how to use foreign labor to make an American product. When the outright mastery of classic Disney animation seemed too difficult, the simple designs and stylized movement pioneered by UPA greatly influenced artists in other countries. In many nations, animated film output was subsidized by the government. This was especially true of nations with socialist economies. Polish animator Jan Lenica said that the Communist government's basic budget for animation broke down to 50 percent for children's cartoons, 25 percent for educational and propaganda films, and 25 percent for short "prestige" or art films to represent the nation in international competitions. Other countries, and even other American states, tried to lure Hollywood business away with promises of tax breaks, low-paid workforces, and government subsidies.

Max Fleischer's attempt to relocate his entire studio to Miami could be called the first runaway production. Fleischer assured financier Paramount studio that the move would help bring down costs, but the opposite occurred As we saw in chapter 4, Max Fleischer had to import everything, get all film stock processed in New York, and offer the highest salaries in the industry to coax talent to Florida. Paramount pulled the plug on the Fleischer brothers, and they moved their studio back to New York City.[5]

In the late 1940s, Disney director Dave Hand moved to England and tried to get several theatrical projects going for a company called GBS under the J. Arthur Rank banner. In the 1950s, former Disney animator Claire Weeks opened an animation studio in India near the original ashram of Mahatma Gandhi. Neither studio lasted very long.

The first truly successful runaway production was *Rocky and His Friends*. When creator Jay Ward started, he had a motto, "Hire the best talent and you cannot fail."[6] After his first project, *Crusader Rabbit*, became the first great animated series for TV, Ward tried to sell another series about a moose and a squirrel that live in Frostbite Falls. The idea was conceived in 1950, but it took years of wrangling and negotiating to make a deal. In 1957, Ward teamed with former Screen Cartoonists Guild activist Bill Scott and an old college friend, Leonard Key. Key had left Shamus Culhane's studio in New York where he was vice president of sales and set up a company called Producers Associates of Television, or PAT.[7]

After completing the pilot episode, Ward and Scott went off to assemble the writing and voice team and left Len Key with the problem of how to make the costs of animation production palatable to sponsors like Lux Liquid and General Mills. In those days one sponsor paid for an entire program. Key had heard of a new idea being bandied about called runaway for below-the-line production. This concept divided Bray's animation assembly line into two divisions: the perceived creative areas such as direction, storyboarding, animation, and art direction—labeled "above the line"—and the more labor-intensive areas not perceived as creative tasks—assisting, inking, painting, backgrounds, checking, and camera—labeled "below the line."

Key decided he had a solution to low-cost animation production. He made a deal through PAT with the Tojo studio in Japan to produce the animation for *Rocky*.[8] Ward's health had collapsed at this crucial moment, and he had to convalesce for a month. He was on record as being against using out-of-town studios, but he was in no shape to argue, and since there was no money coming in, Bill Scott was away doing freelance work. Key and another PAT executive, Roger Carlin, then concluded a deal with General Mills. The cereal company wanted to challenge rival cereal maker Kellogg's, which was sponsoring Hanna-Barbera's very successful *Huckleberry Hound Show*. When Ward and Scott found out about the deal four months later, they were thunderstruck. PAT had pledged to General Mills that they could do half-hour, high-quality TV shows for $8,500 each. This was at a time when a thirty-second commercial cost on average around $9,000. Even with foreign labor it was impossible.

After they had signed the deal and traveled to Tokyo to examine the studio, another problem arose: Tojo studio didn't exist. It was just chalk marks on a vacant lot. The Japanese partners intended to use the startup money to build the studio. When Key and Carlin complained, the Japanese businessmen tried plying the PAT representatives with sake and geishas so they would overlook these middling details.[9] With the clock ticking, Key made a new deal with a studio named Val Mar to do Ward's animation in Mexico City. Mexican millionaire Gustavo Valdez promised to build a studio from scratch just to make the deal. Their actions have never been fully explained, but historian Keith Scott and others have hinted that Key and Carlin were partners in the Mexican studio they were contracting work from.[10]

Ward and Scott were never happy with the Mexico City animation. Scott explained, "Jay had a great respect for American animators, especially animators who really 'animate,' meaning those who understand it's more than just movement, it's acting and performance."[11] Ward may have wanted something like classic *Looney Tunes* movement or even the Hanna-Barbera style, which was being done by their old MGM crew. But Ward and Scott were handcuffed into this deal with PAT to outsource, and Mexico City was willing and able. Bill Hurtz, like Bill Scott an old union man, agreed that Ward was not happy with the situation and was stung by the poor level of the animation coming back. Characters' heads would pop on and off and slide around on the background like they were ice-skating. Feet were slipping on the background as though the character were walking on ice. It needed quite a number of American supervisors to travel south of the border and coordinate the production. When Ward had the chance to produce some Quaker Oats spots in Hollywood, he enjoyed it so much that he and Scott resolved to slowly pull everything back to Los Angeles. Ward vowed he would never get involved with runaway production again. (Actually, the simple animation became one of the charms of the series. It seemed to match the intent of the design and allow the soundtrack full rein.)

Val Mar studio re-formed and renamed itself Gamma Productions. The studio did work for the Total Television Animation Company, based on the East Coast, and did the *King Leonardo Show* and *Tennessee Tuxedo*. Val Mar closed in 1970—donating their leftover cameras and other equipment to the SCG in Los Angeles.

Despite Jay Ward's experiences, the strong dollar ensured that other Hollywood animation producers continued to experiment with doing production in other countries. In 1960, Al Brodax of King Features made a deal to do two hundred new Popeye cartoons, for which he contracted several studios including Larry Harmon, UPA, and Seymour Kneitel, who was running the remains of Paramount. Former Disney director Jack Kinney had some of the cartoons at his company, Kinney-Wolf, when Brodax yanked the work and sent it to be completed at a studio in Italy.[12] Former union activist Selby Kelly tried to create a studio in Mexico with her first husband, Roger Daley. In 1961, Former Terrytoons director Gene Deitch went to Prague, for producer William Snyder.[13] He was assured that if he did not like it, he could come back in ten days. Deitch married a Czech artist named Zdenka and stayed the rest of his long life. After Deitch completed his Oscar-winning short film, *Munro*, Snyder came up with an intriguing idea. MGM realized too late that it had made a mistake in killing the Tom & Jerry unit in 1957. Snyder sold MGM chief Joe Vogel on having Deitch do the Tom & Jerry cartoons in Prague. While theatrical shorts in Hollywood cost up to $40,000 to make, Deitch could do them in Prague for $4,000. Twelve shorts were done this way. The first, *Switchin' Kittens,* premiered in the United States on September 7, 1961. However, Vogel was ousted from MGM, and the new head preferred his cartoons done closer to home.

Japan developed a large cartoon industry after the war. Television and features called anime, tied to comic books and graphic novels called *manga,* were made in Japan solely for Japanese consumption. In 1960, Osamu Tezuka's Mushi studio released the feature film *Alakasam the Great* in the United States. It achieved some success, but his television series *Tetsuan Atomo* or *Astro Boy, Gigantor, Speed Racer, 8th Man,* and *Kimba the White Lion* did better. To the larger U.S. audience, these anime series were little more than curiosities. But they achieved a certain cult popularity. U.S. networks bought TV series from England *(Dodo the Kid from Outer Space),* Australia *(Cool McCool),* and Canada *(The Beatles,* done by CanaWest, a Vancouver subcontractor for Hanna-Barbera).[14] Canada also sent *Rocket Robin Hood,* coproduced with Al Guest by Shamus Culhane and Ralph Bakshi, but it also failed to find a mass audience.

By the mid-1960s, despite the desires of the most profit-hungry executive, doing TV production out of town just didn't seem to work. A 1964 article summed up the problems: "It was found that while production costs are somewhat lower than in the U.S., custom duties and the time-consuming red tape involved in doing business south of the border virtually wipe out these advantages, or any tax gain that might accrue from a venture in a foreign country."[15]

The Hanna- Barbera studio, which had revolutionized limited TV animation, managed to change all that. Hanna-Barbera was booming with new television production, employing most of a workforce left moribund by the collapse of the great theatrical short units. The TV production houses also used smaller subcontracting houses to freelance work that was in town: Hutten & Love, Ron Campbell, Peter Aries, Fred Calvert, Kubiak/West. Some were union-contract studios and some were not, but they paid market rates. By Hanna-Barbera's peak in 1978, the big studio was turning out ten thousand feet of film a week. Even with two thousand employees in its Los Angeles headquarters, three-quarters of the work had to be animated outside the studio. Small wonder *Time* magazine called Hanna-Barbera the "General Motors of cartoons."[16] People ran to and fro with scenes under their arms, there was the oily smell of .05mm animation cels and the constant whirring of pencil sharpeners and the flipping-crinkling sound of paper. Allison Leopold supervised her five hundred inkers and painters by zipping around on roller skates to get things done faster.[17] Many staffers picked up freelance work after hours from small houses that were subcontracting from Hanna-Barbera. I recall working so hard on my freelance assistant work that one day I fell on my bed and slept for twenty-four hours. My roommate thought I was dead.

With all those employees, every break time seemed to feature someone's birthday cake. The union had mandated two coffee breaks a day: one from 10:00 A.M. to 10:15 A.M. and the other from 3:00 P.M. to 3:15 P.M. If you felt a rush of inspiration and wanted to complete a drawing at 10:00, someone would slap down your pencil and say, "Take your break! Your union worked hard to win it."

Hanna-Barbera was the kind of studio that everyone worked in sooner or later. On a typical day, you could talk to Dave Tendlar, who animated for Fleischer on the first Popeye cartoon; Irv Spence, who drew classic Tom & Jerry's; and Hicks Lokey, who animated on Disney's *Fantasia* and *Dumbo*. Art Babbitt and Friz Freleng were there for a while. One day, animator Kevin Petrilak noticed famed animation director Tex Avery pulling into the parking lot. He asked, "Tex, what are you doing here?" Tex glibly replied, "Don't you know? This is where the elephants come to die!"[18] In 1980, suffering from lung cancer, Tex collapsed and died in the Hanna-Barbera parking lot.

By the late 1960s, Hanna and Barbera felt they had maxed out the Los Angeles talent pool and needed to go abroad for more production. In 1971, they created a studio in Sydney, Australia, to subcontract television production. The first Australian project was *The Funky Phantom* for ABC Television.[19] Zoran Janjic was the supervisor. U.S. animators were sent to train the Aussies in Hollywood-style TV animation production. Old MGM artist Barney Posner recalled how, in the early days, the Australians sawed and sanded wood right next to the uncovered animation cameras, the dust jamming the delicate gears and counters.[20]

Despite these early problems, Sydney soon came online and was producing animated footage to rival the quality of Hollywood cartoons. Hanna and Barbera then looked to Taipei, Spain, Mexico, and South Korea for low-cost artists. Nelson Shin set up subcontracting in Taiwan for DePatie-Freleng. When I was a young inbetweener in New York on the Richard Williams's film *Raggedy Ann & Andy* (1977), I met a young artist named James Wang. Jimmy had come from Taipei to learn the animation business. He left his wife and kids with family members in Ohio and lived in the YMCA in Manhattan. He worked constantly and lived on potato chips and Coca-Cola. My fellow inbetweeners and I feared for his health. When we were all in Los Angeles a year later, Jimmy was furiously freelancing for Peter Aries, a Hanna-Barbera subcontractor. Peter said he never saw anyone work so hard. What none of us knew about Jimmy was that his family had good connections in the Taiwanese government that wanted to expand in the film business. When James Wang felt he knew enough about animation, he made a deal with Hanna-Barbera to subcontract animation for a studio he would build in Taipei. His studio, Cuckoo's Nest, grew to be the largest in Asia, employing hundreds. Additional animation work was flowing to Steve Hahn's Hahnho in Seoul Korea, Tokyo Mushi-Shinsha in Japan, Diamex SA in Spain, and Les Kalusa's operation in Poland.

Doing American work overseas inevitably caused cultural and language problems. Misunderstandings of customs and confusions about slang abounded. When someone would write, "Superman rockets out of a window," the artwork that came back had Superman physically assuming the shape of a rocket ship and blasting off. Brad Bird talked about working with Hungarian animators on "Do the Bartman": "I'd say 'cut a foot off here.'" They translate 'Moosh-moosh-moosh—you want to cut your own foot off?' 'No! I said sixteen frames!' Again 'Moosh-moosh-moosh— you want a picture frame?'" In Japan and Korea the process of correcting errors in a scene became a diplomatic dance because telling artists their work was wrong caused them to lose face and go home ashamed. A talented but hotheaded Canadian woman animator once blew up in a Korean studio and shouted, "All of this work sucks!" Criticism was bad enough, but being criticized by a woman in this male-dominated society was too much. The entire Korean staff put down their pencils, stood up, and walked out. That night the producers spent hours telephoning artists individually and apologizing to them so they would be back at work the next day.

When Gaumont had a studio in the Belleville section of Paris, there was an attempt to institute the American custom of fifteen-minute morning and afternoon coffee breaks. But when the concept was explained to the French staff, they immediately dashed out en masse to a little café across the street to sip wine or café au lait. American supervisors at the studio went nuts trying to get them back to their desks in under an hour. They even built them a coffee counter in the studio—with free pastries. But the French artists were determined. They would make up the hour later; they just wanted that quality time in their unique Gallic way.[21]

In 1989, when we were completing *The Little Mermaid* at Disney, some of the ink-and-paint work was sent for completion in mainland China. At that time the protests and government crackdowns at Tiananmen Square occurred. Back in Burbank, our first thought was, "What happened to our artwork?!" Supervisors Leo Sullivan and Beth Ann McCoy were in Beijing where all television and radio contact with the capital was blacked out. Word of mouth had it that something terrible was happening. Back at their hotel, where half the residents were Chinese nationals and half were foreigners, McCoy noticed that every day another Chinese name was missing from the mailbox slots. When she asked the landlord what had happened to Mr. Chen, he responded, "Who is that?" She and Sullivan decided it was time to get out before they became videotape news for some CNN story.[22] They called the U.S. consulate in Shanghai and were among the last Americans evacuated. Later the studio decided that whenever they sent animation overseas, they would first photocopy everything, just in case.

Another time, when Ralph Bakshi was producing the *New Adventures of Mighty Mouse* show, he had a tight deadline to deliver a specific episode. The show was so late in being delivered that there was danger that the air date would be missed. A Canadian supervisor was sent to Korea to get the finished work. Bakshi bought two first-class plane tickets from Seoul to Los Angeles: one seat for the supervisor and the seat next to it for the can of film, so there would be no danger of the film getting lost in baggage. But the supervisor, being a bit of a roué, checked the film as luggage and put a blow-up Godzilla doll in the seat; he used the doll to flirt with the flight attendants. You guessed it. The film was lost in transit, and the show was never delivered. Predictably, Bakshi hit the ceiling when he found out.

LA artists were offered tempting deals if they would go abroad and train artists in Hollywood production techniques. They were paid high salaries, expenses, and per diems. "It was crazy," said development artist

Drawing the Line

Tim G. "I was sitting in India making double what I usually make, and I know the guy next to me is making a bowl of rice for doing the same work."[23] Canadians proved particularly useful as trainers. They were in the main single men and women with few family ties who by virtue of their British Commonwealth passports could work in many parts of the world where Americans would have difficulty: Singapore, Hong Kong, Australia, and the European Union. Wherever you went in the world to visit an animation studio, there probably was a Canadian supervising artist to meet you.

Ironically, while Canadian citizens went overseas in search of adventure, Canada itself had strong nativist regulations protecting domestic film production. For instance, the Canadian-sponsored feature film *Heavy Metal* (1981) was being made at several studios around Canada and in the UK. By the end of production all the available local talent had been used up. The producers wanted to subcontract the final "Taarna" sequence to Los Angeles, but they were prevented by their contracts. The deal that guaranteed subsidies from the national and Ontario provincial governments stipulated that 80 percent of the workers had to be Canadian citizens unless they were unavailable. I was at a cocktail party where the studio's production manager, John Leach, wandered through the crowd mumbling softly, "Do you wanna work on *Heavy Metal*? Nah-hh . . . You don't want to work on that, do you?" The producers had made up their minds to send stuff out, but first they needed to prove they had looked for Canadian artists in good faith. Even in 2003, a friend was offering freelance Canadian storyboard work in Los Angeles, on condition that the artists hired must be Canadian citizens. This was because of the tough Canadian federal content laws that held firm while American trade laws were allowed to evaporate.

Since the 1950s, the Screen Cartoonists Guild Local 852 and the Motion Picture Screen Cartoonists Local 839 had been monitoring attempts to send work out of town. If an ink-and-paint artist in Hollywood made $600 a week plus benefits while a cel painter in the Philippines made $16 a week flat rate, it was obvious that, sooner or later, all such work would go abroad.

There had been several calls from animators to create some sort of protective language in the contracts before it was too late. Former president Ben Washam said that Local 839 should have gone on strike for such a runaway clause in 1969 when all the mainstream animation business was in Hollywood and all the studios were at the union's mercy. But the business agent at the time, Larry Kilty, was a former Disney feature artist who was never that interested in television animation issues. There was a runaway clause in the contract during the contract negotiations of 1969, but it was overshadowed and put aside in the dramatic battle over residuals. The next Local 839 business agent was Lou Appet, an activist from the 1930s who by this point was distracted by the legal challenges being waged against his administration by his disgraced predecessor, Kilty.

In 1978, Appet retired, and the new Local 839 business agent was former Milt Kahl assistant, Harry "Bud" Hester. Layout designer Morris "Moe" Gollub became president. Gollub was in the 1941 Disney strike and had a well-established side career in the 1960s doing cover illustrations for paperback novels like *Tarzan* and *Turok, Son of Stone.* At Disney Gollub was nicknamed the "Strongest Man in the World" because he was the only animation artist who regularly pumped iron in the studio gym.[24] Even when nearing retirement he was a muscular man. The membership also voted in an aggressive, young executive board dedicated to finally getting tough with the studios over runaway production: Ayalen Garcia, Jim Hickey, Gene Hamm, Tom Tataranowicz, Dave Teague, and Steve Zupkas.

In the basic contract negotiations that year, Hester and Gollub demanded a runaway production clause from the studios doing television production. The runaway cause stated: "No Producer shall subcontract work on any production outside the county of Los Angeles unless . . . sufficient employees with the qualifications required to produce a program or series are unavailable."[25] Some members wanted stronger language in the clause, but Hester urged caution. "Even if we win, it won't solve the runaway problem overnight. But it is a foot in the door," he said."[26] The studios concerned were Hanna-Barbera, DePatie-Freleng, Marvel, Ruby-Spears, Bakshi, and several smaller houses. The commercial studios and Disney were excluded because at the time they had no plans for production out of town. Lou Scheimer's Filmation studio prided itself on keeping production in town and signed a "me-too" agreement. This

Drawing the Line

The Hanna-Barbera crew on the roof of the Cahuenga Boulevard studio, 1979. Hanna-Barbera was a wonderful mix of old veterans from the golden age of Hollywood and the young artists who would spark the 2D animation boom of the 1990s. Courtesy of the Office of the Animation Guild, Local 839, IATSE (formerly MPSC Local 839), North Hollywood.

meant they would abide with whatever deal the producers signed with the local. Other studios balked at signing any such clause as a domestic production content guarantee. They had seen similar clauses like this pop up in negotiations for years and had never taken them seriously. They were confident that no serious action would occur because the cartoonists were too divided and too much concerned with their individual self-interest. No one thought the MPSC would actually go that far. After all, animation folk had not gone on strike for thirty-two years.

Against all expectations, on August 7, 1979, MPSC Local 839 went out on strike for the first time in it's history. Hanna-Barbera and the other studio heads expressed their surprise. The Hanna-Barbera production manager, who was known for her bad temper, outdid herself the first day by screaming epithets through the still hallways, throwing chairs, and kicking empty desks in impotent rage. As Hanna himself drove through the picket line, he stopped his car long enough to address striking assistant animator Alex Topete, "I understand exactly what you are going

Animation and the Global Market

Cartoonists' picket line in front of Hanna-Barbera studio 1979. Courtesy of Jim Brummett.

through and sympathize completely." As hundreds of picketers marched around the studio waving their colorful signs, the Los Angeles Police Department sent officers to ensure that the cartoonists didn't get too out of control. LAPD Sgt. Leo Wacker mentioned to Bud Hester that the sticks supporting the strikers' picket signs were too thick and could be used as clubs.[27] Hester was faced with the job of collecting all the signs and redoing them with thinner sticks, but as Wacker watched the group, he came to see that animators aren't by nature violent people. He let the signs stay as they were.

The producers were in a quandary. With the new TV season looming in September, this work stoppage jeopardized their entire production schedule. The Big Three networks at the time were not very understanding about missed air dates. After you signed contracts to provide on-air content, you were responsible if you missed the deadlines. It took years to create an exclusive relationship with a network for Saturday morning work. Punishing lawsuits and severe loss of future work were very real possibilities. The animation producers quickly buckled and agreed to the runaway clause. Contracts were rapidly signed and everyone went back to work. It was a stunning victory for the MPSC. Within a week Ruby & Spears incurred the first $50,000 fine for violating the deal they had just agreed to.

Drawing the Line

Almost as soon as the deal was signed, the producers resolved not to be caught that way again. The producers began planning for the next confrontation when the contracts would run out in three years. Deals were brokered with start-up animation studios in Canada, Taipei, and Korea. As noted earlier, the studios usually hired TV workers for the new season in March and April; in the year of the new contract negotiations, 1982, no one was rehired until late July. The producers wanted to ensure that people were hungry and didn't have the savings to sustain a prolonged walkout. The studios then asked for accelerated work schedules to build up their inventory. This fed the rumors among the drawing desks that Hanna-Barbera's real plan was to send everything overseas and close down their headquarters at 3400 Cahuenga Boulevard altogether.

The MPSC tried to shore up its strength by pressuring its members not to work for nonsignatory studios. An off-limits list was publicized in the monthly union newsletter, the *Pegboard,* and fines were levied on artists who worked for studios on the list. I recall getting my newsletter then quickly turning to the back to see if I was on the list of those suspended. That was usually the only notice anyone got. Between the strikes, the emphasis seemed to be on penalizing members. This tough enforcement policy may have alienated many artists, who began to wonder if the union management had their own interests at heart more than the interests of the union members.

Before 1979, Hanna-Barbera had hired a number of talented young, Canadian graduates of Sheridan College to work at the Los Angeles studio. They were very popular and included many future industry leaders, including Roger Chiasson, Duncan Marjoribanks, Anne-Marie Bardwell, Mark Simon, Chuck Gamage, and Alvaro Gaivoto. During the strike, one of their own Sheridan instructors, Bill Matthews, had the unique experience of carrying a picket sign reading "American Jobs for American People!" After the 1979 strike, the O-1 work permits of all these Canadians were abruptly revoked. They were forced to pull up their roots in Los Angeles, sell their cars and excess furniture, and return to Canada. The studio told them it was the union's fault. A union business rep has the right to contest a work visa, but the feds usually don't allow them to veto so many at once. Conveniently for the studios it seems, these highly skilled Canadians returned home fully trained in Hollywood production techniques so they could immediately start subcontracting work.

Animation and the Global Market

By 1982, as the contract time drew to a close, all in Toon Town held their breath. The studio negotiators demanded removal of the runaway cause. The union demanded it be enforced and expanded. Everyone seemed to be headed toward an impasse, which meant a strike. I remember a friend in Toronto telling me, "We sure hope you go on strike because if you do we've been promised a lot of work up here!" I told him, "Don't worry. I think we're going in with all flags flying." Anyone who could read the signs could see the trap ahead, yet we were going ahead anyway.

On July 31, 1982, a mass meeting of the MPSC was held at the Machinists Hall in Burbank. About four hundred members were present. The main order of business was to take the strike vote. Everyone knew what was at stake. Tempers flared as the debate pro and con raged for hours. Members wanted to know whether, if they voted a strike authorization at that point, there was any wiggle room before they would have to actually walk out. Could there be a second vote? Gollub and Hester explained that the implied threat of imminent strike was our best card to play to force a favorable result in the negotiations, but it did not mean we would definitely have to walk out. Some were confused by all the legal talk. Board member Gene Hamm recalled: "Some people thought we should wait to see if jobs would really go overseas. I got up and said, 'The time is now! When you are being raped, you don't wait until the baby is born to see who the father is!'" Veteran assistant Ilona Kaba asked Gollub bluntly, "Is this *the* vote? If we vote yes, will this be the vote that decides whether we strike?" At the podium Gollub said, "No, this isn't the final vote, we'll have another before we go out."[28]

The other executive board members stood silently and bit their lips. They knew full well Gollub and Hester did intend to go out on strike after this vote, but they knew a no vote would leave them without the muscle to negotiate. The producers could then dictate their terms. They could not risk another vote. Like Themistocles of Athens gambling long to win the victory of Salamis, Gollub decided to take a chance with his members' fate to win final victory.

The debates raged into the hot night until finally up rose Hicks Lokey. The master animator of *Dumbo* and *Fantasia* had come out of retirement in 1978 to make some money to pay for his granddaughter's eye operation. By now he was ancient and bent; he looked like a wrinkled

Local 839 president Moe Gollub, drawn by Dave Tendlar. Courtesy of the Tendlar family.

Appalachian apple doll, but in his heart he was still the lion of every picket line since 1935. Blacklisted by Max Fleischer, blacklisted by Walt Disney, old Lokey had buried them all. The scattered bickering throughout the hall fell silent as he hobbled slowly and painfully up the center aisle toward the guest microphone. Gollub kept calling out, "Hicks, what do you want Hicks?" Lokey would not be rushed. He finally made it up to the mike and delivered the most eloquent address of the evening. *"Shut up and vote!"* The room erupted into thunderous cheers.

The MPSC 839 membership voted by a two-thirds margin to authorize Gollub and Hester to call a strike if needed. Unlike 1979 when a few key television studios were struck, it was decided that the best way for the strike to work was for the entire animation community to go out. Studios that had nothing to do with the quarrel over TV production were to be shut down: Disney working on *Fox and Hounds*; Don Bluth studio ramping up its next project, *East of the Sun and West of the Moon*; Ralph Bakshi doing *Hey Good Lookin'*; Richard Williams on an ABC TV special *Ziggy's Gift*, along with commercial studios like Kurtz & Friends, Duck Soup, and FilmFair. It was felt that inflicting hardship on the other studios would increase pressure on the TV producers to knuckle under.[29]

After several more days of fruitless negotiations, the walkout was set to begin August 5, 1982. At 9:30 A.M., a meeting of the Disney animation department was called. Hester got up on stage and explained that everyone had to go out and picket. Then an executive from corporate management got up to give the company's side of things. Writer Steve Hulett recalled: "Bud left, we shifted uncomfortably in our seats, until a Disney guy in a light blue blazer who was from the Disney World Florida park strolled out and immediately pissed a lot of people off by being evasive about the questions we asked. He seemed to dance around every simple question that was given to him. By the time he was through, everybody was a lot more okay about striking."[30]

The word to strike spread across Hollywood. One by one, the Local 839 shop stewards methodically walked through every office in town and told animators, assistants, painters, checkers, and storyboard artists to lay down their pencils and walk out. You got an empty feeling in the pit of your stomach. This was it. This was real, we're laying it all on the line. Old Disney veteran Bill Keil was the supervisor of the animators at Hanna-Barbera. He may have read the signs that something good was ending

Picketer Helen Barry in front of Hanna-Barbera, 1979. Courtesy of Bronwen Barry.

because he not only went out on strike but also used the opportunity to announce his retirement. The quiet pavement of Buena Vista Boulevard in front of the Walt Disney studios saw its first cartoonist picketers since Walt leapt out of his 1939 Packard and wrestled with Art Babbitt. Animators made up a song based on the Mickey Mouse Club TV theme: "Who's the last one you'd expect to send work overseas? M-I-C-K-E-Y M-O-U-S-E! sent Tron, Taiwan . . ."[31]

DePatie-Freleng studio did very little overseas work if any; Freleng liked to keep his stuff in-house where he could control it. Yet work there stopped too and picketers appeared out front. Filmation Studio head Lou Scheimer had agreed all along that he should keep all his animation production in town. Lou shouldered a picket sign and walked the line among his own employees outside his Reseda studio. His only request to his employees was that the pickets in front of his studio be his people and never strangers. "I was walking the picket line in front of my own studio. Then I saw this Japanese pickup truck drive up with a load of signs reading "Keep Jobs in America!" It was crazy." [32]

Massed pickets in front of Hanna-Barbera, 1982. Ruby-Spears was a union signatory studio started by Joe Ruby and Ken Spears. They did Saturday morning television animation like *Fangface*, *Foofer*, *Q-Bert* and the *Mr. T Show*. Courtesy of Jim Brummett.

Drawing the Line

Even MPSC Local 841 in faraway New York City agreed to stop doing the little bit of Ruby-Spears and Hanna-Barbera subcontract work that it made there. Rick Reinert's LA studio made small educational films and used freelancers in New York. Local 841 business agent Gerard Salvio telephoned animator Nancy Beiman at her Greenwich Village apartment.

Gerald told Nancy bluntly, "You gotta stop working for Reinert!"

Nancy replied, "Why, is he not paying my annuities?"

"No, you're all paid up."

"Then what's the matter?"

"839 is on strike. It's a sister local. You have to go out."

"Gerard, 839 is picketing because they don't want the work sent out of Los Angeles County. I am in Manhattan County. I'd be protesting myself! What do you want me to do, march around my living room hitting myself on the head with a hammer and screaming, 'I am unfair to me'?"

But Gerard was not amused. He insisted.[33]

Once again the sunbaked streets of suburban San Fernando Valley were ringed with crowds of picketers waving brightly colored signs and American flags. Charlie Downs and his wife, Paulette, roller-skated with picket signs. Downs slipped and got a nasty fracture of his drawing hand. A few of the more musically inclined, like John Kimball, Ward's son, played Dixieland jazz on the curb. Actor Ed Asner, who was the militant president of the Screen Actors Guild, visited to encourage the strikers. The new Aurora/Bluth studio was about to release its first feature, *The Secret of Nimh*, so Bluth strikers, who were all former Disney artists, showed up to picket at the Disney studio Buena Vista gates dressed as characters from the film. As Disney CEO Ron Miller drove through the picket lines at Disney, young Bluth animator Dave Spafford leaped onto his car's hood, gave Miller the finger with both hands and shouted, "Up yours, Football Boy!" Miller jumped out of his car, and had not cooler heads prevailed, a fistfight would have ensued. Despite his years in corporate management, Miller was still a formidable presence because he was, after all, a former University of Southern California football player, as Spafford so eloquently alluded to. Spafford smiled in recollection: "As Miller came for me I thought, 'I'm about to get my ass kicked by a millionaire.' That's not something just anyone can say."[34]

Since the Mohawk Valley rules had transformed the way labor disputes were fought, the importance of strikes became more about bad publicity than about choking off a struck studio's product. However, seeing that it had only taken a week for management to buckle in 1979, the MPSC leaders focused their efforts on choking off the output of the studios and paid scant attention to the media. Very little about the strike came through on the local news programs. SAG was having it's own labor troubles as did the football players association. These also helped to keep the cartoonists' strike publicity in the background. Gene Hamm recalled: "It never failed that we would only have a handful of picketers whenever the news media would show up. So while they interviewed Bud Hester, we would direct the picketers behind him to look like we had an army. Our picket signs were double-sided. We had them walk in a tight circle just slightly larger than the video camera range. When they walked past camera, we would have them flip their signs around and walk back the other way. I called it a 'repeat pan.' We used Hanna-Barbera's favorite technique against them."[35]

The other factor affecting the strike effort was the times in America. The 1979 strike was during the Democratic Jimmy Carter administration. The 1982 strike was deep in the age of Ronald Reagan. As Herb Sorrell and his CSU members discovered a generation earlier, the mood of the country had swung conservative, pro-business, and antiunion. No sympathy could be expected from the general public. If the public paid any attention at all to a strike, they regarded it as a nuisance. And the 1947 Taft-Hartley Act made any sympathy strikes of theaters or print media illegal.

The battle finally came down to a race to see whether the studios could get their TV shows completed and make network air dates before the striking artists and their families starved.

The cartoonists' union did not represent all facets of the animation process. Film and sound editing, camera work, acting, dubbing, and processing were all the jurisdiction of separate union locals, most under the IATSE. The MPSC was an IATSE local as well and answered to the international's central governing board and its president. An IATSE local needed two official permissions from the international leadership: the first to take a strike vote, then another to strike.

IATSE international president Walter Diehl had taken over the position once ruled by the ancient Commie-chaser Richard Walsh. Diehl was kept informed about the issues, and he initially gave permission for the strike vote but not for the walkout itself. He did not want this little cartoonists' feud to mess up his upcoming negotiations with the major Hollywood live-action studios for the IATSE basic contract. Waiting for the IATSE general negotiations would have meant waiting until November, when the television season would be over and an animators' strike would have little or no affect on their TV production. They had to strike at least before September. Diehl felt that Local 839 had exceeded its mandate by walking out without his blessing. So he gave his permission for other union workers to cross cartoonists' picket lines.[36] Gollub, Hester, and the union leadership felt betrayed by the IA's position.

Since there was no IATSE support, the picketers marched in the blazing Southern California heat and watched helplessly as the FedEx trucks drove out with work to ship to distant lands.[37] The recording engineers continued to record tracks, the editors continued to cut film, footage continued to be produced, and deadlines continued to be met. As the weeks dragged on and cartoonists' bank accounts shriveled like dry prairie grass, anger was turned toward the MPSC leadership for getting them into this predicament. Local 839 had no strike fund, and the government turned down its request for unemployment benefits. Ronald Reagan, the first U.S. president to come from the leadership of organized labor, ran the most antiunion administration since the days of Jay Gould and the robber barons during Ulysses S. Grant's administration.

As previously stated, the strike shut down not only the TV animation studios but also Walt Disney Feature Animation, Aurora/Bluth, and the little studios that did television commercials. These studios were now populated by twenty-something baby boomers with a sprinkling of aging golden agers at the top. The new animators were too young to remember Walt Disney, Willie Bioff, or the six-day workweek. Many had come right out of school into the rarefied collegiate atmosphere of Disney. They had never experienced the daily blue-collar haggle between a working commercial artist and his client. It's hard to explain to kids making more money than they ever dreamed of for drawing bunnies that they must put down pencils to assure their future. The young Disney novices were not interested in the workings of low-budget TV animation. They could not see ever leaving Disney. They did not understand why their work was being halted for a cause they felt they had no interest in. They thought they had to strike only because Bud, Moe, and Bill Hanna were in some kind of personal grudge fight. When artists don't want to think about the broader implications, the easiest thing is for them to personalize it: Bud versus Bill, and so on. I was one of those angry young people, but with hindsight I see how wrong I was.

Despite all the younger artists involved, the 1982 strike was really the last action controlled by the golden-age generation. Most of the old-timers did not bother to explain what was at stake. It was simpler to fall back upon imposing penalties and discipline to enforce cooperation. Young artist Dori Littel-Herrick said, "I was always pro-union but I didn't know who these people [the union management] were. They weren't on my wavelength and I didn't trust them."[38] Since then, the more I've studied what Lou Appet, Art Babbitt, Bill Littlejohn, and others did to make our union strong, the more I appreciate events, but in the summer of 1982, while walking a picket line on a hot August day with people yelling curses and throwing garbage from their speeding cars, I didn't understand. All my peers and I could see was that our bosses, who patted our heads and gave us money, were at war with some union officers in North Hollywood who wanted dues and threatened fines.

The union meetings during that strike summer seemed monopolized by hard-line mountebanks. The loudest and most militant seemed to carry any argument. The old problem of division between the job categories arose. The animators now began to complain out loud: "Why should we go broke to keep work in town for ink and painters? After all, they didn't stick by us in 1969 when we wanted residuals."

As the long Labor Day weekend passed by, the numbers of pickets dwindled. Many showed up to picket in the morning and stayed only until 11:00 A.M. when the serious summer heat began to peak. The end of the strike seemed to be nowhere in sight. The media campaign about the local, never that strong to being with, dwindled and the public's attention moved on to newer, more novel stories. The unity of the animation picketers began to come apart. The stricken studios called artists at home to ask them to pick up work in secret. The rumors of people scabbing work at home grew. Animator Dave Brain recalls, "At the strike vote meeting Bud [Hester] begged everyone not to work under the table, and everyone dutifully nodded approval. Then they all picked up work illegally anyway." Tom Tataranowicz recalled, "They met in freeway underpasses and passed each other attaché cases filled with drawings. It was like James Bond."[39] Pro-union activists tried to stop the covert scab work by forming a group called the Midnight Patrol. Jim Hickey, Tom Tataranowicz, Gene Hamm, and Ayalen Garcia staked out a subcontract studio like Peter Aries at night and photographed artists sneaking in and out with freelance work. People were photographed and names bandied about. Some dozen artists were brought up on charges and fined hundreds of dollars—a common action in other unions. For example, when John Belushi and Dan Ackroyd tried to polish their script for the film *Neighbors* during the 1986 Writers Guild strike, they were charged by WGA leaders Gary Marshal and Larry Gelbart and fined thousands of dollars.

Hamm recalls: "I made friends with the labor police, who patrol strikes. One day I was on the picket line at Hanna-Barbera and saw someone pull up real fast across the street and dart into Ruby-Spears studio to deliver work. I went over to write down his license number. As I crossed the street I noticed the labor police parking down the street about half a block. Suddenly a Ruby-Spears manager and two big goons emerged from the studio and advanced towards me. Right then I only had two picketers with me. It looked like the goons were going to get me and then take care of the witnesses. The studio manager is in my face, just as the plain clothes labor police come from around the corner. The manager sees them and says, 'Who the fuck are you?' The labor police pulled back their coats revealing the badges that are affixed to their holsters. The manager and his goons made a quick cartoon exit back into their studio."[40]

Meanwhile, on the cartoonists' picket lines, doubts and fears began to fill everyone's hearts. Rumors were rife that everything was going overseas and production would never return to normal. The leadership of Local 839 would meet with the picketers and offer no news of relief but a lot of anecdotes about solidarity and tales of the courage of the PATCO [Professional Air Traffic Controllers Organization] strike. But the PATCO strike failed. Those folks all lost their jobs. The cartoonists' strike seemed to be spiraling out of control.

In early September, the MPSC started to allow some commercial studios that signed a me-too agreement to get back to work before they went bankrupt. They lacked the resources of the large studios. Richard

Striking animator Harry Love making a lunch date with Joe Barbera, 1982. Love was a longtime friend of Hanna and Barbera, and many jokes were made by members of his attempts to remain in their good graces. Drawing by Bob Ogle. Collection of the author

Williams's ABC special *Ziggy's Gift* came within one week of falling under a force majeure clause and becoming an insurance loss. It was completed and won an Emmy.

The Aurora/Bluth studio was still caught up in the romantic excitement of a group of friends taking on the world together. Film critics hailed *The Secret of Nimh* as the highest-quality animation ever seen outside Walt Disney Studios. The sky seemed the limit, but this strike was slowing the forward momentum. Don Bluth would have meetings with his faithful workers in which he would convince them to go to the union meetings and demand a contract with terms extremely favorable to the Aurora/Bluth management. The union leadership didn't want to grant any major concession to Bluth specifically because all the other studios would demand the same. Hamm said: "The Bluth animators were reluctant. They had been promised to get a piece of his film *The Secret of Nimh*. But nothing was in writing. The Bluth animators thought Bluth was going to save animation, that he was the new animation Messiah. I said, 'Maybe Don Bluth is the new animation Messiah. But even God put it in writing!'"[41] The September general membership meeting turned into an ugly exchange that broke into fistfights in the parking lot between unionists and Bluthies.

In poring over the contracts and by-laws, a Disney lawyer came upon an obscure codicil. It was called "financial core," a way union members could legally resign from their own union. It was created for artists claiming a religious deferment from membership. A financial core member would not be allowed to vote or participate in union activities would still be protected by union rules and receive a pension and health benefits. The Disney Company immediately began telephoning its artists at home and telling them about becoming core members.[42] It would mean they could go back to work without any fines or loss of benefits. Layout artist Tom Yakutis recalled getting the phone call, the other party no doubt unaware that Tom was a Local 839 executive board member.

Disney artists asked for a meeting with the union leaders at Bette Davis Park, a little patch of grass and picnic tables at the corner of Sonora Avenue in Glendale. Not satisfied with the answers they were getting, they had one more meeting at the union offices. After a lot of arguing and screaming, the Disney artists asked the union leaders outright about going financial core. The union's attorney, Stuart Libicki, hemmed and hawed but finally agreed; technically it was legal. The union didn't want you to do it, but you could. Steve Hulett remembered, "The air seemed to go out of the room. People made for the doors. Libicki told me later that he knew then that everything was falling apart and that the central issue of the strike, runaway production, was now a dead issue."[43]

The next day, Disney and Bluth feature employees began resigning from 839 in droves. Many were the bright young prospects who would become powerful and influential in the 2D animation renaissance and digital revolution of the 1990s. When one sulky young animator went off on a rant to old Frank Thomas about how much he hated the union, Thomas corrected him, "No matter what, you can't afford to ignore your union." [44] Thomas was pro-Walt in 1941 and he remained so, but he was also once an SCG executive board member. No one recalled that the young animators' mentor on the Disney training program, Eric Larson, had himself been a guild president once. No matter how passionate the argument about keeping work in town, the young ones just didn't buy it. It seemed inconceivable to all of them that someday even Walt Disney features would be done in faraway places like Australia, China, and Canada.

After ten weeks of marching and arguing, the picket lines finally crumbled. The once proud picket signs dipped down into the dust. The MPSC leadership requested talks with the producers and were made to sign a humiliating contract. Gone was any hope of a runaway clause or a closed hiring roster. Seniority clauses were badly compromised. The studios demanded amnesty for all artists who broke the strike and scabbed under the table. Three months later, Hanna-Barbera contested paying health insurance benefits to the scab artists for the hours they worked during the strike. In a cynical act, they published the names of the artists to make their case, even though they had assured them that their acts of betrayal would be kept strictly secret. The unkindest cut of all was that among the names revealed was a member of Local 839's own executive board. This increased the bitterness of the animators toward their union leaders. Like the burghers of Calais who were paraded with nooses around their necks before the conquering English king, the surly

Gag drawing of Hanna-Barbera building being towed to Taiwan as a final solution to outsourcing, 1982, by Bob Ogle. Collection of the author.

animators of MPSC Local 839 finally shuffled back to work on October 16, 1982.

Animators' personal savings were badly depleted, and television production never again returned to pre-1979 levels. Union membership in 1979 was at a high of 2,079. Now it plummeted to just 866 active members. Hollywood producers used the 1982 strike as the pretext to ship as much work out of town as possible. Bill Hanna recalled, "Arbitration ultimately proved that producers were contractually unrestricted by their relations with unions in determining where production was to be done. Our flagship company [Hollywood] was compelled to 'turn it loose' so to speak and commit to an ambitious plan of amplifying our industry to global proportions."[45] An economic recession in 1983 stopped a lot of new television production and added to everyone's misery. Filmation, the studio that refused to send work out of town on principle, shrank down to one wing of its own building to make a season of the TV show *Gilligan's Planet*.

Since 1941, all animation production in Hollywood had been under union contract. A few small fringe operations dared to stay nonunion, but they knew they could not hope to grow without a contract. In the undertow of the 1982 defeat, many small commercial studios pulled themselves out from under the union contract. If they only used the same core group of artists, and those artists felt disconnected from the union, all that was needed was to come up with a good health plan. DIC, a French company, set up shop in Los Angeles in 1983. It was the first large studio to openly thumb its nose at the union. Its workers did only writing, character designs, soundtrack recording, storyboards, and exposure-sheet timing. Everything else was completed overseas—all nonunion—but people desperate for work went there anyway. They specialized in rock-bottom budgets. For example, in 1984 a storyboard artist earned a freelance rate of $1,100 to $1,500 for a cleaned-up storyboard for one act of television (that is, one-third of a half-hour program). DIC declared it would offer only $800 for an act plus some key layout designs. After every veteran storyboard artist told DIC to shove it and there were disastrous results with some inexperienced students, rates were raised to the market value. Still DIC resisted all attempts at unionizing. Even when presented with

276

rep cards and an election in 1999, the studio delayed progress by taking the case to court.

After the lukewarm box-office success of *The Secret of Nimh* and the breakup with his distributor, Aurora, Don Bluth suspended feature operations and shifted production to create two groundbreaking video games, Dragon's Lair and Space Ace. When his union contract was up in 1984, Bluth refused to sign another. He encouraged all his employees to go financial core. Believing in Don's plans for success, they did so overwhelmingly. About the only ones who didn't become core members were Bluth himself and his business partners. After the collapse of the 1980s video-game market, Bluth hooked up with entrepreneur Morris Sullivan and moved his entire studio to Dublin to take advantage of the tax breaks and low-paid English-speaking workforce.

By the 1990s, live-action film production was also being undermined by increased nonunion production. While theatrical film producers sought to cut costs by overseas production, the explosion of the new pay-TV cable channels had a great impact on television. If the audience could choose between hundreds of programs in a time slot, a network could no longer count on getting a lion's share of the viewers. This meant they could not command the same licensing rates from sponsors. By 1995, the fees networks charged for commercials dropped to one-half what they had been. Cable channels soon began producing their own original programming. In the beginning it was pretty primitive stuff. Manhattan Cable once had a show called *Really Nasty George*, which consisted of a man with a video PortaPak following women at random through the streets of Newark, New Jersey, trying to talk them into flashing for his camera. From these humble beginnings, cable eventually gained a reputation for innovative and challenging programming like *Meet Dorothy Dandridge* (1999), *Angels in America* (2004), *Band of Brothers* (2001), and *Rome* (2005). At first much of this programming was low budget and nonunion. Part of the problem was addressed in 1993. IATSE president Tom Short worked out a two-tier pay system for union film workers to create cable productions. A long writers' strike in 1986 and a SAG walkout in 1988 spawned reality shows: cheap programming allegedly without scripts or actors (for example, *Cops*, *Emergency 911*, and *Bad*

Boys). In reality, many reality shows do have actors and scripts but all are working far below union scale.

Through the 1980s the fortunes of MPSC Local 839 continued to sink. In the next negotiation in 1985, the local lost seniority clauses and was omitted from the IATSE bargaining unit, the group that creates the IATSE basic contracts. Many of the union contracts with small commercial houses lapsed, and employers took their studios nonunion. Also in 1985, MPSC Local 841, New York became so weak that it was finally folded into the Cameramen's Local 659 and disappeared. By 1990, MPSC Local 732, Chicago had ceased to be. President Moe Gollub retired. Business agent Bud Hester lost much support and was defeated for reelection by Disney animation writer Steve Hulett in 1987.

The members who had served on Local 839's executive board during the Runaway Wars moved on to other pursuits. Animator Ayalen Garcia returned to visit his native Peru, where he and his wife died in a car crash. Gene Hamm went north to teach at San Francisco State University. He said of his experience during the strike, "All in all it felt good to stand up for something." Tom Tataranowicz soon found himself producing TV shows that required him to work with companies in Asia, where he traveled frequently. He said later: "We lost. A lot of it had to do with people not sticking by the union. There was scabbing everywhere. I mean, I never faulted the companies . . . because it's their job to get work done. But the people, everybody had a bad viewpoint about that strike."[46]

By 1985, Hanna-Barbera was doing a hundred half-hour TV shows a season in eight countries. The Pacific Rim subcontracting studios soon realized that they really didn't need Hanna-Barbera, Marvel, or Ruby-Spears. They could pitch shows to the networks without middlemen. So Tokyo Mushi Shinsha (TMS), Hanho, Sun Woo, and Calico were soon competing against their former partners. When Japan became too expensive, work was subcontracted to Seoul, then mainland China, then the Philippines, Vietnam, North Korea, and India in an ever widening search for artists who would work as cheaply as possible.

In 1984, as part of the studio-wide revival under Michael Eisner, the Walt Disney Company set up its own television animation division and purchased the original Australian subcontract studio from Hanna-Barbera. Although all preproduction, writing, and so on for Disney TV animation was done in Los Angeles, there was never a thought that the bulk of production would not be completed overseas. Overseas production became standard operating procedure throughout Hollywood. Disney Studios explored making low-budget spin-offs of its feature films—"cheapquels"—in Australia and Canada through its TV animation arm. The first successful direct-to-video production was *Aladdin II: The Return of Jafar* (1993), which was a huge hit. While Disney and Warner feature budgets were topping $100 million, the cheapquels were made for $26 million to $30 million and made significant profits, even though they relied upon the audience's memory of classic original films. To the bean counters this was all easy money, and any attention to quality or desire to advance the medium be damned. In 1986 Twentieth Century-Fox and Steven Spielberg released the hit *An American Tail*, a story about an immigrant mouse discovering the American dream. A big-budget, high-quality film, it was completely animated in Dublin with heavy tax breaks and subsidies from the Irish government.

Lou Scheimer alone kept his promise to his staff not to send their jobs overseas; in 1983, Filmation blossomed by creating a boom of syndicated TV series: *He-Man and the Masters of the Universe, She-Ra Princess of Power, Fat Albert and the Cosby Kids, Ghostbusters*. Instead of the usual sixteen-episode season dictated by the networks, syndication demanded sixty-five half-hour shows with little corporate involvement. This meant that instead of offering seasonal employment, Filmation needed people almost year-round. Many artists, cast adrift by Hanna-Barbera, the breakup of DePatie-Freleng after Friz Freleng's retirement, or the big Disney layoff after the completion of *The Black Cauldron* (1984), found a refuge at Filmation.

But in the 1980s larger companies were gobbling up little ones for a quick buck and a tax-loss write-off. In 1987, the Swiss firm L'Oréal-Nestle bought Filmation from Group W Westinghouse so its library could be exploited for European cable television. Scheimer initially favored the sale, thinking it would ease his financial woes, but he later felt he was taken advantage of. After getting the library of old cartoons, the Europeans were not really interested in keeping an American animation studio going. On February 3, 1988, without warning, they closed Filmation and laid off 229 artists. This was done the day before a federal law was to go into effect that mandated sixty days' notice of all plant closings. As sulky artists filed out the doors for the last time, one of Filmation's executives made the unfortunate choice to show off his new silver Jaguar.

By 1989, television shows that were hand-drawn and painted completely in Hollywood had all but disappeared. Only eclectic fringe studios—like John Kricfalusi's, which was making *Ren & Stimpy*—still did TV animation in-house. With the opportunity to practice their craft gone, many unemployed animators drifted away and found jobs in other fields. The artists who had been well paid to go overseas and train foreign animators now discovered that their own positions were redundant. They had nothing left to teach and so were no longer needed.

After eliminating the jobs of hundreds of television artists, the triumphant producers now put the new spin in the press that the only reason they went offshore was that there were not enough qualified artists in LA to keep up with the workload. They really wanted to keep work in America, but they could no longer find the talent, they claimed.

As the 1980s gave way to the 1990s the boom in the volume of shows brought about by new cable cartoon venues like NickToons, Kids WB, and Cartoon Network created new work opportunities. Hanna and Barbera had sold their company to Taft Enterprises, so the studio went to Ted Turner when the maverick billionaire bought up Taft. Turner sent out lawyers to get rid of most of the Hanna-Barbera's old-guard directors and supervisors, men and women who had been with Bill and Joe from the beginning, who had fought the strikers, and who had created years of memorable programming. All were told it was time to go. The hotheaded supervisor who had kicked chairs now actually called the MPSC to ask for help in suing Turner for age discrimination. In 1997 Ted Turner merged Hanna-Barbera into Warner Bros.

Warner Bros. and Cartoon Network began to buy series directly from Asia: *Pokemon, Digimon,* and *YuGiOh*. Warner considered phasing out Hanna-Barbera completely but was convinced not to by executives at Cartoon Network, who said Hanna-Barbera still commanded brand loyalty from the public.[47] Today the company's headquarters at 3400 Cahuenga Boulevard is just a memory to old artists. Warner sold the empty 1964 building to Universal, and for a while there was a fear Universal would tear it down to build a new entrance lane into the Universal City theme park. The preservation society Hollywood Heritage won it historic landmark status in 2004.

Animation and the Global Market

Bill Hanna and Joe Barbera continued to go to their offices even as Hanna-Barbera became little more than some offices and a display case in Warner Bros. Animation. Hanna suffered terribly from Alzheimer's disease in his final years. Once one of the sharpest and most dynamic producers in Hollywood animation, he ended a bewildered shell. Staff members on his floor were briefed about what to do if they came upon Mr. Hanna—Bill and Joe were always "Mr. Hanna" and "Mr. Barbera" to the staff—wandering the stairwells. Hanna died in 2001 at age ninety. Artists who went to his memorial on the Warner Bros. studio lot complained that most of the eulogies were not from Bill's friends but from a seemingly endless line of AOL/Time Warner executives who waxed rhapsodic about how much money the Hanna-Barbera characters were making for them.

In 1998, when I was president of MPSC Local 839, I asked the IATSE to create a Canadian Animation Guild, which was called Local 841, after the collapsed New York local. Attempts to interest local artists in joining failed, and the guild was stillborn. They took the custom T-shirts and listened to the speeches, but no one wanted to rock the boat. That year the all-Canadian-animated Disney feature *Beauty and the Beast: Belle's Special Christmas* outdid the box office of Don Bluth's Irish-animated *Anastasia*. It was a well-known secret that some large Canadian animation studios accepted subsidies and tax breaks from both the provincial and federal governments to foster Canadian film production, then used that clout to get low-bid subsidized American work and send it to Korea, reaping profits all around.

The general public at the turn of the millennium gained a greater appreciation of Japanese anime and manga. The sexy, hard-hitting stories appealed to adolescents raised on shoot-'em-up movies. The societal melding of Asian-African-Caribbean-Gangsta themes in hip-hop culture seemed to join the simple violent code of these cartoon ronin, or masterless samurai. The interactive games of Nintendo, Game Boy, and Sony PlayStation (*Final Fantasy, Suikoden,* and *Xenogears*) drew a mass audience for Japanimation in a way the larger Japanese movies like *Princess Mononoke* and *Spirited Away* did not. Whereas at the beginning of the 1990s you might find one copy of *Akira* or *Robotech* in your local store, by 2004, video stores boasted whole sections of Japanime, for both children and adults. When producer Joel Silver wanted Warner Bros. to greenlight his trilogy of live-action movies, *The Matrix*, he used a copy of Mamrou Oshii's anime film *The Ghost in the Shell* to bolster his argument.

As the 1990s moved on, American audiences got used to seeing the exotic movements and designs of foreign animation. Even the taxpayer-funded Public Broadcasting System (PBS) commissioned animation, not from an American studio, but from Canada because it was cheaper. Local 839 led a large demonstration picket in front of Los Angeles PBS affiliate KCET in 1998, but to no avail. The local affiliate claimed it followed instructions from the network in Washington. PBS program directors in Washington told the press there was no problem.

The amount of live-action production being done outside of Hollywood finally roused the larger live-action film community to anger. They formed the Film & Television Action Committee (FTAC) in December 1998 and, in 1999, marched on the state capitol in Sacramento. (Well, it *is* California, so they drove there.) They demanded action from the state and federal government to protect domestic film jobs. FTAC also clashed with IATSE, which FTAC accused of doing nothing to stop the flow of work to Canada. IATSE's hands were tied because many film and stage locals in Canada were in the alliance and sensitive to all the criticism. Some FTAC activists also criticized the MPSC 839 for not doing enough. They specifically focused their anger on Canada because much live-action work was being done in Vancouver and Toronto. This was a problem for animators, as many of the artists living in Los Angeles were proud Canadian expatriates.

Hollywood animation was losing work not only to other countries but also, in equal measure, to other parts of the United States. *Jimmy Neutron* was made in Texas; *Ice Age* in White Plains, New York; *Final Fantasy* in Honolulu; *Veggie Tales: The Movie* in Chicago; and Pixar/PDI (Pacific Data Images) films in the San Francisco Bay area. "From the mountains, to the prairies, to the ocean, white with foam" animation was being done, virtually all nonunion. In 1960, 90 percent of commercial animation in the United States was done by union artists; by 2000, only Los Angeles, Orlando, and a bit of San Francisco had animators under contract. Those of us in animation explained to FTAC that we had led the way twenty years earlier with our Runaway Wars in 1979 and 1982. Back then, many of the live-action actors and technicians accusing us of lack of will were probably ignoring our picket lines, thinking such problems could never affect them.

Bud Hester said later, "It was never about keeping 100 percent of the work in LA. We knew that was impractical. We just wanted a guarantee that our jobs in Hollywood would be protected before everything went overseas."[48] Bill Hanna wrote, "None of us ever intended or believed that expanding our operations abroad would deprive our own people here in the U.S. of a livelihood."[49]

The issue of runaway production and the demands of the global market is not settled. Disney closed what was once Hanna-Barbera's first overseas studio, in Sydney, Australia, in 2006. Now, Chinese studios are subcontracting to India. Eastern Europe, Argentina, and Israel are vying for a chance to build animation studios. Hollywood cannot build a wall around itself and keep work in. The people of Hollywood have to stiffen the resolve of their state politicians to enact the same kind of nativist leg-

Bill Hanna in 1990. Hanna, who started as a scene checker and supervisor, had a natural gift for organization and timing. He would spend his weekends on his yacht timing animation for TV episodes. Courtesy of ASIFA/ Hollywood Animation Archive, www. animationarchive.org.

islation and subsidies that most of the world's film industries have in their competitive arsenal. And unions have to think beyond the borders and bring good ideas and worker solidarity to the animators of the world.

A few weeks after the Runaway War ended, a party was held at Chadney's Restaurant across the street from NBC in Burbank to celebrate MPSC president Moe Gollub's birthday. The party consisted solely of the hard-core union faithful, the hotspur executive board still licking their wounds over the bitter defeat. The revelers had just gotten their first cocktails when Bill Hanna walked into the room. Tom Tataranowicz said, "It was amazing, he walked straight into the belly of the beast. Surrounded by people who blamed him for their defeat. We all wanted to kill him. Yet there he was, utterly fearless."[50]

Hanna went right up to Gollub and wished him a happy birthday. While Moe was still grasping for words, Bill turned to the angriest board members and warmly shook their hands. "Lousy year this year, let's hope for a better one next year," he said. His little black leprechaun eyes had a twinkle that could disarm the harshest critic. In the end it was just business, nothing personal. After a drink or three, all sense of rancor was gone. Hanna entertained all with stories of his great days of Tom and Jerry at MGM. They were no longer adversaries, just artists sharing stories of their common love of making cartoons.

10

Fox and Hounds

The Torch Seen Passing

"I dunno, Art. Maybe this *is* a young man's medium."
—Wolfgang Reitherman

Films can be important for different reasons: blockbuster box office, the creative apogee of a particular performer, the debut of an innovation. The Walt Disney Studios' 1981 release *The Fox and the Hound* is probably not on many top ten lists for best animated films of all time, but it is uniquely important. It marks the turning point when the golden age artists of *Pinocchio* and *Bambi* passed the torch finally and forever to the baby-boom generation.

The Fox and the Hound is the first Disney animated film that Walt Disney himself had nothing to do with. It was the last major work in which any of the legendary Nine Old Men participated; the three involved were Frank Thomas, Ollie Johnston, and Wolfgang "Woolie" Reitherman. Milt Kahl, Marc Davis, and Ward Kimball had retired or moved from feature animation to other pursuits. Eric Larsen focused on Disney's training program. John Lounsbery, Fred Moore, and Les Clark had died. Other great names of Disney animation like Bill Tytla, Norm Ferguson, Mary Blair, and Ub Iwerks were now only memories. Look at *The Fox and the Hound* today and you'll notice something interesting about the screen credits. It is the last Disney film with no complete roll credits at the end. Credits were for a select few and had moved to the long set-up sequence at the beginning. The names not mentioned are as interesting as those that are.

If you thumbed through the draft scene lists of the film in the Disney

Drawing the Line

Animation Research Library, or if through some form of prestidigitation you could get a full personnel roster of *The Fox and the Hound,* you would see a veritable who's who of modern Hollywood animation power. Among the names are Glen Keane, Don Bluth, Tim Burton, John Musker, Ron Clements, future Pixar head John Lasseter, Joe Ranft, Henry Sellick, Andy Gaskill, Chuck Harvey, Sue Kroyer, Dan Haskett, Jerry Rees, Mike McKinney, Richard Rich, Brad Bird, Bill Kroyer, and Dave Spafford. The first American women animators since the days of Laverne Harding are there—Linda Miller, Diann Landau, Rebecca Rees, Heidi Guedel, and Lorna Cook—as well as the dean of Hollywood life drawing, Glenn Vilppu. Animation union heads Steve Hulett and Earl Kress were writers on the film. Current top studio executives like Don Hahn and Ron Rocha were production personnel. (Also at Disney, but on another project, was animator Andreas Deja, newly arrived from Germany.)

Disney Animation had been in a slow decline since 1959's *Sleeping Beauty.* In 1958, the studio downsized its staff from 500 to 125, and this reduced staff level continued into the mid-1970s. If the studio hired at all it was a very, very selective process. From 1970 to 1977, Disney Animation hired only twenty-one people, and most of them were hired in that last year.[1] To the young artists then beginning their careers it seemed easier to attain nirvana than get into Disney.

Art doesn't require youthful energy. Japanese landscape artist Hokusai, Titian, and Al Hirschfeld did some of their best work at a very old age. Animators like to brag that they'll never retire, that they will draw until they "hit the disc." The Disney artists who visualized Walt's dreams in the 1940s were in the main at the same desks forty years later. White-haired lions to us, they nevertheless were nearing the end of their careers. By the mid-1970s, it was obvious that if something wasn't done soon, Disney Animation would die out with its first generation of creators.

By 1977, most of the graduates of the character animation program at the new California Institute of the Arts (CalArts) were taken on as trainees. The young bloods were brassy, bell-bottom-jeans wearing, longhaired, and iconoclastic. They rode bicycles through the hallways. For the hedonistic disco era they were a well-behaved bunch, but for a sleepy studio whose policy forbidding women to wear pants at work was only changed in 1977, they were a breath of fresh air. The trainees were required to produce two short pencil tests over a nine-month period, and if judged worthy, they would be assigned to a veteran artist to do production. A compromise was worked out with the MPSC, whose rules on seniority did not allow trainees to work on production. Union officers Bud Hester and Moe Gollub were themselves working Disney artists. I recall a friend of mine animating beautiful scenes to be put into *The Fox and The Hound,* but he was being paid less than I was as a cleanup assistant on *Godzilla* and *Yogi's Space Race* for Hanna-Barbera. The old guard of the cleanup artists resented the trainees. They felt that they should be first to move up when the older animators retired. They had waited their turn and now felt that their reward would be to be passed over for some brassy kids.

The master animators commenced to teach the trainees all their secrets while keeping them aware of who was boss. These veterans had learned their craft in the old-fashioned way—tough, no-nonsense butt kicking—and this was to be their method of teaching the young trainees. Many animators have stories of Milt, Frank, or Ollie chewing them out for their mistakes and of being made to feel like idiots. One animator told of being made to stand before his directing animator while he rifled through scene folders, mumbling, "Hmmm, you're not good enough for this one yet . . . you're not good enough for this . . . hmph . . . maybe you can manage this one."[2]

Another time an old sequence director played a cruel prank. He assigned one trainee a test scene that was actually earmarked for the mercurial master Milt Kahl. Of course, when Kahl saw his scene animated by another he exploded, which was the reaction the prankster wanted. The young artist was mortified and went in to see Kahl to apologize as if it were his idea. Milt snapped, "Apology *not* accepted!" When this young animator's periodic review came up, Milt was loud in his recommendation that the man not be promoted.

When Walt Disney died in 1966, the studio passed into the control of Roy Sr. After Roy's death in 1970 the firm was led by Walt's son-in-law, Ron Miller. Walt's widow, Lillian, and other members of the family preferred to remain silent stockholders. Before running one of the largest corporations in Hollywood, Ron Miller was a tight end for the USC football team and later the National Football League's LA Rams. To a studio that had been run by one of the great masters of the medium, submitting to the authority of someone so inexperienced was a challenge; taking orders from a silver-haired, chain-smoking genius was much easier. But Walt was gone, and Disney had to make do.

In 1971, Disney Studios bought the rights to the *Chronicles of Prydain* by Lloyd Alexander, which would become *The Black Cauldron*.[3] All through the 1970s, trade publications announced its development by a new generation of "Nine Young Men," always with the same accompanying artwork done by old visual development master Mel Shaw. The truth was that the remnant of the Nine Old Men felt their young charges just weren't ready for such a difficult and dark story.

Production of *Cauldron* was repeatedly delayed. After *The Rescuers* (1977), the studio did *Pete's Dragon* (1977) and a Christmas special called *The Small One* (1978). Production was again put off while the staff began work on a film based on Daniel Mannix's 1967 book, *The Fox and the Hound*.

The story of Tod, the fox who befriended a hunting dog named Copper, was originally much more realistic. It ended with a hunter nailing Tod's lifeless red pelt to the wall, then euthanizing Copper with his shotgun. The Disney story department softened the tale. The hard-drinking hunter of the book became a sweet, pudgy old lady. Lots of kooky little animals and bitter foes ran around and became pals at the end. This treacly version grated on a lot of the younger story people who wanted to push the envelope into more mature realms.

At the climax of the film, Chief, the Copper's old hound-dog mentor, gets hit by a speeding freight train and drops a thousand feet into a gorge, seemingly to a dark, certain death. This is the motivation for Copper's rampage of grief for his old friend. Yet in the last sequence the old mutt appears okay, having only a little bandage on his paw. Story veteran Vance Gerry argued for the department, "But he gets hit in the kisser with a freight train!" To which Ron Miller and codirector Art Stevens countered, "Geez, we never killed a main character in a Disney film and we're not starting now!"[4]

Codirector Woolie Reitherman, the animator of Monstro the whale in *Pinocchio* and director of *The Jungle Book* and *Aristocats*, was a formidable figure in his twilight years. Even at seventy-plus, he was tall, lean, and dignified, like John Wayne in *Donovan's Reef*. He directed the animation crew with a fat unlit cigar stump clamped all day in his taut jaws, like Sherman when he was burning Atlanta. When the end of the stogie got too chewy, he would snip it off and chew the remaining stump for an hour more. Three-quarters of the way through production of *The Fox and the Hound,* Reitherman wanted to add a new sequence in which Phil Harris and Charro voice two whooping cranes who sing a silly song called "Scoobie-Doobie Doobie Doo, Let Your Body Goo."[5] Lots of live action reference film was shot of the busty Latina chanteuse Charro jumping around in a sweaty leotard. It must have helped the blood pressure problems of a lot of the elder artists. But just about everyone from Ron Miller to the interns hated the song. They thought it was needless and a distraction from the main plot. Reitherman was at last prevailed upon to scrap it. He walked into Art Stevens's office, slumped into an easy chair, and said dejectedly, "I dunno, Art, maybe this *is* a young man's medium."[6] He moved over to developing *Catfish Bend* and in 1985 was killed in a car accident.

By late 1978, veteran animators Frank Thomas and Ollie Johnston had completed their animation on *The Fox and the Hound.* Thomas animated a lot of Tod and Copper as youngsters using dialogue Larry Clemons had written and recorded with the child actors. Johnston had done a lot of work on a sequence in which Chief stomped around the house with his leg in a cast. Unfortunately, most of that sequence was edited out. Their work done, Thomas and Johnston had begun to think more of their book projects, like a book about the techniques of Disney animation, *Disney Animation: The Illusion of Life.* They now felt things at the studio were in good enough shape that they could bow out gracefully. There was no gold watch or black-tie testimonial like Winsor McCay's. Don Bluth took a piece of paper and drew a Mickey that everyone on the crew signed—a low-key way of acknowledging the end of an era, the last animation performances by the members of the magnificent team, the Nine Old Men.

By 1979, the field was clearing for the young Turks, but factions had developed in their ranks. There was a key group of artists devoted to director Don Bluth and his vision for revitalizing the studio. A tall, gaunt man with a wry smile and piercing eyes, Bluth had been at Disney off and on since 1956. Only at Disney would an artist who has been around that long be considered a young Turk. Bluth was an exceptionally good animator. Hired at a time when few younger artists even entered Disney's, he was considered the best hope to guide Disney Animation into the future. Having been groomed in such a strongly paternalistic environment, Bluth saw himself as the new Walt, set to lead the people into the next generation of Disney greatness. Ron Miller and other top management encouraged him in his belief. It was reported by some that Bluth felt he had a duty to restore "family values to animation." His identification with the iconic Walt Disney was so strong he even grew a thin mustache and at one point affected a pipe. (Image-conscious Walt Disney himself liked to be photographed smoking a pipe, but away from the camera he smoked unfiltered Marlboros.) No one was sure whether Bluth was joking or not.

Another group of Disney animators worried about Bluth's influence. So the political lines were set: the Bluthies versus the Mouseketeers. The room where Bill Kroyer, Brad Bird, Henry Selick, and John Musker worked was dubbed the "Rat's Nest" by their detractors. They had a meeting with Miller about the future of the studio, a meeting that Bluth may have interpreted as a challenge to his authority. No one is sure.

In any event, Don Bluth finally came to the conclusion that the films he wanted to make couldn't be done at Disney. He dreamed of bigger mountains to climb. He passed on codirecting *The Fox and the Hound* with Reitherman so he could focus on his independent short *Banjo the Woodpile Cat*. After work, many of the animator friends in his circle labored on the film in Bluth's garage. Ron Miller suspected something and directly asked Bluth whether he planned to resign. Bluth told him no.

Writer Steve Hulett recalled: "I remember wondering if something was up at *The Small One* wrap party held in the studio cafeteria. Miller was there, Diane Disney Miller was there, and Don was in the corner with a wry look on his face. I went over to make small talk with him, and he was pretty distanced and flip. I asked him about a couple of artists I knew who didn't have work assignments and who were nervous about it, and he said: 'Oh, they won't get laid off. Nobody ever gets laid off around here. If they don't work out in animation, they just go over and work for WED [Walt Elias Disney, or Walt Disney Imagineering, where the theme parks are designed and maintained].'"[7]

On his forty-second birthday, September 13, 1979, Bluth, with his partner animators Gary Goldman and John Pomeroy, entered Ron Miller's office and tendered their resignations. Miller's final tactic to try to get Bluth to stay was to offer him his own covered parking space on the studio lot free of charge. Everyone else had to pay. Despite this tempting carrot, Bluth quit, and his followers, amounting to almost one-third of the staff, followed suit. All morning, artists marched into the producers' offices in twos and threes and resigned. After Bluth, Pomeroy, and Goldman, there were Sally Voorheis, Skip Jones, Diann Landau, Heidi Guedel, Linda Miller (no relation to Ron Miller), Dave Spafford, Emily Juiliano, Vera Law, Lorna Pomeroy, and Dorse Lanpher. The coup was complete. Ron Miller was outraged. He felt personally betrayed by these artists, all of whom had been culled from hundreds of applicants, nurtured, and painstakingly trained at studio expense to take their place as Disney lifetime employees. Miller ordered all of them off the studio property by noon that same day. Gathering the remaining staff, he began a speech with: "Now that the cancer has been excised. . . ."[8] Still more young talent, not associated with Bluth but just tired of the infighting, left the studio: Dan Haskett, Chuck Harvey, Bill Kroyer and Sue Kroyer, Jerry and Rebecca Rees, Andy Gaskill, Brad Bird, and John Lasseter.

The Bluth group went on to build a studio and became Walt Disney's chief competitor for the next decade. For years afterward, many Disney artists would not speak to their Bluth studio counterparts. Even at house parties the factions would split into small groups at opposite ends of a room.

Miller pushed the release date of *The Fox and the Hound* back from Christmas 1980 to summer 1981. New artists were hired and promoted to fill the ranks. To make up for the lack of experience of the new animators, much of the quality control would rely upon a corps of veteran assistant animators, including Tom Ferriter, Walt Stanchfield, Chuck Williams, Dale Oliver, and Dave Suding. Like master drill sergeants, they would help their younger charges bring the project, at last, to completion.

Young animator Glen Keane began earning a reputation for himself by re-storyboarding and animating the bear-attack sequence. I've been told the original storyboards were even more dramatic but were toned down by the directors for fear of losing their family G rating. (Even Glen left the studio for a while. He joined other exiled Disney animators on *Alvin & the Chipmunks: The Chipmunk Adventure*.)

Drawing the Line

The Fox and the Hound finally opened to lackluster box office and tepid critical acclaim. The studio moved on, at last, to *The Black Cauldron*, which failed disastrously in 1984. Whereas *The Rescuers* cost $17 million and Bakshi's *Wizards* $10 million, *The Black Cauldron* cost a whopping $45 million. Disney chairman Ron Miller was ousted in the famous 1984 takeover that spawned the Roy Disney–Michael Eisner–Jeffrey Katzenberg era. Ron Miller and his family today own Silverado vineyards in the Napa Valley and make a rather nice chardonnay.

Don Bluth created his own films and scored major hits in conjunction with Steven Spielberg with *An American Tail* (1986) and *The Land before Time* (1988). Like a shot of cold water, his success reawakened Disney management to the potential earning power of animation. The transfer of the medium was now complete. Like an antique jewel, the heritage of Disney Animation passed from the failing grasp of the World War II generation to the impetuous but sure grip of the Pepsi Generation. The road was clear for the animation renaissance of the 1990s.

Camelot

1988–2001

> INTERVIEWER: Don't you feel your talents as an artist
> are being exploited by a huge corporation to make
> even more profits for them?
> ANIMATOR: Yeah, . . . but it's a good picture.
>
> —*Roger Rabbit* animator
> answering *Premiere* magazine
> correspondent Kim Masters, 1988

From 1988 to 1998 while digital animation was taking its first baby steps, traditional hand-drawn animation experienced a renaissance of interest. The public's love of pencil-drawn animation peaked in a way not seen since the 1940s. This created in Hollywood a boomtown atmosphere of fast careers and fast profits that carried within it the seeds of its own destruction.

In 1978, a curator at the Smithsonian Institution telephoned a production executive at Walt Disney Studio in Burbank. He said the Smithsonian was planning an exhibit entitled "Industrial Arts in the Entertainment Industry in the Twentieth Century." They heard that Disney still possessed 1930s-vintage black and brass upright editing machines and a nonmotorized Oxberry camera stand. He asked if Disney would be willing to donate those items for the exhibit. The Disney executive said sheepishly, "But we're still using them." The Smithsonian curator replied, "You're kidding, right?"[1]

This was the state of animation at the Disney studio after Walt's death. Everything was frozen in time. While the rebellious, iconoclastic cinema of the 1960s, influenced by the European new wave, rocked America, Disney slept. While the wild ideas of Ralph Bakshi's *Heavy Traffic*, George Dunning's *Yellow Submarine*, and the blockbuster changes brought about by *Star Wars* changed Hollywood film, Disney slept. Into the 1980s, as Hollywood boiled over with corporate takeovers and junk bonds, the Walt Disney Company acted like the kingdom of Sleeping Beauty. The Disney studio had become a self-replicating creation of its own publicity machine, where Dean Jones and Annette Funicello still smiled all day, women and minorities knew their place, skirts never rose above the knee, and no one uttered a swear word stronger than "gee whillikers." Marc Davis recalled some older supervisors occasionally slipping out for an afternoon of golf. On hot afternoons the Firehouse Five still played Dixieland to the lunch crowd. Custodians knew that the Snow White rotoscope room, where the device from 1937 was still used, as a good place to take a nap.[2] The Creator had been dead for eighteen years, yet animators still addressed production problems with these words, "What would Walt do?" At the time the Smithsonian curator made that phone call, flatbed Steenbeck platter-editing tables had long replaced the old green upright Moviolas in Hollywood. Computers were beginning to make themselves known. In the rest of town every animator had a cassette player to listen to soundtrack tapes, while animators at Disney still relied on "acetates"—thick, record-like 78mm platters that played on a record player, much as they had done when their ancestors were animating *The Three Little Pigs* (1933).[3] Among movie studios Disney's was sixth in overall box office and relied to a great extent on theme-park revenues to keep their books balanced. Into the 1980s, most Disney animators still used hand-cranked pencil sharpeners. The joke around town was, "Some people work at Disney's and some people work in film."

In 1984, after a celebrated power struggle, Roy Disney's son, Roy E. Disney, the producer of the True-Life Adventures series, wrested control of the company from Walt's son-in-law, Ron Miller.[4] Roy and his partners had become adept at the merger-acquisition mania of the 1980s financial scene. Roy had developed a healthy portfolio under his banner company, Shamrock Inc., built on the site of the old UPA studios. Shamrock then was big enough to buy Polaroid Corporation. Roy used his boardroom skills to outmaneuver his cousin Ron Miller, bringing about Miller's resignation on September 7, 1984. When consolidating their control of Walt Disney, Roy and his colleague, Frank Wells, brought high-powered studio executives Michael Eisner and Jeffrey Katzenberg over from Paramount, where the two had been instrumental in helping Barry Diller turn around the fortunes of that sagging behemoth. Now Eisner and Katzenberg were given full powers to toss out, change, destroy—anything, just turn around the fortunes of the House of Mouse.

They immediately set to work bringing in new ideas, new people, and new talent from the rest of Hollywood: top filmmakers like Peter Weir, Woody Allen, and Paul Mazursky and film stars like Bette Midler, Richard Dreyfus, and Robin Williams. George Lucas, Steven Spielberg and Martin Scorsese came in to update theme rides at Disneyland (Star Tours, Captain Eo). When the Eisner-Wells-Katzenberg team looked at the animation unit, their first instinct was to get rid of it. Even with its new trainee program, it still looked like a handful of white-haired old men who turned out a movie every five years. By now most of the golden age artists were gone and its best days seemed to be in the past. They could shut down the animation unit and license the characters to be done overseas for quick cheapie films.

This was one instance where Roy Disney put his foot down. Animation was the heart and soul of Disney and he would not let it die. Modest and self-deprecating (he describes himself as "Walt's idiot nephew"),[5] he nonetheless carries an immense sense of responsibility for maintaining the Disney family legacy. This was hard to express to his corporate-raider, quick-buck colleagues. He got them to at least go over and see what the animation guys were planning.

On September 23, 1984, Michael Eisner, Frank Wells, and Jeffrey Katzenberg were taken by Roy Disney to meet the Disney animation department. They were pitched the storyboards of *Basil of Baker Street*, later renamed *The Great Mouse Detective*. They were won over by the potential of quality animation. Conventional wisdom had been that quality animation was too expensive to be profitable, but they understood that, with the right marketing and tie-ins, big animated films could be the revenue engines they had been in Walt's time. That same day, Eisner dictated the first memos ordering setting up a TV Animation Division. They bought Hanna-Barbera's Australian subcontracting studio and began work on *Tailspin* and *Gummy Bears*. The rest of the LA animation community laughed at Eisner's determination that elitist Disney should deign to compete with lowly Hanna-Barbera, but then TV was where the serious money was.

Don Bluth's independent attempt at his own "Snow White," *The Secret of Nimh* (1982), didn't make big box office, but it did signal that there was one studio in town that could do Disney-caliber animation outside the walls of the Disney studio. This attracted the eye of Steven Spielberg. After the hedonistic hangover from the "anything goes" 1960s and 1970s, Spielberg had shown audiences the way back to high-quality family films. *Jaws* (1975), *Close Encounters of the Third Kind* (1977), *Raiders of the Lost Ark* (1981), and *ET: The Extra-Terrestrial* (1982) appealed to the kid in everyone without being maudlin. After a decade-long diet of socially and sexually controversial films, Spielberg, with George Lucas, made family films cool again. Using Don Bluth's animation team in Ireland, Spielberg produced the animation hits *An American Tail* (1986) and *The Land before Time* (1988), giving Disney its first serious challenge since the Fleischer days. Spielberg also produced the Warner Bros. hit TV series *TinyToon Adventures* (1990) and *Animaniacs* (1993) and the *Amazing Stories* episode "The Family Dog" (1993). The last of these was directed by young Disney artist Brad Bird, who would later bring to the screen *The Iron Giant* (1999) and *The Incredibles* (2004). These were the kinds of projects Disney should have been turning out. Obviously, the key was a good story, memorable characters, and good music.

While Eisner and Wells concentrated on other aspects of the corporation, the animation department was left to Jeffrey Katzenberg. Roy Disney retained the title of president of animation and was involved, but he had Shamrock and his other holdings to manage as well. With the passion of a new convert, Katzenberg became the creative executive who rolled up his sleeves and leaped into the trenches with the animation team. At first he knew little about animation technique beyond reading Frank Thomas and Ollie Johnston's book *Disney Animation: The Illusion of Life*. There was a well-known, albeit apocryphal, story in the hallways that the first time he saw some animation dailies he said, "That's great, now what did the B and C cameras get?" But he came at the task with a demonic energy and a nose like P. T. Barnum's. One old-timer said Katzenberg was the closest thing to Walt since Walt. Jeffrey was a hyperactive bantam in black-rimmed glasses and immaculate white shirt, with a crease pressed into his stonewashed jeans. Like auteur-producer David O. Selznick in a previous generation, Jeffrey Katzenberg didn't bow to custom; he wanted results fast. He had a feeling for what the public wanted. While most of the younger team had been chosen and trained to focus on the principles of creating convincing, lifelike animation in the Disney tradition, Katzenberg and the other filmmakers he brought in, like Robert Zemeckis, declared, "It's about *entertainment first!*" To all of us who had turned the art of realistic movement into a stylized fetish, this was news.

While most studio execs had been content to condescendingly feign interest in what animators do, then quickly leave, Katzenberg was everywhere with opinions about everything: "I don't believe he's in love with her. . . . Guys, guys, ya got nothing here! She should be up in a tree with animals up the ying-yang! I really want ya to fuck me in the heart on this one!" More than once animator Glen Keane said to him, "It's a good thing you can't draw, then there would really be no living with you!"

Gag drawing of Jeffrey Katzenberg in Indian garb for the film *Pocahontas*. Katzenberg liked to give notes to his artists like, "Here she should be in the tree, with animals up the ying-yang." Artist unknown, 1994. Collection of the author.

Drawing the Line

The first time I entered the Disney studio after this sea change, I noticed the effects immediately. Instead of the rigid dress code that made animators look like they bought all their clothes in a golf pro shop, I saw wild jewelry, shaggy hair down to butts, and leopard-print spandex. The women looked even wilder. The atmosphere in meetings had changed, too. In a story meeting I heard Jeffrey good-naturedly call one of his directors a "real sick fuck" (New Yorkese for "Hello"). Jiminy Cricket! What would Bobby Driscoll have said?

There was a downside as well. Michael Eisner had also quietly canceled the policy of awarding longtime animators stock options that slowly made them rich enough to be able to donate entire hospital wings to Saint Joseph's. Obviously he had big plans for the stock. Eisner and Katzenberg moved the animation department out of the ancient headquarters on the main lot that it had occupied since 1939. Now the animation staff had to squeeze into a collection of ugly, faceless warehouses in an industrial park near the Disney Imagineering complex. Disney animators were back in pasteboard dividers and old furniture like in the days before the Hyperion Studio. They wondered if the end of the studio was near.

To many of the traditionalists for whom Disney was not just a company but also a way of life, all this was outrageous. It angered many of the retirees, too. Eric Larson, one of the Nine Old Men and a mentor to most of the young animators, made no secret of his contempt of the studio's new executives. But the results spoke for themselves. Eisner, Katzenberg, and Disney immediately launched the studio into an updated production of *Oliver Twist* with music by Billy Joel. Taglined "The First Disney Cartoon with Attitude," *Oliver & Company* (1988) wasn't a major breakthrough, but it was the shakedown cruise for the young team. It grossed $46 million in North American box office, which was double the usual take for an animated film of the time.

The first big salvo of this new era was 1988's *Who Framed Roger Rabbit?* Gary Wolf had written the novel *Who Censored Roger Rabbit?* in 1976. It was about a Raymond Chandler–esque hard-boiled detective who solved the murder of a cartoon character. Disney Studios bought the rights to the book, but another Disney animator at the time said to me that the studio was never going to make the film. Disney used to buy properties just to make sure no one else used them, the animator remarked, noting that. Disney owned the *Lord of the Rings* throughout the 1960s and never did anything with it. *Roger Rabbit* did indeed molder in a vault until 1984. Then while developing the Disneyland ride Star Tours, George Lucas and Steven Spielberg were allowed by Katzenberg to poke around in the archives, and Spielberg came upon this property. "This is terrific! Why aren't you making this?" he said. In answer to the blank stares all around, Katzenberg and Spielberg made a deal to jointly produce the film and have Spielberg's director-protégé Robert Zemeckis direct the project.

To keep the project midway between Disney and Spielberg's Amblimation, it was agreed that the animation would be done in London with a crew led by Richard Williams. There was a London animation trade union, a division of BECTU (Broadcasting Entertainment Cinematograph and Theatre Union), the British equivalent of IATSE. An accommodation was made for American artists working under Local 839 contracts in London.

During the making of *Roger Rabbit,* a new custom was born. Animation administrator Max Howard bought everyone on the project a customized crew jacket. The London magazine *Time Out* joked that so many wearers of crew jackets milled about the studio area of north London called Camden Town that it seemed to be occupied by a foreign army.[6] The jackets went a long way toward instilling a sense of pride in the unit. At first the studio back in Los Angeles tried to discourage interest in the jackets. When animator Dave Spafford returned to America with one, he was ordered not to wear it to work. Not only did he continue to wear it, but every time someone had to run an errand by the management offices, Dave thrust the jacket onto that person's shoulders: "Here, wear this!" Management finally relented and issued a lighter, Southern California–acclimatized black windbreaker with the familiar red Walt Disney script logo.[7] Soon every studio had to have its own crew jacket; your production simply wasn't serious without one.

Roger Rabbit was the first of many big-budget gambles for Eisner and Katzenberg's Disney. The budget zoomed upward, and the initial test screenings were a disaster. The rabbit and the live action were not seen together until the final compositing, because few of those shots were ready. When test screenings commenced, audiences were forced to judge the film by looking at grainy, empty rooms with props moving by themselves and black-and-white cartoon pencil tests. The audiences didn't understand any of it, so the approval numbers were dreadful. The first theatrical trailer, which tried to be a spoof of film noir conventions, also laid an egg with audiences.

Despite these setbacks and the final mad rush to completion, Katzenberg stood by Spielberg and Spielberg stood by Zemeckis, so the project remained relatively unmolested by upper management. An eleventh-hour crisis occurred when Disney suddenly demanded that the film be distributed as a Walt Disney Pictures release. Robert Zemeckis was against it. At this time the Disney brand on a live-action film had sunk very low in public esteem thanks to dreadful films like *Condor Man* (1982) and *The Black Hole* (1983). Eisner and Katzenberg wanted to use this film to restore the Disney brand name, but Zemeckis thought it would hurt his movie's chances. A compromise was to call it a Touchstone release, Touchstone being then the hipper PG wing of Disney distribution, which had released films like *Splash* (1984).

Who Framed Roger Rabbit? was a huge critical and financial success. It earned four Academy Awards and, at $150 million in North America alone, was the biggest box-office earner of 1988. Eddie Murphy, whose movie *Coming to America* was out at the same time, said to reporters, "Don't ask me 'bout dat damn rabbit!" *Who Framed Roger Rabbit?* proved to a skeptical Hollywood that a high-quality, high-budget cartoon could make the kind of monster profits made by an Arnold Schwarzenegger or Tom Cruise movie.

Meanwhile Richard Williams's Disney London crew, which had been promised more projects if this one hit it big, was laid off. The crew had been assembled from the four corners of the world with the idea that this was a one-shot project. During production, however, upper management decided to urge artists on to greater effort by dangling the carrot of long-term work under their noses. A memo was circulated declaring to them, "Your futures are assured." When the layoff notices filled the studio at the end of production, artists hung the memos on doors as a bitter reminder of the hollow promises of the powerful.

Camelot

Back in Burbank, the regular Disney animation crew wondered if *Roger Rabbit* was just an aberration in the normal pattern of animation releases. It was in keeping with the Lucas-Spielberg style of grown-up boys' fantasies. *Star Wars* (1977) was the Hollywood boomers remembering *Buck Rogers*; *Raiders of the Lost Ark* was the Hollywood kids remembering the cliffhanger serials of the 1930s like *Captain Marvel* and *Spy Smasher*; and *Who Framed Roger Rabbit?* could be called the Hollywood boy's remembrance of classic Looney Tunes of the 1940s. But did it really mean classic animation was back?

The next release, *Oliver & Company* (1988), earned a more understandable profit: $46 million. *Roger Rabbit* could be considered a special case.

The next film in the Disney studio schedule was *The Little Mermaid*. There is a legend that somewhere in the bowels of the studio there was a yellow, crumbling memo from Walt Disney about what fairy tales would and would not make good cartoon features. Supposedly topping the list of don't-do ideas was "The Little Mermaid," followed by "Beauty and the Beast." But, hey, who has time for history? To make *Mermaid*, Katzenberg forged an alliance with the Broadway musical team of Howard Ashman and Alan Menken. While the crew was finishing drawing the film, Katzenberg grandly announced that it was going to be the first animated feature to make $100 million at the box office. The crew all thought he was crazy. Animated films didn't earn that kind of money. In 1989 *The Little Mermaid* made $110.7 million in the United States and $222 million overseas, sparked billions in toy sales, and earned two Oscars. Disney publicity executive Howard Green said that four years after the movie was in the theaters, *The Little Mermaid* merchandise was still selling as if it were new. No one had seen anything like it.

Katzenberg now saw the animated feature as the lifeboat of the American Broadway musical, which had also been in the dumps the last few years. He felt musicals would be the next wave in the 1990s. The Disney artists made lots of jokes about Katzenberg buying the animation rights to *Paint Your Wagon*, *The One and Only Genuine Original Family Band*, and Ross Hunter's *Lost Horizon*. There was a rumor that he was seriously trying to secure the rights for *My Fair Lady* to make something called *My Fair Kitty*.

Drawing the Line

After purging all the production executives from the Ron Miller era, Katzenberg replenished the production ranks with personnel from the Broadway stage. Animators joked that back east on Times Square dancers and musicians must be milling about, wondering why no one had posted the next rehearsal schedule. Why? Because all their production people had left for Hollywood to go torture animators. Katzenberg's lead executive was Peter Schneider, whom he had met while working on the Arts Project for the 1984 Los Angeles Olympics. Schneider said he was called in to meet Roy Disney and for forty-five minutes discussed Roy's passion for yacht racing. "The next thing I knew I was on my way to a meeting with Steven Spielberg over *Roger Rabbit* as the spokesman for Disney Animation!"[8] This was a far cry from the days of production people like Ben Sharpsteen and Card Walker, who were longtime animation veterans.

The influx of theater people had good and bad effects. Some embraced this funny art form and its unique community; others preferred to just ride the gold rush until it petered out, then go back to their real love, the theater.

In the 1990s, the Disney team created some of the most memorable animated films since the golden age: *Beauty and the Beast* (1991), *Aladdin* (1992), and *The Lion King* (1994). *The Lion King* alone generated more than $2 billion worldwide ($350 million in North America) and for a while stood alongside *Jurassic Park* as the most profitable movie of all time. A psychological change had also occurred among the Disney artists. In the 1970s, artists seemed to have a preoccupation with recreating the glory of the past. It was as though the best work ever done in animation had been done before they were born. Ironically, it was old Frank Thomas and Ollie Johnston who wanted to discuss new animated films they saw. Even they noticed it was unhealthy to dwell on the past all the time. Now all the emphasis was on the future and the next film. Everyone looked forward to breaking new ground with each new challenge.

At the same time, big things were happening in Disney's television animation division. Starting with *Aladdin II: The Return of Jafar* (1994) and *A Goofy Movie* (1995), Disney Television Animation produced a series of highly profitable made-for-video movies. The writing and preproduction were done in Los Angeles and the bulk of production completed cheaply outside the United States: Tokyo, Australia, Canada, and Taiwan. Disney's success started the other Hollywood studios salivating. All this profit was accumulated with no major stars like Tom Cruise or Jack Nicholson taking $20 million and 20 percent of net profits. In 1972, 55 percent of the total revenue of the Walt Disney Company was from theme parks; in 1994, 55 percent of the total revenue of the company was from animation. All this success was accomplished with MPSC union animators.

Don Bluth was not the only one working to catch Disney's lead in feature animation. Scenting success, Warner Bros. revived its long-dead animation units, and Paramount (through Ralph Bakshi), Hanna-Barbera, and others weighed in with new feature cartoons: *Rover Dangerfield* (1991), *FernGully: The Last Rainforest* (1992), *Bebe's Kids* (1992), *Cool World* (1992), *Once Upon a Forest* (1993), *The Swan Princess* (1994). Warner Bros. Feature Animation, under former Disney executive Max Howard, built a facility in Glendale with a research library and humidity-sealed archives. Maverick movie mogul Ted Turner bought Hanna-Barbera and tried his own version of playing Walt Disney: *The Pagemaster* (1994) and *Cats Don't Dance* (1997).[9]

All this competition made it fat city for experienced 2D animators. Dingy warehouse industrial spaces with corkboard walls were replaced by offices with matching furniture and scenic views. Salaries tripled and signing bonuses were paid out as studios vied for the small pool of experienced artists. Year-round employment replaced the television season. The money was nothing like a movie star earns, but it was tops for the animation world. Basic union minimum was $1,000 a week; the market rate was $2,500–3,000 a week. Studios wanted to lock talent into a repertory-company system, going from picture to picture. The studio publicity departments, working on the model of Frank Thomas and Ollie Johnston and the Nine Old Men, turned out stories of the new star animators: Glen Keane, Eric Goldberg, Andreas Deja, Will Finn, Kathy Zielinski, Duncan Marjoribanks, Bruce Smith, and many more. Animators got agents and negotiated personal service contracts. The *Wall Street Journal* and *Newsweek* did features on the life of a Hollywood animator. An animator finally got on *Premiere* magazine's list of the 100 Most Powerful People in Hollywood. Glen Keane was number 100, but at least we made the list. The unseen, unknown little gnomes were coming out into the sunlight. For a while it was actually cool to be an animator.

Drawing the Line

What was great for the local animation community was that more studios were getting into animation, and, possibly more important, results showed that any attempt to do a big feature on the cheap overseas had met with failure. Only the high-quality union work in Los Angeles made the monster profits.

Los Angeles began to see a reverse of the runaway period. The finest animation talent in the world was being brought to Los Angeles to augment the crews there. In 1977 my New York accent was the most exotic sound anyone in a studio had ever heard. In 1990, Hollywood studios were a United Nations of artists—French, Irish, Dutch, Vietnamese, Korean, Bulgarian. This worked to the advantage of the cartoonists' union, because people from other countries, especially the Europeans, didn't seem to have the revulsion for trade unionism that Americans seemed to imbibe with their baby formula in the Reagan era. The new artists knew that at home trade unions were the only trustworthy guardians of employees' livelihoods. In 1979, the membership of Local 839 peaked at 1,985 active members. After the strikes and recession, those numbers plummeted to 715 by 1987, but by 1994, the membership was at an all-time high of 3,000 members. If a film flopped, studios, discouraged, would eliminate animation departments; the latest hit would send them back to the table for another try. The sky was the limit, and it seemed like the good times would go on forever.

In 1993, MPSC Local 839, under my leadership and that of business agent Steve Hulett, went to Orlando and helped the Florida artists form their own union as MPSC Local 843, Orlando. The local created a multiple-employer 401(k) plan and provided health benefits for same-sex couples. The union also established contact with the French Syndicat Audiovisuel representing artists in Paris. The Florida and French artists quickly won wage parity with their Burbank compatriots. Union wage scales showing what artists were earning in Los Angeles were mailed to animators as far away as Mexico City and Minsk.

At the same time, the upstart Fox network started a revolution in TV animation. In its attempts to break the exclusive hold of the three major television networks, Fox saved money on censors and pushed the limits of taste with iconoclastic shows like *Married with Children*. In

1987, producer James L. Books hired *LA Weekly* underground cartoonist Matt Groening to develop animated interstitials for Fox's *Tracey Ullman Show*.[10] At first Fox wanted Groening to use his trademark Binky rabbit from his regular "Life in Hell" comic strip, but Groening was reluctant to lose control of his then bread-and-butter character. Instead, he developed a dysfunctional family he called the Simpsons. Rather than use typically low-paid TV animation writers, Brooks went into the world of big-time sitcoms and assembled a team of top writers. Groening used a team of brash young independent animators—David Silverman, Wes Archer, Jim Reardon—anchored by Disney veteran Brad Bird.

After Groening's animated interstitials became the highlight of the *Ullman* show, Brooks's Gracie Films pushed for a regular prime-time series. Fox chief Barry Diller was at first reluctant. There had not been a successful prime-time cartoon show for thirty years, since *Top Cat* was a hit in the sixties. Hanna-Barbera's two attempts to revive the form—*Where's Huddles* (1970) and *Wait till Your Father Gets Home* (1972–1974)—met with minimal results. Diller would have preferred to produce a series of TV specials like the *Garfield* franchise, but Brooks won out, getting a regular series run of nineteen episodes per season.

Originally the grunt work of *The Simpsons*, which debuted in December 1989, was done at the animation studio Klasky Csupo. Gabor Csupo was a Hungarian immigrant with a hatred of unions. He declared to the *Los Angeles Times* he would "slash his wrists rather than sign a union contract." He assembled a team of young animators under Fox-contracted directors and convinced them that not being in the union gave them more flexibility and creative freedom. After two seasons, Gracie Films transferred *The Simpsons* and most of its staff from Klasky Csupo to Film Roman, a company started in 1983 by old Warner's animator Phil Roman, originally to make *Garfield* specials. Phil had been very pro-union when he worked under Bill Melendez, constantly urging Melendez not to send animation work overseas. As the boss, he maintained the show's nonunion culture. He was supported by some disgruntled SCG veterans and some older Disney artists who were in any case already vested in their IATSE pensions. Every other facet of production—sound, editing, camera, and actors—was done by union-contract workers so the show could still sport the IATSE logo on its end credits. In 1998, the show's writers won representation with the Writers Guild of America. By working together the voice actors won great salary bumps. Only the four hundred animators refused any type of collective representation. When upper management fired a popular production manager, the Film Roman artists overwhelmingly signed petitions to keep him, yet taking the next logical step to organize under a union contract seemed totally alien to them. Not until 2004, after the show had been running for an unprecedented fifteen seasons, did the artists finally vote to organize.

The Simpsons became a phenomenon. It was the most successful show on television for more than a decade. Writers like Conan O'Brian and Larry Doyle left for other opportunities, but new blood came in and the show kept going. In 1992, when President George Bush senior referred to Bart Simpson derogatorily in a speech about family values, people voted in droves for his opponent, Gov. Bill Clinton.

A new, hip tone took hold in television animation. *The Simpsons,* John Kricfalusi's iconoclastic *Ren & Stimpy* (1991), and the output of MTV's independent animated showcase, Liquid Television—Peter Chung's *Aeon Flux* (1995), Mike Judge's *Beavis and Butt-Head* (1992)—sparked many imitators. Klasky Csupo recovered from the loss of *The Simpsons* and created *The Rugrats* and *The Wild Thornberrys* shows. The Cartoon Network started in 1990 and created a new audience for old Hanna-Barbera shows like *Space Ghost,* and its shorts program fostered new properties, spawning series from some successful college-student films: *Dexter's Lab, Johnny Bravo, Powerpuff Girls* (originally the *Whupass Girls*). Television boomed with half a dozen prime-time and late-night shows in addition to the regular daytime and cable fare. Disney Channel and Nickelodeon went out to eighty countries twenty-four hours a day. MPSC Local 839 tried several different ways to organize these studios, but the union-hating rebel counterculture was deeply inculcated into their young artists. Most of these small studios had reasons for avoiding signing a contract with the MPSC. The cost of health coverage and pensions for artists would add 30 percent to their costs. After a contract was signed, the IA reserved the right to occasional audits of studios' payroll records, and some contractors didn't want anyone to see anything questionable hidden in their books. Also, many of these little studios had big contracts with union-hating conglomerates like Sumner Redstone's Viacom and Rupert Murdoch's Fox News Corp.

Camelot

The message to avoid union contracts at all costs was sent from New York and Sydney to Los Angeles execs, who relied on a loyal core group of young, hip artists with no emotional connection to the older established animation studio culture. They didn't see the old robber barons pulling the strings. All they saw was their hip studio director with his earring and Save-the-Whales T-shirt; they felt no connection to a union they did not understand. Their shows made them real money, at least for a while, with no health benefits or pensions. Che Guevara said, "It is hard to be a revolutionary on a full stomach." Klasky Csupo's secret was importing animation talent from Eastern Europe, where the slogans of union brotherhood and workers uniting were viewed with suspicion. It sounded too much like the old Soviet-dominated world they had just escaped. After removing most of his employees from the MPSC, Don Bluth moved his studio to Ireland and then to Phoenix. Arizona is a right-to-work state reminiscent of the union-hating Florida of the 1930s that the Fleischer brothers loved so much.

There was no end to the shenanigans used to circumvent basic worker rights in this boom atmosphere. Artists were given contracts with booby traps in the legalese taking away their overtime pay. Some artists were declared in-house freelance workers. Some contracts forbade artists to join a union, a violation of the Wagner Act of 1935; others forbade artists to discuss their salaries, a violation of several California laws. A group of Philippine artists were imported with all expenses paid by an agent who pocketed their salaries and gave them allowances—in effect, indentured servitude that would have been familiar to Rip Van Winkle. A similar group of Korean animators was held in a secret studio on Olympic Boulevard in Koreatown. With millions to be made and most artists ignorant of the basic skills of business negotiations, it was open season. One exec said, "It's Purchasing 101. You talk the client into agreeing to a contract that is not in his best interest." To stay competitive with union studios for top talent, these studios soon instituted their own makeshift health care, dental, and 401(k) plans. These costs rose until the monetary difference for the studios between union and nonunion shrank to almost nothing. But the rancor against unions remained.

First-time animators flush with success saw no need to rock the boat with a union. Despite the fact that the MPSC never expresses any opinion on creative content, this new culture of edgy cartoons was packaged and sold to the workers as only being possible in a nonunion studio.

At a union Christmas party when a member was teased for attending wearing a *Simpsons* (hence nonunion) crew jacket, the young miscreant drew himself up and proclaimed with indignant pride, "This jacket means freedom!" In modern times the Vatican complained about Americans being "cafeteria Catholics," picking and choosing which doctrines to follow. In the same way some younger animators became "cafeteria cartoonists." They could shed copious tears at the memorials for their old mentors like Maurice Noble and Chuck Jones, then ignore their passionate unionism and cheerfully open nonunion studios without seeing any contradictions.

The mainstream contract studios, Disney and Warner, complained about having to compete with these cheap nonunion studios. Peter Schneider teased me at meetings, "Tom, when are you going to do something about these nonunion studios?" The explosion of cable channels meant that sponsorship fees had declined. Where once the kid audience dependably was all watching *Scooby Doo* or *He-Man,* now it was splintered among dozens of channels: Cartoon Network, Kids WB, Nickelodeon, Disney, Boomerang, Discovery Kids, and others. The feds in Washington also drove a stake into the heart of Saturday morning kid-vid with the Children's Television Act, promulgated on July 11, 1996. The creation of longtime lobbying by such pressure groups as Action for Children's Television (ACT), the act imposed such extreme restrictions on children's programming (ACT chairman Peggy Charren singled out animated programs for special blame) that the old networks just stopped most animation production altogether. They switched to local sports and information shows. Most of the audience had gravitated to the cable stations like Nickelodeon and Disney Channel anyway. Saturday morning television revenue, which had once been the reliable staple of the industry, plummeted. Ironically, audiences for the new cable channels were enjoying shows like the *Flintstones* and *Space Ghost,* shows their parents watched. Another effect of the Children's Television Act was that anything edgy enough to have other than an absolute G rating was banned from being advertised on children's programming.

This erosion of union negotiating strength in television occurred just when the feature artists were feeling their oats enough to want to try again to win residuals. Many of the top animators were ready to demand backend moneys in the next basic contract negotiation in 1994. They were angry because the disparity in compensation for the success of the features was becoming glaringly obvious. While a chorus singer in New York on the *Beauty and the Beast* soundtrack got a bonus check from Disney of $175,000, the artist who drew the characters got a one-time unofficial bonus of around $5,000. The artists were suffering from overwork. Wrist wraps for repetitive motion injuries and carpal tunnel syndrome were common. Meanwhile, a number of producers, most of whom entered their jobs completely ignorant of the animation process, began chalking up small fortunes. One artist sarcastically laughed, "When I began at Disney Michael Eisner was only making $2 million a year, now he makes $22 million a year! I'm proud!"

At the request of some directing animators, the MPSC began talking to the star law firm that successfully sued actress Kim Basinger over her breach of contract for the film *Boxing Helena* (1993). Peggy Lee and the Philadelphia Philharmonic had recently won high-profile lawsuits against Disney for the rerelease on video and compact disc of the music from their films *Lady & the Tramp* and *Fantasia*. The MPSC felt if it were to go to war over such a case, it needed some fierce Hollywood legal talent. The attorneys felt the cartoonists had a good case to take public about Disney's inadequate compensation, but after a few meetings with the animators the momentum seemed to stall. Some of Disney's key animators turned around and adopted a politically cautious wait-and-see attitude. Combined with the loyalists who just would never go against the House of Mouse, their defection blew some serious holes in Local 839's effort. With such a sizable portion of the cartoon industry nonunion, there was not enough muscle to go all the way. It seemed to be 1969 all over again. The attorneys finally said to the MPSC leaders, "Hey, you don't have a lot of solidarity, do you?" Once more the effort melted away like the snows in spring. Residuals would remain a dream for a future time.

The end of the second animation renaissance began when Walt Disney CEO Frank Wells went on a weekend skiing trip on April 2, 1994. Wells was a rabid ski fan who had adopted the new beautiful-people fad of avoiding the long waiting lines for ski lifts by chartering a private helicopter to fly to the more remote ski slopes. That morning Billy Joel and his wife, Christie Brinkley, had a scare when their helicopter developed engine trouble midflight on a similar trip. Undaunted, Wells resolved to push on to the slopes. His friend Clint Eastwood was supposed to accompany him, but Clint had to cancel at the last minute. As Wells's helicopter climbed higher and higher through the snow-packed Sierras, some loose packed powder blew off an overhanging escarpment. A freak ice ball was sucked into the helicopter's air manifold, causing the engine to stall and the craft to fall like a stone. No one inside ever had a chance. The helicopter crashed and exploded, killing all on board. Wells's death sent shock waves through the power players of Hollywood. Wells was low key in public, but in boardrooms he was the vital link between all the major players in the Disney success story. His death left a gaping hole in the Walt Disney Company's top management.

After the grief passed, everyone naturally assumed that Jeffrey Katzenberg would move up and assume Wells's position as an equal to Michael Eisner and Roy Disney, but Eisner hesitated. Katzenberg, never good at waiting, began to pester his old partner, even visiting him at his bedside while he was recovering from quadruple bypass surgery. Finally, at the Telluride Film Festival, Eisner gave Katzenberg the bad news: there was to be no promotion. Eisner himself would assume the combined roles of chairman and CEO. Later evidence showed Eisner never had any thought of Katzenberg advancing to Wells's position.

Katzenberg was stunned. This was the partner whom he had given his all for. If he accepted this and went back to his corner, in the world of Hollywood power players he would be seen as diminished, as nothing more than Eisner's golden retriever. Katzenberg's friends Steven Spielberg and music mogul David Geffen advised him not to stay at Disney. His contract option was coming up, and they urged him to join a new partnership they were planning. The animus between him and Eisner and Roy Disney was growing. Animation executives like Peter Schneider and Tom Schumacher were caught in the middle. Their code words for these fights were "Mom & Pop are fighting again."[11] So in late July 1994, just when *The Lion King* was taking off, Katzenberg announced he was leaving the Walt Disney Company. The artists at the feature animation division were stunned. What was going to happen now?

Eisner at first tried to replace Katzenberg with Creative Artists

Camelot

Agency superagent Michael Ovitz, but after a year Ovitz left, doing little but taking a $140 million contract buyout with him. This outraged stockholders, who sued Disney to try to get the money back. Then Eisner tried Joe Roth, but that didn't work out either, and Roth formed Revolution Studios.

In early 1995, Katzenberg joined Steven Spielberg and David Geffen to form DreamWorks SKG, and Katzenberg began aggressively wooing top animation talent away from Disney. Warner Bros. and Ted Turner Animation were also in the market for experienced artists, and a bidding war resulted. Unlike the little cable houses, DreamWorks was a union-contract studio from its birth. In a meeting with MPSC leaders under a tree at his famous adobe offices on the Universal lot, nicknamed the Taco Bell, Spielberg snapped a crisp salute and declared, "We don't have time to fool around, we need to start fast with the best talent that there is. So we are a union studio!"

Disney's legal department contested Katzenberg's cut of *The Lion King* profits, and the disagreement devolved into a bitter court trial. Finally, the court awarded Katzenberg $145 million.

A 1997 *New Yorker* article estimated that what with the lawsuits, the added costs to compete with DreamWorks, and lost revenue, the little snowball in Frank Wells's helicopter cost the Walt Disney Company over $1 billion.

By the year 2000, budgets and staff levels of animated feature films bulged.

When Hanna-Barbera was at its peak, the production staff was minimal. Even Walt Disney Studio animation in the Ron Miller era was administered by three people and a man to hand out pencils and paper. Now in Hollywood every department in a cartoon studio needed a production manager, a production coordinator, two assistant production managers, and a cloud of production assistants. New computers and tracking systems were developed almost per production. Instead of hiring one or two savants who knew where every one of the 1,500-plus animation scenes were in the pipeline at any one time, studios invested ruinous amounts on computerized tracking systems with tech support and additional staff to feed it information. Legal departments also grew by leaps and bounds.

Drawing the Line

Old animator Frank Thomas once sighed: "'Ya know the difference between 1940 and now? In 1940 there were fifty artists to every lawyer, now there are fifty lawyers to every artist."[12] This entire overhead had to be reflected in the film budgets. In 1977 the Richard Williams musical *Raggedy Ann & Andy* went over budget at $4.9 million and Disney's *Rescuers* cost $17 million to make. By 2000, animated film budgets were estimated to be "a million a minute." Budgets of $147 million to $200 million were not unusual.

In 1984 the Disney studio had one crew of 125 artists. By 1989, it had 500, plus the TV animation unit of 175, which worked with Sydney, Tokyo, and Taipei. In 1989 Disney created two feature units to leapfrog one another, then the Florida studio, then the Paris unit, then a separate unit to make *Fantasia 2000*, then another to create *Dinosaurs* (2000). And of course there were contracts with Pixar for five animated films. By 2000 the Disney studio staffing rose to over 2,100 workers.

It was a structure that could not withstand any adversity. And Disney was not the only studio with such big overhead. Warner Bros., Paramount, and Fox's Phoenix studio maintained large crews who sat around reading comic books between films.

At the same time, the corporate owners and stockholders insisted that every animated release be a bigger blockbuster than the previous one. Animation studios were not allowed to make a small film. Live-action filmmakers could have a hit, then a flop, then go on their merry way. A prestige film like *Boys Don't Cry* (1999) could rack up the accolades while doing little business, but the minute animated features hit a tough patch, pundits started writing epitaphs for the entire animation industry. The crew on Disney's *Pocahontas* (1995) was actually depressed after *The Lion King*'s box office soared to $100 million in just ten days; it was just too tough an act to follow. Everyone felt the pressure of the industry mantra "Bigger, better, faster, cheaper."

As the millennium approached, tastes changed, and the world audience finally tired of its steady diet of Broadway musicals à la cartoon. Test audiences groaned aloud when the first tinkly piano notes signaled an impending long song sequence. The studios scrambled to find a successful new formula. They tried to create American anime, or Japanese-style action adventure, but the mass-market nature of Hollywood meant animation could never be as edgy or implicitly sexual as Japanimation.

Camelot

In Japanese anime and manga, characters frequently are slain or mutilated to reappear as robot entities, as Mamoru Oshii's 1995 film *Ghost in the Shell*. No matter how exciting a sequence was, no one ever seriously thought a Disney or Warner character would die—at least not since Bambi's mother. In addition, dynamic new digital visual effects had moved back the borders between live action and animation. If the live-action *Tomb Raider* (2001) and the cartoon *Atlantis* (2001) had basically the same story, except one had sexy Angela Jolie and the other didn't, which do you think young teenage boys would choose?

So, bombs away: *Dinosaurs* (2000), *Anastasia* (1997), *The Emperor's New Groove* (2000), *The Road to El Dorado* (2000), *Atlantis* (2001), *The Iron Giant* (1999), *Titan AE* (2000), *Osmosis Jones* (2001), *Treasure Planet* (2002), *Sinbad* (2004), *Home on the Range* (2004), *Looney Tunes Back in Action* (2003). All these films cost between $50 million and $200 million each and performed poorly for a myriad of reasons.

While 2D hand-drawn films sputtered, CGI studios like Pixar scored hit after hit. *Ice Age* and *Shrek* capped the CGI success, and Klasky Csupo's *Rugrats* films demonstrated that you could now do a hit movie overseas. Looking for someone to blame for the downturn in their fortunes, the big studios turned on their celebrity artists. Those big salaries were now trumpeted in the media as the primary reason their films failed. The castles of sand began to fall. Paramount abandoned animation; Fox got rid of Don Bluth's Phoenix studio. Warner's sold off its infrastructure and decided that if it did more animated films, crews would be hired on a per-project basis like the live-action model.

After Katzenberg's exit, the Disney publicity machine went into overdrive to emphasize that he was not essential to Disney's feature animation success. They used the same time-honored tactics they had employed in Art Babbitt's case. The war between Katzenberg and Eisner, stoked by the press, left many animators hemming and hawing in front of reporters.

The lieutenants Katzenberg left behind at Disney were accustomed to anticipating and taking orders from him. They were now ordered to recreate his intuitive magic—a task that was simply beyond them. Strategic missteps burned millions in development, and, in the end, again the artists became the scapegoats. But the animators had merely done what they were told; they drew the things they were told to draw and developed the ideas they were told to develop.

In 2002 a new rift developed between Roy Disney and Michael Eisner when Roy tried to arrange for his son Kenneth to succeed him on the executive board. Eisner blocked the appointment, then, citing a mandatory executive retirement clause, had Roy forced off the central executive board. On November 30, 2002, Roy Disney and Disney family attorney Stanley Gold resigned from the board after publicly calling upon Eisner to step down. They began an aggressive grass-roots campaign to oust him from the chairmanship. They started a Web site, SaveDisney.com, which was regularly read by thousands of Disney employees and fans. The company's stockholder meetings turned into angry free-for-alls. Because the feature animation division was so close to Roy's heart, when Eisner began dismantling the 2D staff, many interpreted the move as Eisner's way of getting back at him.

Something besides insecurity and confusion was driving upper studio management. The attention the animators got in the Katzenberg-Eisner feud and the new feud between Roy Disney and Eisner had soured the Disney management on the cult of the celebrity artist. The studio began to deemphasize the value of the performing animator and looked for cheaper means to make characters move. The animator was now to be a craftsman functionary like a stage carpenter, nothing more. New executives, brought to Disney fresh out of business school, bragged of their lack of understanding of the medium of which they were now in charge. They could look at a high-quality film like *Lilo & Stitch* (2002) and a low-budget quickie like *Lady and the Tramp II: Scamp's Adventure* (2001) and not see any appreciable difference.

In fact, the release of *Lilo & Stitch* in 2002 was an act of unintended irony. The film, by Chris Sanders and Dean DuBois, is a precocious fantasy about a little Hawaiian girl who adopts an alien from another world as a pet. *Lilo & Stitch* earned over $300 million and was the most successful Disney animated film since *Tarzan*. It was animated at the Burbank and Orlando studios with traditional pencil drawing augmented with some 3D CGI, mostly for the spaceships. It was also colored and composited digitally, as all traditional cartoons had been done since *Rescuers Down Under* (1990). The central theme of the film, which is set in a contemporary native Hawaiian household, is "Ohana means family; family means no one gets left behind or forgotten." While audiences around the world were charmed by this sentiment, Disney management was busy getting rid of their artists.

The Disney animators remember March 25, 2002, as the day when the plans for the massive layoffs were made known. Twenty- and thirty-year animation veterans would lose their jobs. These people had spent their entire professional lives at Disney and never wanted to work anywhere else. For years they had been assured that they were "part of the magic," that Disney was more than just a place to work. They were part of the family. From mere blank paper they had brought to life Ariel, Beast, and Simba and generated billions of dollars for an otherwise sputtering corporation. Some were old enough to have known Walt Disney and were protégés of the Nine Old Men. But they were told by the newly

Disney traditional artists show their anger toward their employers in drawings. Caricature of Michael Eisner and Tom Schumacher, then head of feature animation, 2003. Collection of the author.

minted execs that their careers were now over. It was the biggest massacre of artists since the *Sleeping Beauty* layoff in 1958. One remaining animator said, "I feel like Anne Frank hiding in an attic."

Starting in 2003 Walt Disney Studio laid off 1,400 workers and closed Disney Paris, Tokyo, and Orlando. In 2006 they closed Disney Australia. One senior layout artist was told his option was not being renewed and his job was being phased out, but in the time remaining on his contract, would he consider going overseas to train his replacement? He said in no uncertain terms where studio officials could go. Assistant animator Jacky Sanchez boldly said to the executives, "You guys have the London Philharmonic and you are busting it down to a boy band!" In September 2005 John Musker and Ron Clements, the veteran directors of *The Little Mermaid* and *Aladdin*, ended their employment. Their goodbye party was held in the driveway of the feature animation building. Studio head David Stainton declared: "I know John & Ron still have more classic films in them!" But for the near future they would not be made for Disney. Laid-off effects animator Dan Lund and his partner Tony West created a documentary of their experience called *Dream On, Silly Dreamer*. It was screened for stockholders at a meeting in Minneapolis to thunderous applause. Michael Eisner began a third feud, this one with Steve Jobs and Pixar. On January 29, 2004, after ten months of frustrating negotiations, Pixar announced it was walking away from any further contract talks with the Disney Company. Six days later Pixar chairman Steve Jobs criticized Disney Animation, calling its more recent releases *Treasure Planet* and *Brother Bear* "bombs" and the studio's cheap sequels "embarrassing."

At the annual Disney stockholders meeting on March 3, 2004, in Philadelphia, a whopping 43 percent of polled stockholders demanded that Eisner resign. It was the highest no vote ever recorded for a U.S. stockholders meeting. The meeting was webcast back to the Disney/ Burbank Studio lot where office workers in the cubicles cheered the news. The next day, after twenty-one years, Michael Eisner stepped down from the chairmanship of the Walt Disney Company, and on October 1, 2005, he was succeeded by Robert Iger. Pixar soon resumed contract talks with Disney. Roy Disney was reinstated to the Disney executive board.

Meanwhile, DreamWorks SKG opened big and created an ambitious slate of animated films. The first big efforts, *The Prince of Egypt* (1998) and *Antz* (2000), performed well but not tremendously; *The Road to El*

Dorado (2001) and *Spirit: Stallion of the Cimarron* (2002) disappointed and *Sinbad* (2003) flopped. The DreamWorks attempts at TV animation—*Invasion USA, Toonsylvania* and *Father of the Pride*—all failed. Despite successes like *Shrek* (2001), *Shrek II* (2004) and *Madagascar* (2005), it seemed in retrospect that Disney needed Jeffrey Katzenberg and he needed Disney. Both seemed a little less for their separation.

On September 23, 1994, a party was thrown for Jeffrey Katzenberg to say goodbye to the Disney animation staff. It was ten years to the day that he, Roy, Eisner, and Wells first walked together into the Walt Disney studio. Instead of being on the main studio lot, the party was squirreled away in a far corner of the faceless warehouses of the same Glendale business park where *The Little Mermaid* and *The Lion King* had been made. The function was surreptitiously called an Octoberfest to keep its true meaning a secret from the press. Disney upper management stayed away. As the Disney animators talked to Katzenberg about all the classic films they had made together, Katzenberg's conclusion was, "Hey, it was Camelot."

12

Animation . . . Isn't That All Done on Computers Now?

The Digital Revolution

Gee, that film had such warmth and character in it,
what software were you using?
                            —Technician to John Lasseter

In 1987, former Disney animators Bill and Sue Kroyer created *Technological Threat*, a short cartoon that makes fun of the dawning digital era. The film combines, or interfaces if you prefer, 3D characters and traditional 2D characters. It is about a Tex Avery–style cartoon wolf that works in an office slowly being taken over by pyramid-headed computerized artists. It won awards including an Oscar nomination. And it turned out to be more prophetic than anyone could realize then.

The 1990s had been a boom time for traditional animators; every Hollywood studio had a large crew ensconced in cubicles with pencils wiggling. But as the big-budget hand-drawn musicals failed at the box office, the unique-looking digitally animated films became a novelty with audiences. CGI films like DreamWorks's *Shrek* and *Shrek 2*, Fox's *Ice Age* and *Ice Age: The Meltdown*, Nickelodeon's *Jimmy Neutron*, and IDT's *Hoodwinked* made box-office news. Most especially there was Pixar with an unprecedented record of six blockbuster hit movies in a

© 2006 Kroyer Films, inc.

Pencil-pushing artists face their computer replacement in Bill and Sue Kroyer's Academy Award–nominated short, *Technological Threat* (1987). As funny as the film was, it turned out to be prophetic. Courtesy of Bill and Sue Kroyer.

row: *Toy Story, A Bug's Life, Toy Story 2, Monsters Inc., Finding Nemo,* and *The Incredibles.* The corporate entities controlling Hollywood concluded that only 3D CGI movies are box-office gold mines.

Between 2003 and 2006, DreamWorks, Warner Bros., and Twentieth Century-Fox dumped their hand-drawn animation departments and went digital. Even the Walt Disney studio, which for seven decades had led the way in animation innovations, became just one more confused elephant following the herd. Universal's *Curious George* (2006) became the final mainstream Hollywood cartoon feature to be completely hand drawn. Pencil was now used only for TV storyboards and preproduction design work.

CGI had developed over a half century in myriad unrelated places—in the work of avant-garde artists like Mary Ellen Bute, Philippe Bergeron at the National Film Board of Canada, and UPA artists John and James Whitney; in Defense Department flight simulators; and in university research labs. The history of the development of CGI animation is worthy of book to itself, but this is not the right place.

Animation . . . Isn't That All Done on Computers Now?

While research into computer digital imaging slowly evolved in places like Stanford, Cornell, MIT, and Bell Laboratories, until the 1980s the mainstream film community ignored it. Movie executives would, on occasion, grant an audience to a nerdy technician with the obligatory pocket protector who would try their patience with detailed explanations of the potential of inverse kinematics and wire-frame removal. The low-resolution green fluorescent monitors were too weak to even appear on a film or video; they had to be matted in later. It all seemed too far off, too limited, too time consuming, and above all too expensive to be applicable to serious filmmaking.

In 1983, Jim Blinn, a young artist working for NASA, took CGI a quantum leap forward in front of a world audience.[1] In 1979, two Voyager space probes were launched on a tour of the outer planets of our solar system. NASA needed a simulation film to explain exactly what was happening, especially if the spacecrafts' on-board cameras failed to send back clear images. Blinn's masterful handling of the CG medium created realistic visuals that ran on all major world news outlets covering the event. CGI had earlier been used in the interest of science education in the 1980 Public Broadcasting Service program *Cosmos,* in which Carl Sagan strolled through a virtual re-creation of the ancient Great Library of Alexandria and, in another scene, talked about a churning gas nebula. But it was the Voyager fly-by films that inspired a generation of CG artists the way Winsor McCay's animation of *Gertie the Dinosaur* inspired a generation of traditional animators. At a SIGGRAPH meeting (Special Interest Group on Graphics and Interactive Techniques) in 1985, digital artist Jim Hillin pointed Blinn out to me and said: "Of the top ten most influential computer artists, Jim Blinn is seven."

The 1980s proved to be the pioneering era of CGI. Television provided a great demand for flying logos that zipped and flashed. Traditional animators were more than willing to let them have the dreary work of turning complex geometric images in perspective. Small independent studios popped up like mushrooms, leased some Cray supercomputers, ran up a lot of debt on the speculation of profits, maybe broke some new ground, then went under. CG animator Mike Disa said the evolution of CGI was an endless pattern: "Two nerds take an expensive program and modify it to do something that it was never intended for. It didn't yet look as good as the old-fashioned way, but it was cheaper and faster and that was good enough for the suits."[2] Suits always had trouble with flaky artists and their moods, but they understood the idea of retooling. It was the digital equivalent of a Wild West gold rush—hucksters, nerds, geniuses, and gamblers abounded. Everybody you met at a festival seemed to have *the* program that was going to revolutionize entertainment. As in the early days of network television, the lowly production trainee who sat near the washroom reading technical manuals became the studio expert overnight. A number of experienced, traditionally trained animators like Randy Cartwright, Chris Bailey, Ken Cope, Tina Price, and Mark Mayerson wanted to see how their skills might be applicable to CGI production.

Bob Abel's studio started a new appreciation of character animation with his 1987 ad for the Canned Food Council, "Brilliance," known as the sexy robot ad. Digital Productions, with the aid of ex-Disney animator Bill Kroyer, made the *Hard Woman* rock video for Mick Jagger. Steve Goldberg created the great character short, *Locomotion*, which, along with the Michael Jackson video *Black & White*, created a sensation for morphing. It was the 1980s, when companies bought each other like big fish devouring small fish. A Canadian company, Omnibus, under John Pennie bought out Abel and Digital Productions but accrued mountains of debt in the process (Abel's company alone came with $12 million in debt), so much so that Omnibus quickly was bankrupt by April 1987. One artist called the company Digital-Omnibus-Abel or DOA.

After the bankruptcy, one of Omnibus's creative directors, Dan Phillips, moved to Disney animation and joined Price, Hillin, Goldberg, Paul Janover, and Scott Johnston in helping start Disney Feature Animation's CGI department. The other survivors of the "Omni Bust" formed new studios: Pacific Data Images, Rhythm & Hues, Metrolight, and Jim Cameron's Digital Domain. Some older, traditional service houses like Iwerks and Leon Schlesinger's original firm, Pacific Art & Title, reinvented themselves as CGI houses. Stan Winston's Creature Shop and Jim Henson's company also explored going digital.

The 1980s also saw a boom in video games using simple animation: Pac-Man, Donkey Kong, Q-Bert, and Paw-Paws. Venerable electronic giants like Phillips and Texas Instruments set up animation divisions to create games. While paying top dollar for software engineers and programmers, they balked at the normal salaries even low-paid animators were getting. So they mainly hired kids with no experience but lots of stamina and a copy of Preston Blair's *How to Animate Film Cartoons*. They stuck them in a back room with some huge mainframes and waited for the magic to happen. Meanwhile ex-Disney director Don Bluth, seeing his feature film efforts stalled temporarily, jumped into computer games. He created a sensation with the use of high-quality character animation in his many-layered arcade games, Dragon's Lair and Space Ace. For a while there was talk that the hot video game market spelled the end of hand-held children's toys, but the video game craze burned too hot not to cool off.

By 1985, the public had tired of the glut of look-alike games that were not compatible and tied up the family TV set. CG game empires went down like houses of cards. Arcades closed and truckloads of Atari video cassettes were buried in landfills. Electronic firms that had hired up to 1,500 employees to create games laid them all off just as fast. Magicom, which had partnered with Don Bluth on Space Ace, declared bankruptcy while Space Ace II was still in production, freezing Bluth's assets and dragging him under, too.

Meanwhile, traditional feature animation studios experimented with CGI, but not too seriously for fear of damaging their overhead on endless research and development. Some CGI images were used in the 1982 Nelvana film *Rock and Rule* and Filmation's TV show *Bravestarr: The Legend* (1986).

In 1982, Walt Disney Studios released the feature film *Tron*. The film was directed by Boston filmmaker Steve Lissberger and created by the CG companies Magi, Bob Abel, and Triple I backed up with veteran animator help like Bill Kroyer. Actor Jeff Bridges played a man who was sucked into an arcade computer game and lived out the life-and-death battles enacted by the circuitry. It was the first film where all the settings and motion was done by computer, although the images still had to be printed on cels, painted, and photographed traditionally. In 1983, Disney experimented with creating a 3D version of Maurice Sendak's *Where the Wild Things Are* using computer imaging by John Lasseter combined with traditional animation by Glen Keane. It was an experiment and didn't get Sendak's blessing, so the project was soon set aside.

Drawing the Line

The interest in new technologies improved when the team of Roy E. Disney, Michael Eisner, and Jeffrey Katzenberg took over the Mouse Factory in 1984. The revitalized Walt Disney Company set the pace for the other major animation studios by moving decisively to incorporate computer imaging into its mainstream animated films. While other studios had spotty results when trying to replace traditional animation outright, Disney tried to combine the best qualities of both traditional and digital styles. The results were seen in Big Ben's clockwork gears in the climactic battle of *The Great Mouse Detective* (1986), the revolving ballroom in *Beauty and the Beast* (1991), the tiger head cave and magic carpet in *Aladdin* (1992), and the wildebeest stampede in *The Lion King* (1994).

Moving-camera shots in animation have always been difficult to do. The active camera following Peter Pan dueling Captain Hook on the mainmast was done with minute planning executed by scene planners with slide rules, flawlessly calculating down to the hundredth of an inch. Hand-held shots that made live action so dynamic were almost impossible in animation. The new CGI technology freed the animated film from the simple perpendicular east-west and in-out camera moves and allowed sweeping perspective moves that increased depth and dynamic range.

It wasn't always easy. I recall Katzenberg driving the 3D department crazy about making the CG integrate more seamlessly with the 2D art. Once, on the ballroom sequence for *Beauty and the Beast,* someone thought to bring the producers in early to see the wire-frame structure turning to the music. In place of the character animation to be done of Belle and Beast were two large polygons. When they watched it, Katzenberg reacted to the placeholding polygons. "What the fuck is that? It looks like two big avocado pits!" He left everyone rattled and one designer in tears. The solution was to bring in traditional animator James Baxter to draw a few key poses of Belle and Beast to cover the offending polygons. Otherwise the camera move and structure was exactly the same. This time when they brought Jeffrey to see it he beamed, "There! Now that's much better!"

Soon other animation studios followed Disney's lead. In 1998 for Warner Bros.' *The Iron Giant,* Disney alumnus Scott Johnston created a Toon Render program that blended the 3D CGI elements with the 2D characters so that they were practically indistinguishable. In 2003, for the film *Looney Tunes: Back in Action*, Johnston created Lumo, a program that created realistic shadows on characters without being painted on separate levels. Don Bluth incorporated CGI moves into his *Thumbelina* (1994), and 2D and 3D characters coexisted as well in *Osmosis Jones* (2001), Hayao Miyazaki's *Spirited Away* (2002), Disney's *Treasure Planet* (2002), and Otomo's *Steamboy* (2004).

For television animation, the march of CGI had to wait for less expensive systems to make the creation of digital half-hour shows economically feasible. Television producers didn't have millions of dollars to spend in research and development just to dip their toes into 3D animation, so it was no wonder that the first breakthroughs would come in places far away from Hollywood, places where salaries and overhead were low. The first 3D TV shows appeared in Europe, where France in particular embraced digital storytelling. In 1994, while *The Lion King* ruled the theaters and *The Simpsons* ruled television, a Vancouver-based company, Mainframe, created *Reboot*, the first all-3D animated series.[3] After the series premiered, the Disney Company picked up the show and ran it on ABC for two more years. It then had a new life on the Cartoon Network show *Toonami*. Mainframe went on to create a second all-3D series called *Beastwars: Transformers*, which debuted in 1998. Soon more Canadian 3D shows made it to U.S. television: Nelvana's *Roli Poli Olie* (1998) and Mark Mayerson's *Monster by Mistake*. In 2003, Mainframe created a very high-quality *Spiderman* show for MTV with motion-capture realistic movement and moody noir settings reminiscent of Johnny Romita's comic book.

Visual effects for live-action films transitioned over to CGI several years before animated feature films. When Steven Spielberg started filming the Michael Crichton fantasy *Jurassic Park* (1993), he was going to have the dinosaurs done in the classic Ray Harryhausen stop-motion armature miniatures style. But several renegade CGI artists at Industrial Light & Magic, led by Steve "Spaz" Williams and Richard Taylor, showed Spielberg a dinosaur test totally done in 3D CGI that they had made on their own time. Spielberg was so impressed that he ordered the entire film to be done in CGI. ILM artists put away their beeswax and wire armatures, and on July 9, 1993, the Andersen Optical Printer was shut off.[4] It was the end of an era. *Jurassic Park*, with ILM's animation of the T-rex and velociraptor became one of the biggest worldwide box-office hits of all time.

Advanced PC technology and new terminals called Silicon Graphics (SGI) replaced the older Cray supercomputers. Up until the mid-1990s, most CG work was done with proprietary software that had to be customized from an initial basic package. Several companies tried to create efficient off-the-shelf software systems: LightWave, SoftImage, and the UK's Cambridge Animation Systems' package called Animo. In 1996, the Toronto company Alias merged with the Santa Barbara company Wavefront, developed by Eric Kovacs, and together they created the most widely used 3D software package in Hollywood, the program adapted from Lightwave, now called Maya.[5] By the first years of the new century Maya had become the industry standard for visual effects feature and television CGI animation. Grand live-action spectacles—*Titanic, Gladiator, Troy, Pearl Harbor,* and *Enemy at the Gates*—were now possible because they could be built virtually and manned by synthespians and 3D avatars, which, although they look realistic, move according to the same principles as Mickey and Donald. Vincent Ward's 1998 fantasy *What Dreams May Come* showed actor Robin Williams convincingly moving in and out of oil paintings and other surreal digital landscapes. In 1993, the pilot episode of the TV sci-fi series *Babylon 5*, "The Gathering," used effects by Foundation Imaging. They created realistic visual effects cheaply on smaller PCs, Amigas, and Video-Toasters. The mainstream effects community laughed, but Foundation made the show on time and on budget.[6] This opened the possibility of creating convincing visual effects for television on a tight budget.

The sky seemed the limit. Some predicted the end of set building and locations. One CG animation designer said his goal was to create a love scene between a living sex symbol like Orlando Bloom and a long-dead one like Marilyn Monroe. John Van Vliet, a veteran special effects designer, told me how he was forced to digitize his studio, Available Light, after he lost a routine fire-effects matte job to CG studio R. Greenberg at three times his bid only because the client wanted something CGI. Shortly after Van Vliet lost the bid, the winning studio called him and asked if he wanted to do freelance animation on the job!

In 1988, PDI created a character called Waldo C. Graphic for the *Jim Henson Hour.*[7] This was the first successful character created using a

Animation . . . Isn't That All Done on Computers Now?

technique called motion capture. Instead of an artist intuitively recreating the illusion of natural motion and gravity, an actor was covered with sensors and the patterns of action created made into an animated character in the computer. Motion capture at its best is similar to the old rotoscope technique developed by Max and Dave Fleischer in 1917. PDI's concept was quickly copied by dozens of inventors trying their own version of the motion capture technique. Most failed to financially justify its expensive equipment. When DreamWorks began *Shrek*, it built a large motion-capture set to do the film, but the disappointing results caused them to abandon the technique in favor of regular keyframe animation. To look its best it still needed a good character animator to make sense of the motion.

The Gollum character in Peter Jackson's *The Lord of the Rings* trilogy (2002–2003) grabbed headlines for the performance of the actor-model Andy Serkis, but behind all the hype were many strong traditionally trained animators who shaped the performance: Randy Cook, Andy Schmidt, Shane Prigmore, Richard Baneham, and Doug Henley. To many executives, however, mo-cap seemed the silver bullet to achieve believable animated movement without being dependent on flaky artists. The technique also appealed to hard-core visual-effects producers who understood hard technology and little appreciated animators' droning on about achieving sensitivity and performance. To the producers, character animation was just another visual effect like a breakaway chair or squib. Motion capture was something they understood: sets, actors, hardware. Despite continued disappointing results like *The Hulk* (2003) and *The Polar Express* (2004), motion capture and its offshoot, performance capture, were touted as great breakthroughs in convincing human-like animation.

In 1996, two major CGI events occurred that would impact the future. A company called Macromedia took Final Splash, a program for creating simple Web animation, and created Flash.[8] Flash animation is a way to create simple actions without using overwhelming amounts of data and without having the image break up into jagged lines when enlarged. The other event was the Japanese Nintendo Corporation's reintroduction of the home game system with a 64-bit console that could plug into a computer or a television. After breaking sales records in Japan, selling more that 500,000 units the first day, the Nintendo 64 premiered with similar results in the United States on September 29, 1996. As games became more readily available on CD-ROM, interest in computer and online games increased as well. Sony eventually launched the PlayStation 2, then Nintendo launched the GameCube, and Microsoft followed with the Xbox—the first system to carry a built-in hard drive and an Ethernet adapter. The gaming industry had returned big time. In 2002, for the first time, sales of electronic interactive games outstripped total Hollywood box-office receipts. Game designers started to attain cult popularity. The interactive gaming industry grew by leaps and bounds and brought a lot of new young people into animation. This was in part because the interactive studios were started and manned mostly by engineers who didn't know the mainstream animation talent pool. Also, because the appreciation of quality personality animation was a low priority for the electronics overlords, the original salaries offered were too low to attract serious Hollywood talent. It seemed that unless you worked for a large firm like Microsoft or designed and patented your own hit game, it was hard to make a living in interactive.

While the endless list of digital achievements left film fans lightheaded, what about the behind-the-scenes workers? What about the people who built sets? The people who were extras? They needed to make a living, too. The visual-effects teams had always been stereotyped as big guys with ponytails and universal tools on their belts setting off charges in steel garbage cans. Now many of the old visual-effects teams were being replaced by younger CGI animation teams.

The apologists for CGI pooh-poohed the traditionalists' fears: You are the "glass-is-half-empty" crowd. Change is good. When the time comes, you can always retrain for a better, more lucrative CGI job. What if, however, some thirty-year pro with a credit list a mile long doesn't take to working on a terminal? Then, that's his problem. The academics at the cutting edge of development preferred not to think about that. Businessmen saw something they could understand, retooling and modernization.

In the 1990s, when visual effects people were sullenly putting away their beeswax and sticking their twisted wire armatures on their monitor screens for old time's sake, the traditional animation world was having a revival, as we saw in the previous chapter. It wasn't until the 2D renaissance began to falter that the overextended studios began to look at CGI seriously as the next great wave.

John Lasseter began as a CalArts graduate and part of the Disney studio training program. Along with future Disney greats like John Musker and Glen Keane, Lasseter was trained in the hand-drawn techniques by the Nine Old Men. Rather than go for a career solely in traditional animation, though, Lasseter was inspired by the possibilities of computer imaging, and he began to experiment in the new field.

When he completed his 1983 short film, *Andre and Wally-B*, a breakthrough in computer character animation, technicians said to him, "Gee, that film had such warmth and character in it. What software were you using?"[9] Lasseter moved to the San Francisco Bay Area to work for a new company called Pixar, which had been formed in 1980 by George Lucas to detach his own ILM computer program into a separate entity to explore the possibilities of CGI film and also to develop Renderman, their own plug-in software for retail. In 1984, new Disney chieftains Michael Eisner and Jeffrey Katzenberg negotiated an entente cordiale with Lucas to create the Star Tours ride at Disneyland, among other projects. This détente between the two entertainment giants included a free exchange of ideas and talent.

By 1985, Pepsi executive John Sculley maneuvered Steve Jobs, the CEO of Apple, out of the company he'd help start. Ed Catmul of NO! Incorporated visited the dejected Jobs and suggested he think about starting over and gave him a tip. Catmul told Jobs that George Lucas was grappling with larger concerns at ILM and was losing interest in his small struggling digital satellite. Jobs went to Lucas and bought Pixar from him for $10 million, which for those guys was pocket change. Catmul signed on and Lasseter was given free rein to develop cartoon animation in CG.

Lasseter took all of the skills he had learned from the masters of Disney animation and adapted them to Pixar's production process. While their engineers were developing innovative ways of stretching characters and creating fur and flame, Pixar's story department still used the corkboard-and-pins storyboards that would have been familiar to the 1930s

artists of *Snow White*. Most of the preproduction artwork was traditionally painted and drawn. If you pick up a copy of the book *The Making of
"Finding Nemo"* (2003), you will be hard put to find a drawing made on
a computer. Most of the artwork reproduced is paint, pencil, and pastel.
Lasseter used short films to try out new techniques and train artists. This
emulated Walt Disney's strategy of creating techniques in his Silly Symphonies to apply later to his feature films. In the beginning, the idea of
theatrical success was a secondary concern to marketing. Management
saw the shorts as showcasing the latest breakthroughs of their software
packages. They asked Lasseter and his team to create a film showcasing their new breakthroughs in representing light. So Lasseter created
a film about two lamps, *Luxo Jr.*, in 1986. Then they needed something
to highlight their ability to create reflective metal and cellophane. John
came up with *Tin Toy* (1988). The awards, including the Oscars that the
Pixar shorts won, generated much excitement about the entertainment
possibilities of CGI animation.

On July 11, 1991, Pixar signed a deal with the Walt Disney Company to make five feature films. Disney Studio started regularly sharing
traditional animation artists with Pixar to create films with the Disney
family charm and warmth. For instance, the title of the film *Monsters,
Inc.* (2001) was the idea of Joe Grant, a ninety-three-year-old Disney storyman who had contributed to *Snow White* (1937). Lasseter convinced
Disney veterans like Joe Ranft, Floyd Norman, and Jorgen Klubien and
talented CalArts grads like Andrew Stanton and Pete Docktor to move
north to Marin County. Airlines that specialized in frequent flights between Burbank and the Bay Area did a booming business in shuttling
talent up and down the coast. While other digital houses fixated only on
building better machines to ape what artists do, Lasseter kept Pixar's focus on story and character. His story crew became the envy of Hollywood.
Instead of trying to recreate reality, he created styles that worked within
the limitations of the medium at that time: toys, bugs, fish. Whatever the
formula, the general public loved the results. *Toy Story, Toy Story 2, A
Bug's Life,* and *Monsters, Inc.* became huge hits. In 2003, *Finding Nemo*
($360 million North American box office) surpassed Disney's *Lion King*
($328,423,001) to become the most profitable animated feature film of
all time.

On January 29, 2004, after ten months of negotiations, Pixar announced it was leaving the Disney fold and would strike out for itself after 2005. This helped accelerate the departure of CEO Michael Eisner. Eisner's successor, Robert Iger, made it his first priority to make peace with Steve Jobs and Pixar. Pixar was the first 3D studio to base itself solidly on time-honored 2D traditions and experience, instead of faking what they didn't know. Soon, other studios followed Pixar's lead. Union-contract studio DreamWorks acquired twenty-year-old nonunion warhorse Pacific Data Images (PDI), and together they created the 2001 hit *Shrek*. After ten years of backing Don Bluth's traditional feature films, Twentieth Century-Fox turned to Blue Sky, a small CGI company in upstate New York. Under the direction of Chris Wedge, the studio created the 2002 hit *Ice Age*, which did better box office ($176,387,405) than the live-action Best Picture Oscar winner of the year, *A Beautiful Mind* ($170,708,996).[10] The success came as a complete surprise to Fox. Management at Fox was in the process of selling the company and getting out of animation when the film struck box-office gold. In 2001, for the first time, the Motion Picture Academy gave an Oscar for Best Animated Feature Film. The nominees were all CGI films: *Shrek; Monsters, Inc.;* and *Jimmy Neutron. Shrek* won and entered the history books.

Before these films, back in 2001, the conventional wisdom in Hollywood was that it was impossible to beat Disney in the cartoon features category, and that the only way to create an animated hit is with a presold TV product like *Rugrats* or *Beavis & Butt-Head*. *Shrek, Jimmy Neutron,* and *Ice Age* shattered that logic and spawned a new myth: anything CGI is better than anything drawn on paper. Digital visual-effects houses that maintained a precarious existence on a few farmed-out shots of a live-action movie now saw animated features as the easy way to success. If Pixar, PDI, and Blue Sky could do it, they could do it, too.

Even high-budget CGI flops like *Final Fantasy* (cost $120 million, made $37 million), *The Veggie Tales Movie* (failed to make significant spinach), Disney's *Dinosaurs* ($300 million estimated production costs, U.S. gross, $137.7 million), and *Valiant* (cost $45 million, made $11 million) failed to cool the impression that the only successful cartoons were now done by computer. The digital revolution had caught up with traditional animation.

For the 2D traditional animation crews, the bell began to toll. DreamWorks, Twentieth Century-Fox, and Warner Bros. all transitioned their

331

production to 3D and laid off the artists who weren't getting with the program. After the massacre of March 2002 top Walt Disney animator Glen Keane declared his next project "Rapunzel Unbraided" would only be done 2D. Glen said, "I couldn't walk down the hallway without running into ten different people and them saying 'We're praying for you.'" But studio heads David Stainton and Dick Cook had told him it had to be made 3D. Glen thought long and hard about it and called a meeting of all the remaining Disney animators on April 4, 2004. It was touted as the "best of both worlds" meeting.[11] There pencil animators and 3D animators debated the pros and cons of their medium for hours. At last CG artist Kevin Geiger challenged Glen, "If you can do all this cool stuff that you're talking about, that you want to see in animation, but you have to give up the pencil to do it, are you in?" Glen hesitated, then said, "I'm in." Three weeks later David Stainton told his crew that Walt Disney Feature Animation would not make any more pencil-drawn animated films for the foreseeable future.

Was all this success because CGI was cheaper? Not really. The budget for a CGI film was not appreciably less than that for a hand-drawn film. It seemed to use just as many artists. So what was it? Why the success? Perhaps there was an aesthetic reason. The mania for 3D CGI could also be argued to be a generational thing. Part of the success of CGI films was that they looked new. The post-baby-boom age groups, Gen-X, the Whatever Generation, had been dominated by their parents' music, their parents' movies, and their parents' love of classic cartoons. Maybe the kids who embraced hip-hop and techno-rave saw CGI films as their own classics, something that could not possibly have been done fifty years earlier.

Because the CGI industry developed outside the mainstream Hollywood community, its employer-employee traditions were shaped more by the Silicon Valley–Marin culture than older Hollywood studio–craft guild relationships. The image of J. R. Bray in his starched suit and pince-nez sitting above his workers was replaced with the open-floor boss wearing a Three Stooges T-shirt and showing off Thunderbirds toys on the desk. New categories entered Bray's assembly line: modelers, riggers, compositers. Instead of union breaks and time clocks, it was casual style:

Animation . . . Isn't That All Done on Computers Now?

Birkenstocks, Web surfing, and Ping-Pong. Everyone went bowling or to cookouts. John Lasseter set the tone at Pixar with his Hawaiian shirts. At Pixar's Point Richmond and Emeryville plants, bikes and skateboards were used to get around in the hallways, the way Hanna-Barbera employees of the seventies had used roller skates. The interactive-games artists put up with a lot in the hope that they could, one day, get the chance to create a new hit game that would make them celebrities among their peers like Rand Miller, who created Myst. Their role models were not Art Babbitt and John Hubley but Steve Jobs and Spaz Williams. CG artists multitasked, performing several tasks not specified in more traditional animation categories. Employees were given stock options, profit sharing, and bonuses.

While the moguls who created the studios of the 1930s were reared in the Thomas Edison–Horatio Alger corporate culture, the entrepreneurs who owned the digital studios were reared in the rock-and-roll–LSD–tie-dyed counterculture of the 1960s that preached rejection of older societal institutions. Their Bob Dylan folk guitars sat under their Silicon Graphics workstation tables. Historian John Markoff said, "It is not a coincidence that at the height of the protests against the war in Vietnam, the civil rights movement and widespread experimentation with psychedelic drugs, personal computing emerged." A review of Markoff's book *What the Dormouse Said* remarks that "the same patch of land on the peninsula south of San Francisco that gave birth to the Grateful Dead was also the site of the groundbreaking research leading the way to the personal computer."[12] For both owner and worker, this rejection of the establishment especially meant unions, which they derided as anachronisms of the postindustrial past. Many of the software techs came to Hollywood from the defense industry where they had been developing Star Wars programs until peace with Russia put them out of a job. Thanks to the Taft-Hartley Act barring defense workers from collective bargaining, they also came with a preconditioned antipathy to union membership.

The most important ingredient of the loyalty of CG workers to their bosses was the reintroduction of trust. The large cartoon factories populated with workers with narrowly specialized tasks had become depersonalized. The original rolled-up-sleeves owners like Bill Hanna and Joe Barbera had faded into memory, replaced by swarms of business execs who regarded the production process as a bulk assembly line. Respect for the individual artist was not in the equation beyond a little condescending lip service on special occasions like Christmas. In the CG companies, by contrast, the needs of a small, very customized digital team meant that a key CG artist was depended upon to perform a variety of jobs and solve problems on personal initiative. The artists responded to this trust and repaid management with a fierce loyalty and identification with the company's success.

The myth of the digital lifestyle persisted in employees' minds even as the digital business matured and went Hollywood. When studios get too successful, they can grow large and impersonal. The fun-loving production execs are replaced with business grads trained to limit fraternization with the "creatives." Far from being a new problem, this complaint was voiced by artists at Max Fleischer's studio in 1937 and at Walt Disney in 1941. By the late nineties, the patterns of evolution of the CGI business seemed to be repeating. It went something like this: Three or four young, zitty partners open a small service studio, subcontracting a few effects shots or building a Web site. They work eighty-hour weeks and live on Diet Coke and cold pizza. Then one of the partners predominates, becomes a millionaire, and screws the others. The others continue the eighty-hour weeks and grow embittered. When they complain to a new production flunky, hired to limit access to the boss, they are accused of having an attitude problem and are replaced with lower-paid college interns. The boss eventually sells out to a conglomerate, takes the payoff, and moves to an A-frame chalet in Utah. The old partners start over at the bottom rung with not much to show but eyestrain and a wider butt. *Sic transit gloria mundi.* By 2000, the Wild West days of CGI were over. It was now all big business. In the gaming world, one animator lamented, "The days when two guys in a garage could pitch a cool idea and it gets picked up are pretty much ended."

I recall asking CGI animators in 1993, "What are your issues?" They replied, "We want to be able to multitask and not be pigeonholed into archaic traditional job classifications that are not relevant." A year later, I asked again, "What are your issues?" In the main, they replied, "We want the right to patent and own anything we create." Still later, I asked again, "What are your issues?" This time, the artists were over thirty years old.

Animation . . . Isn't That All Done on Computers Now?

They complained, "We want a life. We want to go home on weekends and see our families."

There wasn't a normal mechanism to steer the new workers toward unions. SIGGRAPH, an organization similar to the Animators Clubs of the 1930s and ASIFA of the 1960s, was formed in 1972 so computer enthusiasts could share information. But, whereas the Animators Clubs evolved into employee unions, SIGGRAPH was conceived by hardcore academic researchers and digi-bohemians as a way to network and share information and didn't move beyond that orientation. Instead, as the high-tech industry boomed, SIGGRAPH evolved from eggheads sharing research papers to a massive tradeshow where industry leaders Microsoft, Silicon Graphics, Apple, and others demonstrated software and recruited.

CGI artists with a decade or more of experience have begun to look nervously over their shoulders as the veteran key animators of traditional animation are learning CG and will be competing for their jobs. Also, they worry that Third World countries have built up 3D studios staffed by low-paid workers to siphon off mainstream work. The high-tech stock bubble and crash of 2002 proved that no CG job lasts forever. When a studio closed its doors, health insurance and profit-sharing perks ended, too. The workers who had believed the hype of the company's mission statement and put their personal lives on hold held pink-slip parties.

Despite all these problems, not many in CG land thought unions could be the answer. When PDI was absorbed by DreamWorks and DreamWorks executives moved north to run production, the old-guard artists met my overtures about unionizing with a broadside of flaming e-mails, still spouting the long-dead Marin lifestyle myth. The poor white-collars didn't want to be associated with something so blue-collar as a labor union. Even though the Animation Guild was created and run by artists, many CG people clung to their stereotyped images of union leaders as hoodlums, images drawn from films like *On the Waterfront*.

By the early years of the twenty-first century, the large corporations that ruled media completed the integration of the evolutionary threads of CGI. Traditional animators were training on computers, character animators were doing visual effects, interactive artists were doing pencil animation, games executives were running traditional studios (e.g., Avi

Ran was running Marvel Productions). The turn-of-the-century years were a time of great change and innovation, but all revolutions create casualties. In all that excitement, what were the human costs?

Before 1989, the largest single category of workers, by far, in an animation studio was ink-and-paint artists. They were, in the main, women who were held back by barriers to moving into the ranks of animator, layout, or direction. Many were single mothers.

In the 1930s, Max Fleischer tinkered with a method to fix animation drawings onto cels and so avoid the need for inkers. In 1936, physicist and inventor Chester Carlson, working in the back of a beauty parlor in Astoria, Queens, invented a process of photographically heat-fixing print onto paper. He sold the idea to a company called Haloid that produced photographic paper for Eastman Kodak. They soon changed their name to the Xerox Company. On September 9, 1940, Ub Iwerks, the animator who created Mickey Mouse, rejoined the Disney Studio. Ub had a love of inventing that led him to apply himself to animation production problems. For instance, in 1932 when his animators were forming a union, he was distracted by trying to build a 3D camera rig using parts from an old Chevrolet. He developed an adaptation of Carlson's Xerox process that allowed animation drawings to be photographed directly onto cels without needing an inker. Interestingly enough, Walt Disney still ensured that Ub animated at least one small scene in each feature for good luck. The first film to feature Xeroxed animation cels was *101 Dalmatians* (1961). Character designer Ken Anderson was so unaware of the consequences that he went over to the veteran inkers and expected them to be as jubilant as he was that because of xerography they would no longer be needed. They didn't share his enthusiasm. By the 1980s, the job classification of inker had all but disappeared except for some artists who created cels of classic characters for sale in galleries. Inkers remained on the payroll at Disney for 1989's *The Little Mermaid* because all the bubbles and water effects around the sea denizens had to be hand-inked.

Cost-conscious studios were concerned about how to reduce costs by reducing the large payroll of artists. To do this, Hanna-Barbera in 1983 funded the Cornell University computer development lab to the tune of $10 million a year to attempt to create a digital coloring sys-

Digital Film Making: How It Works...

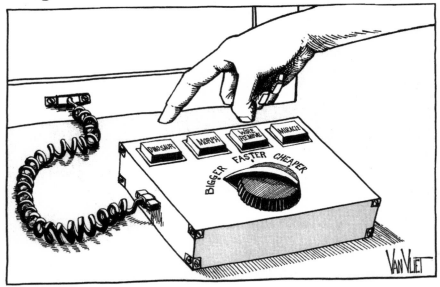

Animator and effects designer John Van Vliet has some fun with some people's misconceptions about what computer animation can do, 1995. Courtesy of John Van Vliet.

tem that would replace traditional paint and cels. When the system was finally ready for *The Smurfs Show*, other studios had already created systems like USA Paint Systems and Animo, making Hanna-Barbera's system obsolete. The Walt Disney studio created its own successful paint system, Computer Animated Paint Systems (CAPS). The last scene of *The Little Mermaid* was their first digitally painted scene. The *Rescuers Down Under* was the first all-CAPS feature. After *Mickey's Prince and the Pauper* (1990), cels and ink and paint became a thing of the past. The capability of the paint system used for *The Lion King* was said to be the color palette of the classic *Pinocchio* raised to the ninth power. In the past, animated characters were provided with a set of day colors and night colors with little variance. With CAPS, art directors were free to literally color compose every one of as many as 1,500 shots separately. Others wondered if the transition to digital images would kill off the boom investment market in old animation cels. By 1990 cels from *Pinocchio* and Bugs Bunny cartoons that used to cost a few dollars were auctioning for tens of thousands. The studios felt that the loss of the cel market was minimal compared to the reduction of film budgets. The mainstream public would be offered printed color serigraphs, which are digital clones of frames of the film, and can be reproduced ad infinitum.

To the businessmen, this new flexibility and wealth of color meant nothing. What the scientists had given them, what they could take to the bank, was that CGI would use fewer artists and be markedly cheaper than traditional feature films. An English company, Cambridge Animation Systems, created a system that eliminated assistant animator and cleanup jobs. By 2006 most of the traditional categories created in 1913 by J. R. Bray—layout, cleanup, breakdown, inbetweener, xerography, checking, opaquer, scene planning, and camera—had all but disappeared. In their places were new designations: artists to model the characters, in effect building the puppet; riggers, who create the controls for their muscles and limbs; digital layout; animators; lighting; and finally the compositers, who assemble all the elements. This crew is backed at all levels by clouds of tech directors, or TDs. These folks provide all types of tech support and keep the system running smoothly. Software engineers are also on hand to create custom solutions to any new visual challenge.

In 1979, the Hollywood Animation Guild had a peak membership of 1,759 active members, of whom 55 percent were ink-and-paint artists. In 1994, The Animation Guild's ranks peaked again at almost 3,000, but a change had taken place. Only 6 percent were ink and paint.[13] Where had all those people gone? True, most of the work in ink and paint was not lost through tech change but had already gone overseas after the Runaway Wars in 1982. If anything, the job of digital painter and color modelers brought a lot of that work back to America because of the skills required to use computers. Studios had been content to gently urge conversion of traditional and CGI skills until 2001. By then several large traditional films like Disney's *Atlantis* (2000), *Treasure Planet* (2001), Fox's *Titan A.E.* (1999), and Warners *Osmosis Jones* (2001) had flopped at the box office while the CGI films like *Shrek* (2001), *Ice Age* (2001) and *Robots* (2005) became big hits and earned the first feature animation Oscar nominations.

The Hollywood players, rather than fault their ideas, went out of their way to blame pencil animation as the cause of all their woes. The large studio financiers focused on the hardware instead of the content and decided animation by pencil was now the equivalent of silent movies. So the veteran animation departments of Walt Disney, DreamWorks, Warner Bros., and Fox were gutted.

Where once it had been a suggestion, now veteran artists with decades of experience were told to learn the computer or face unemployment. No more appeals, no more alternatives. In the Disney animation department, forty-five assistants had to compete for just six CG positions. Another studio trained sixty-six artists to compete for sixteen slots. After the box-office failure of DreamWorks' *Sinbad*, Jeffrey Katzenberg told the *New York Times*, "Traditional animation is a thing of the past."[14]

California state law stipulated that workers displaced by technological change were entitled to additional severance pay. Disney responded by going to court to prove the artists weren't being displaced but were leaving of their own accord. The Animation Guild took Disney to court but lost the case. What wasn't being done digitally was sent overseas to be done by low-wage labor. By 2003, one-third of the members of the Hollywood Animation Guild had lost their jobs, and there were five suicides among the membership. One traditional animator told me bitterly, "I want to feel good about my business again." At the same time the new CGI workers didn't want to be made to feel guilty for the problems of others. They had at last been accepted into the Hollywood mainstream and appreciated for their talents. How could the animation unions help those dispossessed by the elimination of their job categories and at the same time adapt to serve the needs of the new workers?

Although there had been warning signs of major change coming for years, when the digital revolution overran Hollywood, most of the larger live-action traditional crafts unions were still scratching their heads over it. Their leadership was in the main dominated by elderly workers from the golden age of the studio system. They possessed an arrogance of position; anyone desiring change in the industry would have to come to them, and the changes would have to be done by them. Many leaders said that if computers took over, they would merely take a night class to learn the new way. They couldn't see that the CGI world wouldn't wait for them. It had already developed a separate culture nurtured in the Ronald Reagan, union-hating 1980s that did not understand the function of unions in a highly specialized workforce. The corporate media giants were more than delighted to replace their older unionized workforce with the newer union-ambivalent one.

The Hollywood Animation Guild found itself in a better condition to adapt to the change than other Hollywood backstage unions due to the comparative youth of its membership. Because of the generation gap described in chapter 8, by 1992, the average age of the members was thirty-nine. Many union artists who got into CG and CG artists who tasted the benefits of union membership asked that something be done for their brothers and sisters in Digital Land.[15]

I became president of the Motion Picture Screen Cartoonists Local 839 in 1992. During my presidency the MPSC began by reaching out to a number of respected CGI artists who were frustrated by working conditions. In 1994, longtime digital artist Jim Hillin became the first CGI shop steward in animation. The guild demanded representation for tech directors and CG animators in the basic contracts. The CGI departments of the larger Hollywood studios like Disney and Warner Bros. unionized quickly. In 1994, Walt Disney Florida included all CG artists and techs in its contract with Orlando Animation Local 843. DreamWorks went union at its birth. When there was an attempt by some execs to keep the Hollywood-based preproduction of *Shrek* nonunion, 80 percent of its artists signed a petition demanding their union benefits. In 1998, Local 16 Stagehands unionized the digital artists and techs of Industrial Light & Magic.

But the smaller CGI service houses proved more difficult to organize. Company identification and trust of a boss superseded health benefits and decent working hours. Digital studio leaders reacted to the threat of unionization with many tactics that would have been familiar to Burt Gillett or Max Fleischer in the 1930s. They called for loyalty to the team and mistrust of outsiders, created in-house health benefits, and said they'd have to close if they unionized. All this got old-guard loyalists to loudly denounce organizing efforts so the boss could still smile and seem like everyone's friend.

Some Bay Area studios even appealed to regional rivalries: "The Hollywood types want you to unionize so they can come up here and take over your jobs." The same appeal to the new paradigm was used with sound workers in 1933 and videotape workers in the 1950s to justify

staying nonunion. This was ironic because the claims of regional auton-
omy in the face of unionization were being heard while legions of Hollywood production executives were selling their homes in Burbank and
moving to Tiburon and San Rafael to manage the restructured CG businesses. Management also skillfully created a jurisdictional rift between
live-action union locals and the animation guilds. They claimed that CGI
characters were motion-picture visual effects and not cartoons and in
effect were outside the jurisdiction of the Animation Guild. There was
no union local for special-effects animators in live-action movies because
before CGI there had been so few of them. Now Hollywood films were
dominated by digital animation. When confronted with *Titanic, Lord of
the Rings*, and *Who Framed Roger Rabbit?* how do you decide where the
animated film ends and the live-action movie with digital effects begins?
Disney compounded the problem by combining a visual-effects house
named DreamQuest with the Disney animation unit working on the CG
film *Dinosaurs* and called the new entity the Secret Lab. Leaving the
unions to wrestle with this conundrum, the small CGI houses went on
their merry way.

A number of the IATSE film locals were concerned about losing all
their membership to the Animation Guild as everything went digital.
To allay their fears, in 1999 the national leadership under international president Tom Short formed the IATSE CGI Division. This group-
ing allowed cameramen, art directors, and those with other skills who
now work digitally to maintain their individual local membership and
be part of this division. The Secret Lab was their first contract. As early
as 1990, IATSE briefly sponsored a CG retraining group called Hollywood Hands/On, run by Casey Bernay of Local 877 Script Supervisors.
When the states were granted federal money for retraining, the Animation Guild led the way in getting as many members as possible into retraining and subsidizing much of the retraining themselves. A number of
CGI service houses, although remaining nonunion, voluntarily went to
a forty-hour week and started paying overtime to avoid a confrontation
with their people. By the end of my administration, the Animation Guild
went from representing almost no CGI artists and techs to having the
largest number represented by any labor union in the world. My successor as president, Kevin Koch, was a CGI animator who contributed to
hits like *Shrek II* and *Madagascar.*

Drawing the Line

By 2004, the CGI studios discovered the siren appeal of cheap, overseas labor. The immense success of Peter Jackson's *Lord of the Rings* trilogy, using the Weta Workshop facilities in Wellington, New Zealand, proved it was possible to make groundbreaking effects without incurring the high labor costs of California. Delivering the keynote speech at the 2005 SIGGRAPH meeting in Los Angeles, George Lucas proudly announced that his new digital animation facility would make 3D *Star Wars* shows in Singapore. This speech was received coldly by the audience, most of whom were digital artists who could already see their jobs going overseas. Walt Disney Studios built a facility in India. Korea, China, and Israel competed for 3D production. One NewLine executive boasted to me, "The world is now our production company!" CGI artists who stubbornly clung to their union-hating antiestablishment ideals now found themselves helpless to stop the move to overseas production. When they had all the power and influence concentrated in their hands, they might have used their influence contractually to block any attempts to outsource. Now they had no recourse. They found themselves as unemployed as the 2D cel painters of decades ago.

At the same time, the computer games world has grown into a $10 billion business employing as many artists as the film business. This has led to the inevitable overworking of artists in pursuit of ever burgeoning profits. The situation came to a head when a class-action suit was brought by animators against Electronic Arts (EA), the largest computer games company in the world. Originating in Alexandria, Virginia, EA dwarfed other companies with games like The Sims, and quickly announced a move into mainstream entertainment and the opening of new plants in Los Angeles and the Bay Area. Employers worked their animators and programmers long hours via a loophole in the California labor law that permitted the reclassification of creative decision-making employees as supervisors and thus exempt from overtime rules. Employees were mollified with promises of stock options and bonuses. But when the stocks went down in the high-tech bust and a shortage of skilled workers arose, the dissatisfaction grew. By 2004 many industry insiders had come to feel that unionization was only a matter of time.

Rather than listen to union organizers, the digerati first resorted to lawyers. In 2004 animator Jaimie Kirschenbaum filed a lawsuit against EA for unpaid overtime. His attorney argued that Kirschenbaum was an "image production employee" and that because EA was in the entertainment business, it was the tradition and practice in that business to pay workers overtime. In October 2005 the San Mateo County Superior Court agreed with Kirschenbaum, who had left EA. The court ordered the company to pay out $15.6 million in unpaid overtime to its employees. In addition the employees received a onetime ownership grant of company stock, but further stock options and bonuses were suspended. Other lawsuits in the games world such as *Artists vs. Sony Computer Ent. America* and *Software Engineers vs. Vivendi Universal* are pending. Employment attorney Tom Buscaglia was quoted by Animation World Network as telling the *San Jose Mercury News*, "Six months ago I thought unionization would be inevitable in the (videogame) industry, now I'm not so sure."[16] Unions in these areas must ask themselves why they are not leading these efforts but watching from the sidelines. After all, the tradition and practice of the entertainment industry cited in the court cases only exist because unions won them. Without a union standard to measure against, such efforts could never be won. Union organizers have to be better at presenting this case to the employees of the gaming and podcasting industries.

After the departure of Walt Disney's CEO in 2006 the triumph of CGI was complete. Disney announced its purchase of Pixar studios. But who was devouring whom? The leaders of Pixar, Ed Catmull and John Lasseter, were invited down to Burbank to take over the running of its feature animation unit and Walt Disney Imagineering. Steve Jobs was given a seat on Disney's executive board. In effect, the larger studio was admitting it needed help. After some very high-profile bloodletting of senior management, Lasseter and Catmull went to work. They not only restored Disney digital film productions but also rehired John Musker and Ron Clements, the directors of *The Little Mermaid,* to create a new traditional hand-drawn feature, as well as a feature that combines traditional animation and live action, *The Enchanted,* directed by Kevin Lima (*Mulan*).

The story of the digital revolution is not over. It continues to affect the balance of power in Hollywood. Steven Spielberg's prediction of the paperless animation studio has become a reality in many places. No one doubts anymore CGI's right to make magic on the screen. No one challenges the right of CGI artists to be lauded alongside the great artists of Disney and Looney Tunes. Top CG animators like Glen McQueen, Donnachada Daley, and Suni Thankamushy are being joined at the computer by A-list traditional animators like Glen Keane, Tony Fucile, and Duncan Marjoribanks.

The great fusion of traditional and CGI animation continues, our times are but the cusp of change. The career professionals will learn to get along. The novelty will wear off, and conditions will find a new level. Traditional animators grumble but are learning to adapt. At the same time, CGI artists are learning that the film business is still a business. Because your employer looks like you and not like Mr. Spacely from *The Jetsons* doesn't mean he doesn't think like a boss when behind closed doors. Winston Churchill, who dabbled in watercolors, once said, "Art without Tradition is like a sheep without a shepherd, but Art without Innovation is a corpse, something dead."

CG artist Jim Hillin said, "When sound first came in, every movie title card had a big explanation—"This is an RCA Radio-Photophone Process movie"—to distinguish it from a silent film. Eventually it just became a 'movie' again. Now we have traditional films and digital films, one day it will simply be 'movies' again."[17] At the end of the Kroyers' short *Technological Threat*, the robot and the pencil pusher unite to defeat the business guy. Perhaps we may see this prophecy come to pass as well.

Conclusion

Where to Now?

You know what your problem is, Culhane?
You are an Artist!

—Max Fleischer

This book has been written as the art of animation is entering its second century. Decades have rolled by since Winsor McCay, John Randolph Bray, Walt Disney, and Herb Sorrell took meetings in Tinseltown. Pen and pencil have yielded to pixel and stylus, wax recordings to MP3 players, and torn-paper trick films to billion-dollar blockbusters. The generation raised on Felix and Koko gave way to the generation of Dumbo and Bugs Bunny, which in turn yielded to the generation of Ariel and Bart, who yield to SpongeBob and Mr. Incredible. Children will continue to smile and adults to be charmed. Animators will continue to crank out childhood memories by the yard. Meanwhile, behind the bright colors and fun, each generation of cartoonists will deal with the issues of money and business in their turn. They must choose whether to be the users or the used.

What is the future of animation unions in the second hundred years? Is there still a reason for an animation union—an organization that was born of the Great Depression and came of age built on an industrial model? Did the creation of animation workers' benevolent groups really accomplish anything other than make the filmmaker's life more complicated? After all, many artists will want to make art regardless of what they are paid. Do unions merely push conditions past the highest level of cost and so drive work opportunities away from their area?

Animators like to think of themselves as individual artists and tend to ignore the fact that they are frequently part of a corporate entity. With

Grim Natwick's one-hundreth birthday party at the Sportsman's Lodge, 1990. Five hundred artists turned out to celebrate what turned out to be the last great meeting of the Golden Age Generation. Grim had so much fun he died two months later, which is exactly as he had planned. He said to his assistant Dwayne Crowther: "Well, what more do you expect from me? Two hundred?!" Left to right, Friz Freleng, Walter Lantz, Natwick, and Mae Questel, the voice of Betty Boop and Olive Oyl. Collection of the author.

Walt Disney strike fiftieth-anniversary picnic in Johnny Carson Park near the site of the original picketers' camp, Burbank, 1991. Standing, left to right, Bill and Mary Hurtz, George Bodle, Bill Littlejohn (partially hidden), Bill Pomerance, Dave Hilberman, and Libby Hilberman shaking hands with Martha Sigall. Center, unknown and Fini Littlejohn (partially hidden). Seated, Leo Salkin, Art Babbitt, Bill Melendez. Collection of the author.

rare exceptions, like independent filmmaker Bill Plympton, it's impossible outside a corporate structure to amass the capital and resources to create a major motion picture or television series. For the individual animator, the assigned part of the project can be an all-consuming creative challenge. But to the large corporation, the animated film may be but one small part of an overall business strategy. Vast amounts of loyalty and angst can be expended on a company whose management regards its animators as at best the marginal to the company prospectus. The subsequent disillusionment can be difficult to bear.

The condition of being one little cog in a large apparatus has not changed; only the technology has been updated. In the 2D age, films cost millions and needed a small army of artists. Now 3D digital films are at least as expensive and still require hundreds of skilled artists. Labor unions will continue to play a major role in the cartoon industry, no matter how conditions and technologies change. Most animators today have to be versed in the skills of drawing, as well as theater, drama, cinema, and the computer. Just like the artists with John Randolph Bray glaring

Union animators' picket line, Nickelodeon Studios, 1998. Nickelodeon signed a union contract in 2000. Courtesy of Archives of the Animation Guild Local 839, IATSE (formerly MPSC Local 839), North Hollywood.

Conclusion

down at them, most would like not to have to haggle over money. Yet some entity has to exist to champion the rights of the individual artist apart from company concerns. The conditions of the Great Depression, the labor-sympathetic Roosevelt administration, and the coordination of sympathy strikes in the era before the Taft-Hartley Act made the unionizing of Hollywood animation possible. It is debatable whether if the unions had to start from scratch again, they would be as influential. But the new technologies and new generations show the unions frequently do have to start from scratch. I like to believe that if the Animation Guild disappeared today, a new one would rise tomorrow. In cities where the animation union local disappeared, like New York and Toronto, artists' movements to create new organizations are already under way. As long as businessmen hire a multitude of artists and technicians to work on a project, some form of third-party ombudsman to police working conditions will be necessary.

Animators will come to understand that regardless of the system they work in, when the promises of businessmen prove hollow and the words in contracts turn to dust, the artists have only themselves to rely on. Animators in the past have learned not to be loyal to any one company or messianic guru artist but to be loyal to the art of animation, and to seek the respect of their brothers and sisters. This is a lesson artists of the future will come to understand as well.

In writing this book, I've come to see that there were no ultimate heroes or villains in the big animation strikes. Each strike was like a Greek tragedy. If each side sticks to its values and will not see the other's point, the tragic outcome is almost inevitable. Walt Disney, the Fleischers, and Bill Hanna were not bad people. They were self-made men who were proud of surviving the shark pools of Hollywood big business. They liked to think of themselves as benevolent, but when millions of dollars were at stake, their survival instincts took over. They could not see any value in listening to committee delegates of their own artists. The artists for their part were appreciative of the chance to do great work, but they felt their loyalty was being abused and their needs neglected by a distant boss. They wanted to be good employees, but they also wanted to be respected. Mix in strangers from hard-line business and labor as catalysts, and the explosive mixture can ignite.

A union tries to say that all workers should be treated alike, but art

Conclusion

Union animators picket Public Broadcasting System Los Angeles affiliate KCET to protest PBS sending their donation-funded animation work to be done in Canada, 2000. Courtesy of Archives of the Animation Guild Local 839, IATSE (formerly MPSC Local 839), North Hollywood.

demonstrates that some artists are better than others. Trying to serve both concepts sometimes created friction among the union ranks after the initial romantic battle for recognition was won. As I have shown, management time and again played this card to frustrate greater collective gains by the workers. Yet these issues seem to be resolved in labor unions of other performance categories like writers, directors, ballet dancers, and symphony orchestras. So it is an ongoing study. We have a common love of our art form, and we are treated by corporations and the public like a tribe unto ourselves. The companies share information on artists, so why can't artists work together for our common good as actors, writers, and musicians do?

The animation labor unions have to grow and diversify or die. The days when the Hollywood craft unions owned the whole game board and waited for new people to come to them is over. The digital revolution outflanked them and created a new workforce with no heritage of union activism. The only way for unions to win these new people and fight the

Conclusion

Local 839 officers in 1993. Left to right, business agent Stephen Hulett, vice president George Sukhara, president Tom Sito, secretary Jeff Massie. Courtesy of Archives of the Animation Guild Local 839, IATSE (formerly t MPSC Local 839), North Hollywood.

global plantation is to proselytize beyond the confines of their jurisdiction. Could the animation unions have done better if they were not part of a larger labor structure like the IATSE? Probably not. The increased muscle of a national labor organization helped win health benefits and conditions that an isolated local never could have managed alone. The Screen Cartoonists Guild Local 852 tried to go it alone for several years and struggled, finally having to shelter under the cover of the Teamsters in 1970.

George Orwell understood that the best way to affect the present is to understand the past. I hope I have shed some light on a part of the story of American animation that has been rarely discussed. I don't think you can truly understand the evolution of the American animated film without knowing the story of the animation union. Max Fleischer would not have moved to Miami if it were not for the unions. UPA would not have been created if it were not for the unions. The comic strips "Pogo,"

Conclusion

"Sad Sack," and "Dennis the Menace" would not have been born if their creators hadn't left during the Disney strike. Maurice Noble, Jack Kirby, and John Hubley would not have explored their distinctive styles if they had not left their first jobs because of the unions. The television watched by children in the twenty-first century was affected by the citywide cartoonists strikes of 1979 and 1982. I think Herb Sorrell, Bill Littlejohn, and Moe Gollub had just as big an impact on the animation industry as Walt Disney and Chuck Jones.

I don't consider this a definitive study of animation unions by any means. I think there will be more discussion and better efforts than mine. But I hope this begins a dialogue on the position of the individual animator and the animator's role in the larger corporate structure.

Shamus Culhane recalled attending the premiere of Disney's Snow White and the Seven Dwarfs in December 1937. The premiere was a gala affair with many movie stars and huge press and spectators crowding in. As Culhane, in black tie and tails, and his wife walked up the red carpet, he overheard two fans in the crowd who were pointing to him. One said, "Hey, is that somebody?" The other responded, "Nah, that's nobody." This injured Culhane's pride, and he brooded on it as he watched the movie. After the film was greeted with thunderous applause, he thought of those two impertinent stargazers. He concluded: "Screw you bastards. I just created something that will be around long after you two are dead. I am somebody!"[1]

Appendix 1

Animation Union Leaders

Details on early leadership structures are difficult because until 1942 much was underground and their activities clandestine. Not every local maintained a full slate of officers. This list is as comprehensive as I have been able to make it. Abbreviations used are: CADU, Commercial Artists and Designers Union; IATSE, International Alliance of Theatrical Stage Employees and Moving Picture Technicans, Artists, and Allied Crafts of the United States and Canada; MPSC, Motion Picture Screen Cartoonists; SCG, Screen Cartoonists Guild; TAG, the Animators Guild.

1926	The Associated Animators—Bill Nolan, president.
1932	Animators Society—Grim Natwick, president; James Culhane, Bill Carney, Al Eugster.
1936	Animators Union—Ted Pierce, president; Frank Tashlin, vice president.
1937	CADU 20239 (New York)—John Hulley, president; Arthur Post, business agent.
1938–1940	SCG Local 852 (Los Angeles) created—Jack Zander, president; Herb Sorrell, business agent; George Bodle, attorney.
	CADU closed New York Animation Division.
1941	SCG 852—Bill Littlejohn, president; Pepe Ruiz, vice president; George Bodle attorney.
1942	SCG 852—Bill Littlejohn, president; Pepe Ruiz, vice president; William Pomerance, business agent.
1943	SCG 852—Al Amatuzio, president; Dave Hilberman, vice president; William Pomerance, business agent.

Appendix 1

1944   SCG 852—Eric Larson, president; Ade Woolery, vice president; William Pomerance, business agent.
SCG 1461 (New York) created—Gordon Whittier, president; John Gentilella, vice president; Pepe Ruiz, business agent.

1945   SCG 852—Ray Patin, president; Chuck Jones, vice president; Maurice Howard, business agent.
SCG 1461—Gordon Whittier, president; John Gentilella, vice president; Pepe Ruiz, business agent.

1946   SCG 852—Al Gamer, president; Ray Patin, vice president; Maurice Howard, business agent.
SCG 1461—Orestes Calpini, president; Pepe Ruiz, business agent.

1947   SCG 852—Art Babbitt, president; Bob Hathcock, vice president; Maurice Howard, business agent.
SCG 1461—Pepe Ruiz, business agent.

1948   SCG 852—Art Babbitt, president; Bob Hathcock, vice president; Maurice Howard, business agent.
SCG 1461—Gordon Whittier, president; John Gentilella, vice president.

1949   SCG 852—Bill Hurtz, president; John Carey, vice president; Maurice Howard, business agent.
SCG 1461—Jack Zander, president; Harvey Patterson, vice president; Pepe Ruiz, business agent.

1950   SCG 852—Ben Washam, president; Bill Hurtz, vice president; Maurice Howard, business agent.
SCG 1461—Jack Zander, president; Reden Morey, vice president; Pepe Ruiz, business agent.

1951   SCG 852—Ben Washam, president; Barney Posner, vice president; Maurice Howard, business agent.
SCG 1461—John Gentilella, president; Johnny Vita, vice president; Pepe Ruiz, business agent.

1952   SCG 852—Bill Scott, president; Bill Melendez, vice president.
SCG 1461 becomes MPSC Local 841 (New York)—John Gentilella, president; Norman Witlen, vice president; Pepe Ruiz, business agent.

Animation Union Leaders

1953	SCG 852—Ed Levitt, president; Bill Scott, business agent. MPSC 839 (Los Angeles), IATSE created—Bill Shippeck, president; Don Hillary, business agent. MPSC 841—John Gentilella, president; Izzy Klein, vice president; Pepe Ruiz, business agent.
1954–1955	SCG 852—Barbera Begg, president; Bill Scott, business agent. MPSC 841—Lu Guarnier, president; Sam Kai, vice president.
1956	SCG 852—Barbera Begg, president; Bill Scott, business agent. MPSC 841—Lu Guarnier, president; Jim Logan, vice president.
1957	SCG 852—Fred Madison, president; Jerome Bowen, vice president. MPSC 839—Don Hillary, business agent. MPSC 841—Johnny Gentilella, president; Wardell Gaynor, vice president; Pepe Ruiz, business agent.
1958	SCG 852—Fred Madison, president; Bill Perez, vice president. MPSC 839—Donald Hillary, business agent. MPSC 841—John Gentilella, president; Isadore Klein, vice president; Pepe Ruiz, business agent.
1959	SCG 852—William Perez, president; Margaret Julian, vice president. MPSC 839—Larry Kilty, business agent. MPSC 841—Gordon Whittier, president; Wardell Gaynor, vice president; Pepe Ruiz, business agent.
1960	SCG 852—Frank Braxton, president; Margaret Julian, vice president. MPSC 839—Ben Washam, president; Don Foster, vice president; Larry Kilty, business agent. MPSC 841—Gordon Whittier, president; Wardell Gaynor, vice president; Pepe Ruiz, business agent. New Chicago local of IATSE, MPSC 732, formed—Oscar Herz, president; William Bailey, business agent.

Appendix 1

1961   SCG 852—Russell von Neida, president; Robert Maxfield, vice president; Paul Harris, business agent.
MPSC 839—Larry Kilty, business agent.
MPSC 841—Wardell Gaynor, president; Howard Beckerman, vice president; Pepe Ruiz, business agent.
MPSC 732—Oscar Herz, president; William Bailey, business agent.

1962   SCG 852—Russell von Neida, president; Judith Drake, vice president; Bob Leventhal, business agent.
MPSC 839—Larry Kilty, business agent.
MPSC 841—Wardell Gaynor, president; Howard Beckerman, vice president; Pepe Ruiz, business agent.
MPSC 732—Norbert Schulz, president; William Bailey, business agent.

1963   SCG 852—Margaret Selby Kelly, president; Russ von Neida, vice president; Bob Leventhal, business agent.
MPSC 839—Larry Kilty, president.
MPSC 841—Izzy Klein, president; Howard Beckerman, vice president; Pepe Ruiz, business agent.
MPSC 732—Norbert Schulz, president.

1964   SCG 852—Sherman Thompson, president; Russ von Neida, vice president; Bob Leventhal, business agent.
MPSC 839—Larry Kilty, business agent.
MPSC 841—Izzy Klein, president; Howard Beckerman, vice president; Pepe Ruiz, business agent.
MPSC 732—Phil Lepinsky, president.

1965   SCG 852—Ed Levitt, president; Ruth Kissane, vice president.
MPSC 839—Larry Kilty, business agent.
MPSC 841—Dick Rauh, president; Carmen Eletto, vice president; Pepe Ruiz, business agent.
MPSC 732—Phil Lepinsky, president.

1966   SCG 852—Bernard Gruver, president; Bill Littlejohn, vice president.
MPSC 839—Larry Kilty, business agent.
MPSC 841—Dick Rauh, president; Carmen Eletto, vice president; Pepe Ruiz, business agent.
MPSC 732—Phil Lepinsky, president.

Animation Union Leaders

1967–1968	MPSC 839—Larry Kilty, business agent. MPSC 841—Dick Rauh, president; Pepe Ruiz, business agent. MPSC 732—Ronald Alsperger, business agent.
1969–1970	SCG 852 becomes Teamsters Local 986—Dotson Bennett, business agent. MPSC 839—Lou Appet, president; Charlie Downs, vice president; Larry Kilty, business agent. MPSC 841—Irving Dressler, president; Cliff "Red" Augustson, vice president; Al Shapiro, business agent. MPSC 732—William Day Cotter, president.
1971–1973	MPSC 839—Harry "Bud" Hester, president; Moe Gollub, vice president; Larry Kilty, business agent until his impeachment in 1974, when he was replaced by Lou Appet.
1975–1980	MPSC 839—Bud Hester, president; Moe Gollub, vice president (except 1978, when John Kimball was vice president); Lou Appet, business agent. MPSC 841—Noel Sheinberg, president; Lu Guarnier, vice president; Gerald Salvio, business agent.
1981–1982	MPSC 839—Moe Gollub, president; Martha Buckley, vice president; Bud Hester business agent.
1983	MPSC 839—Tom Yakutis, president; Joni Jones Fitts, vice president; Bud Hester, business agent. MPSC 841—Noel Sheinberg, president; Lu Guarnier, vice president; Gerald Salvio, business agent.
1984–1986	MPSC 839—Karen Storr, president; Steven Hulett, vice president; Bud Hester, business agent.
1985	MPSC 841 merged into Local 695 Camera, New York. Name later changed to Local 600 Camera, IATSE.
1987–1988	MPSC 839—Karen Storr, president; Martin Forte, vice president; Steve Hulett, business agent.
1989–1991	MPSC 839—Karen Storr, president; George Sukhara, vice president; Steve Hulett, business agent.
1992–1995	MPSC 839—Tom Sito, president; George Sukhara, vice president; Steve Hulett, business agent.

Appendix 1

1994–2002 MPSC 843 Orlando (created in 1994)—James Parris, president; Brian Lawlor, business agent.

1996–1998 MPSC 839—Tom Sito, president; George Sukhara, vice president; Steve Hulett, business agent.

1998–2001 MPSC 839—Tom Sito, president (until September 2001); George Sukhara, vice president; Steve Hulett, business agent.

2001–2002 MPSC 839 becomes TAG 839—Kevin Koch, president (from September 2001); Steve Hulett, business agent.

2003–2004 TAG 839—Kevin Koch, president; Kathleen O'Meara-Svetlik, vice president; Steve Hulett, business agent.

2005–2006 TAG 839—Kevin Koch, president; Earl Kress, vice president; Steve Hulett, business agent.

Appendix 2

Dramatis Personae

Avery, Fred "Tex" (1908–1980): Influential animation director and comedy surrealist. Born Frederick Bean Avery in Taylor, Texas, to a family that claimed to be descended from Judge Roy Bean, "the Hanging Judge." Avery came to Los Angeles in the early 1930s and worked for Walter Lantz. During some office horseplay, he was hit in the eye with a paper clip and lost his vision in that eye. Moving to Leon Schlesinger's studio in 1935, he first began directing cartoon comedy shorts. Avery's sense of rapid-fire comedy energized the unit and influenced all the other directors. He was a key factor in the development of Bugs Bunny, Daffy Duck, and Porky Pig. He left in 1941 to direct shorts at MGM. Again the manic pace and surreal traits of Avery's humor made his cartoons unique. He created Droopy, the Wolf, and Screwy Squirrel. He left MGM in 1955 and went back to Lantz, where he made Chilly Willy popular. In the 1960s, he moved into the world of advertising and made the famous Raid bug spray commercials. He joined Hanna-Barbera in 1980 to produce the *Kwiky Koala* TV show. He died in 1980.

Babbitt, Arthur "Bones" (1906–1991): Animator and unionist. Art was born in Omaha, Nebraska, of Russian immigrant parents. He became an animator at Paul Terry's in New York in the late 1920s and moved to California to join Walt Disney in 1933. He animated famous scenes like the drunken mouse in *Country Cousin*, the Wicked Queen in *Snow White*, the Mushroom Dance in *Fantasia*, and the stork in *Dumbo*. He led the strike against Disney, leading to a permanent rupture with the studio. After service as a combat Marine in World War II, Art helped set up UPA and animated Frankie in the UPA classic *Rooty-Tooty-Toot*. He later helped establish Quartet Films, where he did award-winning commercials. In 1973, he went to London to train Richard Williams's animation crew; the notes from those master classes are still read.

Bioff, Willie (1900–1955): Hollywood gangster. He was born William Morris Bioffsky in Chicago. Kicked out by his father when he was eleven years old, he drifted into gangs and became a pimp and a bagman. Sent by the Chicago mob to infiltrate Hollywood, Bioff could be seen at the side of major studio heads like Louis B. Mayer as their union expert. He tried to hijack the Disney animation strike negotiations in 1941. After being indicted, convicted, and sent to Alcatraz, Willie turned witness and informed on his former mob bosses. He went into the witness protection program, moved to Arizona, and changed his name to William Nelson. In 1955 he was killed when a bomb planted in his truck exploded.

Blackton, James Stuart (1875–1941): The first American animator. The British immigrant started as a cartoonist, doing a lightning-sketch act in drag as Mademoiselle Stuart in vaudeville. As a reporter for the *Brooklyn Eagle* he interviewed Thomas Edison and was inspired by Edison's experiments in motion-picture films. Blackton talked about persistence of vision with film pioneer Edward Muybridge, then joined Edison, making the first cartoon, *Humorous Phases of Funny Faces* (1906). He also made the first newsreel, started American Vitagraph Company to compete with Edison, made a fortune and lost it, and was finally struck and killed by a bus on Pico Boulevard in Los Angeles.

Bluth, Donald Virgil "Don" (1937–): Animation director, producer. Born in El Paso, Texas, and educated at Brigham Young University, Bluth joined the Walt Disney studio as an inbetweener in 1956. Unemployed as a result of the *Sleeping Beauty* layoff in 1958, he first did Mormon missionary work in South America, then floated around the studios that produced Saturday morning cartoons. Back at Disney in the 1970s, Bluth became a top artist and was groomed to become the studio's senior director. But creative differences made him quit the studio, taking a third of the staff with him. He set up Don Bluth Productions, where he did the animation scenes for the live-action film

Xanadu (1980) and *The Secret of Nimh* (1982). Taking his crew out of the union contract, he continued under several company names as a nonunion signatory His crew animated the breakthrough video game Dragon's Lair, then moved to Dublin, finally settling in Phoenix, Arizona, as a satellite of Twentieth Century-Fox. This studio closed in 2001.

Bray, John Randolph (1870–1977): Pioneering animator. In 1913, he adapted the assembly-line production system to making animated films, creating specialized artist categories like animator, inker, layout, background painter, and checker. Bray took out U.S. patents on animation, arcs, and cycles and sued anybody who violated them, even Winsor McCay. When he died at 107, Mike Sporn a New York studio owner, called me and said: "Well, Tom, it's finally OK to animate. It's now in public domain."

Cobean, Sam (1914–1951): Walt Disney artist who went on strike and helped create publicity for the SCG. After leaving Disney he became an award-winning cartoonist for the *New Yorker*. A collection of his humorous illustrations. *The Naked Truth*, was a best seller. Cobean's life was cut short in a car accident in upstate New York. He was thirty-seven.

Cohl, Emile (1857–1938): French animation pioneer who first proclaimed animation as a distinct and separate art form. Legend has it that Cohl died alone and ignored in a poor flat in Paris when a candle ignited his beard as he was preparing to attend the French premiere of Disney's *Snow White*. A square in Paris was named after him, and subscriptions were raised to create a statue. The sculptor ran off with the money, and the statue was never made.

Culhane, James, later "Shamus" (1913–1994): Animator, writer, and director. Culhane began at J. R. Bray's studio in 1924 and spent the golden age working at all the main studios: Fleischer's, Lantz, Schlesinger's, and Disney. In 1932, he, along with Grim Natwick and several other Ub Iwerks animators, set up the first animators' union. Shamus created the Hi-Ho March in *Snow White* and directed some of the best early Woody Woodpecker shorts as well as *Popeye Meets William Tell* for Famous Studios. After World War II he got into television and created some of the first animated TV commercials for Muriel Cigars. He retired in 1980 and wrote two important books on

Appendix 2

animation: *Talking Animals and Other Funny People* and *Animation: Script to Screen*.

Disney, Roy Edward (1930–   ): Son of Roy Oliver Disney. He produced the True-Life Adventures series under his Uncle Walt and was on the board of the Walt Disney Company. He became a successful investor with his company, Shamrock, and, in 1984, wrested control of the Disney Company from his cousin, Ron Miller. He engineered the revitalization of Disney animation that created *The Little Mermaid* and *The Lion King* but in 2003 was forcibly retired by chairman Michael Eisner from the Disney Company's executive board. He mounted an anti-Eisner grassroots campaign among stockholders and former employees (SaveDisney.com). In 2005, after Eisner's departure, he regained a place on the executive board in an emeritus status.

Disney, Roy Oliver (1893–1970): Brother and partner of Walt Disney. Roy chiefly worked behind the scenes on the business end of the studio. He was chairman of the Walt Disney Company from Walt's death in 1966 until his own in 1970.

Disney, Walter Elias, "Walt" or "Uncle Walt" (1901–1966): Animation filmmaker and creator of the largest studio and company based on animation the world has ever seen. He started his studio in 1923 in Kansas City, Missouri, and soon moved it to Hollywood. His studio pioneered sound cartoons, color, feature-length films, theme parks, and television.

Eastman, Phillip D. (1909–1986): Screenwriter and union activist. Eastman wrote for Disney until the strike, then for Warner Bros. He created Private Snafu for the U.S. Army Air Forces' First Motion Picture Unit and worked for UPA. After he was blacklisted, his friend Ted Geisel (Dr. Seuss) got him into children's books. He wrote *Go, Dog, Go; Are You My Mother?* and *The Big Nest*.

Eisner, Michael (1942–): Walt Disney Company CEO from 1984 to 2005. Son of a wealthy Wall Street investment family, Michael was a protégé of Barry Diller at Paramount and was instrumental in turning around the fortunes of that studio. After gaining control of the Disney studio, Roy Disney and Frank Wells got Eisner and his lieutenant, Jeffrey Katzenberg, to revive the fortunes of the company.

Fleischer, Max (1883–1972) and **Dave Fleischer** (1894–1979): In the

Dramatis Personae

1920s and 1930s, Max Fleischer's studio, based in New York City, was Walt Disney's chief competitor for Toon Town dominance. Their studio produced Koko the Clown, Betty Boop, Popeye, and Superman cartoon shorts. They moved their studio to Florida and tried to compete with Disney by creating feature films like *Gulliver's Travels* (1939) and *Hoppity Goes to Town* (1943). Heavy debt and the shrinking revenues from the World War II market caused their chief creditor, Paramount, to remove the brothers from their studio and reorganize it as Famous Studios. Max retired and Dave went on to direct shorts and educational films. Max's son, Richard Fleischer (1916–2006), became a noted live-action director with films like *Fantastic Voyage* (1967) and *Tora! Tora! Tora!* (1970).

Freleng, Isadore "Friz" (1904–1995): Warner Bros. shorts director. He came from Kansas City with Walt Disney in the silent era. In the 1930s, Friz joined Leon Schlesinger's studio, where he directed some of the most famous Warner Bros. cartoons. In 1965, he started DePatie-Freleng Studio and created *The Pink Panther*, *The Ant and the Aardvark*, and a number of popular Dr. Seuss TV specials. In the 1980s, he returned for a while to Warner Bros. to direct some shorts, then produced television at Hanna-Barbera.

Guenther, Anne (1937–): Disney, Warner Bros., and Chuck Jones background painter.

Gollub, Morris "Moe" (1910–1984): Layout artist, illustrator, and union activist. Gollub was one of the first to sign a union rep card for Disney Studios in 1941 and led MPSC 839 during the Runaway Wars of 1979–1982. When not involved in animation he was one of the more celebrated book illustrators of the 1950s and 1960s. His painting style set the standard for many paperbacks like Louis Lamour's Western cycle, *Tarzan*, and *Turok: Son of Stone*.

Grant, Joe (1908–2005): Son of a cartoonist who worked for the William Randolph Hearst newspaper chain, Grant was the head of the Walt Disney character design department from 1934 to 1949. His artwork was crucial to the development of the big five Disney features. Joe and friend Dick Heumer wrote the film *Dumbo*. His dog Lady was the star of *Lady and the Tramp*. He left Disney in 1949 and started his own graphics company. He returned to Disney in 1991 and contributed to more modern hits like *Monsters Inc.* and *The Incredibles*.

Appendix 2

Just short of his ninety-seventh birthday, he died at his drawing desk, pencil in hand.

Hanna and Barbera, William "Bill" Hanna (1910–2001) and **Joseph Barbera** (1911–): Hanna started in ink and paint and checking while Barbera was a storyman for various studios including Fleischer's and Terrytoons. Partnering at MGM in 1937, they directed the great Tom and Jerry cartoons starting with *Puss Gets the Boot*. After MGM's cartoon unit closed in 1957, they pioneered limited animation techniques to make animation fast and cheap enough for television. They created Ruff & Ready, Huckleberry Hound, Yogi Bear, the Flintstones, the Jetsons, Top Cat, Peter Potamus, the Banana Splits, Scooby-Doo, and many more. Generous to their employees and friends, they nonetheless created methods to send animation work overseas, thus causing much unemployment and hardship. They sold their company to Taft Inc., which in turn sold it to Ted Turner, who merged it with Time Warner.

Hester, Harry "Bud" (1924–): Animator and union business agent. He was a key assistant to famous Disney animators like Milt Kahl. With Moe Gollub, he led MPSC 839 in the Runaway Wars of 1979–1982.

Hilberman, Dave (1907–): Artist, designer, and union activist. Hilberman worked at Disney, where he was one of the strike leaders. In 1947, Walt Disney denounced Hilberman to the House Un-American Activities Committee, saying he was a Communist. Dave was one of the founders of UPA and later Tempo Production in New York. He later settled in Palo Alto, California, and had a long teaching career at San Francisco State College.

Hillin, Jim (1956–): Digital artist and writer and the first-ever CGI shop steward for MPSC 839. His credits include *Beauty and the Beast, Aladdin, Interview with a Vampire,* and *Ghostrider.*

Hubley, John (1914–1977): Great modernist director in animation. Hubley started at Walt Disney Studio doing layouts and backgrounds on *Snow White* and *Pinocchio*. He was very involved in the 1941 strike and left soon after. After World War II, he joined other strike leaders to form UPA, the studio that revolutionized styles in animation. He met his wife, Faith, in 1946. In 1953, Hubley left UPA when parent Columbia Studio enforced the blacklist. He and Faith moved to New York and formed first Tempo, then Storyboard, and finally

Dramatis Personae

Hubley Films, where they created many award-winning independent short films.

Hurtz, Bill (1919–2000): Started at Walt Disney in 1938 and was active in the Disney strike of 1941. Hurtz left the studio after the strike and served in the Army Motion Picture Unit in World War II. He helped start UPA, designed *Gerald McBoing Boing*, and directed the award-winning film *The Unicorn in the Garden*. He was an executive for Shamus Culhane Productions, then joined the Jay Ward studio to direct many of the *Rocky & Bullwinkle* shows.

Iwerks, Ub (Ubbe Eert Iwwerks) (1901–1971): The first great Disney animator. Iwerks designed Mickey and Minnie Mouse and led the animation on all the early sound shorts. He quit in 1930 to start his own company with unscrupulous executive Pat Powers, but after its failure, he returned to Disney in 1940. An inveterate inventor, Iwerks helped develop the Xerox cel system, and his descendants created the CGI house Iwerks Imaging. Some of the earliest union meetings were organized by animators from his crew in 1932.

Jones, Charles M. "Chuck" (1912–2002): Animation director of some of the most memorable Warner Bros. shorts as well as television specials like *The Grinch Who Stole Christmas*. In 1941, Jones threw his support behind the organizing drive of the Cartoonists Guild and after unionizing Schlesinger's he was the Warner's picket captain on the strike line at the Disney Studio. He was an SCG vice president and member of the Hollywood Independent Citizens Committee of the Arts, Sciences, and Professions.

Katzenberg, Jeffrey (1948–): Film executive influential in the Disney renaissance of the 1980s and 1990s and the creation of DreamWorks SKG. Katzenberg started in New York City on the staff of Mayor John Lindsay's presidential committee, then at Paramount became paired with Michael Eisner under Barry Diller. He accompanied Eisner at Frank Wells's invitation to revitalize the Walt Disney Company and was the chief of studio production, including animation, from 1984 to 1994. He started DreamWorks SKG in 1994 with partners Steven Spielberg and David Geffen, and took the company public in 2004.

Kelly, Margaret Selby (1917–2005): Animator, illustrator, and union activist. Born Margaret Selby, she changed her name to Selby Daley when she married Roger Daley, then to Selby Kelly when she married cartoonist Walt Kelly. She joined the Walt Disney studio in 1936 as an inker and painter. A leader in the 1941 Disney strike, she left afterward and went to MGM and Walter Lantz. She maintained Walt Kelly's "Pogo" comic strip after his death. She was president of the SCG in 1963.

Kelly, Walt (1909–1973): Animator, cartoonist. Active in the union strike of 1941, Kelly left Walt Disney's and after a stint in the navy settled back in his native Connecticut to draw comics. His comic book for Western Publishing about Albert the Alligator became the award winning comic strip "Pogo." His famous appeal for environmental activism was, "We have met the enemy, and he is us."

Kilty, Lawrence L. (1922–2002): Controversial business agent of both the MPSC Local 839 and the Screen Cartoonists Guild 852. Forced out of the SCG in 1958 and expelled from Local 839 in 1972 for misappropriation of funds.

Kimball, Ward (1914–2002): Top Disney animator and one of the legendary Nine Old Men. Although Ward did not picket, he supported unionists' issues and urged Walt to make an accommodation with them. Ward created many famous Disney characters like Jiminy Cricket, the Mad Hatter, Pecos Bill, Toot Whistle Plunk, and Boom.

Kinney, Jack (1916–1992): Disney animator. Kinney animated on the 1935 *Mickey's Band Concert* and is known for his direction of the great series of Goofy shorts involving sports, like *Hockey Homicide*. Kinney was laid off from Disney in 1956. He started his own studio in the 1960s and taught animation in New Mexico. His book *Walt Disney and Other Assorted Characters* offers an irreverent look at his time at the studio in the golden age.

Klein, Isadore "Izzy" (1897–1986): Animator who began as a cartoonist for the radical newspaper the New Masses. He worked for Disney in Los Angeles and for Charles Mintz and Terrytoons, where he is supposed to have suggested to Paul Terry the idea of a supermouse, Mighty Mouse. A longtime union supporter and officer, in 1968 he successfully defended New York MPSC Local 841 when business agent Pepe Ruiz wanted to divide it into creative and technical sections.

Koch, Kevin. President of the Animation Guild 2001–present and

Dramatis Personae

DreamWorks animator. Koch's credits include *Madagascar* and *Shrek*.

Kroyer, William "Bill" (1950–): Disney-trained animator who transitioned early into CGI. He created the 1987 Oscar-nominated short *Technological Threat*, as well as the feature film *FernGully: The Last Rainforest*.

Lantz, Walter (1900–1993): Animator who started his own studio with the character Oswald the Lucky Rabbit in 1928. Lantz Production's characters included Chilly Willy, Woody Woodpecker, and Gandy Goose. In 1941, Lantz's studio was the first to sign a union contract with no fuss. Although as early as 1941 he predicted the end of the theatrical short cartoon, Lantz was among the last makers of animated shorts, as late as 1972. He died at ninety-three in 1993.

Larson, Eric (1904–1988): Great Disney animator, one of the Nine Old Men. He was elected president of the SCG in 1944 and in the 1970s mentored many of the top Disney artists who were to spearhead the 1990s revival.

Lasseter, John (1957–): Pioneering CGI animation director. Born in Southern California and schooled in traditional animation in the California Institute of the Arts Disney program, Lasseter fell in love with the possibilities of computer animation on the film *Tron* (1982). In 1986 he moved to Lucasfilm to do effects on *Young Sherlock Holmes*. He became the creative force behind Pixar studios, earning multiple Oscars for films such as *Luxo Jr., Tin Toy, Toy Story, Toy Story 2, Finding Nemo,* and more. In 2006 he was named the creative head of Walt Disney Animation as well as Walt Disney Imagineering.

Lessing, Gunther (1891–1965): Vice president and chief legal counsel for the Walt Disney studio, 1929–1950. He was very influential in the Disney studio's efforts to thwart union organizing in 1941.

Littlejohn, Bill (1909–): Animator and SCG activist and president. Littlejohn was instrumental in the unionizing efforts at MGM and Lantz and in the battle for jurisdiction between the CSU and the IATSE in 1951. He later animated some of the most memorable scenes in John Hubley's films like *Cockaboody* and *The Hole* and was an important animator on Bill Melendez's TV special *A Charlie Brown Christmas.*

Lokey, Hicks (1905–1991): Animator and strong union man who seemed to be everywhere. Hicks was involved with the Van Beuren controversy in 1935, then went to Fleischer's and was a factor in the Fleischer strike. After that he went to Disney, where he did animation on *Dumbo* and the Dance of the Hours in *Fantasia*. Because he was in the Disney strike in 1941, he soon left. Hicks worked at Hanna-Barbera in the 1970s and came out of retirement to participate in the Runaway Wars citywide strikes of 1979 and 1982.

Melendez, Bill (1916–): Animator, director, and unionist. Melendez was born in Mexico and educated in Los Angeles, where he joined the Disney studio as an assistant animator. He was very active in the Disney strike and later was elected guild president. After doing animation for Bob Clampett, Warner Bros. shorts, and commercials, he started his own studio in 1964 to create TV specials like *A Charlie Brown Christmas* and *It's the Great Pumpkin, Charlie Brown* .

Melies, Georges (1861–1938): Former French magician, considered the father of motion picture special effects. Melies introduced the matte technique, dissolves, use of models, and surreal cutting. Carlo Bendazzi said that in a world of documentary filmmakers Melies was the first to view cinema as the realm of the imagination. He died selling chocolates in a Paris railway station.

Natwick, Myron Henry "Grim" (1890–1990): A pioneering artist in the silent era who did the first realistic character animation of women and trained such future luminaries as Chuck Jones, Marc Davis, and Milt Kahl. Natwick drew the illustration for the sheet-music cover for W. C. Handy's "St. Louis Blues," for which he was paid one gold dollar. He started at Hearst Films in 1916, then went to Max Fleischer's, where he created Betty Boop. He went to Walt Disney to create Snow White, then returned to Fleischer's and later went to UPA to create Nelly Bly in *Rooty-Tooty-Toot*. Grim was also one of the earliest animation union presidents, elected in 1932. He lived to be one hundred and was still animating at age eighty-eight on Richard Williams's film *The Thief and the Cobbler*.

Quimby, Fred (1883–1965): Production head for MGM shorts, motion picture theater owner, and Pathé executive. Quimby coordinated MGM's short-film department from 1937 until 1956.

Reagan, Ronald Wilson (1911–2004): Warner Bros. contract actor and president of the Screen Actors Guild; later governor of California and president of the United States, In his role as SAG president he attempted to mediate the war between the CSU and the IATSE. In 1952, he addressed animators at a pro-IATSE rally organized by Roy Brewer. Reagan was SAG leader when actors won residuals in 1960.

Ruiz, Pepe (1914–1993): Cuban-born union organizer. Ruiz began at Disney then went to MGM, where he helped with the overwhelming vote to unionize. He later moved east to help set up the New York CSU guild and led the unsuccessful strike against Terrytoons. In 1952, he made a deal to merge his CSU guild into the IATSE to create MPSC 841. He remained as its business agent until his retirement in 1968.

Schlesinger, Leon (1884–1949): Schlesinger started as a founder of Pacific Art & Title Company but in 1929 won the exclusive contract to produce cartoon shorts for Looney Tunes and Merry Melodies at Warner Bros. He produced all the famous Warner Bros. shorts until his retirement in 1943, when he sold his company outright to Warner Bros.

Scott, Bill (1920–1985): Writer, known as the voice of Bullwinkle the Moose. Scott was also a passionate union organizer who left Disney after the strike and helped set up UPA. He was fired in the blacklist purge in 1952. He teamed up with Jay Ward and wrote many of the funnier Jay Ward comedies. Scott was very involved in the governance of the SCG and its unsuccessful effort to halt the IATSE takeover of the cartoon unions in 1952. He was also involved in ASIFA/Hollywood.

Sigall, Martha Goldman (1917–): An ink-and-paint artist at Leon Schlesinger's in 1936, painting Looney Tunes and Merrie Melodies. Sigall became an inker and moved to MGM in 1943. In 1957, she was one of the first employees of Hanna-Barbera. Her sharp memory even into her eighties has made her an invaluable resource to historians of the period. Martha and her husband, Sol, became docents at the Warner Bros. Museum in 1998.

Sito, Tom (1956–): Animator, teacher, writer. Born in New York City, he attended the School of Visual Arts and the Art Students League. Sito's first film work was as an assistant on Richard Williams's *Raggedy Ann & Andy* (1977). His screen credits include *Who Framed Roger Rabbit?* (1988), *The Little Mermaid* (1989), *The Lion King* (1994),

Shrek (2001), *Garfield* (2002), and *Osmosis Jones* (2001). Sito served three terms as president of MPSC Local 839. He helped organize animators around the United States, including Local 843 Orlando and undertook an unsuccessful organizing effort in Canada. In 2001 he was awarded the title president emeritus of Local 839.

Sorrell, Herbert K. "Herb" (1899–1964): Charismatic organizer from the American Federation of Labor who helped unionize the Hollywood animation studios and led the CSU labor wars in the mid-1940s.

Spielberg, Steven (1943–): One of the great Hollywood film directors and also a great patron of animation. He produced *An American Tail* (1985), *Who Framed Roger Rabbit?* (1988), *Tinytoons* (1990), and *We're Back* (1993). In 1994, he partnered with Jeffrey Katzenberg and David Geffen to form DreamWorks SKG.

Stalin, Joseph (1878–1953): Russian dictator. Born Jozef Djugashvili in Tbilisi, Georgia, he changed his name to Stalin ("man of steel") when he became a revolutionary. He maneuvered himself into power in 1923 after the death of Russian revolutionary leader Nikolai Lenin. Marshal Stalin turned Soviet Russia into a brutal police state and executed millions. His assumed worldwide control of all Communist-Socialist movements alienated most liberal progressives in Western democracies. Stalin kept an extensive network of spies worldwide to collect secrets and undermine other governments. America's fear of Stalin fueled the Hollywood blacklist.

Tashlin, Frank "Tish-Tash" (1913–1972): Born Francis Frederick von Taschlein in New Jersey. His family dropped the "von" during World War I. Tashlin started as an errand boy and cel washer for Fleischer's in 1929. He moved up to animator at Van Beuren, then moved west to Schlesinger's Looney Tunes, where he quickly became one of the more innovative directors. He was an early SCG vice president and left to do story at Walt Disney for two years and, more important, to help promote unionization of Disney artists. He left during the 1941 strike to produce animation for Screen Gems. There he hired many unionists cut adrift after the bitter Disney strike. In 1945, Tashlin joined the Paramount live-action writing team and began a career directing comedy films, including the famous Dean Martin and Jerry Lewis films. His films include *Will Success Spoil Rock*

Hunter? (1956), *The Lemon Drop Kid* (1951), and *The Geisha Boy* (1958).

Terry, Paul (1887–1975): Started at J. R. Bray, then founded his own animation studio in 1921, producing the Farmer Grey or Farmer Al Falfa series. Other Terrytoons stars included Sidney the Elephant, Mighty Mouse, and Heckle and Jeckle. His studio remained in New Rochelle, New York, and unionized after a long, damaging strike in 1947. Terry sold Terrytoons to CBS Television in 1961.

Tytla, Vladimir "Bill" (1904–1968): One of the most influential U.S. animators. His animation for Disney of Grumpy, Chernobog the Devil on Bald Mountain, and Dumbo are famous. Tytla stuck with his friends in the 1941 strike and left Disney in 1943. After stints at Terrytoons and Famous, he started his own commercial studio in New York. In 1964, he teamed up with the Looney Tunes crew to direct the animation on *The Incredible Mr. Limpet*. He suffered a series of small strokes in the 1960s that left him blind in one eye. He died of a stroke in 1968.

Van Beuren, Amadee J. (1879–1937): Early producer and distributor of cartoon shorts. Van Beuren began as a manager of nickolodeon sales. In 1928 he purchased a controlling interest in Paul Terry's Fables Studio, but in 1929 he and Terry parted ways and he went out on his own. Through the 1930s the Van Beuren studio did shorts like *Tom and Jerry* (not Hanna-Barbera's famous cat and mouse), Otto Soglow's *Little King*, and *Sunshine Makers;* he also attempted to remake Felix the Cat. Director Frank Tashlin was so unhappy working for Van Beuren that after he left he created a comic strip about his experiences, "Van Boring." After Van Beuren lost his RKO distribution contract to Disney in 1936, he closed his studio; he died of a heart attack in 1937.

Ward, Jay (1920–1989): Pioneering television animation producer. He created the first made-exclusively-for-TV animated series, *Crusader Rabbit* (1949). Later he produced *Rocky* & *Bullwinkle* (1961) and *George of the Jungle* (1967).

Washam, Ben (1915–1985): Warner Bros. animator, teacher, and union activist. Ben served terms as president of both SCG 852 and MPSC 839.

Whitney, John (1917–1995): With his brother, James (1921–1981), among the fathers of computer animation.

Williams, Richard (1933–): Award-winning animator who led a renaissance in British commercial animation. Williams created the films *A Christmas Carol* (1972) and *Raggedy Ann & Andy* (1977) and the animation for *Who Framed Roger Rabbit?* (1988) and *The Cobbler and the Thief* (1995). His book, *The Animator's Survival Kit*, became a must-have manual for animation artists.

Zander, Jack (1909–): MGM animator who was an early president of the SCG. Zander later owned Zanders Animation Parlour, one of the larger commercial animation houses in New York City from the 1960s to the 1990s.

Zemeckis, Robert L. (1952–): Influential live-action director. Born in Chicago, Zemeckis trained at USC. His screen credits include the hits *Back to the Future, Romancing the Stone,* and *Forrest Gump.* Among his projects involving animation are *Who Framed Roger Rabbit?* (1988), *Polar Express* (2004), *Monster House* (2006), and the animated series *Back to the Future* (1991).

Appendix 3

Glossary

AFL-CIO: North America's largest labor alliance. The American Federation of Labor (AF of L) was organized in the late 1880s by Samuel Gompers to help trade guilds and skilled artisans, while the Congress of Industrial Organizations (CIO) was formed by John L. Lewis in 1931 to help industrial and unskilled workers. At first they were bitter rivals, but they voted to amalgamate in 1951. All the animation unions were affiliated with the AFL-CIO.

AMPWU (Animated Motion Pictures Workers Union): An early attempt by the Artists Union to organize the New York animation studios. The AMPWU unraveled after the 1935 organizing campaign at the Van Beuren Studio failed.

AMPTP (Alliance of Motion Picture and Television Producers): Since 1982 the negotiation body representing the studios. Today it represents 350 production companies.

animatic: A film of the still drawings of the storyboard, matched to an improvised soundtrack to get a rough idea of the final film. Also called a storyreel, Leica reel, or telecine.

animation: The creation of the illusion of movement on film by a variety of single-frame techniques, drawings, clay figures, digital models, etc. From the Latin *anima*, to breathe life into.

Animation Guild, Local 839, Hollywood: The current Hollywood animators' union. Original name: Motion Picture Screen Cartoonists and Affiliated Graphic and Electronic Arts, Local 839. Chartered by the IATSE in 1953 after IA defeated the CSU guilds in a general election among animators. The MPSC changed its name to the Animation Guild in 2002.

Appendix 3

anime: Class of animated films made in Japan with strong cultural and graphic ties to Japanese theater. Also called Japanime. The comic books are called manga. Anime had a strong influence on Hollywood animation in the early 2000s and influenced live-action movies like *The Matrix* (1998) and Quentin Tarentino's *Kill Bill* (2003).

arbitration: A way to resolve labor disputes where both sides agree to submit their claims to a neutral power, usually a judge or mediator. They agree to abide by whatever the judge decides. Binding arbitration means the right to any further appeal is waved.

Artists Union: Originally called the Unemployed Artists Union. Founded in 1929, it was an early radical artists' labor organization set up in New York. Its publication was *Art Front*. The movement was as much about avant-garde aesthetics as socio-political activism. The Artists Union offices were raided and shut down in 1937 when Congress cut off funding of all Roosevelt federal arts programs. The New York Police Department had to drag people out of the building and padlock it.

ASIFA (Association Internationale du Film d'Animation): Animation society started in 1961 by an international group of animators, including John Hubley, Dusan Vukotic, Norman McClaren, Paul Grimault, John Halas, and Feodor Khytruk. In a world polarized by the cold war, it was an international movement for the spread of animation ideas. Today there are twenty-nine ASIFA branches around the world. The ASIFA/Hollywood branch created the Annie Awards in 1972 for achievements in animation.

assistant animator: Sometimes called cleanup, final line, or graphic delineator artist. An artist who cleans up and refines the animator's rough drawings. The animator works quickly, neglecting detail as he represents movement in line drawings. The assistant goes over the animator's drawings, sharpens the detail, and makes sure the character is on model, then assigns the additional between drawings to an inbetweener.

BGs: Animation background paintings. The scenery or stage a character is acting upon.

Big Five films: The first five Walt Disney–produced feature-length cartoons that became money engines for the studio and are considered pinnacles of artistic quality: *Snow White and the Seven Dwarfs*, *Pinocchio*, *Fantasia*, *Bambi*, and *Dumbo*.

Glossary

Big Five studios: Warner Bros., MGM, Paramount, Columbia, and Universal. In the 1930s and 1940s, Twentieth Century-Fox, Disney, United Artists, and RKO were considered smaller players.

blacklist: An unofficial practice of employers to collude to refuse work to individuals because of a political or other agenda unrelated to ability. Used extensively in the anti-Communist investigations of Hollywood lasting from 1947 to 1962. While never officially admitted, this practice is still occasionally employed for personal vendettas—the "You'll never work in this town again!" scenario.

blitzkrieg: German military tactic used in World War II. It means "lightning war"—a rapid, unexpected, and overwhelming attack. The term was used in Screen Cartoonists Guild leaflets during the 1941 strike to describe studios' arbitrary firing of employees.

block booking: A monopolistic practice enforced by the Big Five studios upon their affiliate theater chains and independent movie houses in the 1930s and 1940s. If a theater wished to run a big feature like *Gone with the Wind*, it was compelled to also run the attached cartoon, newsreel, short subject, and B picture. In 1948, the Supreme Court outlawed the practice.

business agent: A salaried elected official of a union whose duties are to maintain the union office and execute the policy enacted by the membership and governing executive board.

CADU (Commercial Artists and Designers Union): New York–based labor union that first struck, then signed a contract with, the Max Fleischer studio.

cels: Clear acetate sheets of roughly 10 1/2" by 12 1/2" upon which animation characters are inked and painted. Invented by Carl Hurd in 1916. Use of cels was the industry norm from the early silent era until they were supplanted by digital imaging in the 1990s.

CGI (computer graphic imaging or computer-generated imaging): The current term for animation, effects, and graphic art produced on a computer rather than with traditional paint or pencil. Sometimes shortened to CG.

checkers: In traditional animation, a category of specialized technicians who review the data and artwork to be photographed, much like proofreaders.

closed shop: A union practice where a studio agrees to hire only union members and all employees working full-time must be union members.

collective bargaining: A legal way of workers getting together and negotiating as a group with their employers.

communism: Political theory created in 1848 by Karl Marx and Frederick Engels. It espoused the idea that society would be better overall if common workers and farmers controlled all political and economic power. Its concepts, like the sharing of private property, were tempting to many impoverished people, but it was viewed with horror by the wealthy and aristocratic classes. Groups and nations that embraced this philosophy found themselves the pariah of the industrial powers. Whenever economic times were bad, such as during the Great Depression, Communist ideology won many adherents. Hollywood flirted with the progressive aspects of communism in the 1930s, and this association brought on the blacklists of 1947–1962. The largest Communist state, Soviet Russia, collapsed in 1991. The remaining Communist countries that accepted corporate investment and trade, like Vietnam and China, were no longer harassed.

CRT (cathode ray tube): The original green-screen computer monitors.

CSU (Conference of Studio Unions): Association of Hollywood backstage union locals formed by radical unions from the FMPC groupings in 1937. The CSU attempted to challenge the representation of Hollywood film workers by the IATSE. The CSU staged several violent industry-wide strikes in 1945 and 1946, but, by 1947, it had collapsed. The Los Angeles animation community was first organized as a CSU group in 1942, then joined IATSE in 1951.

DGA (Directors Guild of America): Originally the Screen Directors Guild.

digital: Like CGI, a general term for production methods using computers in place of traditional mediums. Digi EFX means special-effects shots created on a computer.

director: An animation director is an artist who oversees the creative team on an animated film. The director may storyboard, time out the film, oversee the track recording, and cast and coach the animators.

DreamWorks SKG: Movie studio formed in 1994 after Jeffrey Katzenberg broke with Michael Eisner and left Disney. The Glendale,

Glossary

California, company was founded by Steven Spielberg, Jeffrey Katzenberg, and David Geffen (the SKG of the name). In 2004 the animation division was spun off as a public company and in 2005 DreamWorks was acquired by Viacom and merged into its Paramount Studio division.

executive board: In a union, individuals selected by union members to discuss and set policy. The executive committee can order the business agent to expedite the policies they approve. In Hollywood animation unions, executive board members have included Frank Thomas, Ollie Johnston, Eric Larson, Art Babbitt, and Margaret Selby Kelly.

FMPC (Federation of Motion Picture Crafts): An alliance of independent and radical backstage unions between 1932 and 1937 that challenged the IATSE for the control of Hollywood crafts guilds. After the FMPC broke up, many members reorganized as the CSU.

FMPU (Film Motion Picture Unit): Pronounced "fum-poo." World War II crew of Hollywood animators in uniform set up as the U.S. Army Air Forces 18th Air Force Base at the Hal Roach Studio in Culver City, California, which was nicknamed Fort Roach, to create training films. Directors included Chuck Jones, Frank Thomas, and John Hubley; among the writers was Ted Geisel (Dr. Seuss). The U.S. Navy and the Army Signal Corps also had animation units.

frame: A single photograph on a strip of film. It is also the unit of measure to create individual motions. Twenty-four frames per second is the industry standard. Animators refer to timing animation on "ones," or one photographed frame, or "twos," two frames.

FTAC (Film and Television Action Committee): Political action group formed by Hollywood live-action workers and actors in the 1990s to try to pressure politicians to create laws to keep more production work in Los Angeles.

glamour guilds: The Writers Guild of America, the Screen Actors Guild, and the Directors Guild of America; so named because of the celebrities on their rosters and their independence from any large labor alliance.

Hanna-Barbera Studios: The largest employer of animators in Hollywood, it has been called the "General Motors of cartoon animation."

HICCASP (Hollywood Independent Citizens Committee of the Arts, Sciences, and Professions): A Hollywood association of political liberals. It supported Franklin Roosevelt's New Deal policies. Warner Bros. cartoon director Chuck Jones was a member and Ronald Reagan for a time was on its board of directors. Labeled a Communist front organization by HUAC in 1948, it was reconstituted later in a truncated form as the Independent Citizens Committee of the Arts, Sciences, and Professionals.

HR (human resources): In many large companies, the department responsible for regulating the working conditions and discipline of the staff. Invented in the late 1930s as an Orwellian misnomer for someone who hires, fires, cuts, or raises pay. (See Mohawk Valley rules.)

HUAC (House Committee on Un-American Activities): Originally set up in 1938 as the Martin Dies committee to investigate Fascist movements in America and their potential for sabotage. By 1940, HUAC's emphasis was altered to hunt for Americans who were Soviet Communist spies. As American anxiety over the cold war grew, HUAC's scope enlarged to include Americans with any current or former Communist, socialist, progressive, pro-labor, pro–civil rights, or left-of-center thinkers. While a Congressman, future president Richard Nixon served on the HUAC panel. The committee's enforcement power was never stronger than a contempt of Congress or perjury charge; its chief weapon was ruining a victim's professional career through the resultant blacklist. In the Senate, Sen. Joseph McCarthy (R-Wis.) made similar charges against government and military officials.

IATSE, also IA (International Alliance of Theatrical Stage Employees and Moving Picture Technicians, Artists, and Allied Crafts of the United States and Canada): Since 1893, the alliance of unions of backstage artisans and workers. The animation industry formed union locals within IATSE in 1952 and 1953.

impasse: In union negotiations, the point at which all sides admit they are hopelessly deadlocked and suspend further talks. They can then agree to binding arbitration or resort to industrial actions like a strike or lockout.

inbetweener: In hand-drawn animation, the person who supplied the many intermediate drawings between the animator, who did the extremes or key poses, and the assistant animator, who cleaned up the animation drawings.

Glossary

ink and paint: Artists and technicians who traced the animation drawings onto celluloid sheets, then painted in their colors. Before the 1970s, ink-and-paint departments were staffed mostly by women.

John Reed clubs: During the Depression, informal groups of American radicals who favored workers' rights and desegregation and opposed fascism. John Reed clubs also provided forums for discussions of modernist art theory, poetry, and philosophy. These groups formed the nucleus of radical factions of labor unions like the FMPC, the CSU, and the CADU. They were named after journalist John Reed, a founder of the American Communist Party, author of *Ten Days That Shook the World*, and the only American buried in the Kremlin wall. John Reed's good friend, cartoonist Art Young, was eulogized by Walt Disney. Reed also knew Bill Tytla, the animator of *Dumbo*.

layout artist: Animation artist who from the storyboard draws out and sets up the staging of an animation scene for the animator and background painter.

lockout: A pressure tactic used by employers against union workers. The management tries to head off a strike by closing the shop without warning, locking out the workers.

me-too agreements: Deals signed by employers not wishing to participate in labor negotiations stating that they will abide by whatever conditions are agreed to by the negotiators.

moguls: Nickname for the colorful studio chief executives in the Hollywood golden age: Jack Warner (Warner Bros.), Louis B. Mayer (MGM), Jesse Lasky (Paramount), Harry Cohn (Columbia), Darryl F. Zanuck (Fox), and Carl Laemmle (Universal).

Mohawk Valley rules: Labor tactics suggested by the Rand Corporation in 1935 at the request of the National Association of Manufacturers. NAM asked Rand to come up with new ways of combating the successful union organizing drives and strikes then rampant in America to replace the tactics of police harassment, tear gas, judicial assassination, and militia violence. Rand came up with the idea that labor unions are best fought in the press, where the unions could be made to appear unpatriotic. Also, human resources departments should be set up to give the fictitious appearance that workers have a say in the way their workplace is run. In 1937, ten thousand pamphlets advocating these tactics were distributed to businesses nationwide. The Mohawk Valley rules didn't begin to have an impact until 1945, after the labor peace of World War II ended.

motion capture: Also called performance capture. A CGI version of rotoscope developed in 1988. An actor wears sensors and his movements are registered in a computer. Gollum in Peter Jackson's *Lord of the Rings* films and Robert Zemeckis's *Polar Express* are examples.

MPSC (Motion Picture Screen Cartoonists): Name of IATSE union locals 839 Hollywood, 841 New York, 732 Chicago, and 843 Orlando. In 2001 Local 839 changed its name to the Animation Guild.

New Deal: The blanket title for all the pro-labor, liberal economic policies of the Franklin D. Roosevelt administration, including the Works Progress Administration, the National Recovery Act, the Federal Deposit Insurance Corporation, and the Wagner Act. Conservatives who were opposed to Roosevelt policies were called anti–New Dealers. Some New Deal opponents labeled it the "Jew Deal" because many key strategists like Treasury Secretary Henry Morgenthau were Jewish.

Nine Old Men: Title bestowed by Walt Disney in 1949 on the animators he considered the senior artists of his studio. The term was borrowed from Franklin D. Roosevelt's name for the Supreme Court after it stuck down his National Recovery Act in 1935. At Disney's, the term was a badge of honor for animators Frank Thomas, Ollie Johnston, Ward Kimball, Wolfgang Reitherman, Eric Larsen, Les Clark, Milt Kahl, John Lounsbery, and Marc Davis.

NLRB (National Labor Relations Board): Investigative and enforcement arm of the Labor Department set up in the Roosevelt New Deal years. Unions or managers could appeal to the NLRB if they felt they were being dealt with unjustly. The NLRB's accessibility and effectiveness have seemed to wax and wane depending upon whether a labor-friendly or corporate-friendly administration is in power in Washington.

NRA (National Recovery Act): New Deal legislation enacted by the Franklin D. Roosevelt administration to try to reverse the economic slump of the Great Depression.

opaquers: For years the common industry title for animation cel painters. The paint must be applied until the character is opaque; that is, until light cannot be seen through it.

Glossary

opticals: Traditional special effects created on a bottom-lit camera stand and optical printer. Multiple runs on a strip of film burn a glow on the emulsion to simulate laser rays and heavenly auras. Optical effects became very popular after the success of heavy effects movies like *Star Wars* (1977). Most optical techniques are now done digitally.

organizer: A free-roaming union official whose job is to advise and aid employees in organizing a company—sort of missionary work for unions.

organizing: The procedure for getting union recognition at a given plant or studio. Rep cards are collected from employees. When 50 percent are favorable, a union can request an election. If three-fourths or more of a company's employees sign cards, an election is deemed unnecessary. Negotiations to sign a contract and contract ratification follow.

pan: To move an elongated painted background behind a character moving in place. It can also mean moving the camera in a lateral motion across artwork.

***Paramount* decision:** The 1948 Supreme Court decision declaring the movie industry a monopoly. It was the result of a 1938 suit brought by independent theater owners against the major motion picture producers. The *Paramount* decision hastened the decline of the great studios and the short cartoon.

The Pipeline: Contemporary nickname for the animation production line.

pitch, pitching: Preproduction technique in which a story or development artist takes clients or crew through the story of a film backed by visual aids such as artwork. Walt Disney was considered to be not a strong artist but a great pitchman.

Popular Front: During the 1930s, a blanket term for the plethora of progressive associations, charities, and political clubs that supported President Franklin Roosevelt and his New Deal. Originally a nickname for the coalition of radical leftist political parties that formed the Spanish Republic from 1931 to 1939.

producer: An executive who oversees the financial and personnel end of production.

Rand Corporation: Think tank originally formed to provide research and analysis to the U.S. armed forces that has expanded to work with other governments and private industry on strategic issues. Rand (previously Project Rand) split from the Douglas Aircraft Company to become independent in 1948. The name comes from "research and development." Daniel Ellsberg of Pentagon Papers fame was a Rand employee. Rand devised the Mohawk Valley rules for fighting unions. It was also a key developer of the Internet.

Red Squad: Covert team of rogue Los Angeles Police Department detectives who visited the homes of union organizers, civil rights activists, and other progressives and roughed them up. Started by LAPD chief James E. Davis in 1933. A police commissioner of the era is quoted as saying, "The more the police beat them up and wreck their headquarters, the better. Communists have no constitutional rights, and I won't listen to anyone who defends them" (www.lapdonline. org/history_of_the_lapd/content_basic_view/1109). The unit was disbanded in 1950 in Chief William Parker's departmental reorganization and merged into the Public Order Intelligence Division.

rep cards: Short for request for representation cards, confidential cards employees fill out and mail in to request union representation. Distribution of these cards is the basic method of grassroots union organizing.

right-to-work state: State that has enacted a law preventing unions from creating closed shops. It isn't necessary to join a union to work in a particular company within its borders. Film director and former union activist Cecil B. DeMille supported an unsuccessful effort to create right-to-work status for the film industry in 1944.

rotoscope: Technique of filming live action, then tracing off the movement to create realistic-looking animation. First developed by the Fleischer brothers in 1917.

SAG (Screen Actors Guild): The trade union representing actors in film and theater. Formed in 1933, the guild won recognition by the major Hollywood studios in 1937. Later affiliated with the Screen Extras Guild (SEG) and the American Federation of Television and Radio Artists (AFTRA).

scab: Derogatory term for a worker who crosses a picket line to work or one who takes the job of a worker on strike. In other words, a strikebreaker. In the Reagan 1980s, the media were encouraged to refer to them by the cleaned-up term "substitute worker."

Glossary

scenes: In animation, a single cut of the picture, while in live action or theater a scene can be made up of many cuts and angles. An animation scene is created from one panel of the storyboard and arrives on the animator's desk with layout staging, background reference, and timings determined by the director.

SCG (Screen Cartoonists Guild): Local 852 of the CSU Hollywood guild existed from 1938 to 1979. The East Coast guild Local 1461 lasted from 1943 to 1953. The IATSE Local 839 changed its name to the Animation Guild in 2001.

SIGGRAPH (Special Interest Group on Computer Graphic and Interactive Techniques): The computer animators' society where digital artists and researchers since 1972 have shared information and breakthroughs.

storyboards: Drawings used in planning a cartoon. The drawings are pinned on a wall in a continuity delineating the story's structure. Storyboard artists were known for their ability to write gags as much as for their talent for drawing or cinema. Bill Peet, Mike Maltese, Joe Barbera, Ted Pierce, Cal Howard, and Joe Ranft were top storyboard artists. Also called storysketch. The nickname for drawing storyboards is "boarding."

story department: The Disney concept of creating storyboards for a film, referred to as story rather than storyboarding because in this process there is as much writing as drawing. The earlier Disney features were written entirely on storyboards. Scripts created by writers didn't come into general use in television until the 1970s and in features until the 1980s.

Taft-Hartley Act: Restrictions on the power of unions enacted by Congress in 1947 in reaction to a series of postwar nationwide strikes. Taft Hartley forbade wildcat strikes, ancillary and sympathy strikes in related industries, and jurisdictional strikes, and made unions share the maintenance of their pension funds with employers. It also provided that union officials who were Communist Party members and refused to take a loyalty oath could not remain in office.

tech directors (TDs): Widely used industry name for technical support personnel for the animators. TDs sometimes write code and often troubleshoot problems with the animation software.

techs: Computer systems support engineers, software programmers, riggers, and lighting and technological directors who work on artwork.

Termite Terrace: Affectionate nickname for the dilapidated building at 1351 North Van Ness behind the Warner Bros. Hollywood studio where Leon Schlesinger Productions was based. This was where Looney Tunes and Merrie Melodies were made between 1930 and 1953. After 1953, the building became storage space for local television station KTLA.

traditional animation: Term coined during the digital revolution to describe the precomputer methods of 2D animation production. Animation done by pencils, paper, and paint.

UPA (United Productions of America): An animation studio formed toward the end of World War II that explored modern design styles and subject matter. UPA made breakthrough films like *Gerald McBoing Boing, The Unicorn in the Garden, Mr. Magoo*, and *The Tell-Tale Heart*. The films had a great influence on emerging world animation, particularly in Eastern Europe.

Van Beuren: New York animation studio started by producer Amadee Van Beuren. The Van Beuren studio was the first to be the target of a union organizing campaign and the first studio to be picketed. In 1936, when the studio's major distributor, RKO, transferred its allegiance to Disney, Van Beuren's went out of business.

vis-dev (visual development): Illustrators and/or designers who work with the art director at the earliest stages of production to create the style of a film. Mary Blair, Gustav Tennegren, and Bruce Zick were vis-dev artists. It was once referred to as inspirational art.

Wagner Act: Labor legislation passed in 1935 that said all workers had the right to form unions and bargain collectively and that an employee cannot be disciplined or fired for wanting a union. The act was almost immediately challenged by the National Chamber of Commerce, but the Supreme Court upheld the act in 1937.

Walt Disney Imagineering (WDI): Arm of the Disney Company concerned with the design and creation of theme parks. Several animators, including John Hench and Marc Davis were Imagineers. Also known as WED, for Walter Elias Disney.

WED (Walter Elias Disney): An acronym for the branch of the Disney Company concerned with theme park creation and management.

Also known as WDI, for Walt Disney Imagineering. Workers there are called imagineers.

Weta Workshop: Visual effects unit based in Wellington, New Zealand. Begun in 1993. The workshop created the breakthrough visual effects of Peter Jackson's *Lord of the Rings* (2001) trilogy and *King Kong* (2005).

WGA (Writers Guild of America): Originally the Screen Writers Guild.

WPA (Works Progress Administration): A Franklin D. Roosevelt administration program to fight the Depression. WPA programs offered employment to many thousands, including writers, artists, and actors.

Notes

1. The World of the Animation Studio

Epigraph: John Canemaker, *Winsor McCay: His Life and Art* (New York: Abbeville Press, 1999), 142.

1. Ted Le Berthon, daily column, *Los Angeles Daily Examiner*, August 1, 1938, Screen Cartoonists Guild (SCG) Archives, California State University, Northridge (CSUN).

2. The term "migrant film workers" was coined by John Van Vliet (motion picture visual effects animator whose credits include *Tron*, *Ghost*, and *Hart's War*) in discussion with the author, February 1990.

3. For a more detailed look at the career of John Randolph Bray, see Donald Crafton, *Before Mickey: American Animation, 1898–1928* (Cambridge, Mass.: MIT Press, 1987), chap. 5, "Bray: The Henry Ford of Animation."

4. Taylor's ideas also extended to the field of medicine. When surgeons in the operating theater ask their nurses for "Sponge!" or "Clamp!" they are following Taylor's ideas.

5. Crafton, *Before Mickey*, chap. 5.

6. Crafton, *Before Mickey*, 178; Grim Natwick, in discussion with Dwayne Crowther and the author, July 1989.

7. Shamus Culhane, quoted in Charles Solomon, *Enchanted Drawings: The History of Animation* (New York: Knopf, 1989), 24.

8. Maurice Noble, interviewed by ASIFA/Hollywood series "Evenings with . . . ," 1987, in ASIFA/Hollywood archives.

9. Shamus Culhane, in discussion with the author, December 1993; Joe Grant, in discussion with author, March 12, 2003; Ed Friedman, in discussion with author August 29, 2003.

10. Jack Zander, in discussion with the author, May 1997.

11. Claire Weeks, in discussion with the author, January 1996.

12. Martha Sigall, in discussion with the author, July 26, 2002.

13. Anne Guenther, in discussion with the author, August 27, 2003.

14. John Canemaker, *Before the Animation Begins: The Art and Lives of Disney Inspirational Sketch Artists* (New York: Hyperion, 1996), 79, 105.

15. Leslie Iwerks and John Kenworthy, *The Hand behind the Mouse: An Intimate Biography of the Man Walt Disney Called "the Greatest Animator in the World"* (New York: Disney Editions, 2001), 99.

16. Nat Falk, *How to Make Animated Cartoons: The History and Technique* (New York: Foundation Books, 1941).

17. Howard Beckerman, lecture at the School of Visual Arts, October 1974.

18. Jack Ozark, Max Fleischer animator, in discussion with Tiny Toons producer Richard Arons at Filmation Studios, 1984.

19. Jim Logan, Terrytoons animator, in discussion with the author.

20. Disney animator who wishes to remain anonymous, in discussion with the author, September 1987.

21. Falk, *How to Make Animated Cartoons*, 10.

22. Neal Gabler, lecture at Motion Picture Academy, May 1985.

23. Jack Zander, interview by the author, May 1997.

24. Zander, interview.

25. Martha Sigall, discussion, July 26, 2002.

26. Iwerks and Kenworthy, *Hand behind the Mouse*, 51.

27. Shamus Culhane, *Talking Animals and Other Funny People* (New York: St. Martin's, 1986). Near the same time, the Walter Lantz Studio promoted LaVerne Harding to animator.

28. Art Babbitt, interview by the author, November 1991.

29. Bill Melendez, in discussion with the author, May 21, 2002.

30. Ben Washam, in discussion with the author, August 1978.

31. Bud Hester, in discussion with the author, June 25, 2004.

32. Crafton, *Before Mickey*.

33. Friedman, discussion.

34. Martha Sigall, discussion, July 26, 2002.

35. Friedman, discussion.

36. Dave Fleischer, interview by Joe Adamson. Adamson interviewed Fleischer as part of an oral history for the University of California, Los Angeles, Department of Theater Arts in 1972 as part of "An Oral History of the Motion Picture in America." It is currently in the Special Collections of the UCLA Library.

37. Ward Kimball to Karl Stysz, quoted in Robert Fiore, "The Disney Strike: Inside and Out," *Comics Journal* 180, 1988.

38. A. M. Sperber and Eric Lax, Bogart (New York: William Morrow, 1997).

39. Beckerman lecture.

40. Selby Kelly to Nancy Beiman, *Cartoonists Profiles* (a publication of the National Cartoonists Society), 1983.

41. Heidi Guedel, *Animatrix: A Female Animator—How Laughter Saved My Life* (Bloomington, Ind.: AuthorHouse, 2003).

42. Hester, discussion.

43. Walt Disney married Lillian Bounds, Roy Disney married Edna Francis; both weddings were in 1924.

44. Guenther, discussion.

45. Merle Welton in discussion with animation producer Jan Nagel, February 20, 2004.

46. Guenther, discussion.

47. Guenther, discussion.

48. Ed Friedman and Frank Gonzales in discussion with the author during a celebration at Filmation Studio marking Frank's retirement, June, 1984; and Martha Sigall, discussion, July 26, 2002.

49. Floyd Norman, in discussion with the author, April 13, 2004; Melendez, discussion.

50. Melendez, discussion.

2. Suits: Producers as Seen by the Artists

1. Samuel Johnson, *A Dictionary of the English Language* (1755; reprint, New York: Arno Press, 1979); William Durant and Ariel Durant, *The Age of Voltaire* (New York: Simon & Schuster, 1965), 378.

2. Giorgio Vasari, "Michelangelo," vol. 1, pt. 3 of *Lives of the Artists*, trans. George Bull (New York: Penguin, 1987).

3. Culhane, *Talking Animals*.

4. William Hanna, *A Cast of Friends* (Dallas: Taylor, 1996), 82.

5. This is a famous old animation legend passed on for generations. I've heard the same quote attributed to Max Fleischer and Paul Terry, and to J. R. Bray by a World War I War Department contractor. See Crafton, *Before Mickey*, 148.

6. Joe Adamson, *The Walter Lantz Story: With Woody Woodpecker and Friends* (New York: Putnam & Sons, 1985), 85.

7. Shamus Culhane first told me about this curious payroll formula, and I saw it confirmed in Crafton, *Before Mickey*, 148.

8. Bray's patent was dated January 9, 1914. Bray and McCay continued suing one another until 1932.

9. For a more detailed view of Margaret Winkler, see Crafton, *Before Mickey*, 206–8, 307.

10. Crafton, *Before Mickey*, 321.

11. Many versions are told of what transpired in that hotel suite. Did Sullivan, a violent ex-boxer, in a jealous rage hurl his wife, Marjorie, out the window? Was she trying to get her chauffeur's attention? Did she fall by accident or, in despair at losing both men, did she commit suicide? The record is unclear. See Crafton, *Before Mickey*, 320; Solomon, *Enchanted Drawings*, 37; Pierre Lambert, *Le cartoon à Hollywood: L'histoire du dessin animé* (Paris: Librairie Séguier, 1988), 40.

12. Crafton, *Before Mickey*, 212.

13. Bob Thomas, *Building a Company: Roy O. Disney and the Creation of an Entertainment Empire* (New York: Hyperion, 1998), 6.

14. Crafton, *Before Mickey*, 212; Iwerks and Kenworthy, *Hand behind the Mouse*, 66.

15. Iwerks and Kenworthy, *Hand behind the Mouse*, 87.

16. Bob Givens, in discussion with the author, September 1989.

17. This was one of Chuck Jones's favorite old stories about the cluelessness of upper management. Other times Jones said it was Friz Freleng who originated the story. Chuck Jones, *Chuck Amuck: The Life and Times of an Animated Cartoonist* (Toronto: Warner Books, 1996), 89; Mel Blanc, *That's Not All Folks* (New York: Warner Books, 1988), 76.

18. Jones, *Chuck Amuck*, 89; Maureen Furniss, ed., *Chuck Jones: Conversations* (Jackson: University Press of Mississippi, 2005), 162–63. Chuck says that gag man Cal

Howard first suggested Leon's speech impediment for Daffy Duck and that he should possess Leon's "the world owes me a living" attitude. Some scholars, such as Mark Kausler, dispute the story of Leon's lisp, and no evidence of a lisp is audible on the few film clips that survive of him, but Mel Blanc repeats the same stories in his book *That's Not All Folks*, 234.

19. Jones, *Chuck Amuck*.

20. Jones, *Chuck Amuck*, 92–93.

21. Leonard Maltin, *Of Mice and Magic: A History of Animated Cartoons* (New York: McGraw Hill, 1980), 277; Joe Barbera, *My Life in 'Toons: From Flatbush to Bedrock in Under a Century* (Atlanta: Turner), 65.

22. Zander, discussion.

23. Barbera, *My Life in 'Toons*, 84.

24. John Canemaker, *Tex Avery: The MGM Years, 1942–1955* (Atlanta: Turner, 1996), 26.

25. Bob Kurtz, animator and director, in discussion with the author, May 2003.

26. Shamus Culhane, in discussion with the author, December 1977.

27. Alex Berenson, "The Wonderful World of (Roy) Disney," *New York Times*, February 15, 2004.

28. Dave Pruiksma was a Disney animator whose memorable performances include Ms. Pots in *Beauty and the Beast* and the Sultan in *Aladdin*. The comment was posted on Pruiksma's outspoken Website, www.pruiksma.com, May 8, 2001.

29. An allusion to French king Henry IV of Navarre (1554–1610), the founder of the Bourbon dynasty. He was famous for riding into battle with a large white feather in his helmet. During one battle when his generals asked, "What is the plan, Sire?" he replied: "Just follow the white plume."

30. John Elting, *Swords around a Throne: Napoleon's Grande Armée* (New York: Da Capo Press, 1997), 35.

31. *Variety*, February 21, 1921, cited by Crafton, *Before Mickey*, 198.

32. George Bakes, animator and assistant of Bill Tytla, in discussion with the author, May 1977.

33. Friedman, discussion.

34. Thomas, *Building a Company*, 244.

3. Hollywood Labor, 1933–1941

Epigraph: Maurice Rapf, cited in Otto Friedrich, *City of Nets: A Portrait of Hollywood in the 1940s* (New York: Harper & Row, 1980), 74.]

1. Another version of the origin of *Buried Treasure* was that it was created for a dinner for McCay in 1928 at the Hotel Richmond but the film was not ready in time for the dinner. The effort was organized and partly animated by George Stallings. Animators like George Canata Sr., Rudy Zamora, Raul Barré, Walter Lantz, and the crew of Pat Sullivan's studio also contributed. The artwork disappeared for a time but it was inked and painted and shot in Cuba.

2. The story of the Winsor McCay dinner has been well documented and passed down by animators for years, although the exact quote varies from teller to teller: "I gave you an art and you turned it into a trade. Too bad!" or "Animation should be an art. That's

how I conceived it. But as I see what you fellows have done with it, is making it into a trade. Not an art, but a trade. Too bad!" Howard Beckerman told it to me the first time in his lectures at the School of Visual Arts in 1974. Versions also appear in John Canemaker, *Winsor McCay*, 159; Culhane, *Talking Animals*, 435; and the recollections of eyewitness Phil Klein, courtesy of Leonard Maltin.

3. Emma Goldman didn't do herself any favors by writing a defense of Leon Czolgosz, the anarchist assassin of President William McKinley in 1901.

4. Mike Nielsen and Gene Mailes, *Hollywood's Other Blacklist: Union Struggles in the Studio System* (London: British Film Institute, 1995).

5. "A Short History," in Directors Guild of America Inc., Golden Jubilee 1936–1986, Directory of Members, ed. Ann Zollinger, 12.

6. Steve Tally, *Bland Ambition: From Adams to Quayle—The Cranks, Criminals, Tax Cheats, and Golfers Who Made It to Vice President* (San Diego: Harcourt Brace Jovanovich, 1992), 270.

7. Mike Quin, *The Big Strike* (Olema, Calif: Olema Publishing, 1949).

8. Esther Leslie, *Hollywood Flatlands: Animation, Critical Theory, and the Avant-Garde* (London: Verso, 2002), 130.

9. The hot-potato story of Leni Riefenstahl's visit to the Disney studio was verified to me in an interview with Disney department head Joe Grant, March 12, 2003. It is also mentioned in Leslie, *Hollywood Flatlands*, 123; Leni Riefenstahl, *Leni Riefenstahl: A Memoir* (New York: St. Martin's, 1992); Charles Higham, *Merchant of Dreams: Louis B. Mayer, MGM, and the Secret Hollywood* (New York: D. I. Fine, 1993), 285–87.

10. Higham, *Merchant of Dreams*, 300.

11. Harvey Deneroff, "Popeye the Union Man," PhD diss., UCLA, 1985.

12. Ian Hamilton, *Writers in Hollywood, 1915–1950* (New York: Harper & Row, 1990), 91.

13. Irene Mayer Selznick, *A Private View* (New York: Knopf, 1983), 84.

14. Jack Kinney, *Walt Disney and Other Assorted Characters: An Unauthorized Account of the Early Years at Disney's* (New York: Harmony, 1990), 26.

15. Jack Zander, interview, 1995.

16. Adamson, *Walter Lantz Story*, 84.

17. Hamilton, *Writers in Hollywood*, 92.

18. Hamilton, *Writers in Hollywood*, 93.

19. Hamilton, *Writers in Hollywood*, 93.

20. Hamilton, *Writers in Hollywood*, 97.

21. Sperber and Lax, *Bogart*, 63.

22. James Cagney, *Cagney by Cagney* (Garden City, N.Y.: Doubleday, 1976), 108.

23. Richard O. Boyer and Herbert Morais, *Labor's Untold Story* (Pittsburgh: United Electrical, Radio and Machine Workers of America Press), 1955.

24. The story of the broken IATSE strike of 1933 is recounted in detail in Nielsen and Mailes, *Hollywood's Other Blacklist*.

25. The story of the Hollywood studio extortion racket is well documented in George H. Dunne, *The Hollywood Labor Dispute: A Study in Immorality* (Los Angeles: Conference Publishing, 1949); Friedrich, *City of Nets*, chap. 3; and Nielsen and Mailes, *Hollywood's Other Blacklist*.

26. In accounts of the time Frank "the Enforcer" Nitti was sometimes referred to by his name back in Italy, Francesco Nitto, other times as Frank Nitto.

27. Nielsen and Mailes, *Hollywood's Other Blacklist*, 16.

28. Nielsen and Mailes, *Hollywood's Other Blacklist*, 16.

29. "Striking Cartoonists Declare for F.M.P.C.," *New York Times*, May 16, 1937.

30. David F. Prindle, *The Politics of Glamour: Ideology and Democracy in the Screen Actors Guild* (Madison: University of Wisconsin Press, 1988), 31.

31. For the story of SAG's birth and development, see Prindle, *Politics of Glamour*.

32. Time line, Directors Guild Annual 1986.

33. Culhane, *Talking Animals*, 86.

34. Iwerks and Kenworthy, *Hand behind the Mouse*, 128–29.

35. Friedman, discussion.

36. Culhane, *Talking Animals*, 86.

37. The best resource for tracing the early animation unions in New York and the Van Beuren union troubles is Deneroff, "Popeye the Union Man."

38. Roger Garcia, *Frank Tashlin* (London: British Film Institute, 1994), 188.

39. Deneroff, "Popeye the Union Man."

40. Bill Littlejohn, interview by the author, April 9, 1999.

41. Deneroff, "Popeye the Union Man," 95.

42. Gene Price and Jack Kistner, *The Story of the Hollywood Film Strike in Cartoons* (Los Angeles: Conference Publishing, 1945). This is a self-published book of CSU strike leaflets and cartoons created by two members of CSU Local 644.

43. Deneroff, "Popeye the Union Man," 115.

4. The Fleischer Strike

1. Leslie Cabarga, *The Fleischer Story* (New York: Nostalgia Books, 1974), 11–13.

2. Crafton, *Before Mickey*, 158.

3. Recollections of Dave Fleischer as told to Joe Adamson, An Oral History of the Motion Picture in America, UCLA Special Archives, 1969.

4. Dave Tendlar, interview by the author, May 1985.

5. Solomon, *Enchanted Drawings*.

6. Red Pepper Sam was a vaudeville singer named William Costello. Dave Fleischer had heard him on the radio do a character called Gus Gorilla and hired him to do the famous sailor. Mae Questel recalled he did it for one year, but it all went to his head and he wanted more money as well as a vacation in the middle of production. Tim Lawson and Alisa Persons, "Jack Mercer," in *The Magic behind the Voices: A Who's Who of Cartoon Voice Actors* (Jackson: University Press of Mississippi, 2005), 232; Maltin, *Of Mice and Magic*, 102.

7. Documentary, *The Good Fight*, Noel Buckner, Kino Video, 1984.

8. Grim Natwick in Solomon, *Enchanted Drawings*, 22. The veracity of this anecdote has been challenged by recent scholars, but the anecdote was repeated by Dave Tendlar in 1985 when I interviewed him for ASIFA/Hollywood. Shamus Culhane also repeated the story to me.

9. Culhane, *Talking Animals*, 65. Laverne Harding had been promoted by Walter Lantz at about the same time. Adamson, *Walter Lantz Story*.

10. Newsreel from documentary, *Brother Can You Spare a Dime?* Image Entertainment, 1976.

11. Cabarga, *Fleischer Story*, 141.

12. The overall best resource for details on the Fleischer studio strike is Deneroff, "Popeye the Union Man."

13. Richard Williams, conversation with the author, 1978.

14. Harvey Deneroff, "The Story of Dan Glass," *Inbetweener* (ASIFA/Hollywood newsletter), August 1984.

15. Deneroff, "Popeye the Union Man," 67.

16. Deneroff, "Popeye the Union Man."

17. Deneroff, "Popeye the Union Man," 135; Cabarga, *Fleischer Story*, 142.

18. Dave Fleischer, recollections, UCLA Special Archives.

19. Ellen Jensen, letter to the author, July 1994. In an article in the union newsletter I had called her "a nice little old lady who during the Fleischer Strike had bitten a policeman on the leg" (*Pegboard*, June 1994). Here is her letter to me: "Dear Tom, I didn't bite the policeman on the leg but on the arm until blood flowed. They were wringing both my arms and had just knocked off my hat with a nightstick. Of course the union thought it was great but I felt awful. . . . I am not sweet nor will ever be but an old lady.—Ellen C. Jensen-Klugherz." Collection of the author.

20. Cabarga, *Fleischer Story*, 107.

21. Dave Fleischer, recollections, UCLA.

22. "Movie Studio Strike Voted by 100 Workers," *New York Times*, May 8, 1937, 5; microfilm, UCLA collections.

23. Deneroff, "Popeye the Union Man."

24. Dave Fleischer, recollections, UCLA.

25. Deneroff, "Popeye the Union Man."

26. Deneroff, "Popeye the Union Man."

27. Deneroff, "Popeye the Union Man."

28. Deneroff, "Popeye the Union Man."

29. A good resource for Fleischer in Florida is Harvey Deneroff, "Fleischer's Travels," lecture to the Society of Animation Studies, Museum of Television and Radio, Museum of Television and Radio, 1982; Animation Guild Local 839 office archive.

30. Deneroff, "Popeye the Union Man."

31. Hank Ketcham, *The Merchant of Dennis the Menace* (New York: Abbeville Press, 1990).

32. Ketcham, *Merchant of Dennis*.

33. Jack Ozark, in discussion with the author, September 1984.

34. Deneroff, "Fleischer's Travels"; Cabarga, *Fleischer Story*, 144.

35. Michael Barrier, *Hollywood Cartoons: American Animation in Its Golden Age* (New York: Oxford University Press, 1999).

36. Barrier, *Hollywood Cartoons*, 304. Cabarga, *Fleischer Story*, 192; Solomon, *Enchanted Drawings*, 85.

37. Dave Fleischer, recollections, UCLA.

38. Cabarga, *Fleischer Story*.

39. Dave Fleischer, recollections, UCLA.

40. Richard Fleischer, *Out of the Inkwell: Max Fleischer and the Animation Revolution* (Lexington: University Press of Kentucky, 2005), 139.

41. April 1, 1956, then with Hal Seeger as Out of the Inkwell Production, 1958–1964. Fleischer, *Out of the Inkwell*.

42. August 1, 1972; Fleischer, *Out of the Inkwell*.

43. Deneroff, "Popeye the Union Man."

44. Deneroff, "Popeye the Union Man," 257.

5. The Great Disney Studio Strike

Epigraph: Thomas, *Building a Company*, 220.

Portions of this chapter first appeared in my article "The War of Hollywood—Part 2: The Disney Studio Strike of 1941," in the *Grim Reader*, the newsletter of the Los Angeles Grim Society (www.grimsociety.com), April–May 1996, and are reprinted with the society's permission.

1. Walt Disney was born in Chicago in 1901 and grew up in the farm community of Marcelline, Missouri. At the time of his discharge from the army in 1919, his residence was listed as Kansas City. His family home there was at 3028 Bellefontaine Avenue. His first studio, the Newman Laugh-O-grams company was in the McConahy Building at 1127 East Thirty-first Street. The legend that Walt started the Disney studio in a garage came from the small garage he rented temporarily from an uncle when he first moved to Hollywood in 1923. Check the Web site www.laughograms.com on attempts today to preserve the buildings.

2. Friedrich, *City of Nets*, 16.

3. By many accounts Walt had a penchant for such double-edged humor with his contemporaries. Ward Kimball told me in 1998 about an encounter after top animator Grim Natwick had quit the studio to go to Max Fleischer's in Florida. After a few years Grim was visiting back at the Disney studio. He was having lunch with friends in the studio commissary when Walt came over and clapped him on the back. Walt smiled: "Gee Grim, I really wish you'd come back and work for me again . . . so this time I could fire you!"

4. Bob Thomas, *Walt Disney: An American Original* (New York: Hyperion, 1994), chap 5.

5. Martha Sigall interview by the author, July 2003.

6. Friedman, discussion.

7. Littlejohn, interview.

8. Robert C. Harvey and Gustavo M. Arriola, *Accidental Ambassador Gordo: The Comic Strip Art of Gus Arriola* (Jackson: University Press of Mississippi, 2000).

9. Jack Zander, interview by the author, May 1997.

10. Jones, *Chuck Amuck*, 166.

11. Herbert K. Sorrell, "You Don't Choose Your Friends," oral history transcript. The Memoirs of Herbert Knott Sorrell, Interviewed by Elizabeth I. Dixon, 1961, acquired 1963. Call no. 300.11, UCLA Special Collections.

12. J. M. Ryan, *The Rat Factory* (Englewood Cliffs, N.J.: Prentice-Hall, 1971), 80.

13. SCG Leaflet, Disney Strike Documents, CD988, Motion Picture Screen Cartoon-

ist Local 839, AFL-CIO Collection, Urban Archives Center, Oviatt Library, California State University, Northridge (hereafter MPSC 839, CSUN).

14. Dave Hilberman, in discussion with the author, April 28, 2002.

15. Frank Tashlin, interviewed by Michael Barrier in 1973, in Garcia, *Frank Tashlin*, 157.

16. Iwerks and Kenworthy, *Hand behind the Mouse*, 148.

17. Ward Kimball to Klaus Stzyz, in Fiore, "Disney Strike," 91. Kimball's recollections are very valuable for understanding this period because of his evenhanded view of the issues and because he kept a daily diary as it was happening.

18. Rudy Zamora Jr. in discussion with the author, February 1991; Barrier, *Hollywood Cartoons*.

19. Kinney, *Walt Disney and Other Assorted Characters*, 21; see also Bill Peet, *Bill Peet: An Autobiography* (New York: Scholastic, 1989), 80.

20. Iwerks and Kenworthy, *Hand behind the Mouse*, 80.

21. Claire Weeks, in discussion with the author; Ed Fourcher, in discussion with the author, August 19, 1990; Art Babbitt, in discussion with the author.

22. Bill Tytla, interviewed by Michael Barrier in 1968, did not recall being promised a bonus, so the issue remains controversial.

23. Leslie, *Hollywood Flatlands*, 112.

24. Thomas, *Building a Company*.

25. Ted Le Berthon column, *Los Angeles Evening News*, August 1, 1938, SCG Archives, CSUN Special Collections. Ted Le Berthon in Hollywood daily column in *Los Angeles Daily Examiner*, August 1, 1938, SCG Archives, CSUN.

26. Notes on an exhibit of early television development, the National Film and Television Archive, British Film Institute, Southbank Center, London.

27. Walt Disney, 1956 taped interview by Peter Martin for the book written with Diane Disney Miller, *The Story of Walt Disney* (New York: Dell, 1959). Parts of the interview appeared in an article "My Dad, Walt Disney," in the *Saturday Evening Post*, November 24, 1956. The tapes have been copied and circulated among Disney artists for years. I'd like to thank Disney animator Rick Farmiloe for bringing them to my attention.

28. Barrier, *Hollywood Cartoons*, 281.

29. Leaflet, Animation Guild Local 839 IATSE archives.

30. Kinney, *Walt Disney and Other Assorted Characters*, 138.

31. Oswald the Lucky Rabbit was restored to Walt Disney Co. in a deal with Universal in 2006.

32. Kimball in Fiore, "Disney Strike."

33. For a version of the 1941 strike mainly from Walt's point of view, see Thomas, *Walt Disney: An american Original*.

34. Disney animator Al Eugster's diary courtesy of the Al Eugster Collection and animator Mark Mayerson.

35. Barrier, *Hollywood Cartoons*, 283.

36. Art Babbitt interviewed by Klaus Strzyz in Fiore, "Disney Strike."

37. Dunne, *Hollywood Labor Dispute*, 23.

38. Zander, interview by the author, May 1997.

39. Editor Joe Campana, in discussion with the author, May 2002. Campana is currently completing a book on the addresses of many notable Hollywood cartoon and animation people.

40. Hilberman, discussion, 2002.

41. Hester, discussion, 2003.

42. Thomas, *Walt Disney*, 43; Fiore, "Disney Strike," 80; Barrier, *Hollywood Cartoons*, 284.

44. Thomas, *Walt Disney*, 166; Karl F. Cohen, *Forbidden Animation: Censored Cartoons and Blacklisted Animators in America* (Jefferson, N.C.: McFarland, 1997), 160.

45. Guenther, discussion.

46. Melendez, discussion.

47. Dave Hilberman, discussion.

48. SCG Leaflet, Disney Strike Documents, CD 988, MPSC 839, CSUN.

49. Babbitt to Styzsz, in Fiore, "Disney Strike." Babbitt is the only source for this story.

50. SCG Leaflet, Disney Strike Documents CD 988, MPSC 839, CSUN.

51. Thomas, *Building a Company*, 243–44.

52. The dust bowl comment is a famous statement and was spoken about often in later years. Grant, Littlejohn, discussion. See also Thomas, *Walt Disney*, 166. Six years later Walt Disney recalled it in his HUAC testimony, which is available at www.cnn.com/SPECIALS/cold.war/episodes/06/documents/huac/disney.html.

53. Babbitt in Fiore, "Disney Strike."

54. Grant, discussion.

55. Thomas, *Walt Disney*, 168.

56. Kinney, *Walt Disney and Other Assorted Characters*, 138.

57. Babbitt, discussion.

58. John Canemaker, *Vladimir Tytla, Master Animator* (Katonah, N.Y.: Katona Museum of Art, 1994.)

59. Scrapbook, Disney Strike Documents, CD 988, MPSC 839, CSUN.

60. Ketcham, *Merchant of Dennis*.

61. Garcia, *Frank Tashlin*, 159.

62. Bill Melendez, in discussion with the author, May 21, 2002.

63. Art Babbitt in documentary, *Animating Art*, by Mo Sutton, 1982.

64. Martha Sigall, in discussion with the author, July 15, 2003.

65. Jones, *Chuck Amuck*, 84.

66. Friedman, discussion.

67. Adrienne Tytla, *Disney's Giant and the Artists' Model* (Deep River, Conn.: Valley Press, 2005).

68. Melendez, discussion.

69. Friedman, discussion.

70. Kinney, *Walt Disney and Other Assorted Characters*, 137.

71. David Swift, interview by the author, May 2000.

72. Ketcham, *Merchant of Dennis*.

73. Babbitt in Fiore, "Disney Strike."

74. The Disney-Babbitt confrontation is one of the most dramatic moments in U.S.

animation history. There are many versions as to who yelled what, but all acknowledge that Babbitt said something that made Walt angry enough to go for him. Solomon, *Enchanted Drawings*, 71; Fiore, "Disney Strike," 82; Richard Schickel, *The Disney Version: The Life, Times, Art, and Commerce of Walt Disney* (New York: Avon Books, 1967), 219; Barrier, *Hollywood Cartoons*, 307. Kimball recalled seeing Babbitt yell something on the loudspeaker then run up to Disney's car yelling at him before Walt stopped and got out. Thomas, *Walt Disney*, 169, just says "one of the striking animators."

75. Babbitt, discussion, December 1991.

76. Bill Tytla, interviewed by George Sherman, May 13, 1968, in Didier Ghez, ed., *Walt's People: Talking Disney with the Artists Who Knew Him* (New York: XLibris, 2005), 1:101.

77. SCG Archives, CSUN. Apologists for Walt Disney, if they mention the national boycotts and ancillary strikes at all, interpret them as being organized solely by Herb Sorrell. Thomas, *Walt Disney*, 169.

78. Babbitt, in Fiore, "Disney Strike," 80.

79. Mary Hurtz, in discussion with the author, November 10, 2000.

80. Maurice Noble, Ed Fourcher, Bill Hurtz, in discussion with the author.

81. Ed Fourcher, Maurice Noble, discussion.

82. Dave Hilberman, discussion.

83. The Walt Disney testimony to the FBI about the causes of the strike can be found in U.S. Congressional Committee Hearings (80) H1169–5, 280–90 and is available through the Freedom of Information Act. For a detailed discussion, see Cohen, *Forbidden Animation*, 161.

84. Cohen, *Forbidden Animation*, 162.

85. Fiore, "Disney Strike," 81.

86. "Strike Settlement Seen as Great Victory for Cartoonists, *Variety*, July 10, 1941, SCG Archives, CSUN.

87. Leaflet , SCG Archives, CSUN.

88. Thomas, *Building a Company*.

89. Sorrell, "You Don't Choose Your Friends," UCLA Special Collections.

90. Thomas, *Building a Company*, 148. Thomas claims that Roy Disney shut down the studio at the suggestion of some anonymous Labor Department official.

91. Thomas's version is that "Walt and Roy went to Washington to try and break the labor stalemate." *Building a Company*, 148.

92. Babbitt, discussion; Fourcher, discussion.

93. Babbitt in Fiore, "Disney Strike."

94. Joe Grant, interview by the author, March 12, 2003.

95. Melendez, discussion.

96. Maurice Noble, interview by the author for ASIFA/Hollywood series "Evenings with . . . ," August 21, 1996.

97. Babbitt, interview; Fourcher, interview.

98. Melendez, interview.

99. Fourcher, interview.

100. Grant, interview.

101. Walt Disney, Peter Martin interview, 1956.

Notes to Pages 144–158

102. Garcia, *Frank Tashlin*.

103. George Bakes, Tytla former assistant, in discussion with the author, April 1977.

104. Ben Washam, interview by the author, August 1978.

105. Canemaker, *Vladimir Tytla*.

106. Melendez, interview.

107. *Los Angeles Times*, October 25, 1947, UCLA Microfilm Collection. The complete testimony of Walt Disney is available online atwww.cnn.com/SPECIALS/cold.war/episodes/06/documents/huac/disney.html.

108. Robert Vaughn, *Only Victims: A Study of Show Business Blacklisting* (New York: Limelight Editions, 1996), 85.

109. Walter Francis, "Disney Tells How Reds Tried to Take Over Studio," *Los Angeles Times*, October 26, 1947, 1; UCLA microfilm collection.

110. Hilberman, interview.

111. "Disney Says Reds Ruled His Artists," *New York Daily News*, October 25, 1947. Courtesy of Howard Beckerman.

112. Cohen, *Forbidden Animation*.

113. Harry Tytle, *One of "Walt's Boys": An Insider's Account of Disney's Golden Years* (Mission Viejo, Calif.: ASAP Publishing, 1997), 84.

114. Screen Players Guides for 1942, 1944, USC Doheny Library. Frank Thomas, in discussion with the author.

115. Thomas, *Building a Company*, 220.

116. Grim Natwick, recollection to Steve Worth, 1998.

117. Kimball, in Fiore, "Disney Strike," 95.

6. The War of Hollywood and the Blacklist

Epigraph: "Brewer, Reagan Exhort Cartoonists to Vote IA," *Daily Variety*, January 8, 1952, 8. Courtesy of Michael Barrier.

1. Boyer and Morais, *Labor's Untold Story*, 278. The name Rand stands for R-and-D, or research and development.

2. A great breakdown of events in the War of Hollywood, albeit slanted toward the CSU cause is in Nielsen and Mailes, *Hollywood's Other Blacklist*, 58. More impartial but not as thorough because of its larger scope is Friedrich, *City of Nets*.

3. Friedrich, *City of Nets*, 281.

4. Nielsen and Mailes, *Hollywood's Other Blacklist*, 81.

5. Nielsen and Mailes, *Hollywood's Other Blacklist*; Friedrich, *City of Nets*.

6. Littlejohn, William, in discussion with the author.

7. One rumor circulated by the CSU was that a dozen big men visited Brown in his jail cell. They told the warden they were all optometrists there to give the prisoner an eye exam. The day after this curious eye exam the IA Executive Board met and nominated Richard Walsh to be new IA president. Nielsen and Mailes, *Hollywood's Other Blacklist*.

8. Price and Kistner, *Hollywood Film Strike in Cartoons*, is a collection of mimeographed daily bulletins from the CSU bound and edited by two stalwarts of Local 644 Painters of the CSU.

9. Friedrich, *City of Nets*, 277. It should be noted that many rank-and-file members of the IATSE tried to dispute the policies of the leadership as they had once fought Bioff and Brown. Several IATSE leaders like Jeff Kibre and Gene Mailes and locals like 37 and 683 agitated for real reform. In 1946 Local 683 lab technicians actually broke ranks and joined the CSU pickets. For that, Walsh declared 683 "in a state of emergency." He ordered Roy Brewer to seize its bank holdings and dismiss its leadership. Nielsen and Mailes, *Hollywood's Other Blacklist*, 183

10. SCG Correspondence, CD 988, MPSC Local 839, AFL-CIO Collection, Urban Archives Center, Oviatt Library, California State University, Northridge (hereafter CSUN).

11. Friedrich, *City of Nets*, 248.

12. Paul Buhle and David Wagner, *Radical Hollywood: The Untold Story behind America's Favorite Movies* (New York: New Press, 2002), 202.

13. Sperber and Lax, *Bogart*, 316. This biography focuses some light on the political life of the famous movie star, with particular focus on his attempt to combat the HUAC Hollywood investigation.

14. Prindle, *Politics of Glamour*, 46.

15. Nielsen and Mailes, *Hollywood's Other Blacklist*, 113

16. Price and Kistner, *Hollywood Film Strike in Cartoons*, introductory notes; Nielsen and Mailes, *Hollywood's Other Blacklist*, 128.

17. Sperber and Lax, *Bogart*, 315–19, gives a good detailed description of the Battle of Burbank in front of the Warner Bros. studio.

18. Jeff Massie, in discussion with the author, September 12, 2004. Massie is secretary of Local 839 Animation Guild and his parents, Reg and Nancy Massie, were guild members who participated in the strikes and the Battle of Burbank.

19. Sperber and Lax, *Bogart*, 315.

20. Friedrich, *City of Nets*, 249.

21. "Dozen Injured in Melee at Warners' Entrance; Union Leader Arrested," *Los Angeles Times*, October 6, 1945, 1.

22. Sigall, Friedman, discussion.

23. Sigall, discussion; Nielsen and Mailes, *Hollywood's Other Blacklist*.

24. "Dozen Injured in Melee."

25. "Pickets May Mass at Film Studio Today," *Los Angeles Times*, October 8, 1945, 1.

26. George H. Dunne, *The Hollywood Labor Dispute: A Study in Immorality* (Los Angeles: Conference Publishing, 1949), 12.

27. Sperber and Lax, *Bogart*, 315–16.

28. Sperber and Lax, *Bogart*, 317.

29. Sperber and Lax, *Bogart*, 318.

30. Sperber and Lax, *Bogart*, 318.

31. Sperber and Lax, *Bogart*, 318.

32. Friedrich, *City of Nets*, 279.

33. Nielsen and Mailes, *Hollywood's Other Blacklist*.

34. Sperber and Lax, *Bogart*, 318.

35. Nielsen and Mailes, *Hollywood's Other Blacklist*.

36. Friedrich, *City of Nets*, 279.

37. Friedrich, *City of Nets*, 279–80.

38. Prindle, *Politics of Glamour*, 47.

39. Prindle, *Politics of Glamour*, 47–48. The Teamsters also changed sides after Teamster LA leader Joe Touhy negotiated with Joe Schenck, the same exec who was pardoned by President Truman for dealing with Willie Bioff. Records show Schenck put Touhy on the Twentieth Century-Fox payroll at $400 a week for the months it took to break the strike. Friedrich, *City of Nets*, 281.

40. Friedrich, *City of Nets*, 281.

41. Dunne, *Study in Immorality*.

42. Walt Disney, Peter Martin interview, 1956.

43. HUAC, the House Committee on Un-American Activities, began as a special committee in 1938 but was made a standing body. HUAC was the body that investigated Hollywood. In the Senate, the Permanent Subcommittee on Investigations of the Senate Committee on Government Operations was chaired by Senator Joseph McCarthy, the infamous Commie-chasing Republican demagogue from Wisconsin. McCarthy's committee focused on government workers and the military. See Vaughn, *Only Victims*, 119.

44. Larry Ceplair and Steven Englund, *The Inquisition in Hollywood: Politics in the Film Community, 1930–1960* (Berkeley and Los Angeles: University of California Press, 1983), 157.

45. Kevin Starr, *Embattled Dreams: California in War and Peace, 1940–1950* (New York: Oxford University Press, 2002), chap 10.

46. Gary Wills, *John Wayne's America: The Politics of Celebrity* (New York: Simon & Schuster, 1997), 196.

47. Sperber and Lax, *Bogart*, 354.

48. Sperber and Lax, *Bogart*, 357.

49. Friedrich, *City of Nets*; Sperber and Lax, *Bogart*, 363.

50. Jay Rivkin, interview by the author, 2004.

51. Friedrich, *City of Nets*, 324.

52. Sperber and Lax, *Bogart*.

53. Patrick McGilligan and Paul Buhle, *Tender Comrades: A Backstory of the Hollywood Blacklist* (New York: St. Martin's, 1997).

54. The memorial for progressive cartoonist Art Young was held in New York on January 27, 1941. It was attended by leading intellectuals such as Carl Sandburg, Langston Hughes, Ernest Hemingway, and Paul Robeson. It has been alleged that Walt Disney was present at the event, but all that can be corroborated was that he donated funds for it.

55. Sol Sigall, in discussion with the author, July 15, 2003.

56. Starr, *Embattled Dreams*, 289.

57. McGilligan and Buhle, *Tender Comrades*.

58. Tytla, *Disney's Giant*.

59. Selby Kelly to Nancy Beiman, *Cartoonists Profiles*, a publication of the National Cartoonists Society, 1983.

60. Victor Navasky, *Naming Names* (New York: Penguin, 1991), 83.

61. Ezra Goodman, *The Fifty Year Decline and Fall of Hollywood* (New York: Simon & Schuster, 1961.)

62. Cohen, *Forbidden Animation*, 190–91

63. Sperber and Lax, *Bogart*.

64. Vaughn, *Only Victims*.

65. Wills, *John Wayne's America*, 198.

66. During the 1937 labor battles between IATSE and FMPC, the Herbert Stewart CP/USA card was in the possession of Jeff Kibre, a CIO organizer and acknowledged Communist Party member. After he refused to appear on a Los Angeles subpoena, the LAPD Red Squad raided his home and took things they considered evidence, including the card. Years later, someone within the LAPD sold the card to an IATSE lawyer, who gave it to Roy Brewer. Prindle, *Politics of Glamour*, 46.

67. Friedrich, *City of Nets*, 282; Prindle, *Politics of Glamour*, 46.

68. Kevin Roderick, *The San Fernando Valley: America's Suburb* (Los Angeles: Los Angeles Times Books, 2002), 126.

69. I'd like to thank Martha and Sol Sigall and Mark Kausler for first making me aware of the Community Projects affair.

70. Roderick, *San Fernando Valley*, chap. 9.

71. Obituary of Wah Ming Chang, *Variety*, December 24, 2003.

72. Bill Hurtz, in discussion with the author.

73. "Brewer, Reagan Exhort Cartoonists."

74. "Brewer, Reagan Exhort Cartoonists."

75. SCG pamphlet, MPSC 839 Archives, CSUN. Bill Scott, better known as the voice of Bullwinkle the Moose, wrote passionate and articulate articles on the IATSE-SCG issue.

76. "NY Screen Cartoonists Guild Joins IATSE," *Daily Variety*, February 28, 1953, 3.

77. "NY Screen Cartoonists Guild Joins IATSE."

78. "NY Screen Cartoonists Guild Joins IATSE,"

79. Ben Washam, recollection to the author, August 1978.

80. Gene Deitch, "UPA, Back to the Future," *Animation World Magazine*, May 22, 2003 http://mag.awn.com/index.php?article_no=1414; excerpt from Gene Deitch, How to Succeed in Animation (Don't Let a Little Thing like Failure Stop You!), http://gene-deitch.awn.com.

81. Barrier, *Hollywood Cartoons*.

82. Cohen, *Forbidden Animation*, 181. Cohen goes into great detail about the HUAC investigations and their effect on Hollywood animation as well as the National Film Board of Canada.

83. Dave Hilberman, in discussion with the author, April 28, 2002.

84. Deitch, *How to Succeed in Animation*.

85. Culhane, *Talking Animals*, 321. Culhane doesn't mention the name here of the blacklisted writer, but it was Phil Eastman.

86. Kelly, *Cartoonist Profiles*.

87. Dave and Libby Hilberman, in discussion with the author, April 28, 2002. Herb Klynn, in discussion with the author, September 1999.

88. Vaughn, *Only Victims*.

89. Other animation people who testified and named names were Schlesinger background artist Bernice Prolifka and her husband, Eugene Fleury, who taught in the Dis-

ney art program. HUAC made them high-profile "friendly" witnesses. They trotted the couple out so often that at one point Eugene Fleury complained, "Congressman, isn't there anyone else in Southern California who could do this besides my wife and myself?" Cohen, *Forbidden Animation*, 171.

90. Melendez, interview.

91. Cohen, *Forbidden Animation*, 183.

92. Hamilton, *Writers in Hollywood*, 204.

93. Observed by the author at the 2000 Academy Awards. Shortly before Kazan stepped out, I talked with other filmmakers, including an instructor of the American Film Institute. "Are you going to applaud? Nah, I'm not!!" was the general tone of the conversation.

7. A Bag of Oranges

Epigraph: Mannie Davis, quoted in Maltin, *Of Mice and Magic*, 143.

1. Maltin, *Of Mice and Magic*, 123.

2. Falk, *How to Make Animated Cartoons*, 17.

3. Crafton, *Before Mickey*, 149.

4. Maltin, *Of Mice and Magic*, 121.

5. Maltin, *Of Mice and Magic*, 122.

6. For details on the Terrytoons Strike, I'd like to thank SCG Local 839 secretary Jim Carmichael and 841 business rep Pepe Ruiz for preserving and donating extensive files from the SCG to the archives at CSUN in 1979, and Harvey Deneroff for writing the first concise summary of the events.

7. Howard Beckerman, lecture, School of Visual Arts, September 1975. Another version of this story attributes the quote to Leon Schlesinger. See Maltin, *Of Mice and Magic*, 121.

8. Maltin, *Of Mice and Magic*, chap. 4; quote is from p. 142.

9. Jim Logan, in discussion with the author, May 1982.

10. Terrytoons Strike, Summary of Events, CD988, MPSC 839 Archives, CSUN.

11. Howard Beckerman, Cliff "Red" Augustson, in discussion with the author.

12. Maltin, *Of Mice and Magic*, chap. 4.

13. Logan, discussion.

14. Maltin, *Of Mice and Magic*, 137.

15. MPSC 839 Archives, CSUN.

16. Logan, Augustson, discussion.

17. Cohen, *Forbidden Animation*, 164.

18. Minutes, General Membership November Meeting 1947, Terrytoons, MPSC 839 Archives, CSUN.

19. MPSC 839 Archives, CSUN.

20. Maltin, *Of Mice and Magic*, 143.

21. "NY Screen Cartoonists Guild Joins IATSE."

22. Gene Deitch, "Tom Terrific 1958 Production Plan," *Animation World Magazine*, June 10, 2003, http://mag.awn.com/index.php?ltype=Columns&column=career&article _no=1769; excerpt from Deitch, *How to Succeed in Animation*.

23. Jules Feiffer, lecture to National Cartoonists Society, San Antonio, May 30, 2001.

24. Local 839 guild secretary Jeff Massie to author, 1990.

25. Maltin, *Of Mice and Magic*, 143.

8. Lost Generations

Epigraph: Anne Guenther, in discussion with the author, October 12, 2003.

1. Corny Cole, in discussion with the author, September 16, 2003.

2. Thomas, *Building a Company*, 222–23. The original filing in U.S. district court, made July 20, 1938, was Petitioners v. Paramount Pictures Inc. et al. Defendants. The other defendants listed were RKO, Warner Bros., Twentieth Century-Fox, Columbia, Universal, and United Artists. See Goodman, *Fifty-Year Decline*, 433.

3. In 1941 there were 7,000 television sets in the United States; ten years later, there were 15 million. See www.tvhistory.tv.

4. Sperber and Lax, *Bogart*, 419.

5. Walt Disney, Peter Martin interview, 1956.

6. ASIFA/ International Journal, Expo/67 Montreal Canada, 1967; ASIFA/Hollywood Archives.

7. Art Babbitt, interview by Michael Barrier, June 2, 1971. Animation Guild Local 839 Office Archives.

8. For a good analysis of the Taft-Hartley Act, see Priscilla Murolo and A. B. Chitty, *From the Folks Who Brought You the Weekend: A Short, Illustrated History of Labor in the United States* (New York: Free Press, 2003), 233–39; and George Lipsitz, *The Rainbow at Midnight: Labor and Culture in the 1940s* (Urbana: University of Illinois Press, 1994), 171–79.

9. Goodman, *Fifty-Year Decline*, 96.

10. Chuck Jones, *Chuck Amuck: The Life and Times of an Animated Cartoonist*. Toronto: Warner Books, 1996, 277.

11. Maureen Furniss, ed., *Chuck Jones: Conversations* (Jackson: University Press of Mississippi, 2005), 27.

12. Furniss, *Chuck Jones: Conversations*, 67; see also Howard Beckerman, *Animation: The Whole Story* (Mattituck, N.Y.: Amereon House, 2001), 88.

13. Barrier, *Hollywood Cartoons*, 538.

14. Tom Ray, animator, in discussion with the author, May 12, 1993.

15. Bud Hester, in discussion with the author, June 25, 2004.

16. Anne Guenther, interview by the author, August 27, 2003.

17. "Elmer Plummer: Artist and Imagineer," an interview for a creative writing assignment at California Institute of the Arts, November 24, 1982, by filmmaker Steve O. Moore. Courtesy of Steve O. Moore.

18. Carl Bell, interview by the author, June 29, 2005.

19. Bill Hurtz, interview, ASIFA/ International Journal, Expo/67 Montreal Canada, 1967, ASIFA/Hollywood Archives.

20. Eddie Izzard, *Dress to Kill* DVD, HBO, 1999.

21. Kinney, *Walt Disney and Assorted Other Characters*, 185–86.

22. Cole, discussion.

23. Solomon, *Enchanted Drawings*, 278.

24. All three films were released in 1972.

25. Phil Young, in discussion with the author, February 2003.

26. Phil Mendez, interviewed by the author for the series "ASIFA/Hollywood Evenings with . . . ," May 1990.

27. Deneroff, "Popeye the Union Man."

28. Bob Kurtz, in discussion with the author May 2003.

29. *ASIFA Journal*, Montreal Expo '67.

30. Chuck Harvey, in discussion with the author, June 1985.

31. S. C. Ringgenberg, "Bobby London and the Air Pirates Follies," www.comic-art.com/intervws/londart.htm; www.mrcranky.com, Tigger Movie forum.

32. For the story of Larry Kilty, I had exclusive access to the relevant papers, transcripts, and correspondence of the MPSC 839 archives, as well as the recollections of Bill Littlejohn, Bud Hester, Dave Brain, Corny Cole, Willie Ito, and Anne Guenther and the back issues of the union newsletter the *Pegboard* from the collections of Mark Kausler.

33. Cole, discussion.

34. Mark Kausler, discussion with author, June 2003.

35. Cole, discussion.

36. Cole, discussion; Willie Ito, recollection, 2003.

37. *Pegboard*, 1969, Animation Guild Local 839 Office Archives.

38. Animation Guild Local 839 office archives contain a complete transcript and minutes of the Kilty inquiries.

39. Trial minutes, May 10, 1972, Animation Guild Local 839 office archives.

40. IATSE ruling transcript, May 20, 1972, Animation Guild Local 839 office archives.

41. Ben Washam, discussion with the author, July 1978.

9. Animation and the Global Market

Epigraph: Anne Guenther, in discussion with the author, October 12, 2003.

1. Nielsen and Mailes, *Hollywood's Other Blacklist*, 21.

2. William Moritz wrote extensively on the Axis animation effort in a series of articles in *Animation World Magazine* (www.awn.com) in 1995.

3. Tissa David, interview at School of Visual Arts, February 1975.

4. Adolf Galland, *The First and the Last* (New York: Bantam, 1967).

5. Culhane, *Talking Animals*, 43.

6. Keith Scott, *The Moose That Roared: The Story of Jay Ward, Bill Scott, A Flying Squirrel, and a Talking Moose* (New York: St. Martin's, 2000), 67.

7. Scott, *The Moose That Roared*.

8. For the genesis of Rocky the Flying Squirrel and Bullwinkle, see Scott, *The Moose That Roared*.

9. Scott, *The Moose That Roared*, 67.

10. Scott, *The Moose That Roared*, 106.

11. Scott, *The Moose That Roared*, 106.

12. Kinney, *Walt Disney and Assorted Other Characters*, 185.

13. Gene Deitch, "Tom & Jerry: Produced in Prague," *Animation World Magazine*, April 10, 2002, http://mag.awn.com/index.php?ltype=Special+Features&category2=Production&article_no=1376; excerpt from Deitch, *How to Succeed in Animation*.

14. Karen Mazurkewich, *Cartoon Capers: The History of Canadian Animators* (Toronto: McArthur, 1999), 95.

15. Scott, *The Moose That Roared*.

16. Barbera, *My Life in 'Toons*.

17. Barbera, *My Life in 'Toons*.

18. Kevin Petrilak, in discussion with the author, May 1980; Hanna, *A Cast of Friends*, 190.

19. Hanna, *A Cast of Friends*, 198.

20. Scott, *The Moose That Roared*, 62.

21. Keith Ingram, in discussion with the author, May 1994.

22. Beth-Ann McCoy, in discussion with the author, March 1991.

23. Anonymous animator, in discussion with the author, April 1997.

24. Hester, in discussion with the author, June 25, 2004.

25. Jeff Massie, in discussion with the author, June 12, 2004.

26. Hester, in discussion.

27. Hester, in discussion.

28. Steve Hulett, in discussion with the author. July 1, 2005; Massie, discussion.

29. Producers regularly negotiate and strategize as a body through their association, the AMPTP, the Alliance of Motion Picture and Television Producers.

30. Hulett, discussion.

31. Gene Hamm, in discussion with the author, July 3, 2005.

32. Lou Scheimer, in discussion with the author, June 2004.

33. Nancy Beiman in discussion with the author, October 2004.

34. Dave Spafford, in discussion with the author, October 1989.

35. Hamm, discussion.

36. Massie, discussion.

37. This didn't happen at Disney because the studio was also being picketed by Teamsters at the same time. The truckers would simply spread nails and slash the tires of trucks trying to pass through their picket lines.

38. Dorrie Littell Herrick, in discussion with the author, September 23, 2003.

39. Tom Tataranowicz, in discussion with the author, August 30, 2003.

40. Hamm, discussion.

41. Hamm, discussion.

42. Hulett, discussion.

43. Hulett, discussion.

44. Ed Gombert, in discussion with the author, June 1994.

45. Hanna, *A Cast of Friends*, 202.

46. Tataranowicz, discussion.

47. Linda Simensky, in discussion with the author, May 1998.

48. Hester, discussion.

49. Hanna, *A Cast of Friends*, 201.

50. Tataranowicz, discussion.

10. Fox and Hounds

Much of this chapter I expanded from my article "Disney's *The Fox and the Hound*: The Coming of the Next Generation," *Animation World Magazine*, November 1998, www. awn.com/mag/issue3.8/3.8pages/3.8sitofox.html. Elements are reprinted with permission of Animation World Network.

1. Aaron Berger of Animanagement, address to MPSC 839 membership, October 1993.

2. Glen Keane, in discussion with the author, 1990.

3. Leonard Maltin, *The Disney Films*, 4th ed. (New York: Disney Editions, 2000).

4. Vance Gerry, in discussion with the author, 1990.

5. Thom Enriquez, in discussion with the author, 1992; Steve Hulett, in discussion with the author, July 1, 2005.

6. Enriquez, discussion; Hulett, discussion.

7. Hulett, discussion.

8. Dorse Lanpher, in discussion with the author, November 1989.

11. Camelot

1. Unnamed Disney artist, in discussion with the author, 1987.

2. Lou Scarborough, in discussion with the author, 2005.

3. Steve Hulett, in discussion with the author, July 1, 2005.

4. For the story in detail, see John Taylor, *Storming the Magic Kingdom: Wall Street, the Raiders, and the Battle for Disney* (New York: Knopf, 1987).

5. Deborah Solomon, "Reanimated," *New York Times Magazine*, February 22, 2004.

6. *Time Out*, November 23–30, 1988.

7. Dave Spafford, in discussion with the author, October 1988.

8. Schneider also had a 5:30 A.M. meeting with Katzenberg and a quick meeting with Eisner, where the chairman told him, "Either it will work out or we'll fire you." Stewart, *Disney War* (New York: Simon & Schuster, 2005), 73.

9. *Cats Don't Dance* was the last movie credit of Hollywood legend Gene Kelly, who was an adviser on the dance sequences.

10. Allan Neuwirth, *Making 'Toons: Inside the Most Popular Animated TV Shows and Movies* (New York: Allworth Press, 2003), 33–41.

11. Stewart, *Disney War*, 178.

12. Frank Thomas, in discussion with the author, September 1995.

Chapter 12: Animation . . . Isn't That All Done on Computers Now?

Epigraph: John Lasseter, remarks at Frank Thomas memorial, El Capitan Theater, Hollywood. September 29, 2004.

1. Solomon, *Enchanted Drawings*, 292;

2. Mike Disa, in discussion with the author, March 17, 2003.

3. Mainframe *Reboot* Web site, www.reboot.com.

4. John Van Vliet, digital effects artist, in discussion with the author, May 1990.

5. Jim Lammers and Lee Gooding, *Maya 4.5 Fundamentals* (Berkeley, Calif.: New Riders, 2003).

6. Mike Disa, interview by the author, 2003.

7. Karl Cohen, "Milestones of American Animation in the Twentieth Century," *Animation World Magazine*, January 1, 2000, http://mag.awn.com/?article_no=1079

8. Sandro Corsaro, *The Flash Animator* (Berkeley, Calif.: New Riders, 2001).

9. John Lasseter, address at Frank Thomas memorial.

10. Figures from ShowBizStats.com.

11. Laura Holson, "Has The Sky Stopped Falling at Disney?" *New York Times*, September 18, 2005.

12. John Markoff, *What the Dormouse Said: How the Sixties Counterculture Shaped the Personal Computer* (London: Viking, 2005), cited in Andrew Leonard's review, "California Dreaming: A True Story of Computers, Drugs, and Rock 'n' Roll," *New York Times*, May 7, 2005.

13. Statistics provided by Animation Guild Local 839, IATSE.

14. *New York Times*, interview, July 16, 2003.

15. Hulett, discussion.

16. "EA Settles Overtime Lawsuit," Animation World Network, October 6, 2005, http://news.awn.com/?newsitem_no=15076.

17. Jim Hillin, in discussion with the author, May 1986.

Conclusion

Epigraph: Culhane, *Talking Animals*, 231.

1. Culhane, *Talking Animals*, 183.

Bibliography

Archive Collections

John Canemaker Collection, New York

Herald Examiner Photo Collection, Special Collections, University of Southern California, Doheny Library

Chuck Jones Life Foundation, Irvine, Calif.

Mark Kausler Collection, Los Angeles

Los Angeles Times Photo Archives, UCLA Special Collections

Motion Picture Screen Cartoonists Guild (MPSC), Local 839, AFL-CIO, Urban Archives Center, Oviatt Library, California State University, Northridge

Office Archives of the Animation Guild, Local 839 IATSE (formerly the MPSC 839) North Hollywood

Books and Articles

Adamson, Joe. *The Walter Lantz Story: With Woody Woodpecker and Friends.* New York: Putnam & Sons, 1985.

Barbera, Joe. *My Life in Toons: From Flatbush to Bedrock in Under a Century.* Atlanta: Turner, 1996.

Barrier, Michael. *Hollywood Cartoons: American Animation in Its Golden Age.* New York: Oxford University Press, 1999.

Barten, Egbert, and Gerard Groenveld. "Reynard the Fox and the Jew Animal." *Animation World Magazine,* October 1, 1996. Available at http://mag.awn.com/index.php?ltype=Special+Features&category2=Production&article_no=941.

Beckerman, Howard. *Animation: The Whole Story* Mattituck, N.Y.: Amereon House, 2001.

Bibliography

Bendazzi, Giannalberto. *Cartoons: One Hundred Years of Cinema Animation.* Bloomington: Indiana University Press, 1996.

Blanc, Mel. *That's Not All Folks!* New York: Warner Books, 1988.

Boyer, Richard O., and Herbert M. Morais. *Labor's Untold Story.* Pittsburgh: United Electrical, Radio and Machine Workers of America Press, 1955.

Buhle, Paul, and Dave Wagner. *Radical Hollywood: The Untold Story behind America's Favorite Movies.* New York: New Press, 2002.

Cabarga, Leslie. *The Fleischer Story.* New York: Da Capo Press, 1988.

Cagney, James. *Cagney by Cagney.* Garden City, N.Y.: Doubleday, 1976.

Canemaker, John. *Vladimir Tytla, Master Animator.* Biographical notes to the Vladimir Tytla exhibition at the Katonah (N.Y.) Museum of Art, September 18–December 31, 1994. Katonah, N.Y.: Katonah Museum of Art, 1994.

———. *Before the Animation Begins: The Art and Lives of Disney Inspirational Sketch Artists.* New York: Hyperion, 1996.

———. *Tex Avery: The MGM Years, 1942–1955.* Atlanta: Turner, 1996.

———. *Winsor McCay: His Life and Art.* New York: Abbeville Press, 1999.

———. *Disney's Nine Old Men and the Art of Animation.* New York: Disney Editions, 2001.

Ceplair, Larry, and Steven Englund. *The Inquisition in Hollywood: Politics in the Film Community, 1930–1960.* Berkeley and Los Angeles: University of California Press, 1983.

Cohen, Karl F. *Forbidden Animation: Censored Cartoons and Blacklisted Animators in America.* Jefferson, N.C.: McFarland, 1997.

Cole, Lester. *Hollywood Red: The Autobiography of Lester Cole.* New York: Ramparts, 1981.

Corsaro, Sandro. The Flash Animator. Berkeley, Calif.: New Riders, 2001.

Crafton, Donald. *Before Mickey: American Animation, 1898–1928.* Cambridge, Mass.: MIT Press, 1987.

Culhane, Shamus. *Talking Animals and Other Funny People.* New York: St Martin's, 1986.

Deitch, Gene. "How to Succeed in Animation: (Don't Let a Little Thing like Failure Stop You!)" Animation World Network, July 2003, http://genedeitch.awn.com.

Bibliography

Deneroff, Harvey. "Popeye the Union Man." PhD diss., UCLA, 1985.

———. "The Story of Dan Glass." *Inbetweener,* August 1984.

Dowlatabadi, Zahra, and Catherine Winder. *Producing Animation.* Boston: Focal Press, 2001.

Dunne, George H. *The Hollywood Labor Dispute: A Study in Immorality.* Los Angeles: Conference Publishing Company, 1949.

Elting, John. *Swords around a Throne: Napoleon's Grande Armée.* New York: Da Capo, 1997.

Falk, Nat. *How to Make Animated Cartoons: The History and Technique.* New York: Foundation Books, 1941.

Fiore, Robert. "The Disney Strike: Inside and Out." Includes interviews by Karl Styszs. *Comics Journal,* March 1988.

Fleischer, Richard. *Out of the Inkwell: Max Fleischer and the Animation Revolution.* Lexington: University Press of Kentucky, 2005.

Friedrich, Otto. *City of Nets: A Portrait of Hollywood in the 1940s.* New York: Harper & Row, 1980.

Furniss, Maureen, ed. *Chuck Jones: Conversations.* Jackson: University Press of Mississippi, 2005.

Galland, Adolf. *The First and the Last.* New York: Bantam, 1967.

Garcia, Roger. *Frank Tashlin.* London: British Film Institute, 1994.

Geirland, John, and Eva Sonesh-Kedar. *Digital Babylon: How the Geeks, the Suits, and the Ponytails Fought to Bring Hollywood to the Internet.* New York: Arcade, 1999.

Ghez, Didier, ed. *Walt's People: Talking Disney with the Artists Who Knew Him.* 2 vols. New York: XLibris, 2005.

Goodman, Ezra. *The Fifty-Year Decline and Fall of Hollywood.* New York: Simon & Schuster, 1961.

Guedel, Heidi. *Animatrix: A Female Animator—How Laughter Saved My Life.* Bloomington, Ind.: AuthorHouse, 2003.

Hamilton, Ian. *Writers in Hollywood, 1915–1950.* New York: Harper & Row, 1990.

Hanna, William, with Tom Ito. *A Cast of Friends.* Dallas: Taylor, 1996.

Harvey, Robert C., and Gustavo M. Arriola. *Accidental Ambassador Gordo: The Comic Strip Art of Gus Arriola.* Jackson: University Press of Mississippi, 2000.

Higham, Charles. *Merchant of Dreams: Louis B. Mayer, MGM, and the Secret Hollywood.* New York: D. I. Fine, 1993.

Bibliography

Iwerks, Leslie, and John Kenworthy. *The Hand behind the Mouse: An Intimate Biography of the Man Walt Disney Called "the Greatest Animator in the World."* New York: Disney Editions, 2001.

Jones, Chuck. *Chuck Amuck: The Life and Times of an Animated Cartoonist.* Toronto: Warner Books, 1996.

———. *Chuck Reducks: Drawing from the Fun Side of Life.* New York: Warner Books, 1998.

Kerlow, Isaac Victor. *The Art of 3-D Computer Animation and Effects.* 3rd ed. New York: Wiley & Sons, 2003.

Ketcham, Hank. *The Merchant of Dennis, Dennis the Menace.* New York: Abbeville Press, 1990.

Kinney, Jack. *Walt Disney and Assorted Other Characters: An Unauthorized Account of the Early Years at Disney's.* New York: Harmony, 1990.

Lambert, Pierre. *Le cartoon à Hollywood: L'histoire du dessin animé américain.* Paris: Librairie Séguier, 1988.

Lammers, Jim, and Lee Gooding. *Maya 4.5 Fundamentals.* Berkeley, Calif.: New Riders, 2003.

Lawson, Tim, and Alisa Persons. *The Magic behind the Voices: A Who's Who of Cartoon Voice Actors.* Jackson: University Press of Mississippi, 2005.

Leslie, Esther. *Hollywood Flatlands: Animation, Critical Theory, and the Avant-Garde.* London: Verso, 2002.

Lipsitz, George. *The Rainbow at Midnight: Labor and Culture in the 1940s.* Urbana: University of Illinois Press.

Maltin, Leonard. *Of Mice and Magic: A History of Animated Cartoons.* New York: McGraw Hill, 1980.

———. *The Disney Films.* 4th ed. New York: Disney Editions, 2000.

Mazurkewich, Karen. *Cartoon Capers: The History of Canadian Animators.* Toronto: McArthur, 1999.

McGilligan, Patrick, and Paul Buhle. *Tender Comrades: A Backstory of the Hollywood Backlist.* New York: St. Martin's, 1997.

Murolo, Priscilla, and A. B. Chitty. *From the Folks Who Brought You the Weekend: A Short, Illustrated History of Labor in the United States.* New York: New Press, 2003.

Navasky, Victor S. *Naming Names.* New York: Penguin, 1991.

Neuwirth, Allan. *Makin' Toons: Inside the Most Popular Animated TV Shows and Movies.* New York: Allworth Press, 2003.

Bibliography

Nielsen, Mike, and Gene Mailes. *Hollywood's Other Blacklist: Union Struggles in the Studio System.* London: British Film Institute, 1995

Norman, Floyd. *Son of Faster Cheaper: A Sharp Look Inside the Animation Business.* Los Angeles: Vignette Multimedia, 2005.

Peet, Bill. *Bill Peet: An Autobiography.* New York: Scholastic, 1989.

Price, Gene, and Jack Kistner. *The Story of the Hollywood Film Strike in Cartoons.* Los Angeles: Conference Publishing, 1945.

Prindle, David F. *The Politics of Glamour: Ideology and Democracy in the Screen Actor's Guild.* Madison: University of Wisconsin Press, 1988.

Quin, Mike. *The Big Strike.* Olema, Calif.: Olema Press, 1949. Reprint, New York: International Publishers, 1979.

Riefenstahl, Leni. *Leni Riefenstahl: A Memoir.* New York: St. Martin's, 1992.

Roderick, Kevin. *The San Fernando Valley: America's Suburb.* Los Angeles: Los Angeles Times Books, 2002.

Ryan, J. M. *The Rat Factory.* Englewood Cliffs, N.J.: Prentice-Hall, 1971.

Schickel, Richard. *The Disney Version: The Life, Times, Art, and Commerce of Walt Disney.* New York: Avon Books, 1967.

Scott, Keith. *The Moose That Roared: The Story of Jay Ward, Bill Scott, a Flying Squirrel, and a Talking Moose.* New York: St. Martin's, 2000.

Selznick, Irene Mayer. *A Private View.* New York: Knopf, 1983.

Sigall, Martha. *Living Life Inside the Lines.* Jackson: University Press of Mississippi, 2005.

Solomon, Charles. *Enchanted Drawings: The History of Animation.* New York: Knopf, 1989.

Sperber, A. M., and Eric Lax. *Bogart.* New York: William Morrow, 1997.

Starr, Kevin. *Embattled Dreams: California in War and Peace, 1940–1950.* New York: Oxford University Press, 2002.

Stewart, James B. *Disney War.* New York: Simon & Schuster, 2005.

Tally, Steve. *Bland Ambition: From Adams to Quayle—The Cranks, Criminals, Tax Cheats, and Golfers Who Made It to Vice President.* San Diego: Harcourt Brace Jovanovich, 1992.

Taylor, John. *Storming the Magic Kingdom: Wall Street, the Raiders, and the Battle for Disney.* New York: Knopf, 1987.

Bibliography

Thomas, Bob. *Walt Disney: An American Original.* New York: Hyperion, 1994.

———. *Building a Company: Roy O. Disney and the Creation of an Entertainment Empire.* New York: Hyperion, 1998.

Thomas, Frank, and Ollie Johnston. *The Illusion of Life: Disney Animation.* New York: Abbeville Press, 1981.

Tytla, Adrienne. *Disney's Giant and the Artists' Model.* Deep River, Conn.: Valley Press, 2005.

Tytle, Harry. *One of "Walt's Boys": An Insider's Account of Disney's Golden Years.* Mission Viejo, Calif.: ASAP Publishing, 1997.

Vaughn, Robert. *Only Victims: A Study of Show Business Blacklisting.* New York: Limelight Editions, 1996.

Williams, Richard. *The Animator's Survival Kit.* London: Faber & Faber, 2001.

Wills, Garry. *John Wayne's America: The Politics of Celebrity.* New York: Simon & Schuster, 1997.

Index

Abel, Bob, 48, 322–23
Academy Award, 111, 135, 187, 195, 300, 320, 410
Academy of Motion Picture Arts and Sciences (AMPAS), 63, 331, 394
Adams, Elmer, 120, 162
Addams, Charles, 88
Aladdin (1992), 8, 302, 316, 324, 364, 396
American Federation of Labor (AF of L), 11, 12, 59, 65, 75, 83, 93, 104, 118, 130, 133, 139, 169, 182, 185, 201, 370, 373
Anastasia (1997), 281, 313
Anderson, Ken, 111, 145, 336
Animation Motion Picture Workers Union (AMPWU) 71, 72, 74, 75, 373
animators: African American 28–29; Asian, 28, 211; gay, 29; Hispanic, 28; women, 23–28
Apodaca, Ruben, 28
Appet, Lou, 72, 84, 85, 91, 98, 241, 242, 244, *245*, 259, 271
Aragon, Ray, 28
Association Internationale du Film d'Animation (ASIFA), 194, 335, 369, 374
Association of Motion Picture and Theatrical Producers (Association of Motion Picture

and Television Producers) (AMPTP), 178, 416
Augustson, Clifford "Red," 202, *205*, 357, 410, 411
Aurora/Bluth Studio, 270, 273
Avery, Fred "Tex," 13, 19, 43, *109*, 164, 196, 223, 226, 255, 319

Babbitt, Art, 21, 52, 74, 109, *112*, 115, 117–22, 124, *128*, 130, *131*, 133, 136, 138–39, 142–43, 147–51, 181, 186, *188*, 198, 199, 216, 222, 223, 224, 232, 233, 255, 267, 271, 313, 333, *346*
Bakshi, Ralph, 50, 229–31, 235, 254, 257, 259, 265, 292, 294, 303
Balaban, Barney, 178, 217
Barbera, Joe, 11, 34, 42–44, 46, 50, 199, 217, *273*, 281, 333
Barré, Raoul, 11, 21, 51, 397
Battle of Burbank, 160–66
Beauty and the Beast (1991), 281, 301, 302, 309, 324
Beiman, Nancy, 27, 268, 394, 408, 414
Betty Boop, 1, 13, 20, 32, 66, 69, 72, 78–79, 96–98
Bioff, Willie, 65–68, 115, 135–36, *135*, 138, 155–56, *157*, 178, 240, 270
Bird, Brad, 48, 234, 256, 286, 290, 291, 296, 305

415

Index

blacklist, 153, 178, 181, 187, 189–91, 193–95, 207, 222–23, 235, 238, 246; in Canada, 179

Blackton, J. Stuart, 36, 247, 250, 360

Blanc, Mel, 41, 219, 388, 396

Blinn, Jim, 321

Bluth, Don, 48, 221, 265, 268, 270, 273–74, 277, 281, 286, 289–92, 296, 303, 307, 313, 323, 325, 331

Bodin, Sadie, 72–74

Bodle, George, 117, 118, 121, *128,* 136, 155

Bogart, Humphrey, 164, 172, 176, 181–82

Bonifacio, Charlie, 235

Bosustow, Steve, 133, 144, 187, *188,* 189, 222

Bowsky, Willie, 87, 90, 99

Braxton, Frank, 28–29

Bray, John Randolph, 9, 11–12, 34, 36, 77, 78, 197, 199, 224, 248, 251, 332, 338, 345, 347

Brewer, Frances, 24, *25*

Brewer, Roy, 159–60, 164, 166, 168, 170, 181, 185–86, 192–93, 195–96, 210, 240–41

Browne, George, 65–67, 155–56, 178

Brucker, Eli, 90, 98, 232

Buchwald, Sam, 43, 52, 85, 92, 97, 201

Buckley, Jack, 120, 148

Buried Treasure (1927), 58

Capone, Al, 65, 155–56

Carmichael, Jim, 360, 410

Carpenters Union, 59, 65–66, 168

Cartwright, Randy, 234, 322

Casey, James F., 140, 141

Catmull, Ed, 329

CBS (Columbia Broadcasting Network), 210, 211, 227, 229, 371

CGI, or CG (Computer Graphic Imaging), 84, 328, 329, 331–35, 338–44

Chang, Wah Ming, 183, 409

Charlie Brown Christmas, A (1965), 4, 145, 227, 367, 368

Churchill, Frank, 30, 234

Churchill, Winston, 223, 344

Clements, Ron, 234, 286, 316, 343

Cohl, Emile, 9, 36, 247

Cohn, Harry, 178, 187, 193

Cole, Cornelius "Corny," 241, 411, 412, 413

Cole, Lester, 192–93

Columbia Pictures, 23, 49, 74, 130, 168, 178, 186, 187, 193, 219, 222, 364, 375, 379, 411

Commercial Artists and Designers Union (CADU), 71, 75, 83–86, 88–90, 92–94, 97, 99, 200

Communism, 129, 146, 177, 181, 184

Communist Party/USA, 71, 82, 160, 169, 172, 177, 178

Communists, 59, 60, 63, 82, 89, 104, 119, 139, 145–48, 153, 159–60, 164, 169, 172–73, 176–81, 185, 189, 193, 195, 204, 217, 250; anti-Communists, 23, 160, *180,* 189, 194, 210

Conference of Studio Unions, (CSU), 67, 74, 104, 131, 155–60, 166, 168–71, 376

Congress of Industrial Organizations (CIO), 26, 133, 158, 201, 373, 409

Crandall, Roland "Doc," 90

Crowther, Dwayne, 346

Culhane, James "Shamus," 12, 16–18, 33, 36, 44, 69, 74, 81, 90, 95, 190, 223, 234–35, 251, 254, 345, 351

Daily Worker, 82

Index

Darling, Charlotte, 118, 192
Davis, Marc, 52, 124, 139, 220, 233, 234, 285, 294, 368, 380, 384
Deep Throat, 229
Deitch, Gene, 187, 189–90, 211, 223, 253
De Mille, Cecil B., 50, 162
De Mille, William, 63
DePatie, David, 219
DePatie-Freleng Studio, 29, 43, 219, 224, 255, 259, 267, 279
DIC Entertainment, 276
Diehl, Walter, 269–70
Dies, Martin, 171–72
Directors Guild of America, (DGA), 69, 376
Disa, Mike, 49, 321, 415, 416
Disney, Lillian, 287
Disney, Ray, 62, 142
Disney, Roy E., 45, 149, 292, 294–96, 302, 310, 314, 316–17, 324
Disney, Roy O., 13, 26, 51, 62, 101, 103, 129, 136, 141–42, 144, 149, 214, 222, 287
Disney, Walt, 11–15, 17–20, 23, 26, 33, 37–38, 40–42, 44, 47, 48, 49, 50–53, 57, 60–61, 69, 81, 97–98, 102–3, 110–15, 118–23, 130, 133, 134, 136–40, 142, 143, 145, 147, 148–50, 155, 160, 171, 172, 175, 177, 186, 199, 215–16, 220, 222, 233, 265, 270, 285, 287, 290–91, 301, 303, 315, 330, 336, 345, 348, 351
Disney Miller, Diane, 290
DreamWorks SKG, 8, 10, 27, 43, 311, 316–17, 319, 320, 327, 331, 335, 339
Dunne, George, 116, 117, 181, 185

Eastman, Phil, 144, 184, 187, 188, 189–90

Eikleberry, Larry, 3
Eisner, Michael, 20, 45, 278, 292, 295–96, 298, 300, 309–11, 313–17, 315, 324, 329, 331
Engel, Jules, 17, 144, 188, 189, 234, 250
Eugster, Al, 10, 14, 38, 69, 90, 95, 115, 353, 403

Famous Studios, 22, 43, 66, 71, 75, 78, 83, 97, 144, 200, 230
Fantasia (1940), 13, 17, 108, 113, 114, 115, 117, 121, 142, 145, 149, 223, 228, 255, 263, 309, 359, 368, 374
Fantasia 2000, 312
Federation of Motion Picture Crafts, (FMPC), 66, 67, 74, 85, 93, 135, 157, 195, 376, 377, 379, 409
Federation of Screen Cartoonists, 115, 117, 119–20, 149
Figlozzi, Don, 202
Film and Television Action Committee (FTAC) 282, 377
Filmation Studio, 43, 53, 224, 226, 259, 267, 276, 279–80, 323
Film Motion Picture Unit (FMPU), 143, 377
Finding Nemo (2003), 68, 320, 330
Fitts, Joni Jones, 357
Flash animation technique, 327
Fleischer, Dave, 21, 22, 78, 81, 83
Fleischer, Lou, 93, 96, 97
Fleischer, Max, 11, 13, 15–18, 20–21, 37, 48, 50, 57, 58, 61–62, 77, 79, 81–82, 84; and strike, 52
Fleischer Animated News, 80, 84
Fleischer Animator's Club, 83
Freleng, Isadore "Friz," 19, 29, 44, 46, 61, 102, 109, 126, 187, 218, 219, 255, 267, 279, 346

Index

Friedman, Ed, 16, 70, 126, 161
Friedman, Lillian, 20, 24, 81, 90, 99
Fritz the Cat (1972), 229, 230

Galland, Adolf, 249
Gamma Productions, 253
Gertie the Dinosaur (1914), 36, 57, 197, 321
Gillett, Burt, 72–74, 340
Glass, Dan, 61, 84
Goebbels, Josef, 249
Goldberg, Eric, 8, 232, 235, 303
Goldberg, Steve, 322, 323
Gollub, Moe, 118, 259, 263, *264*, 265, 270, 278, 284, 287, 351
Gompers, Samuel, 11–12
Grant, Joe, 47, *48*, 124, 144, 330, 363, 393, 398, 403, 405
Great Upheaval, 12
Green, William, 65, 169
Greirson, John, 179
Groening, Matt, 305
Guedel, Heidi, 26–27, 234, 286, 291
Guenther, Anne, 24, 27, 213, 220, *221*, 244
Gulliver's Travels (1939), 94, 96
Gyssling, Georg, 60

Hamm, Gene, 259, 263, 269, 272, 273, 278, 414
Hanna, Bill, 11, 34, 42, 46, 217, 241, 247, *248*, 260, 271, *273*, 275–76, 280–81, 283, 284, 333, 348
Hanna-Barbera studio, 16, 28, 43, 44, 99, *221*, 223–24, 226, 234, *248*, 252, 254–56, 259, 260, *261*, 262, 265, *266*, *267*, 268–69, 272, *275*, 278–81, 287, 295–96, 303, 305–6, 311, 333, 336–37
Harding, LaVerne, 24, 27, 286, 394, 399

Heckle and Jeckyl, 13, 199, 371
Hench, John, 148, 186, 234, 384
Hester, Harry "Bud," 220, 244, 259, 261, 263, 265, 269–71, 278, 283, 287, 357, 364, 394, 403, 412, 414
Hilberman, Dave, 108, 118–19, *128*, 130, 136, 144, 147, 184, 187, 189, 192, *346*, 354, 364, 402–5, 409–10
Hillary, Don, 185–86, 239, 355
Hillin, Jim, 321–22, 340, 344, 364, 416
Hitler, Adolf, 13, 43, 60, 85, 113, 147, 154, 156, 166, 177, 249
Hollywood Canteen, 154
Hollywood Independent Citizens Committee of the Arts, Sciences and Professions (HICCASP), 23, 177, 377
Hollywood Legion Hall, 121
Hollywood Legion Stadium, 68, 169, 173, 177
Hollywood Reporter, 138, 166
Hoover, J. Edgar, 172, 181
Hoppity Goes to Town (1943), 363
House Committee on Un-American Activities (HUAC), 145, 148, 171–72, 174–76, 178, 179, 181, 184, 186–87, 189–95, 210, 235, 378, 403, 405, 407–10; and Walt Disney, 136, 147
Howard, Cal, 43, 95, 199, 383, 396
Howard, Maurice, 146, 184, *191*, 192, 354, 356
Howard, Max, 45, 299, 303
Hubley, John, 19, 120, 129, 143–45, 184, 187, *188*, 190, 192, 194, 223, 333, 351, 364, 365, 367, 374, 377
Hughes, Howard, 215
Hughes, Langston, 63, 408
Hulett, Steve, 265, 274, 278, 286,

290, 304, *350*, 357–58, 414–16
Hulley, John, 83, 353
Hurtz, Bill, 6, 19, 109, 121, 129, 144,
    147, 151, *188*, 193–94, 215, 224,
    225, 241, 252, *346*, 354, 365, 409,
    412; and Mary Hurtz, 404

Ickle Meets Pickle (1942), 199
International Alliance of Theatrical
    and Screen Engineers (IATSE),
    2, 14, 24, 25, 54, 58–59, 62,
    65–68, 74, 80, 83, 93, 98–99,
    105, 135, 142, 155–61, 164, 166,
    168–71, 180–81, 185–88, 193,
    195, 202, 207, 210–11, 214, 217,
    238–46, 260, 269–70, 277–78,
    281–82, 299, 305, 341, 347,
    349–50, 353, 355–57, 367, 369,
    373, 376–78, 380, 383, 387, 398,
    403, 406, 409, 411, 413, 416
International Brotherhood of
    Electrical Workers (IBEW), 59,
    65–66, 157
Ishii, Chris, 28, 124, 144, 154
Ito, Willie, 240, 389, 412–13
Iwerks, Ub, 1, 15, 17, 19, 37, 40, 43,
    69, *70*, 102–3, 109, 285, 322, 336,
    361, 365, 390, 394, 396, 399, 402

Jobs, Steve, 316, 329, 331, 333, 343
Johnson, Carl, 112
Johnson, Johnny, *163*, 164,
Johnson, Samuel, 31, 395
Johnson, Tom, 84, 87–88, 90, 99
Johnston, Eric, 178–79
Johnston, Oliver "Ollie," 124, 139,
    148, 285, 289, 296, 302–3, 377,
    380, 392
Johnston, Scott, 322, 324–25
Jones, Charles M. "Chuck," 4, 6, 16,
    18–20, 23, 27–28, 42, 46, 48–50,

98, 106, 109, 126, *127*, 143, 153,
    193, 196, 215, 218–19, 226–27,
    231–32, 308, 351, 354, 363, 365,
    368, 377–78, 387, 389–90, 396,
    402, 404, 412
Jones, Dean, 294
Jones, Skip, 291
Jones, Volus, 123

Kahl, Milt, 30, 83, 111, 124, 145, 186,
    220, 231, 235, 259, 285, 287, 364,
    368, 380
Katz, Ray, 20, 62
Katz, Sam, 178
Katzenberg, Jeffrey, 45–46, 292,
    295–302, *297*, 310–11, 313–14,
    317, 324, 329, 339, 362, 365, 370,
    376–77, 415
Kazan, Elia, 195–96, 410
Keane, Glen, 1, 234, 286, 291, 297,
    303, 323, 329, 332, 344, 415
Kelly, Gene, 168, 176, 218, 415
Kelly, Margaret Selby Daly, 6, 24,
    108, 120, *128*, 144, 178, 253, 356,
    365–66, 377, 394, 408
Kelly, Walt, 124, 144, 190–91, 366,
    410
Ketcham, Hank, 95, 124–25, 129,
    144, 390, 400, 404
Key, Leonard, 251–52
Kilty, Larry, 185, 239–44, 259,
    355–57, 366, 412–13
Kimball, John, 268, 357
Kimball, Ward, 6, 23, 110, 115, 124,
    129, 139, 148, 151, 285, 366, 380,
    394, 401–4, 406
Kinney, Dick, 124–25
Kinney, Jack, 61, 114, 129, 226, 253,
    366, 390, 398, 402–4, 412–13
Kirby, Jack (Kurtzberg), 88, 98–99,
    351

Index

Klasky Csupo studio, 305–7, 313
Klein, Earl, 194
Klein, Izzy, 72, 201, 210, 355, 356, 366, 397
Klein, Phil, 72, 74, 144, 192
Klynn, Herb, *188*, 192, 410
Kricfalusi, John, 48, 208, 231, 235, 280, 306
Kroyer, Bill, 286, 290–91, *320*, 322–23, 344, 367
Kroyer, Sue (nee Nelson), 27, 286, 291, 319, *320*, 344
Kurtz, Bob, 4, 43, 224, 233, 396, 412
Kurtz & Friends, 43, 265
Kurtzberg, Jacob. *See* Kirby, Jack
Kuwahara, Bob, 28, 211

LaCava, Gregory, 11
Laemmle, Carl, 62, 379
LaGuardia, Fiorello, 82, 89, 93
Lantz, Walter, 11, 13, 34, 37, 57, 62, 74, 103–4, 113, 215, 220, *346*, 359, 366–67, 387, 394–95, 397–99. *See also* Walter Lantz Studio
Larson, Eric, 124, 148, 200, 234, 275, 298, 354, 367, 377
Lasseter, John, 33, 46–48, *53*, 234, 286, 291, 319, 323, 329–30, 333, 343, 367, 415–16
Lawson, John Howard, 175–76, 194
Laupenberger, Roy, *107*
League of Women Voters, 146–47
Le Berthon, Ted, 7, 113, 393, 402
Lessing, Charles, 66
Lessing, Gunther, 61, 114–15, 117–19, 121–23, 126, 139, *141*, 144, 148, 214–15, 367
Libicki, Stuart, 274
Lion King, The (1994), *14*, 27, 302, 310–12, 317, 324–25, 330, 337, 362, 369
Littlejohn, Bill, 71, 73, 104, 106, *116*, 117–18, 128–29, 136, 145, 185, 194, 223, 239, 241, 271, *346*, 351, 353–54, 356, 367, 399, 401, 403, 406, 412
Little Mermaid, The (1989), 1, 29, 68, 257, 301, 316–17, 336–37, 343, 362, 369
lockouts: definition of, 379; and impasse, 378; and Looney Tunes, 106, *107*, *109*; and Schlesinger, 106, *107*; and Terrytoons, 202
Logan, Jim, 199, 201, 202, 204, *206*, 230, 355, 394, 410–11
Lokey, Hicks, 6, 71, 74, 84, 89–90, 94, 99, 144, 255, 263, 265, 367
Looney Tunes. *See* Schlesinger, Leon, studio
Los Angeles Police Department (LAPD), 4, 67, 159, 162, 181, 261, 382
Los Angeles Times, 163–64, 166, *167*, 173, 305, 387, 405, 407, 409
Lucas, George, 49, 239, 295–96, 299, 329, 342

Malloy, Tommy, 65–66
Maltin, Leonard, 390, 396–97, 399, 410–11, 415
Mannix, Eddie, 42, 166
Marjolie, Bianca, 16
Massie, Jeff, *350*, 407, 411, 414
Massie, Nancy, 161
Massie, Reg, 129, 161
Matthews, Bill, 235, 262
Matthews, Blainey, 163–64, 166
Maya (3D software), 326, 390, 415
Mayer, Louis B., 15, 19–20, 61–63, 65, 68, 82, 102–3, 115, 160, 172, 175, 178, 360, 379, 389, 398

Index

Mayerson, Mark, 322, 325, 403
McCarran-Walters Act (1952), 179
McCarthy, Edward, 87
McCarthy, Sen. Joseph, 177, 191, 194, 408
McCarthy anti-Communist hearings, 23, 194
McCay, Winsor, 7, 9, 36, 48, 50, 51, 57, 58, 197, 289, 321, 345, 361, 388, 393, 395, 397
McClaren, Norman, 179, 194, 374
McCormick Press Corporation, 173
Melendez, Bill, 4, 21, 28, 46, 119, 126, 145, 183, 185, 193, 226, 227, 245, 305, *346*, 354, 367–68, 394–95, 403–5, 410
Melies, George, 368
Mendez, Phil, 29, 230, 412
Merry Melodies. *See* Schlesinger, Leon, studio
Messmer, Otto, 17, 38, 39, 40, 69
MGM Studio, animation unit, 13, 15–17, 19–20, 22, 34, 42–43
Mintz, Charles, 16, 20, 22, 37, 40, 114, 366
Miret, Gil, 235
Mohawk Valley rules, 154, 159, 268, 378–80, 382
Momotaro God Blessed Sea Warriors (1943), 249
Morgan, Frank, 67–68, 130
motion capture, 78, 325–27, 380
Motion Picture Screen Cartoonists Local 839: formed, 186; relations with SCG, 210, 238, 240; strike of 1979, 260; strike of 1982, 265
Motion Picture Screen Cartoonists Local 841: folded into Camera Local, 278; formed, 210
Motion Picture Screen Cartoonists

Local 841 (Canada), 2
Motion Picture Screen Cartoonists Local 843 (Orlando), 99
Musker, John, 234, 286, 290, 316, 329, 343

Nash, Ogden, 62
National Association of Manufacturers (NAM), 153, 379
National Film Board of Canada (NFB), 179, 320, 409; and blacklist, 179
National Labor Relations Board (NLRB), 74, 85, 91–93, 95, 104, 115, 117–20, 159, 166, 185, 201–2, 217, 244, 380
Natwick, Myron "Grim," 1, 20, *32*, 69–70, 90, 95, 98, 105, *112*, 150, *191*, 231–33, *346*, 353, 361, 368, 393, 399, 401, 406
New Masses, 177, 366
New York Daily News, 146, 173
New Yorker magazine, 144, 311, 361
New York Times, 66, 89, 339, 396, 398, 400, 415–16
Nickelodeon Studio, 306, 308, 319, *347*
Nine Old Men (Disney artists), 124, 151, 285, 288–89, 298, 303, 315, 329, 366–67, 380, 388,
Nitti, Frank, 65, 115, 156, 398
Nixon, Richard, 23, 174, 176, 237, 378
Nizer, Louis, 85, 90–92, 94
Noble, Maurice, 5–6, 13, 120, 133, 143, 234, 308, 351, 393, 404–5
Nolan, Bill, 17, 69, 353
Nordberg, Cliff, 129
Norman, Floyd, 29, 53, 248, 330, 391, 395

Omnibus, 322
Osmosis Jones (2001), 313, 325, 338,

370
Ozark, Jack, 18, 95, 394, 400

Pacific Data Images (PDI), 282, 322, 326–27, 331, 335
Paramount Studios, 23, 38, 52, 61, 66, 79, 93–97, 103, 169, 214, 218, 220, 231, 251, 253, 295, 303, 312, 313, 362–63, 365, 370, 375, 377, 379; animation and, 33; Paramount decision, 217, 250, 381, 411
Parker, Dorothy, 4, 63, 119, 128, 175, 237
Partch, Virgil "Vip," 21
Patin, Ray, 226, 354
Patterson, Ray, 225
Perkins, Frances, 91, 159
Peterson, Ken, 148
Petrilak, Kevin, 255, 413
Pierce, Ted, 103, 186, 353, 383
Pinocchio (1942), 13, 18, 99, 113, 145, 222, 285, 288, 337–38, 364, 374
Pixar, 46–47, *53*, 282, 286, 312–13, 316, 319, 329–33, 343, 367
Plummer, Elmer, 222, 412
Plympton, Bill, 347
Pocahontas (1995), 8, *297*, 312
Pomerance, Bill, 146–47, 184, 192, *346*, 354
Post, Arthur, 83, 90, 93, 353
Powers, Pat, 40, 365

Quimby, Fred, 15, 20, 42–43, 106, 368

Raggedy Ann & Andy (1977), 2, 8, 50, 256, 312, 369, 372
Rand Corporation, 154, 379, 381–82, 406
Reagan, Ronald, 4, 168–69, 177, 182, 185, 195, 241, 269–70, 304, 339,

368–69, 378, 382, 406, 409
Reed, John, 71, 178, 379; and John Reed clubs, 71, 157, 379
Rehberg, Eddie, 202, *203, 205,* 207
Reitherman, Wolfgang "Woolie," 124, 285, 288–90, 380
Ren & Stimpy, 231, 280, 306
Residuals, 241–42, 244, 259, 271, 309, 369
Return of Jafar, The (1993), 279, 302
Rhythm & Hues Studio, 322
Rivkin, Jay, xiv, 108, 175, 187, 408
RKO, 61, 74, 168, 215, 371, 375, 384, 411
Rocky & Bullwinkle Show, 227, 228, 365, 371
Rocky and His Friends (1959), 224, 251
Rogers, Roy, 159
Roosevelt, Franklin Delano (FDR), 15, 59–62, 67, 68, 71, 82, 85 139, 159, 160, 171–73, 193, 201, 348, 374, 378, 380, 381, 385
Rotoscope, 78, 96, 294, 327, 380, 382
Ruby-Spears Studio, 99, 259, 261, 267–68, 272, 278
Ruiz, Pepe, 104, 186, 200–201, 207, 210–11, 239–40, 353–57, 366, 369, 410
runaway production, 3, 99, 118, 241–42, 247, 250–51, 253, 259, 261, 263, 274–75, 278, 283–84, 304, 338, 363–64, 368

Salvio, Gerard, 239, 268, 357
Scheimer, Lou, 44, 46, 53, 259, 267, 279, 414
Schenck, Joe, 115, 408
Schenck, Nicholas, 66, 155–56, 178
Schlesinger, Leon, 19–22, 28, 33, 40–41, 61–62, 79, 106, 109, 322, 369,

Index

396, 410; and studios (Looney
Tunes and Merry Melodies), 13,
16, 40–41, 359, 363, 369, 384

Schneider, Peter, 45, 302, 308, 310,
415

Schumacher, Thomas, 29, 45, 310,
315

Schwartz, Zack, 120, 144, 187, 189,
192, 235

Scott, Bill, 5, 32, 143–44, 183, 185,
187, *188*, 193, 228, 251–53,
354–55, 369, 391, 409, 413

Screen Actors Guild (SAG), 1, 66, 69,
130, 169, 268, 368, 377, 382, 398

Screen Cartoonists Guild Local 852
(SCG), 74, 104, 113–14, 118,
120, 141, 153, 155, 158, 184–85,
200, 226, 245, 258, 350, 366, 375,
383, 393

Screen Cartoonists Guild Local 1461
(New York), 200, 201, 202, 207,
209, 210

Screen Directors Guild. *See* Directors
Guild of America

Screen Gems, 97, 125, 130, 144, 370

Screen Publicists Guild, 135, 141

Screen Writers Guild. *See* Writers
Guild of America

Selzer, Eddie, 22, 41–42, 193

Selznick, David O., 297

Selznick, Irene Mayer, 391, 398

Selznick, Lewis, 34

Sigall, Martha, 20–22, 27, 103, *107*,
154, 184, 193, *346*, 369, 391,
393–95, 401, 404, 407–9

Sigall, Sol, 177, 184

SIGGRAPH (Special Interest Group
on Computer Graphic and
Interactive Techniques), 321,
335, 342, 383

Silverman, David, 208, 235, 305

Simpsons, The, 45, 305–6, 308, 325

Sinking of the Lusitania (1917), 9,
36, 58

Sito, Tom, *350, 358*

Smith Act, 179, 180

Snow White and the Seven Dwarfs
(1937), 13, 16, 20, 52, 74, 94,
110–13, 142, 144, 150, 222, 232,
248–49, 294, 330, 351, 359, 361,
364, 368, 374

Society for the Preservation of
American Ideals, 145, 160,
172–73

Society of Independent Motion
Picture Producers (SIMPP), 214

Sorrell, Herb, 67, *116*, 117–18, 120–
22, 129–30, 136, 140, *141*, 142,
146, 158, 160, *163*, 164 168–71,
181, 185, 196, 207, 240, 269, 345,
351, 353, 370, 402, 404–5

Spafford, Dave, 234, 268, 286, 291,
299, 414–15

Spielberg, Steven, 46, 49, 240, 279,
292, 295–96, 299–302, 310–11,
325, 343, 365, 370, 377

Stewart, David Ogden, 119, 135, 179

strikes: CSU citywide strike of 1945,
158; CSU citywide strike of
1946, 168; CSU citywide strike
of 1946–47, 168; Disney studio
strike, 5, 99, *122, 132, 140, 141*,
259, *346*, 351, 365–66, 368, 370,
389, 394, 402–6; Fleischer studio
strike, 52, 77–100, 128, 204, 210,
232, 368, 399–400; FMPC strike
of 1937, 67, 74, 85, 93, 135, 157;
IATSE projectionists strike of
1935, 65; IATSE strike of 1933,
65; MPSC strike of 1979, 99, 118,
242, 244, 247, 260, *261*, 262, 265,
266, 269, 363–64, 368; MPSC

strike of 1982, 2, 3, 99, 118, 247, 262–63, 265, *267*, 269, 271, *273*, *275*, 276, 338, 351, 363–64, 368; Terrytoons strike of 1947, 5, 197, 202, *204, 206, 208, 209*, 210, 211, 369, 371, 410

Sullivan, Marjorie, 38, 395

Sullivan, Pat, ix, 37, 38, *39*, 199, 397

Superman (Fleischer cartoon series), 96, 363

Swift, David, 129, 144, 404

Taft, Robert, 216, 217

Taft-Hartley Act, 181, 204, 217, 238, 269, 333, 348, 383, 411

Takamoto, Iwao, 28, 154

Taras, Marty, 84, 85, *87*, 98, 230

Tashlin, Frank, 6, 19, 33, 72, 103, 108, 125, 130, 144, 353, 370–71, 389, 399, 402, 404–5

Tataranowicz, Tom, 259, 271–72, 278, 284, 414

Teague, Dave, 3, 259

Teamsters, United Federation of, 133, 157–58, 166, 237, 350, 357, 408, 414; and Screen Cartoonist Guild, 245

Teletactics, 8

Tendlar, Dave, 83, 89–90, 99, *221*, 225, *245*, 255, *264*, 399

Terrace, Termite, 21, 22, 41, *107*, 218, 384

Terry, Paul, 11, 17, 21, 50, 57, 72, 197, *198*, 199, 201–2, *203*, 204, 207, 209–11, 216, 359, 366, 371, 395

Terrytoons Studio, 5, 13, 28, 71–72, 144, 197–211, 216, 219–20, 231, 253, 364, 366, 369, 371, 394, 410–11

Thomas, Frank, 124, 139, 143, 148, 150–51, 274, 285, 289, 296, 302–3, 312, 377, 380, 392, 406, 415, 416

Thomas, J. Parnell, *174*, 194

Tom Terrific, 211, 411

Topete, Alex, 260

Toy Story (1995), 320, 330, 367

Trumbo, Dalton, 63, 175, 194

Twentieth Century-Fox, 49, 62, 67, 178, 361, 375, 408, 411; and animation, 279, 320, 331

Tyer, Jim, 71, 202, *205, 208*, 209

Tyre, Milton, 186

Tytla, Vladimir "Bill," 17–18, 52, 118, 120, 124, 128, 130, 143–45, 150, 178, 190, 198–99, 201, 219, 223, 233, 285, 371, 379, 388, 397, 402, 404–5, 408

Unemployed Artists Association (UAA), 71, 374

United American Artists, 95, 135

United Artists Studio, 144, 219, 375, 411

United Auto Workers, 159

United Productions of America (UPA), 4, 13, 144, 186, 384

Van Beuren, Amadee, 37, 74, 371

Van Beuren Studio, 16, 71–75, 84, 198, 202, 216, 368, 370, 372, 384, 399

Van Vliet, John, 326, *337*, 393, 415

Variety, 135, 138, 172, 175, 219, 397, 405–6, 409

Vernick, Edith, 24, 99

Wagner Act of 1935, 73, 84, 85, 87, 91, 92, 97, 118, 121, 142, 156, 201, 217, 307, 380, 384

Waldman, Myron, 83, 89, 100

Index

Waldo C. Graphic, 326
Waldorf Declaration (1947), 178–79
Wall Street Journal, 82, 230, 303
Walsh, Bill, 156, 202
Walsh, Frank, 202
Walsh, Richard, 158, 159, 166, 195, 241–42, 269, 406
Walt Disney Studio (Walt Disney Company), 8, *17*, 20, *37*, 40, 45, 47, 51, 69, *71*, 74, 79, 99, 113, 115, 120, 121, 134, 136, 142, 145, 150, 201, 218, 220, 223, 232, 234, 267, 273, 285, 293, 311, 316, 320, 323, 337, 342
Walter Lantz Studio, 32, 95, *214*, 361
Ward, Jay, 11, 224, *225*, 227–28, 239, 245, 251, 253, 365, 369, 391, 413
Warner, Harry, 215
Warner, Jack, 63, 163, 174–75, 178, 219, 379
Warner, Sam, 41
Warner Bros. studio, 8, 13, 17, 19–20, 22–23, 27–28, 37, 40–42, 62, 106, 114, 125, 126, 143, 145, 158–64, *161, 162,* 166, 168, 172, 178, 185–87, 193, 198, 215, 218–19, 223, 227, 234, 235, 279–82, 296, 303, 305, 308, 311–13, 320, 324, 331, 338–40, 362–65, 368–69, 371, 375, 378–79, 384, 388, 407, 411–12
Washam, Ben, 21, 28, *107*, 145, 215, 235, 244, 259, 354–55, 371, 394, 405, 409, 413
Wayne, John, 160, 172, 181, 288, 392, 408–9
Wells, Frank, 45, 295–96, 309–11, 317, 362, 365
Weiss, Bill, 202, 207, 209–11
White Rats, the, 67
Whitney, John and James, 320, 371

Who Framed Roger Rabbit? (1988), 8, 50, 232, 298–301, 341
Williams, Richard, 2, 48–50, 54, 83, 149, 229, 231–32, 256, 265, 273, 300, 312, 360, 368–69, 372, 392, 400
Williams, Steve "Spaz," 325, 333
Wilson, John, 227
Winchell, Walter, 189
Winkler, Charles, 37
Winkler, Irwin, 195
Winkler, Margaret, 37, 78, 395
Writers Guild of America (WGA), 1, 69, 147, 155, 176, 272, 306, 377, 385
Woolery, Ade, 144, 223, 354
Works Progress Administration (WPA), 63, 85, 380, 385

Yakutis, Tom, 274, 357
Yellow Submarine (1968), 228, 294
Young, Phil, 234, 412

Zamora, Rudy, xiv, *14*, 28, 106, 110, 183, 397, 402
Zander, Jack, xiv, 20, 42, 61, 118, 198, 223, 353–54, 372, 393–94, 396, 398, 402–3
Zanuck, Darryl F., 62, 63
Zemeckis, Robert, 8, 297, 299, 300
Ziggy's Gift, 8, 265, 273
Zupkas, Steve, 259